Human Resource Development
As We Know It

Routledge Studies in Human Resource Development

EDITED BY MONICA LEE, LANCASTER UNIVERSITY, UK

HRD theory is changing rapidly. Recent advances in theory and practice, how we conceive of organisations and of the world of knowledge, have led to the need to reinterpret the field. This series aims to reflect and foster the development of HRD as an emergent discipline.

Encompassing a range of different international, organisational, methodological and theoretical perspectives, the series promotes theoretical controversy and reflective practice.

Human Resource Development As We Know It

Speeches that Have Shaped the Field

Edited by Monica Lee

Routledge
Taylor & Francis Group

NEW YORK   LONDON

First published 2012
by Routledge
711 Third Avenue, New York, NY 10017

Simultaneously published in the UK
by Routledge
2 Park Square, Milton Park, Abingdon, Oxon OX14 4RN

Routledge is an imprint of the Taylor & Francis Group,
an informa business

Library of Congress Cataloging-in-Publication Data
   Human resource development as we know it : speeches that have shaped
the field / edited by Monica Lee.
       p. cm. — (Routledge studies in human resource development ; 20)
   Includes bibliographical references and index.
   1. Personnel management.   2. Human capital.   I. Lee, Monica, 1952–
   HF5549.H7835 2011
   658.3—dc23
   2011035079

ISBN13: 978-0-415-89618-4 (hbk)
ISBN13: 978-0-203-12685-1 (ebk)

Typeset in Sabon by IBT Global.

Printed and bound in the United States of America on acid-free paper by
IBT Global.

This book is dedicated to my family for their help, support and patience—especially to Chas, who is a real star.

This book is also dedicated to the HRD family—who, together, create and foster the emergence of what we know as HRD.
May we succour it well.

Contents

PART I
Conecptualization

PART II
Location

PART III
Implementation

PART IV
Value'ation

PART V
Visualization

Summary   306

MONICA LEE

Figures

Foreword by Jim Stewart
Chair of the University Forum for HRD

It is a great pleasure to write a foreword to this collection of speeches. What lies ahead of you, assuming you are reading the forewords and, if so, before you read the chapters, is in my judgment, a celebration. Monica Lee has done the HRD community a significant and important service in producing this collection of the major thoughts and contributions of the most influential thinkers and writers on HRD over the last twenty years or so. But, more than that, Monica has produced a demonstration and justification of the impact and influence of academic and professional practice in HRD which celebrates the positive progress the subject has made and the associated differences made in the lives of employees and citizens across the world.

We often debate the distinction between theory and practice, between academics and professionals, between professional bodies and academic associations. There are no such distinctions. As Monica shows in her introduction, both the AHRD and the UFHRD had early links with professional bodies, and these links remain. In the UK, for example, the majority of academics representing member universities of the UFHRD are also members of the CIPD, the professional body for HRD practitioners. Many are also very active in the work of the CIPD. The workshops and seminars of the UFHRD are commonly attended by professional practitioners. But these examples are not really my point. Again, as Monica points out, the thinking, perspective, beliefs and values related to HRD of people who heard the speeches collected here have been changed by the experience of hearing the arguments of the speakers. Who are the people who heard these speeches? They are for the most part academics who teach HRD. What do these academics do when their thinking, perspective, beliefs and values related to HRD have been changed? They change their teaching of HRD professionals. And, whereas most of the speeches collected here have not been published before, those who delivered the speeches also research and write about HRD and publish books and articles which are then read and used by academics and students in their joint exploration of HRD practice. So, this collection is for me an account of the progress and improvements that have been achieved by the 'academic' associations of UFHRD and AHRD in professional HRD practice. That for me is also a cause of celebration.

An additional celebration comes from the fact that these speeches still resonate with current issues and challenges in HRD. The words spoken one or five or ten years ago are still relevant and speak to current practice as much as they did to practice when the speech was originally delivered. Monica's request to contributors to address the past and current context helps to achieve that relevance. So too does Monica's organization and structuring of the chapters. But more than that, it is the results of hard thinking presented in the speeches that ensure enduring value for their ideas and arguments. A keynote speech or a Professorial Inaugural Lecture is not something taken lightly by anyone, and so we know those in this collection were carefully thought through before they were delivered. Each speech and the collection as whole deserve attention which will provide a pay off in new insights and ideas on and for practice.

We have here a brief but very salient summary of the history and development of HRD across the world. Monica Lee and the contributors deserve our thanks for producing such a work. I hope readers will join in the celebration by recommending the work to colleagues and friends who have an interest in and who care about the future of HRD. This book contains influences on the past which will still be influencing HRD for many years to come.

Foreword by AAhad M. Osman-Gani, PhD

Chair, Asia-Pacific Network of Human Resource Development and Coordinator of Academy of HRD (Asia Chapter)

This is a unique book, which contains many keynote speeches presented at international conferences on various thematic issues related to HRD. The chapter contents enlighten the readers about the trends and developments in the dynamic field of Human Resource Development. Congratulations to Monica Lee for taking such an initiative and producing a great book by providing a sound conceptual structure for it. In today's global arena of HRD, HCD and manpower development, continuous discussions and debates are observed among scholars and practitioners about conceptualizations and boundaries of the field. The foci and contents of several keynote speeches reflect those discussions, and analyses of such debates might provide further insight and clarification for continuing healthy intellectual discourse (without expecting a quick consensus to emerge soon!).

In the Asia-Pacific region, tremendous growth has been observed in the scholarly domain of HRD through the developments of new programs and courses in various institutions of higher learning, as well as in increasing scheduling of academic conferences, workshops and symposia on many topics relevant to HRD. In the HRD professional field, significant developments have also been seen, which can be noticed from increased numbers of announcements about HRD or HCD (human capital development) conferences and congresses, calls for consulting opportunities and rapidly growing online discussion groups, portals and other professional activities related to HRD work. This book has successfully captured many of those developments occurring in the dynamic Asia-Pacific region and beyond. Through the book the reader can experience a taste of the deliberations that have happened in the HRD-related conferences, even though they were not able to be physically present at the sessions.

My heartfelt commendations to Monica Lee for her great contributions to the HRD field through publishing this book, in addition to her other contributions in the past! I strongly recommend HRD scholars, students and professionals to use the book for their own professional development, as well as for referring it to their students, colleagues and clients who have interests in HRD issues. The ideas presented in the keynote speeches, which have been effectively captured in this book, can provide significant inputs in developing and implementing new HRD programs and interventions. My suggestion, therefore, for HRD consultants and practitioners is to study the contents of this book.

Foreword by Darlene Russ-Eft
President of the Academy of Human Resource Development (AHRD)

The title of this book is rather impressive, but we might want to add that this represents HRD as We Knew It and Continue to Know It. Regardless of the title, the contents are even more impressive. Monica Lee has succeeded in assembling the keynotes of many of the HRD thought leaders from across the United States, the United Kingdom, Europe, Asia and Australasia. Thus, the book represents a compendium of the ideas, conceptualizations and recommendations for future work that have guided the field and will help to guide the field in the future.

In her introduction, Monica makes reference to the fact that many of us have commented on particularly impressive keynotes. For example, I can recall a lively debate during one of the early conferences of the Academy of Human Resource Development (AHRD) that occurred between Karen Watkins and Dick Swanson. As one might expect, Karen argued for the predominance of learning as an HRD goal, whereas Dick argued that performance should be the goal. I still wish that someone had been able to capture that debate, along with the corresponding audience comments, on YouTube. Of course, that technology was not available then, nor was it available for many of these keynote speeches.

But, through Monica's leadership and the willingness of these various keynote speakers, we now have the luxury, pleasure and intellectual stimulation of seeing their ideas in print. In addition to providing some of the context of these thoughts, each author has indicated what has transpired since that keynote was delivered. Furthermore, Monica has identified not only the timing of the keynote, but she has also indicated the major theme being discussed. So, we now have a roadmap of HRD research and thought through time.

My one regret is that we only have the speaker's comments in writing. Watching a movie at home enables you to understand the storyline, but it fails to provide you with a sense of the audience reaction. The same is true with this compendium. We can never know the comments and questions that came from the audience or the remaining questions and comments that were discussed in the hallways (and dare I say bars or pubs) throughout the conference. For the full effect, one would have had to participate in these conferences. But, at least, this compendium gives all of us a chance to taste some of the kinds of discussions that took place in each of the conferences. And I hope that we can use these ideas and their implications to shape our future work.

Introduction

Monica Lee

If you are a sharp-eyed reader who likes to start toward the end of a book, you might have noticed that in Chapter 21 I allude to the way in which this book came about. At an excellent conference in 2006 a group of us were standing around discussing some of the speeches we had heard, both at the conference and on previous occasions, that seemed to have an element of gravitas—speeches that were re-visited and found their way into the verbal history of the field—yet often did not get as far as the published literature. If parts of them were published, it was in a more sanitized and literate form—losing the raw statement of the personal; the views and experience that had made them so attractive to the seated audience.

This book, therefore, arose out of the feeling that HRD was now old enough to have a history, but that this was largely verbal—and it was only rehearsed at the times when the elders in the field got out their pipes and slippers, sat by the blazing log fire and swapped stories and took stock. Well—a nice image, but I guess most of the contributors here would not consider themselves to be quite so ancient! Before I talk more about the book, what do I mean about HRD being 'old' enough to have a history? HRD is coming of age. Recently there have been several journal contributions[1] looking at the roots of HRD and exploring its development. All the presentations in this book have been given either by members of University Forum for HRD (UFHRD); the Academy for HRD (AHRD); or the Asian Network; or they have been given at the conferences of these networks. So I shall first say a little bit about the development of these networks.

The UFHRD in the UK, and the AHRD in the US, formed, unknown to each other, within a couple of years of each other. Both have old, and similar, roots. The Academy of Human Resource Development (AHRD) was founded on May 7, 1993, and sprung from the Professor's Network of the American Society of Training and Development (ASTD) and the (US) University Council for Research on HRD. The combined goal of wanting to advance the profession through research and scholarship realigned the two groups into the newly formed and independent Academy of Human Resource Development. The AHRD first published the journal *Human Resource Development Quarterly* (HRDQ) in 1990, and held its first conference in 1994. The AHRD is a network of individuals, whereas the UFHRD is one of universities (with a few individual members), but essentially they are very similar.

The UFHRD emerged from the UK professional body The Institute of Training and Development (ITD)[2] in the late 1980s, spurred on by, and in liaison with, the government introduction of national competence based vocational qualifications (NVQs). It was best described as a voluntary network or an informal association of universities seeking to provide dual masters-level academic and professional qualifications. This group of universities was formalized in 1992/3, initially as the Euston Road Group, and shortly afterward as the UFHRD.

In 1994 the European Council of Ministers decided to adopt measures to establish a common framework of objectives for community action. This influenced a wide range of Europe-wide initiatives, including EURES-FORM. Euresform was established by UFHRD (with CIPD involvement) and was initially funded by the European Union to develop a system based on the achievement of learning outcomes that certified that HR professionals were, among other skills, able to work internationally. This was achieved successfully, and master's degree students from across Europe received the Euresform certificate, jointly awarded by all the participating institutions, accrediting academic and professional status.

The Forum had a pattern of workshops, seminars and short conferences throughout this period, in the UK and some in the rest of Europe, and supported the establishment of the journal *Human Resource Development International* (HRDI) in 1996, with the first volume appearing in 1998. Three lone members of the UFHRD attended the AHRD conference in 1997. The AHRD became involved with HRDI and supported the Forum's first truly international conference at Kingston University, London, in 2000. The Euresform initiative finished in 2000 as European priorities and funding changed. Its influence, however, is still evidenced by the cross-European nature of UFHRD (which now incorporates Euresform) and the pattern of hosting of the annual conferences, which alternate between the UK and the rest of Europe.

Since then the UFHRD and AHRD have been active in participation and sharing in each other's conferences, publishing activities, research collaborations, teaching initiatives and so on. The AHRD has expanded to support an Asian network, with the first conference in 2002, and a network in the Middle East and North Africa (MENA) whose first conference was in 2010. They have also included two more journals in their portfolio—*Advances in Developing Human Resources* (ADHR) in 1999 and *Human Resource Development Review* (HRDR) in 2002. Typically, each conference is attended by about forty to fifty different nationalities, and these conferences provide an important point of contact, cooperation and collaboration, and a catalyst for developments in the field, across all countries involved.

People have been 'doing' what could have been called HRD for many years, but these activities were not then conceptualized as HRD, and so I look to the early 1990s, when these networks were formed, as the time at which HRD crept into the academic arena. The field of HRD has developed largely through academics, scholars and reflective practitioners from across the world coming together, engaging in new debates and actively looking for ways to collaborate. It can be said, therefore, that these conferences are at the forefront of a global network of universities, professional bodies, organizations and individuals that are engaged in HRD, and these conferences have had a major effect upon the way in which the field of HRD has developed since the start of its academic popularization in the 1990s.

As conferences play a large part in the mixing process, so do the conference organizers look to the keynote speakers to provide the spark that mutates a relaxed coming together of people into a thriving and energetic event from which further development emerges. The choice of keynote speaker is often one of the harder parts of conference organization, and a good keynote speech is often one of the more lasting memories of the conference. Good keynote speeches often remain just a fond memory, and inaccessible to those who were not there. They are a forthright statement of the expert's view—stimulating, provocative, up-to-the-minute, designed to be spoken (not written)—and thus they are often not published. As the research for this book showed, many people link memorable keynotes to changes in their research, practice, career path or even life view!

Now that HRD is maturing, there is a need to recapture some of those earlier moments—both as a form of archive, and also to shed light on the path that has been followed. In order to set this in motion, I emailed all of the members of the main academic/practitioner networks and asked them to comment on which keynote speeches had most affected their thoughts, their progression, their understanding and practice of HRD, and whether they would like to see these collected in a book. There was a strong positive response to my email from members across each of the networks. Many people came back to me with suggestions of speeches that had been pivotal to their thinking. Many people gave examples of how these speeches had changed their approach to the field, sometimes their careers, and in a couple of cases, their lives.

There was unanimous support for the idea of collecting the speeches into a book, and the majority of respondents also thought that such a book would be useful as a supplementary source for their students, and of interest to practitioners. There were also many suggestions about what speeches should be included in the book, with a large amount of agreement between respondents about which were the most influential speeches. I have followed these recommendations in putting this book together. Several presentations that were not given in conference venues were also highlighted by respondents. Three of these were Inaugural Professorial Lectures (IPL)—these are large open-access lectures (available to colleagues and the general public) given as part of the acceptance of a professorial post. A fourth IPL, by Sally Sambrook, has yet to occur, but is included here anyway. There were several suggestions that some of her earlier presentations be included, but, because of the nature of this book, she and I felt that this speech would best address these requests.

I am pleased that I was able to persuade nearly all the named presenters to contribute to this book. A few respondents might find their favorite speech missing, as two people were no longer in a position to contribute a chapter. I am sad not to be able to include them, but I trust that as you read this book you will find much to intrigue you. I would point out that the contents of this book have been dictated by the respondents to my questions—hence the emphasis in the title 'HRD as *WE* know it.'

It is my intention that these speeches remain challenging and provocative, and retain a sense of spontaneity and immediateness, and that, as you read them you can easily imagine the voices of the authors talking to you across a hushed auditorium. Of course, some of the early speeches are now quite dated, and so I have asked each of the authors to do more than just replicate what they said when they gave the speech. Insofar as these speeches are milestones along the path of the development of the field, the authors have been asked to comment at the beginning of their chapter on the context of their speech and where their speech was positioned in relation to the field of HRD at the time it was given. I have also asked the authors to add a final section to their chapter looking at how the field, and their thinking, has developed since they gave their speech. In this way I trust that the book will be a resource, not only for those who wish to re-live their pivotal moments, but also for anyone interested in exploring and charting the development of the field.

OVERVIEW OF THE SPEECHES

To start with I considered organizing the speeches chronologically, so that the focus might be on tracing the development of concerns that are current in the field of HRD. That seemed a bit too broad-brush, in that different nations started with different understandings of HRD, and these differences have rippled along through the years—to take just one line of progression would be to say that there is just one interpretation of HRD. I then wondered about organizing the speeches around nationality, so that we could see how clumps of national trends have developed—but, as you can see in Figure 0.1, there is not much coherence to the idea of national influence—at least at the level of keynote speeches. I should, perhaps, have expected this, given that the people asked to give keynote speeches tend to be those who are expanding the area in some way.

Figure 0.1 also seems to show that the keynotes that make the most impression are those that come from a different network—those that

YEAR	Conceptualization	Location	Implementation	Value'ation	Visualization
2000	Monica Lee UFHRD (Kingston University, UK)				
2001				David Megginson IPL (Sheffield Hallum University, UK)	
2002					Gary McLean ASIA (Bangalore, India)
2003		Chartchai Na Chiang-mai ASIA (Bangkok, Thailand)			Rob Poell UFHRD (Toulouse University, France)
2004	Tomas Garavan UFHRD (Limerick University, Ireland) Yvonna Lincoln AHRD (Austin, Texas USA)	Nigel Haworth & Jonathan Winterton UFHRD (Limerick University, Ireland)		Gary McLean UFHRD (Limerick University, Ireland)	Monica Lee ASIA (Seoul, South Korea)
2005				Gene Roth & Darren Short AHRD (Estes Park, Colorado, USA), Darlene Russ-Eft UFHRD (Leeds Metropolitan University, UK)	
2006					
2007			Larry Dooley ASIA (Beijing, China)		
2008			Chanin Vongkusolkit ASIA (Bangkok, Thailand)	Jamie Callaghan UFHRD (Lille, France)	
2009	Paul Iles IPL (Leeds Metropolitan University, UK)	Sharon Turnbull IPL (Worcester University, UK), AAhad Osman-Gani ICCCR (Jammu, India)	Dawn Robinson & Sharon Mavin UFHRD (Northumbria University, UK)		
2010					K. Peter Kuchinke UFHRD (Pecs, Hungary)
2011	Sally Sambrook IPL (Bangor University, Wales, UK)		Nicholas Clarke UFHRD (Gloucestershire University, UK)		

Conference Network

AHRD (Academy for HRD conferences, USA) (2)

ASIA (Academy for HRD Asian Network conferences)(5)

ICCCR (International Centre for Cross-Cultural Research, India)(1)

IPL (Inaugural Professorial Lectures, UK)(4)

UFHRD (University Forum for HRD, UK and rest of EU) (10)

Home Country of Speaker

3 USA

3 Asian, 1 UK, 2 US

4 UK

3 EU, 1 NZ, 4UK, 4US

Figure 0.1 Speeches by year, conference, nationality and part in the book.

bring a different perspective. Of the twenty two speeches here, only two are from the AHRD conferences, Yvonna Lincoln and Gene Roth and Darren Short. While each of these speakers is from the US, Yvonna was invited from a different field of study, and Gene and Darren's presentation was highly experimental—neither was your standard fare. US speakers, however, have made an impact on the other networks, as, in total, they account for eight of the chapters in this book. In a similar way, the

Asian and UK/EU networks account for sixteen chapters (six and ten, respectively), but the majority of speakers are not home grown, with three from Asia speaking in the Asian network, and three people from the UK speaking in the UK. The picture is not quite so clear-cut when Inaugural Professorial Lectures are considered, as they are part of career progression in the UK, and so are located there, but I hold that the basic premise stands—the speeches that stand out are those that challenge us and provide us with something new. I therefore decided that the speeches needed to be organized conceptually.

I have organized the chapters into five parts, based upon the overall focus of the keynote, and within each part I have organized the speeches chronologically so that we can see a development of ideas. The parts are:

1. Conceptualization. Those with a focus on the nature of HRD and how it is conceived.
2. Location. Those with a focus on how HRD is located within the wider field.
3. Implementation. Those that look at practical aspects of 'doing' HRD.
4. Value'ation. Those with a particular focus on the values, emotions and spirit of HRD.
5. Visualization. Those with a focus on the future and the way forward for HRD.

Conceptualization

This part starts with an early speech of my own, in which I questioned the scientistic and definitional paradigm of HRD, one that appeared to give HRD the legitimacy it sought as it developed its academic roots, but also one that denied the very nature of HRD. This is followed by a speech from Yvonna Lincoln, who makes a similar argument from a different perspective—that of evaluation and research methodology. She urges HRD researchers to consider the use of interpretivist and qualitative methodologies. Both of these early speeches are concerned with what HRD might 'mean' and how we might examine that. Speaking in 2004, Thomas Garavan considers global HRD, and the understanding of HRD within international and multinational concerns, establishing the notion of International or IHRD. By 2009, and Paul Iles's speech, our focus is upon HRD as an aspect of leadership development and talent management, within the arms of IHRD. The last speech in this part is that of Sally Sambrook, who reflects on the more recent area of Critical HRD, as built upon multi-faceted notions of an HRD that vary with circumstances. Thus Sally's work takes us in a spiral, much further along from 2000, but incorporating the early challenges posed by Monica Lee and Yvonna Lincoln.

Location

This part considers how HRD is located within the wider field. To some extent it addresses the situated nature of HRD that is alluded to in the previous part. This part starts in 2003 with Chartchai Na Chiangmai's examination of HRD in Thailand, in which he presents a model of holistic management of human resource development, based around the development philosophy of Sufficiency Economy. These proposals for national development link both to National HRD examined by Gary Mclean, Chapter 15, and to Chapter 11 in which Chanin Vongkusolkit describes the implementation of many of the ideas raised here. Chapter 7, by Nigel Haworth and Jonathan Winterton, recounts a speech given in 2004, in which they jump to the level of NHRD to examine supra-state HRD strategies in the EU and APEC regions. They found that despite fundamental differences in the underlying economic objectives of the two approaches and in the means by which the HRD policies are developed, there were important lessons they could learn from each other. We then move to 2009, and the last two speeches in this part. AAhad Osman-Gani maintains the international focus that emerged in 2004 with the Limerick conference (Chapters 3, 7 and 15) and examines factors affecting international managers' adjustment and performance in overseas assignments. This resonates strongly with the following part, 'Implementation,' and, finally, Sharon Turnbull's examination of the qualities that different cultures bring to the notion of leadership, resonates with the fourth part, 'Value'ation.'

Implementation

This part starts more recently than did the previous parts. It could be that discussions of practice had a shorter influence upon the respondents than did other topics, but I would be surprised if that were the case—particularly as many of the speeches in other parts have a lot to say about implementation, and the speeches I have placed here also tie in closely with other areas. Perhaps this is an interesting anomaly for you, the reader, to ponder. Be that as it may, the section starts with a speech by Larry Dooley that he gave in 2007, which examines the impact of emerging technologies and e-learning on talent management within organizations. We might expect any speech on technology to be out–of–date within a couple of years, yet his analysis remains valid and pertinent. This is followed by Chanin Vongkusolkit, who, as CEO of Banpu in Thailand, gives a detailed account of corporate social responsibility and governance for sustainable development within his company, which links closely with Chartchai Na Chiangmai's examination of HRD in Thailand in the previous section. The next chapter follows a similar theme of strategic organizational development within a different cultural context. It recounts a 2009 speech given jointly by Sharon Mavin and Dawn Robinson, who together outline a journey of change within SAGE (where Dawn is head of Learning and Development). This joint presentation, by an academic and practitioner, represented the strength of the research and practice partnership they had developed. The last chapter in this part is a recent speech by Nicholas Clarke, looking at leadership development in a variety of situations, and from that, positing the need for a multi-level perspective in evaluation and research—which resonates with the threads of leadership and complexity that permeate these speeches.

Value'ation

The speeches in this part have a particular focus on the values, emotions and spirit of HRD. The first, Chapter 14, was given in 2001 by David Megginson and examined the notion of spirit in organizations. He grounds this in discussion of coaching and learning communities, thereby resonating with discussions of leadership in other chapters. In 2001 the focus was on the interface between individual and the organization; by 2004, and Gary McLean's speech, it was shifting to a wider screen, looking at the development of nations through HRD (NHRD) and the values associated with that. Development in the practice of HRD was supported in 2005, but the call for the inclusion of humor within our work, was made, in a memorable and humorous manner, by Gene Roth and Darren Short. In the same year, on a different continent, Darlene Russ-Eft was asking us to examine our values as we use evaluation within organizations, emphasizing the challenges of addressing the multi-dimensional values of multiple stakeholders. The last chapter in this part is based on a speech given by Jamie Callahan in 2008. She examines the emotions of leadership, looking at their management and manipulation from a critical perspective, thereby particularly resonating with Sally Sambrook's work in Chapter 5, and Sharon Turnbull's in Chapter 9, as well as discussions of leadership throughout this book.

Visualization

This final part starts in 2002 with Gary Mclean speaking at the first conference of the Asian Network about his view of future trends in HRD from a global perspective. Have these trends been realized nearly ten years later? With a focus on the individual, similar to David Megginson in Chapter 14, Rob Poell, speaking a year later, puts forward the vision that are organizations should be there to make people happy. He examines this notion, and proposes areas for further study. In contrast, Monica Lee, in 2004, adopts a macroscopic view and argues that HRD cannot be cocooned from global changes such as those in the climate, technology and population. Finally, both for this section and the speeches in the book, in his speech in 2010 K. Peter Kuchinke brings together the twin threads of human flourishing and global trends that have woven through each section.

Good speeches, however, often have a wide focus—and so there is a fair amount of overlap between the parts and the chapters, with topic areas, such as 'leadership' being addressed in several parts. In order to bring coherence to the whole, each part will start with a short introduction that locates its contents and builds bridges to other parts. I will also try to pull it all together in a summary section at the end of this book.

Speeches don't usually have many references, and you will notice that I have asked each of the contributors to use endnotes rather than references, to avoid breaking up the text, and thus keeping it more-speech-like. However, this does abuse my academic soul! I have therefore, and unusually, gathered all the references in a final section to this book—thereby providing a wider map of sources used by some key people in the field. Read and enjoy!

NOTES

1. Stewart, J., M. Lee and R. Poell. (2009) 'The University Forum for Human Resource Development: Its history, purpose, and activities,' *New Horizons in Adult Education and Human Resource Development* 23(1), 29–33.
2. The ITD shortly afterward merged into the current professional body—the Chartered Institute for Personnel and Development.

Part I

Conceptualization

The chapters in this section have a particular focus on the nature of HRD and how it is conceived. This section starts with an early speech of my own, in which I questioned the scientistic and definitional paradigm of HRD, one that appeared to give HRD the legitimacy it sought as it developed its academic roots, but also one that denied the very nature of HRD. This is followed by a speech by Yvonna Lincoln, who makes a similar argument from a different perspective—that of evaluation and research methodology. She urges HRD researchers to consider the use of interpretivist and qualitative methodologies. Both of these early speeches are concerned with what HRD might 'mean' and how we might examine that. Also speaking in 2004, Thomas Garavan considers global HRD, and the understanding of HRD within international and multinational concerns, establishing the notion of International or IHRD. By 2009, and Paul Iles's speech, our focus is upon HRD as an aspect of leadership development and talent management, within the arms of IHRD. The last speech in this section is that of Sally Sambrook, who reflects on the more recent area of Critical HRD, as built upon multi-faceted notions of an HRD that varies with circumstances. Thus Sally's work takes us in a spiral, much further along from 2000, but incorporating the early challenges posed by Monica Lee and Yvonna Lincoln.

1   A Refusal to Define HRD

Monica Lee

In this chapter I use I use the example of a MSc in HRD that I designed to illustrate that although at times it is necessary to define HRD for political or social reasons, there is a strong case that HRD should not be defined on philosophical, theoretical and practical grounds. To proffer definitions of HRD is to misrepresent it as a thing of being rather than a process of becoming. I suggest that we need to look to the notion of emergent HRD and enjoy the ability to live with negative capability!
(1st International Conference on HRD across Europe, Kingston University, London, UK, 2000)

CONTEXT

The ideas that I explore here were first aired in 2000 as part of a UK Research Seminar Series sponsored by the Economic and Social Research Council (ESRC) on *Human Resource Development: The Emerging Theoretical Agenda and Empirical Research*, which I jointly convened with Jean Woodall and Jim Stewart. The aim of the seminar series was to provide a forum in which HRD scholars and scholar-practitioners could debate leading-edge research in HRD in a more relaxed environment than can be provided by the typical academic conference schedule. The majority of participants were UK and European, although speakers were attracted from across the globe. HRD was still in its infancy, and these seminars had the enthusiastic atmosphere of fostering and exploring a new and challenging way forward. Three books in the 'Studies in HRD Series' arose from these seminars, as did many papers and, also, UFHRD's system of annual conferences.

I was founding editor of *Human Resource Development International* (HRDI), and it had been going for a couple of very successful years with lots of contributions, alternative perspectives and debates within its pages. One of the central debates revolved around what the definition of HRD 'ought' to be. The underlying presumption was that without definition HRD would never be considered a valid academic discipline. I found this very frustrating, for reasons that I explore below, and so I decided to challenge this view head-on when I spoke at the ESRC seminar series.

THE PRESENTATION: A REFUSAL TO DEFINE HRD

Hello. I want to use this time to argue that on philosophical, theoretical, professional and practical grounds HRD should not be defined, and that to do so is to misrepresent HRD as a thing of *being* rather than a process of *becoming*.

I will start with an example. In the early 1990s I started a master's course at Lancaster University in the UK (MSC in HRD by Research). I designed this to lead to both professional and academic qualifications for international cohorts of senior HRD professionals, via a series of intense week-long workshops, interspersed with research projects in their organizations. They knew there was no set syllabus before they started, that the course 'material' would spring from them; however, each cohort followed the same basic pattern of group dynamics. In the first workshop people were getting their bearings—by the second workshop two months later, after they been back at work and started to reflect upon links between the academic and professional sides of their lives, the feel of the group would change—ravenous for knowledge and demanding of the tutors. What was it they were meant to be learning! Why was I refusing to give them the tool kit!

The defining of HRD became paramount in most people's minds. It was as if they believed that once they knew the definition of HRD then they would understand what HRD 'is'. They would then be able to manage their jobs, and the course—their future study and work roles will be laid out in front of them, such that so long as they know where the path was, they could achieve excellence through sheer hard work. These views shifted quite rapidly, but for that workshop, they held that if I failed to define HRD for them, then, as course designer and leader I would be preventing them from achieving—furthermore, they questioned, how could I design a course without knowing what I was doing? Despite (at times, intense) pressure I have succeeded in refusing to define HRD for the last twenty years, and this event represents a rehearsal of the justifications that I used then, and since, for my obdurate behavior. I will argue that HRD is tacitly 'defined' by our experiences; it is situation specific and dynamic; it is in a state of becoming; and exploration of it merits an emergent approach.

I shall tie this account around that of the master's program that I mention above. This program was terminated after running for only four cohorts, yet, unlike many master's programs, it generated income and proved to be extremely successful with the students, many of whom say that it has fundamentally changed their lives. The problem was not quality, either, as the majority of students achieved exceptionally good academic results, even though several came with very little prior academic experience. The problem was that it adopted a philosophy and practice fundamentally different from that of 'normal' academe.

THE PHILOSOPHICAL CASE FOR REFUSING TO DEFINE HRD

I used the design of this program to explore some of my ideas of adult educa-tion, and, having only recently joined university life after twenty years work-ing for others and myself in the field, I did not fully realize quite how unusual my ideas would seem to the 'system.' I designed my master's program in accordance with how I understood my role as an HRD professional, and as an 'educator' of others. It seemed to me that while I carried a central core of understanding from each experience that came my way, 'I', and 'my under-standing' shifted and changed according to that experience—and each expe-rience influenced, and was influenced by, future experiences. I could never say 'this is the organization,' 'this is my role,' and 'this is what I am doing' as I could never manage to complete or finalize any of these states.

Similarly, as an educator, I could not identify with any firm body of knowledge and say 'this is what is needed.' I could see that people needed knowledge, but that most of what they needed would be situation specific —the knowledge needed by an Angolan participant would be very differ-ent from that needed by someone working in Hong Kong. People work-ing multi-nationally needed different knowledge and skills than did those working with SMEs; working in the voluntary sector appeared fundamen-tally different from working with the corporate fat cats, and so on. I could see that people needed different knowledge and skills, and that they would need to shift and change—to emerge into new roles and 'selves.' However, I could not build a course that specified that—instead I built one that refused to specify—or at least, the only specification was for the areas of focus on the different workshops, the form (not the content) of the assessed research projects and international placement and the form of process that occurred over the different days of each workshop.

The program consisted of eight four-day workshops over one and a half yours, and was assessed through three guided work-based research proj-ects, an international placement, a learning log and a dissertation. Follow-ing a Kolbian pattern, I designed the process of each workshop to force a focus on the academic [theory], followed by one on the professional (self within group) [reflection], and then the individual [planning], before the return to work [experience]. During the first two days of each workshop I invited specialists who I knew would present different views to come and talk to the group about the topic of that workshop (half a day each), with specific instructions to be controversial and to follow their pet theories. For each half day the group lived in the world of that specialist—and, given the diversity of each group, there was lots of discussion and hard questioning. I would refuse to clarify, and insisted that all persons had to come to their own decisions on the differing views presented.

I was very determined in ensuring that the third day shifted to one of *no* content. It was called 'academic debate' as it was set aside for the group to work with the ideas from the previous two days and with their own processes, contextualizing theory with practice. This was, initially, hard for the partici-pants, and proved to be very hard for co-tutors (more of that later). The major-ity of participants came from commerce-based pressured lives where they had to be doing something. Quite often the group got 'stuck,' and occasionally I would jump in with some exercise or idea to shift them, but despite the real pain sometimes associated with the processes of self within group, each group eventually came to value the creation of a reflective space in this way.

While the whole program was based on principles of action learning,[1] the fourth day made this more explicit. The group split into sub-groups of about six people each, and these were run as a facilitative action learning set. Each person would have about an hour (even if they said they didn't want it!) in which to address whatever issues they wished. These normally started as work issues, but quickly shifted to individual/group issues, and then, over the next year, moved increasingly toward issues associated with completing the dissertation!

I designed the course like this because it felt like the best way to foster reflective practitioners able to develop and marry best practice with academic credibility and personal strength. I was not fully aware, at the time, of my underlying philosophical assumptions in doing so, or the extent to which they would be alien to the majority of my immediate academic community.

As Chia[2] states, '*Contemporary Western modes of thought are circum-scribed by two great and competing pre-Socratic cosmologies or 'world-views', which provided and continue to provide the most general conceptual categories for organizing thought and directing human effort. Heraclitus, a native of Ephesus in ancient Greece, emphasized the primacy of a change-able and emergent world while Parmenides, his successor, insisted upon the permanent and unchangeable nature of reality.*'

Parmenides's view of reality is reflected in the continued dominance of the 'belief that science constitutes, by far, the most valuable part of human learning and accomplishment.' This leads to an atomistic conception of real-ity in which 'clear-cut, definite things are deemed to occupy clear-cut definite places in space and time'; thus causality becomes the conceptual tool used for linking these isolates, and the state of rest is considered normal, whereas movement is considered as a straightforward transition from one stable state to another. The metaphysical basis for the organization of modern thought and the perpetration of a system of classificatory taxonomies, hierarchies and categories which, in turn, serve as the institutionalized vocabulary for representing our experiences of reality is rooted in a *being* ontology. This is associated with a *representationalist* epistemology in which formal knowl-edge is deemed to be that which is produced by the rigorous application of the system of classifications on our phenomenal experiences in order to arrive at an accurate description of reality. In other words a *being* ontology is con-ceptualized with one 'true' reality, the units of which are tied together in a causal system. The truth is out there; we just have to find it!

In contrast, the Heraclitean viewpoint offers a *becoming* ontology in which how an entity *becomes* constitutes *what* the actual entity *is*; so that the two descriptions of an actual entity are not independent. Its 'being' is constituted by its 'becoming.' This is the principle of process. "The 'flux of things is one ultimate generalization around which we must weave our philosophical system."[3] Within such a *process* epistemology the individuals involved feel themselves to be significant nodes in a dynamic network and are neither merely passive receivers nor dominant agents imposing their preconceived scheme of things onto that which they apprehend.[4] All are the parts of the whole, and the parts, and the whole, change and develop together. From this point of view, there are both one and many realities, in which I 'myself' come into being through interacting with these and am constituted within them, and the knowing of these is never final or finished. A personal quality necessary for 'living' within such a process epistemology could be that of John Keats's 'negative capability.'[5] This quality involves the resisting of conceptual closures and the desire to stay with the open-endedness and indeterminacy of experience. Conceptual resistance thereby creates the necessary 'space' for the formulation of personal insights and managerial foresight.[6]

These notions gave me a peg on which to pin my understanding of why my program did not suit some of my colleagues: it (and I) was coming from a fundamentally different philosophy from that which they adopted. In essence, my world was one of becoming, while theirs was one of being. A program that generated its own content was fine by me, but anathema to them, as was a program in which the process was structured but the (majority of the) knowledge wasn't, in which the 'students' had full responsibility for their own work and in which the 'teachers' role was to enforce negative capability rather than closure.

I was lucky to start the program with staff who accepted this way of working. Unfortunately they were not core to the department (or 'traditional' academics) and were replaced by colleagues who found it very hard to understand why I placed any importance on what they saw as 'anti-academic-activities' such as refusing to structure the third day or to define my terms. This replacement was partly political (and I won't go into that here) but also occurred because of the sheer dominance of the Parmenidesean viewpoint within academe. The insistence upon there being only one reality or one 'right' way meant that there was no room for alternative paradigms. Indeed, for some, there was no ability to see that alternative paradigms existed, let alone understand that they might be associated with different (but equally valid) forms of operationalization.

Philosophically, then, I do not wish to define HRD because to do so would be alien to my worldview.

THE THEORETICAL CASE FOR REFUSING TO DEFINE HRD

My theoretical case for refusing to define HRD is that I do not believe that it can be done in a meaningful way. Most would agree that, to be meaningful, the definition of something needs to encapsulate the properties or qualities of that which is being defined, such that it can be recognized uniquely from the definition and thereby distinguished from what is not being defined. This sort of description of what a definition might be, however, is, in itself, one of *being* rather than *becoming*. We could, however, say that a definition of something need not be fixed or permanent, but instead, it could take the form of a working definition-if enough people use a word in a particular way, and know what one another mean by it, more or less, then there is tacit agreement about the meaning of that word and its qualities, such that it could be deemed to be *becoming* defined.

We might, therefore, get a rough feeling for a word by looking at the way in which it is used. I once attempted to develop a working definition of the word 'development.'[7] I examined promotional literature aimed at HRD professionals and found four different ways in which the word 'development' was used. In the first approach that I identified, 'development as maturation' was used as if to refer to a pre-determined 'stage-like' and inevitable progression of people and organizations. 'Development' is seen as an inevitable unfolding—and thus the 'developmental' force is the process itself, which, in turn, defines the end-point. The 'system,' be it an individual, a group or an organization, is seen as being a coherent entity with clearly defined boundaries existing within a predictable external environment—the organization is discussed as if it were a single living element, whose structures, existence and change are capable of being completely understood through sufficient expert analysis. Concepts such as empowerment and change-agency are irrelevant in an approach that is essentially social determinism, with no place for unpredictable events or freedom of individual choice.

In the second, 'development as shaping,' people are seen as tools who can be shaped to fit the organization. Here, development is still seen to have known end-points, but these are defined by someone or something external to the process of development. The organization is stratified, and 'senior' management define the end point for 'junior' management—the wishes of the corporate hierarchy create the developmental force. This approach assumes that there is something lacking, some weakness or gap, that can be added to or filled by the use of the appropriate tools or blueprint, and that such intervention is necessary. Individuals (their aspirations and their values, as well as their skills) are malleable units that can be molded to suit the wider system. 'Empowerment' and 'individual agency' can be part of the developmental agenda, but not in their own right they are acceptable developmental end-points only if ratified by senior management—'empowerment' becomes a tool to enhance performance and decision making (within limits).

'Development as voyage' is a life-long journey upon uncharted internal routes in which individuals construe their own frames of reference and place their views of self within this, such that each of us constructs our own version of 'reality' in which our 'identity' is part of that construct. This can be described as an active process in which individuals are continually re-analyzing their role in the emergence of the processes they are part of, and in doing so also confronting their own ideas, unsurfaced assumptions, biases and fears while maintaining a core of ethicality and strong self concept.[8] 'Development' involves a transformative shift in approach that enables critical observation and evaluation of the experience, such that the learners are able to distance themselves from it rather than 'replay' it—experiencing becomes a way of restoring meaning to life.[9] The external world (including organization and management) might mirror or catalyze 'development,' but it is the individual who is the sole owner and clear driving force behind the process. 'Empowerment' would be within the individual's own terms, and might have little regard for organizational objectives.

'Development as emergent' is the fourth approach that I identified. Here 'development' is seen to arise out of the messy ways by which societal aspiration becomes transformed into societal 'reality.' It encompasses individuals' unique perceptions of themselves within a social reality which is continuously socially (re)constructed; in which individuals dynamically alter their actions with respect to the ongoing and anticipated actions of their partners and in which they negotiate a form of communication and meaning specific and new to the group and relatively un-accessible or un-describable to those who were not part of the process.[10] 'Self-hood' is a dynamic function of the wider social system (be it a family grouping, a small- or medium-sized enterprise, a large bureaucracy, or a nation—or parts of each), and as that system transforms so do 'I.' Emergent development of the group-as-organization is seen to be no different from development of any social system, and is not consistently driven by any single sub-section (be it senior management or the shop floor). Discussion about planned top-down or bottom-up

		IDENTITY	
		UNITARY	CO-REGULATED
END POINT	**KNOWN**	MATURATION: Development through inevitable stages.	SHAPING: Development through planned steps.
	UNKNOWN	VOYAGE: Development through internal discovery.	EMERGENT: Development through interaction with others.

Figure 1.1   A 2x2 matrix of 'Development.'

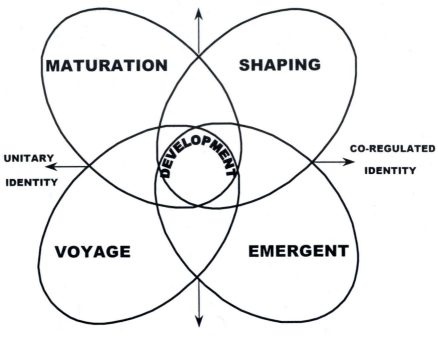

KNOWN DEVELOPMENTAL END-POINT

MATURATION   SHAPING

UNITARY   CO-REGULATED
IDENTITY   IDENTITY

DEVELOPMENT

VOYAGE   EMERGENT

UNKNOWN DEVELOPMENTAL END-POINT.

Figure 1.2   Four forms of 'Development.'

change is irrelevant, as the words themselves imply some sort of structure to the change. This approach is, of course, in direct conflict with traditional ideas that organizational change is driven by senior management; however, there is empirical support for rapid, discontinuous transformation in organizations being driven by major environmental changes.[11]

It would be very simple to place these in a nice 2x2 matrix, as such:

The 2x2 matrix is pervasive and well understood in management, but it is a tool of being, rather than becoming. The lines are solid and impermeable, the categories fixed. Alternatively, we could examine these areas as areas of concentration, in which it is as if the most concentrated 'essence' of that which we are examining is in the centre of the area, and, as it diffuses outward, it mingles with the essences of the other areas.

Despite finding alternative ways of representing these findings, which might meet problems of how to represent the sorts of working definitions associated with becoming, we cannot avoid the fact that there appear to be four fundamentally different working definitions of 'development.' Each of these carries with it a particular view of organization, and of the nature and role of HRD, and each is used under different circumstances. When talking of our own development we normally address it as if it were a voyage. When senior managers talk of organizational development they normally talk of it as if it were shaping. When social theorists talk of development they normally adopt a maturational or emergent perspective (depending upon their theoretical bent). Development' is clearly not a unitary concept.

THE PROFESSIONAL CASE FOR REFUSING TO DEFINE HRD

The many ways in which the word 'development' can be used indicates the many different roles that the professional 'developer' might adopt. For example the role of the developer in the maturational system has the sureness of the (relatively) uninvolved expert consultant who charts the inevitable unfolding of the stages. The developer within a shaped system is the process expert who can not only clearly help senior management identify an enhanced future, but can also apply the tools necessary to ensure that such a future is achieved. Such developers sell a 'better' (and otherwise unobtainable) view of the future (to individuals, groups and organizations)—and the blueprint to get there. Those that are being 'developed' are encouraged/ molded to meet the end criteria, regardless of whether such criteria are enhanced skills, positive attitudes or the achievement of corporate objectives. The role of the developer within the system as voyage is one of helping others to help themselves (see, for example, Rogers).[12] The developer brings 'expert' skills that help the individual recognize their self-imposed bounds and widen their horizons, but does so without calling upon the 'power' of expertise that describes a particular path and endpoint as 'best' for the individual concerned. In emergent systems there is little role for a 'developer' as the developer holds no 'unique' or special status. Developers are as similar and as different as each other member is, and although they (perhaps) have fewer vested interests in political machinations (and thus might be able to view circumstances more objectively), they are as directly involved in the life of the organization as any of the individuals they are supporting in co-development.

Let us step back for a bit, and take a Parmenidesean view of the world, and examine what is meant by the definition of HRD. In this worldview we have the 2x2 matrix rules, and four different definitions of the word 'development,' only one of which can be what we really 'mean' (the other three need to be renamed—but that is not important to us here). When we talk about '*Human Resource* Development' however, the situation becomes clearer. A 'human resource' is a commodity—something to be shaped and used at the will and needs of the more powerful. The role of the HRD professional is clear, and, by implication, so is the nature of organization and management. Senior management set the objectives within a clearly defined organizational structure, in which HRD is a subset of the larger

HRM function. If we accept the common meaning of the words then there is no alternative to HRD as an activity and profession in which development is about shaping individuals to fit the needs of the organization (as defined by senior management). Integrity, ethics and individual needs are not important within this conceptualization (and need only be considered if the circumstances call for hypocritical lip-service to them).

A Parmenidesean definition of HRD, therefore, might be along the lines of 'the shaping of the employees to fit the needs of the employer.' This definition of HRD effectively limits HRD to 'training.' It is questionable, however, whether that definition was ever fully adopted by the HRD professions. It is, perhaps, the professional and qualificatory bodies, more than any others, that feel the need to define HRD. They need to do so, as, in order to patrol their boundaries and maintain their standards, they need to establish what those standards are. Some might still see HRD in this way, but for many, the profession has (slowly) moved on to incorporate notions of integrity and ethics, and also to reflect, at least in part, the notion that people are central to the organization, and thus the strategic role that their development can play.

The professional bodies have, in general, adopted a practice-based view of HRD, in which they attempt to promote what they see as 'best practice' (within their own contexts) through the establishment of their professional standards. In establishing professional standards, however, they run the risk of strangling growth in the profession by stipulating so closely what the practice of HRD is, that it is unable to become anything else.

The master's in HRD program that I mentioned earlier did offer professional recognition; however I tried to avoid the limiting nature of 'professionalization' by working with other members of EURESFORM[13] to establish professional recognition through the attainment of learning outcomes, rather than standards. This meant that the individuals took responsibility of evidencing that they had met the outcomes (either during the course or otherwise) and the learning outcomes could be rapidly adjusted as the needs of the profession changed. This system continues to operate and provide European professional recognition, but appears to be slipping more toward what is, in effect, the 'validation' of courses and back-door standardization. Negative capability is VERY hard to foster![14]

THE PRACTICAL REASON FOR REFUSING TO DEFINE HRD

Pressure toward standardization and thus the defining of HRD seems an inevitable part of professionalization and qualification structures. However, as illustrated in 1996,[15] 'standardization' across disparate systems of HRD is likely to have been achieved through cultural imposition, with the accepted 'standards' or definition in practice, belonging to those cultures with the loudest voices. Even if the rhetoric is of the dominant culture, the practice often remains that of the hidden, or underlying, culture.[16] The idea, therefore, of a generally acceptable definition of HRD achieved via the processes of standardization becomes particularly unrealistic when we look at the degree of variation in practice across the globe. It is simply not practical.

If we abandon the notion of establishing a single working definition of HRD, we still have open the possibility of defining HRD according to what actually happens in different situations, thereby attempting to establish situated working definitions. Some people need and use such definitions for their jobs, but as soon as these definitions are encased in course brochures, syllabi, professional standards, organizational literature or other such statements of fact, they stop becoming and ARE. As discussed above, however, HRD theorists and professionals are increasingly talking and acting as if the process that we call HRD is dynamic and emergent.

Perhaps the only way to address the need to encapsulate what is meant by 'HRD' is to refrain from 'defining' as the encapsulated meaning includes elements that are much wider than 'real' HRD as seen in a Parmenidesean worldview. Instead we should seek to draw permeable outlines around this complex of activities that we all know and, for want of any other term, choose to call HRD.

EMERGENT HRD

One way of addressing this issue this might be to focus again on the 'emergent' system of development. I describe this as reflecting the messy ways by which societal aspiration becomes transformed into societal 'reality.' Society 'develops' with no clear end-point and with its emergent activities as the drive behind change, rather than the edicts of the hierarchy.[17] From this perspective, HRD could be seen as that which is in the processual bindings of the system, which links the needs and aspirations of the (shifting) elements of the system, between and across different levels of aggregation, as they are in the process of becoming

Throughout the master's in HRD I felt unable to explain this concept in a way that it made sense in abstract terms—my method of 'explaining' it was to maintain negative capability, and let it emerge, each person putting it into his or her own words and situations. 'HRD' was different for all people and emerged out of their experiences—*'It is not enough to insist upon the necessity of experience, nor even of activity in experience. Everything depends upon the quality of experience which is had . . . every experience lives in further experiences.'*[18]

I was lucky to be able to run my master's course as I did for four cohorts . . . most institutions wouldn't have even accepted its notion of self-generating content. Having ensured that its systems of verification and quality management were sufficient, the University was happy for it to continue indefinitely. It was particular individuals who caused it to close, largely through fear of the different and a desire to control the uncontrollable. The Heraclitean *becoming* lost to the Parmenidesean *being,* in a fight in which the becoming was gagged and the being held the power!

By virtue of this chapter, while acknowledging how very hard it is at times to live in a Heraclitean world, I wish to redress the balance and propose that, certainly as far as 'HRD' is concerned—there is no alternative. I will not define HRD because it is indefinable, and to attempt to define it is only to serve political or social needs of the minute—to give the appearance of being in control.

THE AFTERMATH

This speech was well received and the debate became more heated. I decided to put pen to paper and submitted these ideas to the refereed section of the Academy of HRD Conference in the US in 2001. There were two reviewers, both of whom suggested outright rejection—one because it was not relevant to HRD, and the other because I used dated sources (the Greek philosophers!). Luckily for me, the Stream chair overrode these and accepted the paper. Even more luckily, it was chosen as one of the top ten outstanding papers of the conference.[19] Following that success I then wrote it for journal publication, where it got accepted as part of a special edition on Defining HRD, and also won an award for the best paper of the year in the journal. I have to add that although the paper was first published in HRDI,[20] I played no part in any of the refereeing or awarding processes, and the award came as a very pleasant surprise to me. Since then it has been re-published in a couple of collections.[21]

Although I still refuse to define HRD, I have, since then, attempted to address what I think might constitute HRD and explore what might lie at roots of HRD, both in further speeches and publications.[22] I have also taken further ways of working with alternative methodologies by which to make sense of our world, ones more in line with becoming than being![23]

Looking back, I think that while my speech did open up the discussion about definitions it also had a deeper effect. Prior to that, words like ontology, epistemology and paradigm had not really impacted upon the field at all—they certainly were not evident in the literature. By referring to the underlying assumptions of the dominant worldview I was also encouraging these to be exposed and questioned. I like to think that this speech helped to kick-start a more critical approach to our theory and practice.

NOTES

1. Monica Lee. (1996) 'Action learning as a cross-cultural tool,' in Jim Stewart and Jim McGoldrick (eds.), *Human Resource Development: Perspectives, Strategies and Practice*, London: Pitman, 240–260.

2. Robert Chia. (1997) 'Process philosophy and management learning: Cultivating "foresight" in management,' in John Burgoyne and Michael Reynolds (eds.), *Management Learning*, London: Sage, 71–88.
3. Alfred North Whitehead. (1929) *Process and reality*. New York: Free Press, 240.
4. Robert Cooper. (1976) 'The open field,' *Human Relations* 29(11): 999–1017.
5. And at once it struck me, what quality went to form a man of Achievement . . . meaning Negative Capability, that is when a man is capable of being in uncertainties, mysteries, doubts, without any irritable reaching after facts and reason. From John Keats, letters of 21 December, 1817, in Duncan Wu, *Romanticism: An Anthology*, 3rd ed., illustr., 1351 Blackwell: Oxford.
6. Alfred North Whitehead. (1933) *Adventures of ideas*. Harmondsworth: Penguin.
7. Monica Lee. (1997) 'The developmental approach: A critical reconsideration' in John Burgoyne and Mike Reynolds (eds.), *Management learning*, London: Sage, 199–214.
8. Paul Adler. (1974) 'Beyond cultural identity: Reflections on cultural and multicultural man,' *Topics in Culture Learning, Vol. 2*. Honolulu: East-West Culture Learning Institute.
9. Fyodor Vasilyuk. (1984) *The psychology of experiencing: The resolution of life's critical situations* (English trans., 1991). Hemel Hempstead: Harvester Wheatsheaf.
10. See Peter Checkland. (1994) 'Conventional wisdom and conventional ignorance,' *Organisation* 1(1): 29–34. Ian Fogel. 1993 *Developing through relationships: Origins of communication, self and culture*. Hemel Hempstead: Harvester Wheatsheaf. Monica Lee. (1994) 'The isolated manager: Walking the boundaries of the micro-culture,' *Proceedings of the British Academy of Management Conference*, Lancaster: 111–128.
11. Elaine Romanelli and Michael Tushman. (1994) 'Organisational transformation as punctuated equilibrium: An empirical test,' *Academy of Management Journal* 37: 1141–1166.
12. Carl Rogers. (1951) *Client centred therapy*. Boston: Houghton Mifflin. Carl Rogers. (1959) 'A theory of therapy, personality, and interpersonal relationships as developed in the client-centred framework,' in Sigmund Koch (ed.), *Psychology: A Study of a Science, Vol. 3*, New York: McGraw-Hill.
13. Through the auspices of a European Community Research Grant.
14. Sadly EURESFORM and the European Professional Certificate ceased to operate in 2004.
15. Monica Lee, Hugo Letiche, Robert Crawshaw and Michael Thomas, eds. (1996) *Management education in the new Europe*. London: Routledge.
16. Monica Lee. (1998), 'Understandings of conflict: A cross-cultural investigation,' *Personnel Review* 27(3): 227–242.
17. Monica Lee. (1997) 'Strategic human resource development: A conceptual exploration,' *Academy of Human Resource Development Conference Proceedings*, ed. Rich Torraco., Baton Rouge, LA: Academy of HRD, 92–99.
18. John Dewey. (1938) *Experience and education*, New York: Collier Books. (Collier edition first published 1963.)
19. Monica Lee. (2001) 'A refusal to define HRD,' in Rob Poell (ed.), *Defining the Cutting Edge—Top 10 Outstanding Papers*, 3–12.
20. Monica Lee. (2001) 'A refusal to define HRD,' *Human Resource Development International* 4(3): 327–343.
21. Monica Lee. (2004) 'A refusal to define HRD,' in *New Frontiers in Human Resource Development*, Jean Woodall, Jim Stewart and Monica Lee (eds.),

London: Routledge, 27–40. Monica Lee. (2011) 'A refusal to refine HRD,' in *Fundamentals of Human Resource Development*, David McGuire, Tom Garavan and Larry M. Dooley (eds.), SAGE Publications, in press.

22. Monica Lee. (2002) 'The evolution of HRD,' in *Human Resource Development in Asia: Trends and Challenges*, U. Ed Pareek, A.M. Osman Gani, S. Ramnarayan and T.V. Rao (eds.), New Delhi: Oxford and IBH Publishing, 695–702. Monica Lee. (2002) 'The complex roots of HRD,' in T. Rocco (Ed,), *Defining the Cutting Edge—Top 10 Outstanding Papers of 2002*, 3–12. Monica Lee. (2004) 'Complex archetypal structures that underlie the 'Human Condition,' *Organisational Transformation and Social Change* 2(2): 49–70.

23. Robert J. Schalkoff. (2011) 'Metaphor as used by noted HRD scholars at the Pecs 2010 conference,' *Human Resource Development International* 14(3): 347–351. Darren Short. (2010) 'An interview with Monica Lee,' *Human Resource Development International* 13(3): 361:374. Monica Lee. (1999) 'The lie of power: Empowerment as impotence,' *Human Relations* 52(2): 225–262. Monica Lee. (2001) 'On seizing the moment as the research question emerges, ' in Jim Stewart, Jim McGoldrick and Sandra Watson (eds.), *Understanding Research into HRD*, London: Routledge, 18–40. Monica Lee. (2003) 'On codes of ethics: The individual and performance,' *Performance Improvement Quarterly* 16(2): 72–89. Monica Lee. (2009) 'On the loss of a room: An autoethnographic assay of fact,' *Human Resource Development International* 12(3): 343–349.

2 In and Out of the "Black Box"

Human Learning, Contextual Performance and Qualitative Research

Yvonna S. Lincoln

The suggestion is proffered that we do not know how to access what is in the human mind (the "black box") unless we engage the other, asking what she or he is thinking. It is only then that researchers in human resource development can begin to understand the deepest human needs, wishes and desires that affect human performance in the workplace. Five related issues are taken up: the major issues confronting the field of human resource development; the problem with "measuring" learning, especially in the workplace; performance as a desired outcome vs. performances of the postmodern, saturated self, which has many choices about identities, roles, enactments, self-presentations; the relationship of human resource development to higher education, which is a supersaturated project in human resource development itself, and; what qualitative methods can help us to unlock and understand about human beings and being human.
(11th AHRD Conference, Austin, Texas, USA 2004)

CONTEXT (WRITTEN BY MONICA LEE)

As Yvonna pointed out in her keynote, she was invited in 'from the outside' (around where I live, the farming community term it "from off"!). She cannot write about either the context or the aftermath of her keynote as she is not part of the field of HRD. I am, however, very keen to include her keynote in this book for several reasons that I will discuss at the end of this chapter. For the moment, I will just point out that this keynote was given in 2004 in an AHRD[1] conference, at a time when the field of HRD and the US-based academic HRD networks in particular were heavily aligned with positivistic approaches to enquiry and standardization of the reporting of results. This was so, to the extent that some US journals would not accept alternative formats in their publications. At this time a brave few were looking at qualitative methodologies—but they were a small minority.

THE KEYNOTE

Good morning, and thank you for inviting me here. I think I was invited here to talk about qualitative methods, but as I tell my own students, the question of methods is always secondary to the question of the question. If you can frame your question elegantly and parsimoniously, then the question of what methods might be used to pursue the answer to the question will flow from that process. As a consequence, whereas I do want to talk about qualitative methods, and suggest some ways in which they might be useful in your practice, I have some other things I want to say in addition.

Let me first admit that I don't know your field. In preparation for this issue, I suspect many of you in the audience helped. I asked a good colleague if she would make me a little list of what she believed to be the three or four most important issues facing scholars of human resource development today. She says that in preparation for doing that, she and a graduate student phoned "a number of senior scholars and journal editors" in your field and posed my questions to them. Thus, I am indebted to those of you, and to my colleague in the department, who provided enormous help in focusing me on your own discipline's problems; without you, this would have been merely a talk about how you might find qualitative methods useful. You have provided me, however, with extremely fruitful background; I hope that I do not use this rich material too loosely or casually or carelessly, and thus betray your hard work. Or hers.

First, I want to say something about your issues, because they are almost all of them 'black box' issues—as, I might add, are all human and social questions. In part, virtually every question nominated by researchers in your field has to do, in part, with what is going on in the human mind. The human mind is the ultimate "black box"—an endlessly processing, macro and granular emotional-rational computer, adventuring throughout its environments with a set of conserved memories, strategies, successes and failures upon which it draws constantly, making sense as it goes. This means that however good your theories grow to be, they will never be perfect. In some instances, they will be less than useless.

Second, we have no way of assessing the length or breadth of human learning. What we know is that we all know more than we know we know. We can assess in the micro whether individuals have learned what they need to know to perform a given set of tasks. We can find out whether their performance is deemed satisfactory by those who make judgments of those performances. But we cannot, finally, I think, assess what a person knows, or the sum of the human learning which has taken place.

Third, I want to talk about performance. I believe when human resource development practitioners and theoreticians talk about performance, they are talking about an individual's ability to perform successfully in some arena, usually related to the workplace. But other theoreticians are talking about performance in a slightly different way, and I want to simply throw that out, and have you think about it.

Fourth, I want to make some mention of the relationship of your problems to my own discipline, because they are quite similar, and because you face many of the issues we face, and often bemoan.

And finally, I will talk a little about qualitative methods, because I do think they could be useful to you, if for no other reason than that every good qualitative researcher comes face-to-face, at some time or another, with the limits of human knowledge and human knowability, with the vast unpredictability of life and the futility of one more chi-square and what that might tell us about human performance.

INTO THE 'BLACK BOX'

In the final analysis, what human resource development researchers are trying to do, I believe, is to understand humans in organizational contexts sufficiently to be able to work at improving individual efficacy so as to enhance organizational performance. It's not a bad idea, in theory. Help humans learn how to be more effective and efficacious at their work performance, and the cumulative impact of that will be higher-producing organizations and workplaces.

The major problem, of course, is that you're working with human beings. Humans bring with them attitudes, values, beliefs, motivations, hopes, fears, worries and other characteristics which have marked their individual lives, and which affect their performance in the workplace. No amount of testing, performance evaluations or other "measures" are going to alter those things. The one thing which holds the hope of effecting change in human performance is meaningful, effective contact with other human beings—contact which has the possibility of changing the ground rules. In this sense, we are probably best served by Vroom's theories on expectancies. We can examine more closely what sorts of issues in the workplace hold instrumental values, and which hold expressive values, and we can ask about manifest and latent attitudes and values, to try to determine what kinds of issues affect what kinds of people, in which kinds of value structures.

Let me give an example. In my own career, I have encountered people who are not performing well. When I'm in charge of the reward structure—as I am from time to time—I try the usual means to encourage better performance: public recognition, merit pay or withholding merit pay, other kinds of emoluments which are generally considered "rewards" in the academic environment: good teaching schedules, less teaching in favor of more research time, higher teaching rewards, more travel monies—carrots and sticks in differing proportions. And seemingly, nothing works. People do not teach better, despite having a highly-ranked Center for Teaching Excellence which would enable them to improve. People do not begin, or resume, research careers, despite the higher merit money consistent with research and publication activities. Clearly, there are values, opinions, beliefs, attitudes at work in these instances which have nothing to do with organizational goals, standards, performance measures or reward systems. Human resource development might tell me how to find the value systems that are so at variance with academic life in research universities. But HRD will not do so with tests and measurements, with psychological scales or with the standard performance evaluation systems.

I ran across the best statement on this issue some while back in the work of Neil Postman. Postman is one of my favorite authors, principally because he exposes me to new ideas, in readily accessible and non-technical language which I can immediately use. Listen to him on tests and measurements:

> the first instance of grading students' papers occurred at Cambridge University in 1792 at the suggestion of a tutor named William Farish. No one knows much about William Farish; not more than a handful have ever heard of him. And yet his idea that a quantitative value should be assigned to human thoughts was a major step toward constructing a mathematical concept of reality. If a number can be given to the quality of a thought, then a number can be given to the qualities of mercy, love, hate, beauty, creativity, intelligence, even sanity itself. When Galileo said that the language of nature is written in mathematics, he did not mean to include human feeling or accomplishment or insight. But most of us are now inclined to make these inclusions. Our psychologists, sociologists and educators find it quite impossible to do their work without numbers. They believe without numbers they cannot acquire or express authentic knowledge.
>
> I shall not argue here that this is a stupid or dangerous idea, only that it is peculiar. What is even more peculiar is that so many of us do not find the idea peculiar. To say that someone should be doing better work because he has an IQ of 134, or that someone is a 7.2 on a sensitivity scale, or that this man's essay on the rise of capitalism is an A- and that man's is a C+ would have sounded like gibberish to Galileo or Shakespeare or Thomas Jefferson. If it makes sense to us, that is because our minds have been conditioned by the technology of numbers so that we see the world differently than they did. Our understanding of what is real is different. Which is another way of saying that embedded in every tool is an ideological bias, a predisposition to construct the world as one thing rather than another, to value one thing over another, to amplify one sense or skill or attitude more loudly than another.[2]

If we want to know about the black box in any meaningful way, then we are going to have to ask about it. To construct learning as primarily the result of a test or a test score, or to measure it as a smooth performance of a task, is to cast human learning and performance in a technology discourse which blinds us to other, perhaps more meaningful, understandings of learning and performance. Most of what I know about why individual performance is so at odds with the context, I learned by asking, in a conversation. I understand HRD is conflicted regarding whether the more important role is for learning or for performance, but I parse it differently. Learning leads to performance, but until we understand what lessons people learned before they got to us, we will not understand how to improve performance. There is only one way into the black box, and that is to engage the black box in a conversation with us.

THE PROBLEM OF HUMAN LEARNING

There are two kinds of human learning (perhaps more): those the results of which we can see, and those which we cannot see, or if we see them, they are rare. The first I call social learning, because its results are exhibited in the social settings in which we locate ourselves—home, the workplace, school, religious groups, public spaces and places. The second kind of learning I call "habits of the heart," after Robert Bellah's famous book with his colleagues.[3] In the socially learned situations, we see what others have learned by how they interact with each other, and in the workplace, by how they carry out their assigned tasks. Learning in those instances is fairly easy to observe, even if not measure, and we can calculate what kinds of learning is occurring, and how well training or education is doing its job.

Most of the time, this kind of learning is what human resource development takes as its major interest, theoretical and practical. It is, however, more of the second that interests me, simply because of its power to undermine, sidetrack, obfuscate or derail the former.

Moreover, we know from the work of Howard Gardner that there may be multiple forms of intelligence, each suited to different learning styles, different kinds of performances and different forms of assessments regarding when and how learning has taken place.[4] New research emerging on "emotional intelligence" is giving us some new tools for examining how and under what circumstances people "learn" sensitivity to and empathy for others, which can be powerful tools for understanding how to help people learn.[5]

The implication of this is that until a focus on learning can take in the whole person—with its social learning and also its personal learning—it will miss much of what it takes to understand learning, or how to work in less interventionist, that is, manipulative, and more interactive ways to help individuals improve their performance. My own sense is that, between the findings of cognitive psychology, neuroscience, brain research and other scientific activity, we are only at the frontier of understanding human learning, not at the end. Incorporating the new sciences into the entire learning-performance continuum can only strengthen human resource development, not dilute or distract it. Broadening the focus of research into human development will make for a messier, but also a richer, context for the discipline.

PERFORMANCE AND PERFORMANCES

Human resource development, I am told by my colleagues, is greatly concerned with performance. I would like to propose that thinking about performance is somewhat narrow. (In case you can't guess, I'm headed toward a larger point here.) Qualitative researchers, and interpretivists more specifically, have tackled some of the thornier issues surrounding representation. By representation, I simply mean the pictures we provide of people, contexts, organizations, and other social settings. Ethnographers and other social scientists are increasingly aware of the "meaning-distances" between what is said and what is the lived experience of research participants. The semioticians have made us acutely and painfully aware of just how far apart the word is from the thing.

At the same time, criticisms from philosophy, particularly from those who criticize the essentializing nature of so much of our representational work,[6] have made us sensitive to the fact that categories which we considered immutable and transcendental—categories such as race, gender, language and the like—are themselves socially produced and socially producing *performances* (see, for instance, Judith Butler on the performance of sexuality,[7] or Bryant Alexander, on the performance of blackness).[8] What such insights do for us is to make us uneasy about *assignment*. Assigning individuals to categories, or even to performances, is a highly fluid, slippery and impermanent activity.

Nowhere is this more slippery and uncertain than in acting as though *performance*—as in work performance, or human performance—were some meaningful and semi-permanent category, when *performances* might be the more elusive, but realistic, consideration. Ken Gergen makes the point that not only are we confronting the "death of the author," we are also confronting the "death of the individual," a construct growing out of the Enlightenment's concern with the autonomous cognizing intelligence.[9] He argues that identity, which twentieth-century psychology considers to be the kernel or core of humanness, is far more fluid and amenable to variety than we have assumed. Gergen says:

> individuals [may] harbor a sense of coherent identity or self-sameness, only to find themselves suddenly propelled by alternative impulses. They seem securely to be one sort of person, but yet another comes bursting to the surface—in a suddenly voiced opinion, a fantasy, a turn of interest, or a private activity. Such experiences with variation and self-contradiction may be viewed as preliminary effects of social saturation. They may signal a *populating of the self,* the acquisition of multiple and disparate potentials for being. It is this process of self-population that begins to undermine the traditional commitments to both romanticist and modernist forms of being. It is of pivotal importance in setting the stage for the postmodern turn.[10]

Until we take full account of what the postmodern turn may signal for human performance/performances, we will not understand fully why our theories do not guide practice. Practitioners deal daily with the "saturated self," and with the "multiphrenia" that virtually unlimited opportunities and choices creates, while the exigencies and necessities of a theory or theories make it appear that relationships between people and things are far simpler, more linear, more causal and more direct than they can ever be in life. As abstractions, theories are of necessity primarily mathematical representations of a far more complex set of options, choices, identities and realities than any of us imagines.

YOU'RE JUST LIKE THE REST OF US: THEORETICIANS VS. PRACTITIONERS

That takes us to theory. As you might well have guessed, I have some reservations about theories, broadly and more narrowly. I speak as both a practitioner (of evaluation and of field inquiry) and a theoretician (of qualitative methods, interpretivism and postmodern inquiry). I have a lot of experience with theory. I teach it all the time. like playing with theory. For me, theory is both a serious activity, and my personal Schmoo. When it's the latter, I like knocking it down and watching it spring up again. And I can tell you from nearly thirty-five years in the scholarly life, theory isn't all it's cracked up to be.

Show me a really strong and effective practitioner, and I'll show you tacit knowledge and intuitive logics-in-use at work.

For me, it is not either/or. We need theoreticians. We need practitioners. We need theoreticians who are learning from practitioners. Who was the famous person who said: "Show me a society which values its philosophers more than it values its plumbers, and I shall show you a society where neither its theories nor its pipes hold water." Speaking as a part-time practitioner and a part-time theoretician, I can tell you that some of the most valuable theoretical lessons I learned I did not learn in my office, mulling over theory. I learned them dealing with what I believed to be "practical" problems in the field (mostly in evaluation practice). It was only after encountering the same problem, in multiple guises, that I began to see the "principle" behind the issue, and then was ready to begin theorizing in some meaningful way.

In human resource development, as in all the rest of social science, the only really meaningful theorizing about learning and performance derives directly from the lived experience of real human beings, in real organizational and community contexts, with real pluralistic complexity. The practitioners know this, so we have to learn from them if our theories are to hold water.

It makes no sense for theoreticians to say that practitioners are insufficiently grounded in theory to be truly useful. That happens in my evaluation community all the time: theoreticians argue that practitioners don't know enough about theory to be actually practicing responsibly. The practitioners quite reasonably respond: Fine. Let's see *you* earn a living by practicing, Ms. Theoretician. Another one of those peculiar and singularly useless arguments. For my money, the theory-practice divide was always a silly one. The circular logic of research → theorizing → *praxis* → research seems to make far more sense. And whereas I wouldn't hold my own career up as a model for any sane person, I would suggest that academic theoreticians need to be far more involved in practice, even if only to provide firsthand experience to graduate students, than they often are, and furthermore, that they need to be involved with practice where practice can lead to significant problems on which one might work. This means, for me, communities, neighborhoods, non-governmental organizations (NGOs), charitable organizations and the like. It is both more fun, and more lucrative, to work on corporate boards, of course. But corporate boards are rarely where the theory-practice rubber meets the road. Some of my own richest field experiences came from places where I earned the least money, and came the closest to participatory action research, with clients and participants taking an active role in nominating arenas of interest, and research and evaluation questions which they thought would offer the best information for their needs.

QUALITATIVE RESEARCH, OR HOW DO WE KNOW WHAT WE KNOW?

In the preceding sections, I have tried to foreshadow what you will hear here. I mean by that talking about the "black box" of the human mind, and appropriate ways to come to know about what is in there. Meaning, too, that I have tried to draw a distinction between performance and *performances*, to help you think both more broadly and more fluidly about how your own theories might contribute to essentializing human behavior in ways which undermine your work. I have tried, too, to indicate that, as a relatively new discipline, you should avoid at all costs the costs of drawing too sharp a divide between theoreticians and practitioners. These two communities need to be in constant interaction with each other, and when that doesn't happen, practitioners should go back to school and become involved with theory, and theoreticians should take on some service projects which expose them to the rigors of practice, in real-life contexts, where people need hard, slogging help to overcome practical problems to realize their fullest potential.

There are several ways, then, that you can use qualitative methods to get a better handle on what you do. First of all, the recent federal emphasis on a return to experimental methods should be seen for what it is: a return to "high modernism,"[11] some presumably "Golden Age" where research was still pure and inviolate. It is a form of methodological and paradigmatic denial, couched as an effort to rid research of its ideological impurities, while reinscribing an ideology of the detached and disinterested observer and the objectivity of statistical methods. Whereas I have no particular argument with quantitative methods, and have often found them useful myself, I do have an argument with those who claim that such methods are the only reliable way to scientific truth. With Laurel Richardson,[12] I would claim that there is no single method, no single paradigm, no single set of strategies which will yield absolute and whole truth. The best we can hope for is a partial truth, a slice of truth, which more closely approximates reality than some other slice. And I would argue that statistical models provide a kind of knowledge farther from lived experience than models dedicated to capturing lived experience in the terms of those who live the experience.

I would also propose that we grow farther and farther from the modernist world of the Enlightenment day by day. This means that our models of reality, and our paradigms for inquiring into those realities, probably need to be more closely aligned with the zeitgeist of our own era than they do with the Eisenhower era. We are living, as someone said, in the era of the *posts*: postmodernism, post-industrialism, post-emotionalism, post-insularity, post-colonialism, post-identity. Much as we might find it gracious, charming or comforting to go back, we cannot. We live, work and play in the age into which we are born. It makes sense, if the focus is on human learning and human performance, to try to couch our most important questions in ways which are well-matched to the era in which the problems have arisen. We have no choice but to deal with the "saturated self" in a postmodern, largely post-industrial, post-colonial and globalized context.

We might also think about moving beyond the confines of the business community so often and so well served to other places where human resources are becoming increasingly important. In a time when the advice to "Think globally, but act locally" has become a reality, new and important sites for such development work might include the kinds of places I mentioned earlier: communities, community organizations, town and small city governments, non-governmental organizations, social service agencies, educational organizations, charitable organizations, colleges and universities. In such contexts, highly abstract experimental method strategies are relatively meaningless. More qualitative, interactionist, interpretivist and narrative methods seem to be better suited and more responsive to participants' experiences. "Data-near" methods appear to have more power than "data-distant" methods, and this likewise suggests that qualitative strategies may exhibit more power, and ultimately more rigor, than what we are accustomed to in the academy.

The increasingly global focus of work among social scientists likewise suggests that we look at our practice more thoughtfully. It is one thing to fly to Boston and spend three days with a corporate board; it is quite another thing to fly to India to do so. The necessity to move gracefully and sensitively across cultural boundaries—even here in the US—implies a willingness to use culturally sensitive and relevant methods, methods which take into account vast differences in the mindsets of participants. The ability to suspend our own cultural frames and to interact with respect with other cultural frames dictates methods which are characterized by reciprocity, sympathy and interpersonal awareness.

Some of us will work even farther afield, with indigenous populations, groups and agencies. For such individuals, methods with the maximum amount of openness and the largest capacity for incorporating divergent thinking tend to be the most useful, and qualitative methods appear to exhibit the best fit here likewise. Given the criticism of Linda Tuhiwai Smith regarding the traditional methods of Western social science, we are probably better off to leave them at home. She says,

At a common sense level research was talked about both in terms of its absolute worthlessness to us, the indigenous world, and its absolute usefulness to those who wielded it as an instrument. It told us things already known, suggested things that would not work, and made careers for people who already had jobs.[13]

This tells us about all we need to know about conventional Western methods and the way they are viewed among indigenous peoples, so we know we have our marching orders there. Clearly, conventional methods associated with and characterizing Western social science have already got a bad reputation, and unless we want to ruin our own, we'd best not be taking the old hussy out when we move among post-colonial peoples.

Smith's critique really revolves about methodology as a form of control, particularly in its power to regulate, taxonomize and legitimate certain forms of knowledge as superior over other forms.[14] The criticism is particularly sharp in encounters with non-Western peoples, with groups from underrepresented populations, with Western and non-Western minorities, but it applies to all sorts of people: women, elderly people, poor people, immigrants, the urban working class. Methods that communicate, however subtly, that group knowledge and ways of knowing are inferior—however much rooted in daily lived experience—to academic knowledge leave us on slippery and dangerous ground. Such methods undermine the multiple epistemologies that circulate freely outside academic circles, and that have rich cultural, embodied and gendered heritages all their own. Methods which suggest that multiple ways of knowing are sought and appreciated, that social research is a collaborative venture, that researchers and the researched can freely trade off the roles of teachers and learners without loss to either party, create openness and authenticity in research processes, and prompt intellectual and social justice.

There are likely many other ways you will find to consider whether research you are passionately interested in pursuing might be more appropriately or wisely undertaken via an interpretivist paradigm and qualitative methods. Reflection on what it is we want and need to know may even possibly lead us to methods which are new to our research, or even to invent methods—a process, incidentally, which is ongoing—or new frameworks, paradigms, models or epistemologies. The last word has not been written—not on theory, not on practice, and certainly not on methods.

Consider this an invitation.

Thank you.

THE AFTERMATH (WRITTEN BY MONICA LEE)

One of the key reasons why I wanted to include Yvonna's work in this book is because this keynote struck a chord with a lot of people! During my survey of what keynotes to include, it was mentioned again and again as having had a profound influence upon the way individuals approached their research. Since that time Yvonna's call for an interpretivist paradigm and qualitative methods has been answered, and, as can be seen in later chapters in this book, such a vocabulary is now commonplace.

I also wanted to include this because I think it illustrates nicely something I will reflect upon in the summary to this book—it seems to me that the field of HRD has learned a great deal from "people from off." Perhaps it is the mystique of the outsider, but there is something compelling about bringing such new thoughts into the conference arena, and, as in this case, the field would be much poorer without such mixing.

NOTES

1. 11th AHRD Conference, Austin, Texas, US, 2004.
2. Neil Postman. (1993) *Technopoly: The surrender of culture to technology.* New York: Vintage Books, 13.
3. Robert N. Bellah et al. (1985, 1996) *Habits of the heart: Individualism and commitment in American life.* Berkeley: University of California Press.
4. Howard Gardner. (1993) *Frames of mind: The theory of multiple intelligences.* New York: Basic Books.
5. Daniel Goldman. (2000) *Working with emotional intelligence.* New York: Bantam Books.
6. Diana Fuss. (1989) Essentially speaking: Feminism, nature and difference. New York: Routledge.
7. Judith Butler. (1993) *Bodies that matter: On the discursive limits of "sex."* New York: Routledge.
8. Bryant K. Alexander. (2005) 'Performance ethnography: The reenacting and inciting of culture,' in *The Handbook of Qualitative Research, 3rd ed.*, Norman K. Denzin and Yvonna S. Lincoln (eds.), Thousand Oaks, CA: Sage, 3:411–442.
9. Kenneth J. Gergen, *The Saturated Self: Dilemmas of Identity in Contemporary Life* (New York: Basic Books, 1991).
10. Kenneth J. Gergen. (1991) *The saturated self: Dilemmas of identity in contemporary life.* New York: Basic Books, 68–69.
11. Anthony Giddens. (1989) *The consequences of modernity.* Cambridge: Polity.
12. Laurel Richardson (2000) 'Writing: A method of inquiry,' in *The Handbook of Qualitative Research, 2nd ed.*, ed. Norman K. Denzin and Yvonna S. Lincoln (eds.), Thousand Oaks, CA: Sage, 1:516–519.
13. Linda Tuhiwai Smith. (1999) *Decolonizing methodologies: Research and indigenous peoples.* London: Zed Books, 3.
14. Linda Tuhiwai Smith. (1999) *Decolonizing methodologies: Research and indigenous peoples.* London: Zed Books.

3 International, Comparative and Cross-Cultural HRD
Challenges for Future Research and Practice

Thomas Garavan

International Human Resource Development (IHRD) is conceptualized as consisting of three distinct strands: international, comparative, and Cross-cultural. These three strands informed the thinking behind the selection of the conference theme. The purposes of this chapter are threefold: to outline how international comparative and cross-cultural HRD was chosen as the theme of the conference; to present the content of the keynote speech, and finally, to explore how international, comparative and cross-cultural HRD has developed since 2004. IHRD is about examination of HRD in a world-wide context. However, in 2004 it could best be described as a subject matter in the embryonic stages of its development. Since 2004, steady growth has occurred in a number of the strands that were the focus of the presentation. In this sense therefore, this chapter contributes to the IHRD debate by clarifying the landscape of the discipline in 2004 and in 2011. It describes covered and uncovered topics as well as the research approaches and methodologies adopted by HRD scholars.
(5th International Conference on Human Resource Development across Europe: International, Comparative and Cross-Cultural Dimensions of HRD, Limerick, Ireland, 2004)

CONTEXT

The keynote presentation that forms the core of this chapter was presented at the Kemmy Business School, University of Limerick, Republic of Ireland, on May 27, 2004, at the 5th International Conference on Human Resource Development Research and Practice across Europe. A total of 275 delegates from twenty-nine countries attended the conference. Two particular aspects of the attendees are worthy of mention as part of setting the scene for the conference. There were approximately a hundred delegates from the US, which represents a record attendance for US delegates since the inception of the conference. Second, an invitation was sent to HRD practitioners in Irish MNCs and indigenous firms to attend the conference. Almost fifty HRD professionals took up the invitation. The conference theme generated 240 scholarly contributions.

As conference chair, I began thinking about the conference theme soon after the fourth annual conference which took place in Toulouse. I engaged in a process of consultation with colleagues within the Kemmy Business School and peers within UFHRD and AHRD. Agreement was quickly reached that the theme International, Comparative and Cross-Cultural HRD would be an appropriate one. The conference theme was prompted by recognition within the HRD academic and practitioner communities that the processes of globalization and internationalization had significant implications for what aspects of HRD were researched, how they were researched and the issues that arose for MNCs who implemented HRD on a global basis. My thinking about the conference theme was very much influenced by two academic contributions in the HRD literatures. These were by Lori Peterson and by Carol Hansen and Ann Brooks.[1] Both papers highlighted significant gaps in knowledge about IHRD. A review of published papers between 1994 and 2004 revealed few contributions which dealt with IHRD issues. I was also conscious of the debates occurring in other social science disciplines such as HRM and OB. Given the emerging evidence on the value of an international perspective on HRD, it was notable that very little work had been undertaken up to 2004 in defining and delimiting the nature and scope of IHRD.

A survey of the literature up to 2004 revealed approximately twenty papers that addressed HRD using an international, comparative or cross-cultural approach. The call for papers for the 2004 conference argued that organizations increasingly operated in an international and global context. This changed context challenged HRD scholars and practitioners to confront international, comparative and cross-cultural type analysis, something that was already in operation in other social science disciplines. The conference theme incorporated three distinct but linked strands or trajectories of HRD that have in the interim increasingly come to define and shape the field. For the purposes of the conference call, IHRD was defined as understanding HRD practices and research in the context of internationalization, and the increasingly significant impact of global firms and MNCs. Comparative HRD was defined as focusing on understanding national or country context such as HRD systems, structures and policies and how they influenced approaches to HRD. Cross-cultural HRD was defined as focusing on understanding the nature and relevance of societal culture in explaining and understanding HRD practices. Societal culture is assumed to be relevant in explaining similarities and differences in the way HRD is defined and researched.

The HRD literature up to 2004 was preoccupied with defining the concept of HRD. Difficulties in defining the concept arose from (and still do) the broad domain of the field, which covers several research areas and different levels of analysis and is relatively young as an academic discipline. Various scholars such as Gary McLean and Richard Swanson have tried to offer comprehensive definitions that seek to integrate the different dimensions that HRD involves[2]. In terms of levels of analysis, HRD up to 2004 was conceptualized in two ways: (i) a micro orientation that focused on functional issues, and (ii) a macro perspective that analyzed HRD from a strategic viewpoint.

Globalization and the internationalization of firms' activities introduce new research and practice questions to the HRD debate. These included differences between global, regional and local HRD strategies, the emergence of diversity, the question of whether HRD should contribute to social as well as economic goals and debates around the expatriation process. Scholars had also begun to acknowledge that HRD could be conceptualized differently in different countries and different societal contexts. Scholars in other disciplines such as HRD and OB had started to highlight a variety of factors that potentially led to diversity of thinking about HRD. These include institutional factors within countries and regions, different development trajectories, the emergence of cross-cultural frameworks, in particular the work of Hofstede,[3] and the emergence of MNCs as a globalizing influence. What is most perplexing in the IHRD context is the very limited concern given to the role of the MNC. They are organizations that need to be global and local at the same time. However, the HRD literature up to 2004 largely ignores the MNC as a shaper of HRD practices.

The three objectives underpinning the key note speech were: (1) to review how the discipline of HRD had evolved; (2) to explore the different strands of IHRD; and (3) to identify the issues that need to be addressed in research and practice domains within each strand.

THE KEYNOTE SPEECH

The field of IHRD is in the embryonic stage of development. It is currently characterized as operating at a somewhat basic level. The primary focus is on defining the field, identifying how it differs from HRM and identifying its theoretical foundations. To date there is a clear preference toward the behavioral perspective as the theoretical foundation of the field. The behavioral perspective has proven valuable in providing descriptions of HRD but also in explaining and predicting HRD variables. HRD research to date makes the assumption that the behavior of employees is a key element of HRD strategy as well as an important element in explaining the performance contribution of HRD. Scholars have highlighted the importance of human capital theory and the resource-based view of the firm in identifying and measuring key concepts. Well-developed human resources are considered to be a source of competitive advantage. It is difficult to draw any definitive conclusions about the state of the field of HRD; however, a number of observations can be put forward. HRD is a relatively new field of study. The term 'HRD' first appears to have been used in the mid 1960s in the context of a discussion on human capital. The purposes of HRD have traditionally been defined in terms of the learning and performance of individuals, teams and organizations, and there is a strong focus on formal

HRD activities. There is very little consideration of the informal in early writings on HRD. There is a strong emphasis on US-centric definitions. These US-centric definitions, however, are insufficient to capture the complexity of HRD. Different dimensions of behavior are highlighted in US and European approaches. US academics emphasize the importance of psychology, education and economics, whereas in Europe the focus is on culture, leadership and learning. This suggests a multi-disciplinary subject area. The boundaries of HRD are relatively fluid at this time. It has strong overlaps with organization behavior, HRM and organization development.

There is a lack of attention to contingency and contextual factors in HRD research. Context is multifaceted and includes economic and sectoral factors, cultural factors, and country characteristics, organizational and individual dimensions of context. There are significant differences between research designed to test rather than build theory. Theory-building HRD research has, to date, shown a clear preference for quantitative tools based on data obtained from questionnaire surveys with one point in time measurement. Theory-building research, on the other hand utilizes an inductive logic in analysis, extracting evidence from interviews, direct participation and analyzing data using qualitative methods.

Overall, HRD is a theoretical field of study; however, there is a lot of work yet to be undertaken to define and measure core concepts and to understand the context under which certain relationships occur. Internationalization has highlighted a new set of activities and issues not considered in research to date, but which will drive future discussions about IHRD. It is these issues that I now consider in the next part of this speech.

THE RESEARCH AND PRACTICE STRANDS OF HRD

I will now consider the three strands of IHRD and what they suggest for both the research and practice of HRD.

International HRD

International HRD focuses on understanding HRD in the context of the MNC. The growing importance of the MNC and the focus on complex global strategic decision making has resulted in an interest in the relationship between IHRD and business performance. This has given rise to a strategic perspective on HRD. The emergence of a strategic perspective on IHRD can be attributed to a number of factors: HRD is considered to be an important component of effective strategy implementation, IHRD can be important to enable the MNC achieve its goals and there is recognition that the characteristics of MNCs will influence HRD practices. As I have already alluded to, there is a dearth of research on IHRD in the MNC context. The IHRD stream represents the most significant gap in the literature at this time. There are a large number of unanswered questions. I will set out what I see as some of the more pertinent ones here:

- How do MNCs develop their workforces in order to secure competitive advantage?
- How can HRD be of value in helping the expatriation process and international assignments?
- What factors explain the diffusion of HRD practices throughout the subsidiaries of the MNC?
- Where are IHRD activities located within the MNC and what discretion do subsidiaries have in terms of the implementation of HRD practices?
- What type of structural arrangement is best suited to IHRD in the MNC?
- What factors shape how MNCs develop their leadership populations?
- How do IHRD practices change to adapt to labor market requirements and changes in the MNCs competitive strategy and changes in the local environment?
- What are the IHRD issues that emerge in the context of international joint ventures, mergers and acquisitions?

There is much to be learned about the dynamics of IHRD in MNCs. It is likely that there may not be a uniform implementation of IHRD within MNCs. However the scope for research within this strand is considerable.

Comparative HRD

A small number of cross-country studies that compare HRD practices have been published. The comparative strand of research typically focuses on national systems characteristics and how they influence organization-level HRD practices. These studies focus on single-country descriptions or compare a number of countries. The work undertaken by Gary McLean[4] represents examples of both approaches. The majority of comparative studies tend to be descriptive and do not focus on explaining the importance of these differences for the outcomes for individual organizations or societies. There is a lack of a comparative framework that can capture the diversity and complexity of IHRD structures, processes, policies and outcomes across nations or countries. A review of the IHRD literature suggests a number of dimensions that may be relevant. These include the reliance on internal versus external labor markets, the question of whether performance or welfare is emphasized in the workplace, the linkages among governments, employers and trade unions and the extent of regulation of the employment relationship.

An important issue in the context of comparative IHRD concerns convergence or divergence. Convergence theory basically postulates that global market and technological forces induce nations or countries to implement similar approaches to HRD. Over time, there will be a homogenization of institutions and HRD practices within developed countries. In order to evaluate and understand the context specific nature of HRD in different national settings, it is necessary to be clear about the factors that should be considered. A number of questions that need to be addressed include the following:

- How do we distinguish between national culture and national institutions?
- What level of analysis is appropriate for the conduct of cross-national comparisons? Should studies focus on the level of the state, the level of the firm or the individual level?
- What are the gaps between policy and practice in different national contexts, and what factors explain these gaps?
- How do we ensure equivalence in terms of function, concept, category and variable, uniformity of data collection methods and time frames?
- What are the main determinants of IHRD policies and practices in a cross-national context
- How can we test the convergence-divergence theses in the field of IHRD?

Effective comparative studies of HRD need to engage with a multiplicity of factors including national culture, national institutions, the industry sector and business environment. Different configurations of these variables will impact firm-level and individual-level characteristics and outcomes. It is likely that there will be a complex interplay between actual HRD policies and practices and the surrounding national factors and organizational factors. It should however be acknowledged that whereas comparative IHRD research is essential for the credibility of the field, it essentially is very difficult to undertake.

Cross-Cultural HRD

The literature has developed different frameworks to analyze how different national cultures can influence IHRD. The cross-cultural perspective has generally focused attention on the cultural distinctiveness of practices, beliefs and values shared by a country. It assumes that culture and values act as boundaries that allow interaction and socialization within them. Cross-cultural perspectives assume that societies or countries will vary in the types of institutions and approaches to HRD and those variations reflect different traditions, values, attitudes and experiences. Culture is typically measured through various value dimensions[5]. This approach is not, however, without criticism, and it is acknowledged that culture is highly elusive, difficult to operationalize and measure.

Two culture frameworks are commonly found in the HRD literatures. The Hofstede conceptualization is by far the most popular. The four dimensions—power, distance, uncertainty avoidance, individualism / collectivism and masculinity / femininity—are considered valuable in understanding HRD practices and outcomes. These four dimensions have been utilized to study HRD; however, they are not without faults; they have been criticized by Baskerville[6] because they do not capture the richness of national culture and they are viewed in a static rather than a dynamic way

Culture has also been conceptualized in terms of context—low and high context cultures. Hall (1976)[7] described low-context cultures as ones that value clear, explicit and written forms of communication. Anglo-Saxon and Northern European countries fall into this category. In high-context cultures, the external environment and non-verbal cues are considered important to communication. There are however few studies that have used this categorization to study HRD practices.

The development of cross-cultural frameworks continues. A very recent example is the GLOBE project. This project sets out to develop a multi-dimensional framework to explain cultural similarities and differences. It makes an important distinction between values 'as it is' and 'as it should be.' This framework has not yet been integrated into HRD research; however, it has the potential to prove valuable in exploring differences and similarities in HRD across countries.

A number of important questions are suggested for IHRD by these cultural frameworks:

- How do cultural values explain the importance that is attached to HRD, the content of training practices and the types of training methods that are utilized?
- What impact does culture have on individual learning styles? Do HRD specialists need to approach the design and delivery of training differently to account for cultural differences?
- How does culture influence the way in which individuals assess HRD outcomes? It is possible that some cultures have short- versus long-term orientations in assessing the value of HRD.
- Is HRD more culture bound than other HRM practices? Given that many development practices focus on interpersonal relationships, it is likely that they will be more embedded in the local culture.
- It is likely that culture will influence the way HRD is conducted. Given that many development processes are relational-based, the extent and type of feedback may be influenced by the nature of the culture. In this context, individualist cultures may be more amenable to direct feedback, whereas in collectivist cultures, the emphasis may be on more indirect and informal feedback processes.
- Culture will likely influence what is discussed in developmental activities. It is possible that individualist cultures will show a preference for discussing potential and performance issues whereas in collectivist cultures, these issues are less likely to be considered.

The questions that I have suggested here are indicative and do not in any way capture what we do or do not know about culture in a HRD context. However, it is appropriate to point out some of the difficulties associated with the cross-cultural perspective on IHRD. Three particular difficulties should be highlighted. The cross-cultural perspective may over-simplify national cultures and their influence on HRD. It is difficult to make a clear distinction between cultural values and institutions. It is generally acknowledged that institutions include cultural attitudes and values. The cross-cultural perspective is a difficult one to operationalize in methodological terms. The robustness of measures and the over-reliance on dimensional models of culture like the ones I have outlined earlier may reduce the potential to reach strong conclusions about the influence of culture on HRD. We have not yet encountered studies that use multi-level models to investigate the impact of culture on HRD policies and practices.

CONCLUDING REMARKS

My attempt in this keynote speech has been to invite you to consider the current state of IHRD as a discipline and to explore strands along which it may develop. The three strands that I have discussed—international, comparative and cross-cultural HRD—are familiar to this audience today as currently there is evidence of all these three strands in the literature at this time. What I hope this speech has done is to illustrate the current embryonic state of the IHRD literature and the lack of research within the field that is truly international in focus. Moreover, in closing, let me point out that the field has not engaged in the type of analysis that other social science disciplines have undertaken. It is perhaps appropriate to say that this gap is inevitable given the relative newness of the field of HRD as an academic discipline. Enhancing the academic robustness and status of IHRD would also be beneficial to practitioners in MNCs that are increasingly highly interdependent, knowledge-creation entities. HRD practitioners in MNCs will most likely in the future have to work across organizational boundaries and add value in a variety of ways. They will have to transfer HRD policies and practices across national borders and adapt these policies and practices to attract local employees and develop behaviors that are aligned with the cultural values of the location.

As a discipline IHRD has not reached the point where it is possible to talk about global HRD. The distinctions between what is considered international and global HRD are difficult to identify at this time. We have had little or no discussion of what global HRD might look like. The need to adopt a contextual approach to the study of IHRD is acknowledged as necessary; however, there is currently very little evidence of this approach in the literature. IHRD has not yet focused on demonstrating its performance contribution, something that appears to be a major preoccupation of

IHRM. Indeed, it is difficult to reach a conclusion concerning what might constitute a set of IHRD practices in this context. A lesson that emerges from the IRHM literature is that universal approaches to the study of IHRD will not prove particularly useful. A more useful approach will abandon the one size fits all and engage with context. I would propose that there is value in pursuing such an approach in the future.

AFTERMATH: THE EVOLUTION OF HRD SINCE 2004

I made this keynote speech in 2004, in a context where there was relatively little discussion of IHRD as a distinct strand of research and practice within the overall field of HRD. In the interim, it is arguable that the field of IHRD has progressed at a modest pace. There are major gaps in our understanding of IHRD. A number of significant papers have been published in the interim; however, we do not have an agreement as to what constitutes the scope of IHRD as a field study. Questions that arise include the following: Is IHRD about the development of an international workforce such as expatriates, cross-cultural teams and specialists involved in knowledge transfer? Is IHRD about the role played by institutions such as national HRD, professional bodies, governments and world agencies? Is it about something more than simply a focus on the MNC, or does it embrace issues such as social development and a contribution to the betterment of society, or is IHRD developing people on a global scale?

It is clear that we need to consider an approach to IHRD that incorporates a number of these features:

1. IHRD needs to actively engage with the political, social, economic, cultural and institutional context within which it takes place.
2. Research needs to explore how cultural and national differences influence the experience reality of IHRD.
3. It is important that comparative factors are not over-emphasized at the expense of understanding national differences.
4. Research will need to investigate the role of distinctive national and local solutions to IHRD issues which MNCs and other institutions have to address.
5. There needs to be an emphasis on exploring the 'how' of IHRD rather than simply focusing on the 'what.'

The field of IHRD has to a certain extent, since 2004, mirrored the evolution that has taken place in IHRM. Since that time a number of significant publications have taken a comparative cross-cultural and significantly less so international perspective. There is significant growth in research that explores HRD in a country context and that accounts for institutional, political and economic systems within the country studied. There is an increased level of

Subsidiary Level	Firm Level			Sector Level	Country Level		Regional Level	Global Level
	Contingency Variables	Firm Strategies & policies	HRD strategies & policies		National Culture	Institutional		
• Resources unique to the subsidiary. • Local labour relationships. • Role of subsidiary managers. • Degrees of autonomy and discretion. • Subsidiary initiatives and relationships	• Strategy – structure configuration. • Age of Organisation. • Size of Organisation. • Nature of Organisation • Status and Ownership of Organisation • Product life cycle stage of Organisation • Level of technology. • Structure • Presence of Unions. • Presence of HRD dept. • Presence of HRD strategy. • Industry characteristics • Stakeholder Interest	• Strategy type and content. • Internal labour markets. • Level of devolution • Nature of work flexibility	• Developmental strategies. • Leadership development. • Workforce development. • Competency frameworks • Resource allocation for HRD activities.	• Common sector strategies. • Sector specific knowledge. • Unique skill requirements of sector • Merger activity. • Labour mobility. • Talent deficits • Capital mobility.	• Common values & norms of behaviour in society. • Assumptions that shape managers perceptions. • Management styles. • Approach to cultural diversity.	• National labour laws. • Trade union influences. • Educational and vocational training policies. • Labour market professional bodies. • Employer bodies. • Trade bodies, Government institutions and voluntary bodies. • Professional organisations	• Regional nature of MNC's. • Regional trade barriers. • Regional inter-firm alliances. • Regional trade groupings – EU & NAFTA • Regional MNC strategy. • Regional focused perspectives on doing business.	• International Institutions. • International joint-ventures and strategic alliances. • Globalisation of Business. • Technological change. • International labour mobility. • International labour market regulations. • International benchmarking • Global competition.

Figure 3.1   Conceptualizing international, comparative and cross-cultural HRD: levels of analysis, and key variables associated with each level.

interest in Asia, the Middle East and Africa; however, there are large gaps in our understanding concerning HRD in Latin America, Eastern Europe and Russia. It is likely that we will see an increased emphasis on emerging and developing economies and Latin America, given the shift in foreign direct investment (FDI) that is increasingly focused on countries such as Brazil, Chile and Argentina. Comparative IHRD research is increasingly more sensitive to context, in particular, single country socio-economic systems studies.

There is significant growth in cross-cultural IHRD research. These studies in the main have focused on national culture as a paradigm to understand HRD practices. Various studies have used national cultural frameworks proposed by GLOBE, Hofstede, etc., to understand HRD practices. These studies, while useful, have reinforced the traditional country focus. If the HRD academic community are to enhance the field by exploring regional and global levels of analysis, then traditional cultural frameworks may not prove useful. Current notions of cross-cultural analysis will need to be revised if research is to be conducted at regional and global levels of analysis.

Less common are studies that focus on IHRD in the context of the MNC. As indicated earlier, the reasons for this trend are perplexing. There are major gaps in the current HRD literatures concerning how MNCs develop a geographically dispersed workforce and utilize development as a strategy for competitive advantage. There is relatively little discussion of HRD issues related to international assignments, expatriation at subsidiary or firm levels of analysis. Research at the regional and global levels of analysis would significantly enhance our understanding about how common institutions and regulations at a regional level influences IHRD. Additionally, how relevant are levels of social and political integration within a region? One could contrast the EU with NAFTA, for example. Global-level research challenges the field to investigate the contribution of HRD to world-wide issues such as CSR, world hunger and poverty, inequality in society and the management of HRD activities using global rule sets. Figure 3.1 presents a set of variables that may be explored at these levels of analysis.

Conclusions

In future, theoretical development of IHRD must continue to explore the levels of analysis that currently characterize the field; however, theory development must also extend the levels of analysis to focus on sector, regional and global levels. These represent significant gaps in the literature. Robust research around new units of analysis will serve to enhance the field and facilitate the incorporation of world-wide institutional influences, movements such as CSR, fair trade, globalized work practices and consideration of social as well as economic issues. This will include a focus on issues such as the impact of international development agencies, NGOs and voluntary and non-profit organizations. Such a focus will help establish what Beverley Metcalfe and

Chris Rees called an independent domain of IHRD:[8] research that is linked to HRM but has well-defined boundaries. The lack of discussion of the MNC in IHRD leads me to conclude that there are significant ideological differences between the IHRD and IHRM communities. The MNC and the performance paradigm are the predominant focus of IHRM at this time, whereas IHRD has engaged with a learning paradigm and more socially oriented concerns. We need to consider both in order to capture the complexity of the globalized world. We also have a major gap in our understanding of the interaction between subsidiary, firm, country, sector, regional and global levels. These latter levels of analyses represent both our challenge and our opportunity.

NOTES

1. Carol Hansen and Ann Brooks. (1994) 'A review of cross cultural research on human resource development,' *Human Resource Development Quarterly* 5(1): 55–74. Lori Peterson. (1997) 'International HRD: What we know and don't know.' *Human Resource Development Quarterly* 8(1): 63–79.
2. Gary N. McLean. (2004) 'National human resource development: What in the world is it?' *Advances in Developing Human Resources* 6(3): 269. Richard A. Swanson and Edward. F. Holton. (2009) *Foundations of human resource development*: Berrett-Koehler Publishers: San Francisco
3. Geert Hofstede. (1984) *Culture's consequences: International differences in work-related values*, Vol. 5. London: Sage.
4. Gary N. McLean, and Laird McLean. (2001). 'If we can't define HRD in one country, how can we define it in an international context?' *Human Resource Development International* (3): 313–326.
5. Examples of such value dimensions are suggested by Geert Hofstede. (1980. 'Culture and organizations,' *International Studies of Management and Organization* 10(4): 15–41; Shalom Schwartz. (1994) *Beyond individualism/collectivism: New cultural dimensions of values*. Newbury Park, CA: Sage; Alfons Trompenaars and Charles Hampden-Turner. (1998) *Riding the waves of culture: Understanding cultural diversity in global business*. New York: McGraw-Hill.
6. Rachel Baskerville. (2003) 'Hofstede never studied culture,' *Accounting, Organizations and Society* 28(1): 1–14.
7. Edward Hall and Elizabeth Hall. 1976 'How cultures collide,' *Psychology Today* 10(2): 66–74.
8. Beverly Metcalfe and Chris. J. Rees. (2005) 'Theorizing advances in international human resource development,' *Human Resource Development International* 8(4): 449–465.

4 Leadership Development and Talent Management
Fashion Statement or Fruitful Direction?

Paul Iles

The chapter explores concepts of leadership development and talent management. Management education and development is littered with concepts that have been passing fashions or fads; which ideas have staying power? The1980s saw a burgeoning interest in management development, allied to the expansion of business schools and a proliferation of management courses. The management development movement emerged, with management presented as a practical set of skills to be learned. But since the 1990s commentators have questioned whether management development is enough. There has been a renewed emphasis on leadership development and on the transformational ability to individuals to change the fortunes of organizations, in everything from police forces to multinational companies and from failing schools to city mayoralties. Organizations are increasingly competing for talent, especially leadership talent. Is 'talent' what really drives reputations, and success? Can the character of a leader really make a difference? Can leadership development make a difference?

I ask, for both leadership and talent management - who are the trendsetters and who are the trend followers? I draw on empirical work on the leadership development of CEOs in the UK, on talent management as a fashion, and on conceptions of talent management in China, the planet's fastest growing economy, drawing primarily on social capital and neo-institutional theory. I explore whether in the rush to develop leaders and manage individual talent, there is a danger of overlooking the development of collective processes and structures-culture, structure, trust, networks and social capital- to ensure winning teams and organizations. I seek to develop a way of looking at both leadership development and talent management in more social, collective and emergent terms than is currently the case. (Inaugural Professorial Lecture, Leeds Metropolitan University Rose Bowl Leeds November 11th, 2009)

CONTEXT

This chapter is based around my inaugural professorial lecture given in the Rose Bowl, Leeds Metropolitan University, Leeds, UK, November 11,

2009. An academic tradition in the UK and other countries such as Australia and New Zealand is to hold a series of inaugural professorial lectures with the broad aim of promoting and celebrating the academic reputation of professorial staff; in most cases it is used to introduce the research of newly appointed professors to a wider audience, both within and outside the University. It is usually chaired by the vice-chancellor or other senior University staff and is open to colleagues, the public and a wide-range of invited guests from industry, the professions and government.

With a background in organizational psychology and HRD, I have long been interested in leadership, and in particular in leadership development; more recently I have become interested in a more recent concept, that of talent management. It has been argued in recent years that both leadership and talent management are necessary to organizational effectiveness in all sectors; indeed they have been recently promoted as panaceas for a range of organizational problems and challenges, ranging from failures in schools and hospitals, the need to 'turnaround' companies or universities and the need to win the 'war for talent' so as to ensure that key staff that 'can make a 'difference' and 'add value' to organizations can be recruited, retained and deployed effectively. In 2009, many such claims for the necessity of leadership and talent management were being made by many HRD practitioners and consultants. What interests me here is to what extent these claims are substantive, or merely a fashion; are leadership and talent management crucial to organizational success, or are they merely a 'fad' or 'fashion,' to be promoted rapidly and then dropped as initial enthusiasm for their efficacy wanes?

THE PRESENTATION: INTRODUCTION

In this inaugural professorial lecture I will explore to what extent leadership development and talent management are 'fashion statements' or fruitful directions for HRD; in particular I will explore:

- How are they different from management/ HRM?
- How can institutional theory help show whether organizations are influenced to adopt practices such as leadership development and talent management to adapt to their institutional environment?
- To what extent do current models and practices in leadership development and talent management reflect over-individualized concepts that over-emphasize human capital development at the expense of social capital development?
- Would an alternative conception of leadership development and talent management provide a more fruitful new direction for HRD?

Like any management discourse and set of practices, management education and development are littered with concepts that have been passing fashions; which ideas have staying power? The1980s saw a burgeoning interest in management development, allied to the expansion of business schools and a proliferation of management courses such as the MBA. The management development movement emerged, with management presented as a practical set of skills (later termed 'competences') to be learned, with an emphasis on management development, management competencies and managerial assessment. Management seemed to be a rational, technical activity with underpinning skills, knowledge and 'competencies' that could be learned and applied. Commentators argued that a major explanation for the UK's relatively poor economic performance since the 1950s lay in poor management, the lack of modern management skills and the low quantity and quantity of management education and development in the UK, as compared to its leading competitors.[1] The 1980s and 1990s saw a similar growth in 'human resource management' or HRM as a distinctive way of managing people, different from and superior to 'personnel management.'

However, since the 1990s commentators have questioned whether management/ management development is enough and whether HRM was able to respond to the new challenges of the new millennium. There has been a renewed emphasis on leadership development, and on the transformational ability of individuals to change the fortunes of organizations, in everything from police forces to multinational companies and from failing schools to city mayoralties. Organizations are also increasingly competing for talent, especially leadership talent, and 'talent management' or TM has also become increasingly fashionable. Is 'talent' what really drives reputations and success? Can the character of a leader really make a difference? Can leadership development make a difference?

In this inaugural I ask, for both leadership and talent management— who are the trendsetters and who are the trend followers? I will draw on my recent empirical work on the leadership development of CEOs in the UK[2] on bibliometric studies of TM as a fashion[3] and on talent management in China, the planet's fastest growing economy.[4] I will also look forward to explore whether in the rush to develop leaders and manage individual talent, there is a danger of overlooking the development of collective processes and structures-culture, structure, trust, networks and social capital to ensure winning teams and organizations. I will seek to develop a way of looking at both leadership development and talent management in more social, collective and emergent terms than is currently the case as a more fruitful direction for HRD.

1. LEADERS, LEADING AND LEADERSHIP

I will begin by distinguishing between leaders and leadership on the one hand, and leader and leadership development on the other.[5] I then argue that leadership development has often been equated with leader development, with the resulting focus upon the individual, as against attending to the social, political, collective and other contexts of action and meaning. Social capital theory is drawn upon in order to help conceptualize and apply leadership development in context, where the emphasis is upon understanding and building relationships and networks, coordinating activities and developing commitments. On the basis of a critical review, I argue that leadership development as theorized and as practiced has too often been equated with leader development. This has resulted in a focus upon the individual, as against attending to the social, political, collective and other contexts of action and meaning. The upshot of this has been that there has been a misallocation of resources in the attempt to develop leadership capacity. I note that there is a dearth of critical studies of approaches to leadership development, despite the increasing interest shown in the phenomenon in recent years. Leadership development is argued here to be about the development of leadership processes in context, as well as the development of leaders as individuals. Leader development can be seen as involving the enhancement of human capital, while leadership development is about the creation of social capital, extending the collective ability of people to effectively undertake leadership roles and processes, and helping them to understand how to join and build social networks, develop commitments and access resources. These 'leadership roles' come both with and without formal authority. It is thus necessary to understand and act on the interactions between the 'leader' and the social, economic and political environment, with 'leadership' being an emergent property of this interaction.

A currently very influential model of leadership compares 'transactional' leaders, exercising contingent reward and management by exception, with 'transformational' leaders, exercising idealized influence and inspirational motivation in a ' charismatic-inspirational' style.[6] Such leaders stimulate organizational members intellectually and give them individualized consideration. However, in many studies, no practicing leaders are actually observed, and the specificity and generalizability of the instruments used to assess leadership have often been questioned. Students of 'managerial behavior' have often criticized 'leadership' researchers for focusing on what leaders 'should' do, not what they actually do.

Frameworks such as those above in my view carry with them the danger of once again proposing a 'one best way' of leadership and of de-contextualizing it, in particular by seeing it in terms of a set of individual leadership 'competencies. Such a model is rooted in a strong US, male and private-sector view of the 'heroic leader.'[7] Particularly post-Enron and the global banking crisis, such a model is open to serious challenge. Recent work has also stressed the importance of 'emotional intelligence' to leadership, especially transformational leadership; people vary in their capacity to process emotional information and relate it to wider cognitions, an ability often now called 'emotional intelligence' or EI, and often linked to leadership and business success.[8]

Instead of focusing on the personal qualities of leaders, I think we need to focus on the leadership challenges faced by communities, societies and organizations in a more collective way; that is, on developing leadership rather than developing leaders. In contrast to focusing on solo leaders, usually 'heroic,' 'transformational' and 'charismatic' CEOs, we need to explore shared, dispersed or 'distributed' leadership, where reciprocal influence processes operate and team structures and empowerment are seen to grow in importance.[9] Leadership involves collaborative relationships leading to collective action; a shared process of enhancing collective and individual capacity to effectively perform work roles. In this view, the leadership actions of any one 'concentrated' focal individual leader are much less important than the collective leadership provided by members of the team or organization. Such distributed leadership can be delegated; it can involve co-leadership or peer leadership. This is in my view a useful entry point for HRD, as such leadership is grounded in interaction and communication, and actors are seen as active constructors of knowledge as members of communities of practice.[10]

2. LEADER DEVELOPMENT VERSUS LEADERSHIP DEVELOPMENT

My central argument in this part of the lecture is that 'leadership development,' while increasingly fashionable, has tended to be equated with 'leader development', involving HRD activities like coaching, mentoring and outdoor development focusing on the training and development of the individual competencies, skills and attributes of the leader. There is a lack of empirical research on the effectiveness of different approaches to leadership development, while there is a growing interest in new approaches to leadership development. There is however a plethora of approaches to management development, from the formal (MBA, management training courses) through to development centers and outdoor development to the informal (on-the-job learning, coaching, mentoring). How appropriate these approaches are to leadership training and development is open to question, as little research and evaluation have taken place.

What are commonly called 'leadership development' programs are often in fact 'leader development' programs, often involving a mixture of competency models, psychometric assessments of personality, emotional intelligence and team management preferences, 360-degree feedback, communication skills training, coaching, mentoring, motivational speeches and outdoor development. Although clearly fashionable, and perhaps even useful as 'leader development,' my view here is that 'leadership development' will involve attention to more collective and contextual processes. Many currently popular leadership development practices (like 360-degree feedback, mentoring and action learning) were in fact originally developed and implemented in organizations for other reasons, such as to improve performance management, enhance socialization and increase productivity. The most popular approaches, following the individualized, competence-based models of leadership discussed earlier, have reinforced the message that leadership development is all about developing the personal attributes or competencies of leaders.

I draw here upon a distinction I developed in the 1990s between manager development and management development; 'management development is generally taken as referring to manager development, but it is important to distinguish between the two.[11] Management development can also refer to the processes in which the manager is engaged, not just to the individual manager. Consequently, if an organization wishes to improve its performance, it needs to find ways of training and developing the teams that manage the organization collectively. Management development can then be used to refer to the development of management processes and the collective skills of those involved in their operation, including changes to career development, work allocation, communication channels and organizational planning processes. What I wished to stress was that all these initiatives require the acquisition of skills by the individual managers and changes to the management processes used by the organization. Both manager and management development are necessary, but should not be conflated.

In similar fashion, I want to argue here that 'leadership development' involves the development of leadership processes in addition to the development of individual leaders. We need to link leader development, based on enhancing human capital, to leadership development, based on creating and developing social capital, a concept first developed in community studies to explain neighborhood survival through personal relationships and collective cooperation.[12] Unlike 'leadership competencies,' we cannot regard social capital as a commodity, and one sole actor or 'leader' cannot have 'ownership rights.' I see leadership development as helping people to understand how to build relationships, access resources, coordinate activities, develop commitments and build social networks. By leadership roles I mean both those that

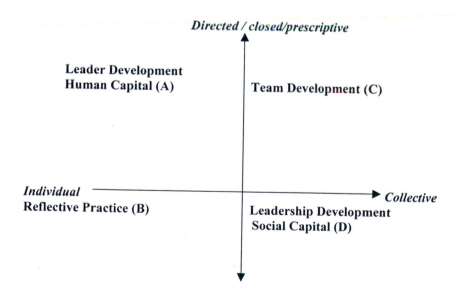

Figure 4.1   Modes of leader development.[13]

come with and without formal authority. By leadership processes I mean those that enable groups of people to work together in meaningful ways-a bit like co-authorship, rather then single authorship. Most current 'leader development' programs make few connections to organizational context; I see leadership development as involving an analysis of the complex interactions between the 'leader' and the social and organizational environment. Leadership is a social process of engaging members of a community, an effect rather than a cause, and an emergent property of social interaction in context. Leadership development therefore involves using social/ relational processes to help build commitments among members of a community of practice; this may be internal and/or external to the organization. In HRD, we need to focus on building the networks and relationships created through interpersonal exchanges that enhance cooperation, resource exchange and social capital.

In summary, I have argued in this section for making a distinction between leader development (developing individual-level intrapersonal competencies and human capital) and leadership development (developing collective leadership processes and social capital in the organization and beyond). Leadership development therefore involves relationships, networking, trust, and commitments, as well as an appreciation of the social and political context and its implications for leadership styles and actions. I have developed this idea here by proposing a typology of modes of leadership development using two axes: how 'closed' or directed' versus how 'open' or 'organic' the approach adopted is, and whether it mainly addresses individual human capital development ('leader development'), or collective social capital development, termed 'leadership development' (see Figure 4.1).

Whereas individual approaches see leading as a contribution of one actor, collective approaches such as I am advocating here see leadership as a collective phenomenon. Directed or closed/prescriptive approaches predefine the direction along which interventions will develop through predetermined paradigms (e.g., most organization development (OD) or team-building interventions, and competence frameworks). In organic, open or emergent approaches, participants can shape outcomes through emergent group/ personal development. As Figure 4.1 shows, some approaches in quadrant A (e.g., competence frameworks) can be classified as individual/directed; others associated with reflective practice can be put into Quadrant B, for example, mentoring and coaching, as individual/open approaches (although mentoring can potentially also build social capital).

More collective approaches can also be seen as either directed (e.g., team-building according to pre-determined models, Quadrant C) or as open (e.g., action learning/research or 'leadership development' focused on developing social capital, Quadrant D). In my view, leadership development can usefully involve more attention to collective and contextual processes (Quadrants C and D), not just individual processes (quadrants A and B).

One final observation to conclude this section: surprisingly little has been written on the leadership development of chief executives and other senior managers, despite the fact that in recent years we have seen much more interest in leadership. In my view, the deployment of ethnographic research methods will better inform our understanding of the above sorts of practices, using participant observation, diaries and in-depth interviews over an extended period to focus on executives' experience of and reflections upon their leadership development. Such approaches have also not often been used in studying the increasingly fashionable area of 'talent management' or TM, to which I now turn.

3. TALENT MANAGEMENT

Talent management (TM) has attracted increasing attention from academics and practitioners in recent years.[14] One line of debate has been whether TM is merely a re-packaging of what already exists, not being distinct from traditional HRM/D practices or disciplines. It is a term in common currency today, yet it did not appear until the late 1990s, when McKinsey and Company first referred to it in their report *The War for Talent*. TM is now said to be critical to organizational success, giving organizations a competitive edge through the identification, development and redeployment of talented employees. TM is often projected to be the next core competency in HR domain expertise and a key role for the corporate HR function, especially in the global firm.[15]

Yet most writing about TM has come from consultants and practitioners, rather than from academic research, and a number of critical questions remain for further empirical research and theoretical development. These include what is meant by TM, how TM differs from earlier approaches to managing people and what drives organizations to adopt TM. To date, the TM phenomenon has not been subject to a significant degree of critical scrutiny, and there has been relatively little empirical research into the nature and application of talent and TM strategies in organizational practice and the issues arising from this. Given the number of consulting firms engaging in talent management and the growing numbers of articles and books on the topic, one might also believe 'talent management' is a well-defined area of practice supported by extensive research and a core set of principles. However, this is not the case.[16]

TM requires HRD professionals and their clients to understand how they define talent, whom they regard as "the talented" and what their typical background might be; this appears to have been difficult to achieve in practice, as organizations often derive their own conceptualization of what talent is, rather than accept a universal or prescribed definition. Defining talent has proved to be a challenging and problematic business for commentators; has this also been the case for defining talent management? The short answer is 'yes.' In my view three broad strands of thought regarding TM can be identified, often associated with a particular theoretical or disciplinary base:

1) *TM is not essentially different from HRM/D*; both involve recruiting, selecting, training and managing people.

2) *TM is integrated HRM with a selective focus*; the focus is here not on the whole workforce but on a select group or segment, termed 'talents.' This perspective often builds on work in marketing on 'employer branding.'
3) *TM is organizationally focused competence development through managing flows of talent through the organization*; the focus here is on developing a talent mindset throughout the organization, building on earlier concerns with 'succession planning.'

4. IS TM A FRUITFUL NEW DIRECTION FOR HRD?

In my view, HRD practitioners have long shown concerns about the status and legitimacy of the occupation; I think this is connected to the range of titles HRD has been given over the years, such as employee development, people development, workforce development, training and development, learning and development and HRD. These have reflected changing conceptions and fashions about the nature of the occupation/discipline. HRD has often been accused of being vulnerable to fashionable 'fads,' falsely offering panaceas, rather than being based on sound evidence and robust theory; instead of new professionals turning to models and theories from a body of understanding of what works and why, they often turn to a fad-driven body of literature of what sells. Is talent management (TM) such a fad? Has there been an element of 'management fashion' about this development, or has this reflected some real change at the level of HRD practice?

HRM was also represented as a radically new approach to managing people, demarcated sharply from traditional personnel management. Does TM represent a radically new approach to managing and developing people, or is it too 'old wine in new bottles'? Many of the key ideas promulgated by TM practitioners, such as assessment centers, succession planning and 360-degree feedback, are not new, stemming from the 1950s. Is TM another management fad which has gained currency through fashion rather than through relevance and value?

In my view, we need to capture the contrasts in perspective which can be detected in the TM literature between, on the one hand, an exclusive versus inclusive people focus, and, on the other, a focus upon organizational positions as against the people themselves. As with our discussion of leadership development, combining these contrasting perspectives results in the four-quadrant model captured in Figure 4.2, outlining four main perspectives on TM: (i) exclusive-people; (ii) exclusive-position; (iii) inclusive-people; (iv) social capital. Here I see interest in talent management as being driven by increasing interest in knowledge and human capital, changes in the global labor market, changing values, changing demographics and changing technologies. This leads organizations to design TM systems for specific purposes (e.g., attracting/retaining talents, ensuring continuity of talent flows, facilitating organizational competence development). This in turn leads them to focus on how to design a talent pool and how to introduce specific

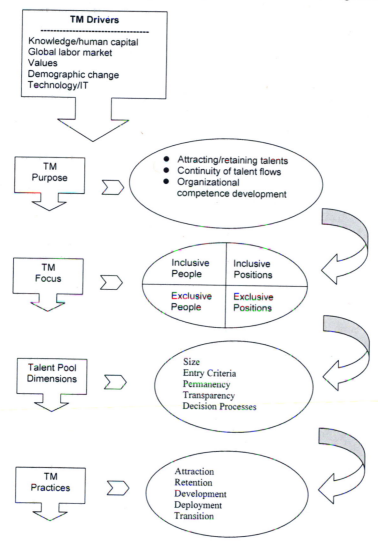

TM Drivers

Knowledge/human capital
Global labor market
Values
Demographic change
Technology/IT

TM Purpose

- Attracting/retaining talents
- Continuity of talent flows
- Organizational competence development

TM Focus

| Inclusive People | Inclusive Positions |
| Exclusive People | Exclusive Positions |

Talent Pool Dimensions

Size
Entry Criteria
Permanency
Transparency
Decision Processes

TM Practices

Attraction
Retention
Development
Deployment
Transition

Figure 4.2   Talent management framework.[17]

HRD/HRM practices associated with talent management. An important question is what is the focus of TM; does it focus on positions or people? Does it focus on an inclusive or on an exclusive approach?

a) Exclusive-people This TM perspective takes a relatively narrow view of talent: those people who have the capability to make a significant difference to the current and future performance of the organization. It adopts a position similar to definition 2, 'TM is integrated HRM with a selective focus.' On this view it is not possible for everyone in the organization to be considered as a talent and managed accordingly; talented employees are seen as fundamentally different from others in terms of their current and past performance and competence, as well as their potential. Talent is neither title nor position-related; it is based on segmentation—the division of the workforce into sections to be treated differently, such as through differentiated 'employee value propositions.'

b) Exclusive-positions This perspective on TM also takes a narrow/exclusive position, but on a different basis, going further than definition 2 in its focus on selectivity. The talent-defining process is here closely coupled with the identification of 'key positions' in the organization. The starting point of TM is the identification of strategically critical jobs ('A positions'); only those people ('A players') occupying those positions can be considered talents, who should receive a disproportionate level of financial and managerial investment. Ideally a 'perfect match' of 'A players' and 'A positions' is then expected to contribute to 'A performance'.

c) Inclusive-people In contrast, this perspective takes an 'inclusive' stance, often from 'humanistic' considerations, that potentially everyone in the organization has 'talent,' and that the task is to manage all employees to deliver high performance, closer to definition 1, TM as similar to HRM/D. This inclusive 'whole workforce' approach to TM seems comparatively rare in practice; opportunities are essential, as talent requires an opportunity to be displayed, and regular opportunities need to be provided for everyone to learn, grow and strive to fulfill their potential.

d) Social capital This perspective follows the critique of leadership development outlined earlier by viewing the majority of TM writing as too dependent on an individualistic orientation, seeing talent essentially as a form of human capital. This neglects the importance of context, social capital and organizational capital in relation to organizational performance, over-stressing individual talents (the attributes or characteristics of individuals), and downplaying the role of such factors or contingencies as teams, cultures, divisions of labor, leadership and networks in giving talent direction and opportunity. It is closest to definition 3, 'TM as organizational competence development.' In empirical research on seven international enterprises operating in Beijing, China, I found one adopting an 'inclusive-people' definition; most of the companies adopted an 'exclusive-people' definition, although the three international consultancies I studied tended to adopt an 'exclusive-position' perspective on TM. One in particular was moving toward a more 'social capital' perspective.[18]

5. IS TM A FASHION STATEMENT?

One approach to researching the TM phenomenon is to assess whether it can be seen as a management or HRD fad or fashion by using print media indicators and bibliometrics, based on the premise that the number of publications on an organization concept in the course of time reflects managerial interest in the topic. This technique has been applied to a range of phenomena, such as BPR, quality circles and the learning organization. I obtained journal article counts using the key words 'talent management' from a search of the Emerald and Business Source Premier databases between 1985 and 2009, using them as a proxy for the development in popularity/fashion of the phenomenon.[19] They revealed a dramatic increase in the numbers of articles relating to TM over this period, as Figure 4.3 shows. In 2009 there were 379 articles related to TM in Emerald and 650 in Business Source Premier, compared to 130 in Emerald and 229 in Business Source Premier in 2000.

This suggests that TM is a management fashion whose popularity has yet to peak, let alone fall; is TM just another in a long line of management fashions, doomed to lose its popularity after reaching its peak?

I also argue that the management fashion phenomenon can be seen from three main perspectives: aesthetic, substantive vs. symbolic and institutional. I find the institutional perspective to be the most useful, as it explains how organizations become increasingly similar to each other.[20] The concept of *isomorphism* best captures this homogenization process: organizations in the same or similar social, economic and political contexts come to resemble each other over time. Firms face institutional pressure from government regulators, professional associations and social networks as well as competitive pressures from other organizations, competing not only for resources and customers, but also for political power and institutional legitimacy, that is, for social as well as economic 'fitness.' Three institutional mechanisms influence organizational decision making: coercive, normative and mimetic. Coercive mechanisms arise from pressures exerted by political contexts and the challenge of legitimacy, from formal and informal pressures exerted by other organizations upon which they are dependent and societal cultural norms. Normative mechanisms refer to the articulation between management policies and the professional background of employees in terms of educational level, job experience and craftsmanship. Professional networks, such as professional and trade associations (e.g., the CIPD in the UK) help define and promulgate norms about organizational and professional behavior, creating pools of individuals who not only share common expectations, but also occupy similar positions across a range of organizations and possess a similarity of orientation and disposition. Normative isomorphism is reinforced by the process of filtering personnel; many professional career tracks in organizations are carefully controlled and monitored (both at entry and throughout the career path) so that individuals in similar positions across organizations tend to have similar biographies in terms of education, skills, work experience, and ideology.

Finally, mimetic mechanisms refer to imitations of the strategies and practices of competitors as a result of uncertainty; these are the mechanisms most often referred to in institutional theory discussions of management

	Number of articles published during the Year					
	1985	1990	1995	2000	2005	2009
Business Source Premier	16	18	84	229	590	650
Emerald	0	1	73	.130	274	379

Figure 4.3   Article count of 'TM' citations between 1985 and 2009.[21]

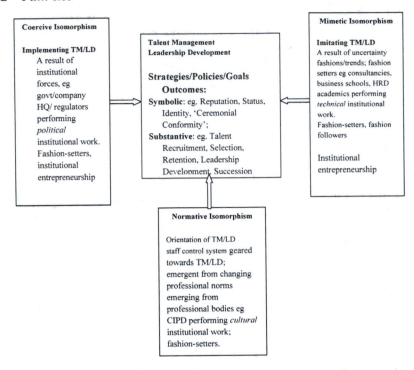

Figure 4.4 Understanding isomorphism in talent management and leadership development.[22]

fashion, as organizations model themselves on other similar organizations in their field, those perceived to be more legitimate or successful. Later, fashionable managerial techniques may be diffused unintentionally, for example, indirectly through employee transfer or turnover, or explicitly by organizations such as consulting firms or industry trade associations. In particular, managers' decisions to embrace new ideas are often informed by collective beliefs about rational or progressive managerial practice, shaped by idea providers such as consultants or gurus 'translating' practices into specific organizational contexts through the actions of professional groups and consultants. A management fashion such as TM then becomes 'unfashionable' by becoming an institution, becoming relatively permanently diffused as a result of the 'institutional work' performed by such actors. An institutional infrastructure is then built within and across organizational fields, to which actual and potential adopter organizations are exposed. Figure 4.4 displays how such processes may work for both TM and leadership development.

A generator of isomorphism in international HRD can be multinational corporate policies relating to subsidiary's practices. The HRD policies of international organizations may reflect national, institutional and/or cultural contexts, emerging common global practices or the dual effects of transnational and national contexts. In my research on TM as a fashion in China[23] I found little evidence of normative isomorphism (HRD/HRM practitioners came from a wide variety of disciplines, functions and career routes, without a powerful professional body such as the CIPD in the UK), but I did find some evidence of coercive isomorphism, with companies urged by national and local governments through seminars and conferences to adopt a talent mindset as part of a drive to upgrade China's skill and knowledge base as it sought to move up the value chain away from dependence on low-skill, low-value labor. There was more evidence of coercive isomorphism from corporate headquarters, with the US/UK/Canada-based companies urging their subsidiaries to adopt policies they had already devised for global application. The companies also claimed little influence from 'mimetic isomorphism,' stating that they were not adopting TM for reasons of boosting HRM/HRD's credibility or status; they also denied they were they fashion followers in imitating consultancies or other companies (they did acknowledge they might be fashion leaders themselves for local and domestic companies).

6. CONCLUSIONS

I conclude by arguing that both talent management and leadership development may display features of a management fashion. Both may appear to be both rational and progressive and effective means to valued ends; they may also seem new or improved in relation to older techniques. There is a lack of clarity and agreement in the literatures on both areas as to their nature, definition and scope; such ambiguity is a key feature of a management fashion for a number of commentators, as it allows 'interpretative flexibility' on the part of those adopting new ideas, and potentially greatly increases their scope for diffusion. At the same time, flexibility enhances market opportunities for fashion setters to extend diffusion through claiming specialist expertise in interpreting and resolving this ambiguity. 'Fashion followers' may then be vulnerable to ideas promulgated by 'fashion setters,' such as consultants and 'gurus' trading in fashion, utilizing persuasion and image manipulation and translating ideas into methodologies and techniques, while creating appetites for solutions. When management fashions lose their novelty, they do not necessarily disappear, but may still help develop solutions to organizational puzzles/challenges; perhaps incorporated into emerging fashion demands, or morphing into regular management practices, perhaps under new labels. The point of differentiation between a fad or institution may be related to the age or novelty of the practice, as new practices are often old fads.

Finally, it may be noted that a fashion may become 'unfashionable' by becoming an institution, relatively permanently diffused as a result of the 'institutional work,' with an institutional infrastructure built within and across the organizational fields to which actual and potential adopter organizations are exposed.

To conclude, I want to note that an empirically informed study designed to address the sort of questions outlined above runs the risk of relying on management rhetoric via interview or questionnaire surveys of managers ('TM/LD is a good thing and we are practicing it in this company'). If managers, HRD practitioners or consultants are asked if TM/LD has been adopted for 'fashionable' reasons, they are hardly likely to admit it; it is in the interests of all parties to argue that its introduction is to solve 'real' ('substantive') organizational problems. In addition, given the varying definitions and interpretations attached to TM/LD, careful interpretation will be necessary. Thus, empirical work may need to adopt other more subtle, 'indirect' approaches, such as longitudinal/multiple organizational levels/repeat visits, participant observation, discourse/ethnographic analyses, and network analyses in order to address some of the research questions I have outlined today.

AFTERMATH

Since 2009 several studies, including my own papers on talent management as a fashion and talent management as a fashion in China,[24] have been published, which allow me to reflect on the changes since this speech, and especially on what the practitioner implications of such research might be. Since 2009, a number of studies on both leadership development and talent management have been published, and attention is being given to the return of 'the war for talent' as economic conditions improve. One key point is that organizations and HRD practitioners should not just 'jump on the TM/LD bandwagon' because TM/LD is fashionable, or practiced by high-status, high-reputation organizations, or seems a way to give the profession greater credibility, or is the professional 'flavor of the month.' They should ask what questions/issues TM/LD is designed to address/solve; are they, for example, issues of branding, attraction, retention, leadership development or succession planning? If TM/LD seems to deliver appropriate solutions, practitioners should then consider what form TM/LD should take, given the mission and culture of the organization—should there be an 'exclusive' focus on a select few 'talents,' probably recruited as 'high-potential,' and who should receive disproportionate investment in HRD/LD, or should there be an 'inclusive' focus on developing everyone in the organization? Should the organization identify a few select positions as key/mission-critical, and tailor HRD/LD efforts to those positions? Or should it focus HRD/LD on building wider organizational competence and social capital? Whatever choice is made, practitioners, in their dealings with putative TM/LD 'institutional entrepreneurs' and 'fashion setters' such as consultants and gurus, need to critically examine the evidence base for claims of effectiveness or success, and the robustness of the theoretical underpinnings for such claims.

Finally, since 2009 there has been continuing interest in talent management in particular, including my own publications on talent management in

China,[25] and talent management as a fashion.[26] In addition, there has been a special issue of the *Journal of World Business* on global talent management in 2010, a book on global talent management[27] and a special issue on talent management in the Asia–Pacific region, among other publications. In addition, leadership development is of continued interest to researchers and practitioners (e.g., special issue of *The Leadership Quarterly*, June 2011). So although both areas show some evidence of fashion, it is clear that they cannot be regarded as short-term fads. Both areas hold continued promise as topics that can contribute to organizational effectiveness, and no doubt will continue to attract attention from HRD practitioners and researchers and show evidence of considerable investment by organizations themselves.

NOTES

1. Andrew Thomson, Christopher Mabey, John Storey, Colin Gray and Paul Iles. (2001) *Changing patterns of management development in Britain.* Oxford: Blackwell.
2. Paul Iles and David Preece. (2006) 'Developing leaders or developing leadership? The Academy of Chief Executives' Programmes in the North-East of England,' *Leadership* 2(3): 317–340. David Preece and Paul Iles. (2009) 'Leadership development: Assuaging uncertainties through joining a leadership academy,' *Personnel Review* 38(3): 286–306.
3. See Paul Iles, David Preece and Chuai X. (2010) 'Talent management and HRM in multinational companies in Beijing: Definitions, differences and drivers,' *Journal of World Business Special Issue 'Global Talent Management'* 46(2): 179–189.
4. Paul Iles, David Preece and Chuai X. (2010) 'Talent management and HRM in multinational companies in Beijing: Definitions, differences and drivers,' *Journal of World Business Special Issue 'Global Talent Management'* 46(2): 179–189.
5. David Day. (2000) 'Leadership development: a review in context,' *Leadership Quarterly* 11(4): 581–611.
6. Bernard Bass. (1985) *Leadership and performance beyond expectations.* Cambridge: Harvard University Press.
7. Beverly Alimo-Metcalfe and John Alban-Metcalfe. (2001) 'The development of a new Transformational Leadership Questionnaire,' *Journal of Occupational and Organizational Psychology* 74(1): 1–28.
8. Daniel Goldman. (1996) *Emotional intelligence.* London: Bloomsbury.
9. Peter Gronn. (2002) 'Distributed leadership as a unit of analysis,' *Leadership Quarterly* 13(4): 423–451.
10. Etienne Wenger. (1991) *Situated learning.* Cambridge: Cambridge University Press.
11. Margaret Dales and Paul Iles. (1992) *Assessing management skills: A guide to competences and evaluation techniques.* London: Kogan Page.
12. Jane Jacobs. (1961) *The Death and Life of Great American Cities.* New York: Random House.
13. Adapted from Jeff Gold, Rick Holden, Paul A. Iles, Jim Stewart and Joyce Beardwell, eds., (2009) *Human resource development: Theory and practice,* Basingstoke: Palgrave, fig. 11.2.
14. Ed Michaels, Helen Handfield-Jones and Beth Axelrod. (2001) *The war for talent.* McKinsey and Company, Inc. Harvard: Harvard Business School Press

15. Hugh Scullion and David Collings, eds. (2011) *Global talent management*. New York: Routledge.
16. Robert Lewis and Robert Heckman. 2006 'Talent management: A critical review,' *Human Resource Management Review*16(1): 139–154.
17. Adapted from Paul Iles, Chuai X and David Preece. (2010) 'Talent management and HRM in multinational companies in Beijing: Definitions, differences and drivers,' *Journal of World Business Special Issue 'Global Talent Management'* 46(2): 179–189, fig. 1.
18. Paul Iles, Chuai X and David Preece. (2010) 'Talent management and HRM in multinational companies in Beijing: Definitions, differences and drivers,' *Journal of World Business Special Issue 'Global Talent Management'* 46(2): 179–189.
19. See Paul Iles, Chuai X and David Preece. (2010) 'Talent management and HRM in multinational companies in Beijing: Definitions, differences and drivers,' *Journal of World Business Special Issue 'Global Talent Management'* 46(2): 179–189.
20. Paul DiMaggio and Walter Powell. (1991) *New institutionalism in organizational analysis*. Chicago: University of Chicago Press.
21. Adapted from Paul Iles, David Preece and Chuai X. (2010) 'Is talent management a management fashion in HRD? Towards a research agenda,' *Human Resource Development International* 13(2):125–146, table 1.
22. Adapted from Paul Iles, David Preece and Chuai X. (2010) 'Is talent management a management fashion in HRD? Towards a research agenda,' *Human Resource Development International* 13(2):125–146, fig. 3.
23. See David Preece, Paul Iles and Chuai X. (2011) 'Talent management and management fashion in Chinese enterprise: Exploring case studies in Beijing.' *International Journal of Human Resource Management*, 22(16): 3413–3428.
24. David Preece, Paul Iles and Chuai X. (2011) 'Talent management and management fashion in Chinese enterprise: Exploring case studies in Beijing.' *International Journal of Human Resource Management*, 22(16): 3413–3428. Paul Iles, David Preece and Chuai X. (2010) 'Is talent management a management fashion in HRD? Towards a research agenda,' *Human Resource Development International* 13(2):125–146. Paul Iles, Chuai X and David Preece. (2010) 'Talent management and HRM in multinational companies in Beijing: Definitions, differences and drivers,' *Journal of World Business Special Issue 'Global Talent Management'* 46(2): 179–189.
25. David Preece, Paul Iles and Chuai X. (2011)'Talent management and management fashion in Chinese enterprise: Exploring case studies in Beijing.' *International Journal of Human Resource Management Volume 22,(16)*: 3413–3428. Paul Iles, Chuai X and David Preece. (2010) 'Talent management and HRM in multinational companies in Beijing: Definitions, differences and drivers,' *Journal of World Business Special Issue 'Global Talent Management'* 46(2): 179–189.
26. Paul Iles, David Preece and Chuai X. (2010) 'Is talent management a management fashion in HRD? Towards a research agenda,' *Human Resource Development International* 13(2):125–146.
27. Hugh Scullion and David Collings, eds. (2011) *Global talent management*. New York: Routledge.

5 What's So Critical about Human Resource Development?

Sally Sambrook

This delayed inaugural professorial lecture presents a summary and reflection on my work around human resource development, and particularly critical approaches to HRD. I consider two notions of the term critical and how this might apply to HRD: first, why is it a critical time for HRD; and second, how can we adopt a more critical perspective to our teaching, research and practice—particularly as I argue Higher Education is a site of HRD practice, and can shape HRD practice in other work contexts. I move from commonplace understandings of critical—in the sense of life and death, or offering a critique—to a focus on critical issues and theories underpinning approaches to learning and development. I offer a very brief review of critical theory, considering two influences on critical HRD —Critical Management Studies and Critical Pedagogy—and identify implications for teaching, researching and practising HRD. Although these are presented separately, I argue they are intertwined. I review my own position as a lone critical voice in a traditional British Business School, but hope to persuade colleagues that they too are HRD practitioners and invite them to consider alternative ways of seeing and doing HRD.
(Inaugural professorial lecture at Bangor University, Wales, UK, 2011)

THE CONTEXT

The presentation I describe here is my delayed inaugural professorial lecture. It draws together several presentations that I have given previously and much of my research and thoughts that have developed over the last few years.

Currently, I work at Bangor Business School, which is steeped in the tradition of accounting, banking and economics—in fact, it used to be called the School of Accounting, Banking and Economics (SABE) and only changed its name in the last ten years or so. We are structured in two 'divisions'—financial studies and business studies. The business studies team, which I lead, has only fifteen faculty. For example, until January 2011, I was the only lecturer in Human Resource Management. We have a few other colleagues who teach and research themes broadly associated with organizational behavior, and a growing body of faculty in marketing. But across the school, the paradigm is very much positivist with a dominant focus on quantitative studies.

Please don't misunderstand me. I'm very happy at Bangor Business School; it's just that there are few people I can connect with to talk about my research. My topic is HRD—'Oh, that's just HRM.' My approach is interpretative, qualitative—drawing on ethnography, discourse analysis, autoethnography and critical management 'but where are your linear models, structural equations?' So, I feel I need to make efforts externally to pursue and progress my research, teaching and managerial practice. That's why it's vital to attend conferences, particularly HRD but also critical management and ethnography. This enables me to continue conversations with like-minded scholars talking a similar language. I also try to engage in other networks, such as the 'Management Education Research Group' and 'Ethnography Knowledge Platform' hosted at Liverpool University. It's important that we don't just speak to one another, but also extend our critical conversations into other disciplinary domains, connecting critical issues in human resource development with wider debates in managing and organizing. Here, there are opportunities for HRD to shape other areas and for other areas to help shape HRD. It's also important, in the broader, generally positivist organization and management community, to stake a claim for alternative views of epistemology and ontology and open up space for more innovative, interpretative approaches to studying and practicing HRD.

You could argue that I am a lone HRD scholar in the Business School. Yet, I view higher education (HE) as a site of HRD practice. As academics, we facilitate the learning and development of not only our students, but also of our colleagues. So perhaps I am not alone in that respect. Could I persuade my banking colleagues they practice HRD, too, in the classroom and in individual performance reviews, for example? Where I certainly feel alone and somewhat powerless is as a critical voice. I am the only critical scholar, in a mass of 'others' in the sense of the orthodox bankers, economists and econometricians, and I should also include my fellow marketing and OB colleagues. Perhaps it is my local positivist context that stimulates my need for criticality. Perhaps it is also the intense focus on accounting, banking and economics, topics partially responsible for much of the current global financial crises and corporate corruption. By looking outside my School, and engaging in the University Forum for HRD and the American Academy of HRD, I am able to connect with others to engage in the critical matters concerning human resource development.

THE PRESENTATION: WHAT'S SO CRITICAL ABOUT HUMAN RESOURCE DEVELOPMENT?

Thank you for inviting me to speak. What I'd like to share with you today is a summary and reflection on my work around human resource development, and particularly critical approaches to HRD, and then, I hope to stimulate some debate. But as Kiran Trehan and Clare Rigg[1] recently note, it is still unclear whether CHRD 'constitutes an incremental development of, or radical departure from, HRD.'

As a discourse analyst, I'm particularly interested in words, and the word critical is no exception. In 2004, I wrote and asked 'Is this a critical time for HRD?'[2] where I explored different interpretations of the word. As lecturers, we often critique—in the sense of judging, assessing—our students' work. As lecturers, we are often asking our students to engage in critical thinking, critical action learning and critical reflection, adopting a more critical pedagogy. As an HRD researcher, there are debates about the very term HRD, and that 'it' is in a critical (near death) state—perhaps challenged by a dominant HRM and/or burgeoning coaching profession, for example. I remember Wendy Ruona and John Walton[3] debating this at the American Academy for HRD several years ago, and this still has not been resolved. For example, can we sensibly use the terms 'resource' and 'development' in the same title? Does one imply a focus on performance and the other on learning, and are the two mutually exclusive or symbiotic? From a practice perspective, we are operating in a global, capitalist economy and so is anything other than performance an unnecessary, costly social responsibility? This suggests a hard, calculative approach. Critical HRD practice attempts to challenge the hegemony of capitalism by opening spaces to question taken-for-granted assumptions, and consider more carefully why and how learning is encouraged and facilitated in work organizations. However, as Tim Hatcher and Monica Lee[4] ask, how can we resolve the conflict between democratic values and undemocratic workplaces? How can this more—perhaps soft—emancipatory orientation fit the dominant capitalist economy? I like Tony Watson's[5] idea that we could develop a 'soft' hard approach, whereby capitalist goals can be met but in more humanitarian ways.

CONCEPTIONS OF 'BEING CRITICAL'

I'd like to consider two notions of the term critical and how this might apply to HRD: first, why is it a critical time for HRD; and second, how can we adopt a more critical perspective to our teaching, research and practice—particularly as I argue higher education is a site of HRD practice, and can shape HRD practice in other work contexts. So, I have moved from commonplace understandings of critical—in the sense of life and death, or offering a critique—to a focus on critical issues and theories underpinning approaches to learning and development.

To address the first issue, WHY is this a critical time for HRD—because of a failure of orthodox HRD, or a lack of critical influence within the field of HRD? We need only look to the corruption in North American companies such Enron, the recent global financial crises in the UK, Greece, Portugal and

Ireland, a culture of bribery in the Indian economy and human rights issues in China to see there is widespread greed and human violation in contemporary work organizations. Who could support the pursuit of corporate goals such as selling mortgages to people who clearly cannot afford to pay them, or taking risks with health and safety to cut operational costs? Yet, HRD extends beyond multi-nationals and in some of these countries HRD is part of national socio-economic plans, and so of even greater importance. There is a growing voice that challenges us to question the interests served by HRD interventions—what goals, and whose goals are we pursuing? Laura Bierema and Michelle D'Abundo[6] talk of HRD as being the conscience of an organization, and how HRD professionals can help senior managers develop more ethical and sustainable organizational activities. Would this help—organizations, individuals and HRD itself? Or is this a laudable but naïve ambition in a capitalist context? Perhaps that depends on how we might become more critical.

So, second, HOW can we adopt a more critical perspective? In line with the view of Monica Lee[7] who advocates a becoming ontology for HRD, I would propose that this can occur through various ways of 'becoming' critical. Orthodox HRD, which has perhaps supported—and certainly not challenged—many of the recent dubious organizational practices, can be explored and expanded through more critical approaches to research, practice and pedagogy. Of course, these three activities are closely related and share their roots in critical theory (CT). Some, such as Jean Woodall,[8] have argued that critical theory has been noticeably absent in HRD theorizing. I'd like to very briefly summarize the role of critical theory in HRD, and the influence of critical management studies (CMS) and critical pedagogy (CP), before sharing some experiences of critical pedagogy, research and practice, in the contexts of higher education, health organizations and education. including critical thinking, critical reflection, and action learning sets.

APPLYING THE CRITICAL TO HRD

As a professor of HRD, it is a pleasure to be invited to examine doctorates and I am especially delighted when they focus on critical HRD. Recently, I was the external examiner for Allan Ramdhony, at Napier University. He noted the limited attention to CT in HRD research, and proposed an *unmediated* approach. He advocated reverting to core critical theory literatures, such as the Frankfurt School—a form of self-reflective social theory rooted in a dialectical mode of thinking, which seeks to expose ideologies and social contradictions that are potentially oppressive. I asked how we could actually achieve a completely unmediated approach—after all, we all perceive and interpret things in different ways and impart our personal biases. But his approach reminded me that critical HRD has been largely shaped—or mediated—by two bodies of thinking: critical management studies (CMS) and critical pedagogy (CP). Critical management studies (CMS), as its label suggests, adopts a management perspective, focusing on oppressive managerial practices. CMS has emerged largely in Europe and its proponents tend to be located in business schools. With the interest in CMS, growing attention has turned to HRM, and more recently to HRD. In contrast, critical pedagogy (CP) adopts a pedagogic perspective, focusing on oppressive teaching practices in adult learning. This has developed mainly in North and South America; its proponents are usually located in schools of education, where many what we might call HRD scholars reside.

In the UK, I would argue that critical HRD has been more influenced by CMS. There is an established history of thinking 'critically' in management.[9] Gibson Burrell[10] reviews this work and notes that critical theory is associated with challenging 'rational' organization practices and replacing them with more democratic and emancipatory practices. This involves identifying weaknesses and limitations of orthodoxy, the need for self-reflexivity, the empowerment of a wider range of participants to effect change and explanations of social phenomena that are multi-dimensional, recognizing the tensions in and contradictions of managing and organizing . . . and I would add learning and development activities. However, as Carole Elliott and Sharon Turnbull[11] argue, 'Despite the influence of the critical turn in management studies on HRD in the UK, HRD has nevertheless neither been subject to the same degree of critical scrutiny as management and organization studies, nor has it gathered together a significant mass of followers that might constitute it as a 'movement' in its own right.' They were, I think, the first scholars in the UK to consider HRD from an explicitly critical perspective and introduced their ideas at the American Academy.[12]. However, I would suggest that others, myself included,[13] were engaged in a critique of the subject of HRD and orthodox ways of conceptualizing and researching it, along with colleagues such as Monica Lee in her defiant refusal to define HRD. Our nascent resistance and critique were captured by Carole and Sharon, who were 'concerned that the methodological traditions that guide the majority of HRD research do not allow researchers to engage in studies that challenge the predominantly performative and learning-outcome focus of the HRD field. . . . We seek to unpick the assumptions behind the performative orientation that dominates much HRD research . . . We therefore perceived the need to open up HRD theory to a broader range of methodological and theoretical perspectives.' This first critical session in the US was followed by a 'Critical HRD' stream at the 2003 CMS conference,[14] and critical HRD has also become a regular theme in the European HRD conference, which I have led with various colleagues.

Why become critical? Billig[15] argues that, 'Basically, when academics apply 'critical' to their own paradigm, discipline or theory, the label tends to signal two related messages:

(a) the new paradigm/discipline/theory includes social analyses, particularly the analysis of social inequality;

(b) the 'critical' paradigm/discipline/theory is opposing existing paradigms/disciplines/theories, which among other failings, fail to address social inequalities. As such, the critical paradigm signals its 'other'—the mainstream, apparently uncritical paradigm.'

So, we need to carefully consider why we engage in this 'other' approach: to bring in more social analyses of learning and development in the workplace; and to challenge the mainstream, orthodox approach. I have always felt uncomfortable about a 'them and us' approach—I'm not sure I want to be an 'other' and I argue that both the orthodox and critical voices should be heard and tolerated. If we begin to consider our own 'critical' approach as best and above critique, I think we are in danger of becoming the next orthodoxy. However, I do think there needs to be space for our critical voice.

This brings me to what we might call a critical turn in HRD. Over the last five or so years, there has been a huge increase in scholarly activity around critical HRD. Clare Rigg and colleagues[16] state there are four main reasons for this critical turn, in response to:

1. the predominance of 'performative values'
2. an unbalanced reliance on humanist assumptions, and an instrumental view of personhood and self
3. 'impoverished' HRD research, dominated by positivism, the reification of organizational structures, and independent of human agency, and
4. an HRD curriculum and pedagogy which pay minimal attention to issues of power and emotion.

CHRD IN PRACTICE?

So these are the reasons why. In terms of how, Tara Fenwick[17] proposes an integrated foundation of CHRD, based on four interrelated precepts that 'do not exist in isolation but , , , intertwine dynamically in organizational and academic practice.' These are:

1. The purposes of workplace reform are aligned with equity, justice, and organizational democracy
2. Knowledge is treated as contested, political and non-performative
3. Inquiry is focused on denaturalizing organizational power and knowledge relations and
4. Prevailing conditions are subject to reflexivity and critical challenge[18]

These themes, from a North American adult learning scholar, reinforce Fournier and Grey's work[19] in CMS. In the UK, Claire Valentin,[20] one of the few British HRD academics located in a School of Education, argues critical HRD encompasses:

1. Insight (recognition of the specific, contextual socio-political dimension)
2. Critique (challenging oppressive ideologies and dominant forms of research) and
3. Transformative redefinitions (an emancipatory intent, and the practical application of research).

This last point is crucial. If we are serious scholars we must not shy away from critiquing CHRD itself. I've been robustly questioned at conferences and job interviews about the ability of critical HRD to change practice. It's all very well in theory. In theory, it's easy to problematize HRD, rather than solve practical problems. Claire Valentin[21] talks of critical HRD lacking practical application. Tara Fenwick[22] questions whether critical HRD is isolated, lacks impact and is elitist. I have also pondered whether it is just grand utterances, and all talk?

In practice, Russ Vince[23] has argued that HRD practitioners ignore the wider politics of organizing; others note the contradictions of attempting to achieve social justice *versus* stakeholder wealth, and Stephen Brookfield[24] talks of the resistance, and potentially disruptive consequences, of critical HRD.

So, how does this translate into teaching, research and practice? Although I shall discuss these separately, I firmly believe that these three are inextricably linked. For example, in my teaching, I draw on my own and other research from the critical HRD community. Some of this research has been conducted in collaboration with HRD practitioners. HRD practitioners can become students, on masters' and doctoral programs. These are all connected; however, for clarity, I'll try to consider each separately in turn.

Research

Orthodox HRD research is dominated by the 'scientific' approach employing an inappropriate use of methods from the natural sciences within social sciences. I have argued that this creates epistemological, ontological and methodological problems.[25] Critical scholars call for other ways of 'seeing' and researching HRD, drawing upon more interpretive philosophies and innovative methods among the growing range of alternative interpretative, collaborative approaches, and through different lenses.[26] Our aim is to achieve this 'critical turn,' through transformative ways of researching to expose power relations and oppression in HRD practices—and HRD research. One way is through critical constructionism, which calls for the practical application of critical theory. An exciting way I am developing my research is through autoethnography, which is one of the most conspicuous anti-theses of positivism. I am also suggesting—but not imposing—autoethnography to doctoral students, fully appreciative of the difficulties of conducting such 'wacky' research in our orthodox business school.[27]

Teaching

In the UK, much HRD teaching occurs in business schools, where the curriculum is dominated by the CIPD performance orientation. Critical teachers call for HRD to retain its identity and independence from mainstream HRM. In adopting a critical pedagogy, we can focus on radical content and/or radical process. We could be teaching the *content* of critical HRD, such as structures of power, domination, emancipation, equality of opportunity and access to learning opportunities, and/or role modeling *process*. This involves examining our own power relations with students. Again, this transformation is not unproblematic in attempting to achieve democratic relationships between teachers and learners, and non-hierarchical forms of assessment, for example, and can lead to disruptive consequences such as dissonance, which Stephen Brookfield[28] refers to as the 'dark side' of critical reflection. Higher education is a potential site of critical HRD, fraught with politics and emotion. But, perhaps this is even more contentious for practitioners in other work organizations.

Practice

Kiran Trehan[29] is concerned that whereas critical approaches have been introduced in pedagogy, little appears to have been transferred to HRD practice. However, Clare Rigg[30] cautiously notes that critical management learning can develop critical managers, making the link between what we can do as HRD teachers and how this can influence HRD practice in other organizations. However, Clare, Kiran and Jim[31] do recognize that there is a disconnection between CHRD theory and practice—as being critical is 'not so easy to expedite in practice as to articulate in theory.' Critical constructionism calls for the practical application of critical theory and arguably offers what Brookfield[32] talks of as the 'flexible pursuit of beautiful consequences.' As scholars, we need to ensure our contributions are relevant to the practical 'wicked issues' in contemporary organizations. We also need to be aware of how attempts at critical HRD are received in organizations, often met with resistance from dominant groups, whose interests may be thwarted by changes in power. There is also the danger of assimilation, where critical HRD is stripped of its 'socio-political element' and emancipatory potential to be converted into a managerial toolkit to serve the interests of those in power while 'leaving the superficial impression that a more critical approach has been applied' to the HRD process.[33] Adopting critical constructionism addresses what Russ Vince[34] identifies as the political dimension. What is the role of HRD practitioners? Do they have a hand in potentially reinforcing control and manipulation? Are they mere implementers of corporate strategy or do they have a voice in shaping more ethical, meaningful work, supported by learning and development opportunities negotiated with employees? Should HRD interventions serve the purpose of freeing humans—perhaps from capitalist exploitation and employment degradation, as O'Donnell and colleagues[35] suggest? Can HRD practice be emancipated from its own *performance* cage?

CRITICAL PEDAGOGY

Having briefly outlined the implications of critical HRD in research, teaching and practice, I'd now like to share some examples with you that connect all three. As a professor of HRD, I am invited to examine PhDs, where I witness glimpses of critical HRD practice. I'd like to share just one example, which draws upon Allan Ramdhony's PhD[36] conducted in the British National Health Service (NHS). Allan applied my concept analysis, to identify the antecedents, attributes and consequences of attempts to develop critical HRD. Drawing on the Frankfurt School of Critical Theory, he identified twelve CHRD roles. In particular, he noted what Mats Alvesson and Hugh Willmott[37] termed micro-emancipation, through the establishment of critical action learning sets, or CALS. These are micro-emancipatory, non-elitist, and non-performative versions of standard action learning sets, free from domination and power asymmetries, [38] and built on free discourse as advocated by Habermas in his notion of ideal speech situation.[39] Such humble, local activities can provide valuable 'small wins' or incremental gains for CHRD practice within the day-to-day experiences of organizations while reducing the risk of a full-blown opposition from dominant groups. They can be used, as Tara Fenwick[40] suggests, to target specific oppressive practices, and help avoid utopian visions and moral evangelism.

This is just one example, but critical HRD in practice is making a small and cautious start. In addition, Tara Fenwick[41] notes some critically oriented development work in organizations, suggesting that sites of critical HRD may already exist in practice if not in name, however peripherally. Again, higher education is a prime site of critical HRD practice. Here, where our students have the potential to become future critical HRD practitioners—and managers—there are several conceptions of 'being critical' that we can introduce, including developing the ability and confidence to critique, to engage in critical thinking, critical reflection and critical action learning sets, as I've just mentioned. I'd now like to share some examples of this critical HRD pedagogy.

As a former nurse, I had an opportunity to develop an MSc in Health and Social Care Leadership in what was then the School of Nursing at Bangor University. This was a brand-new program, designed in collaboration with senior managers, health and social care stakeholders. With a blank canvas, I aspired to move toward a critical pedagogy.[42] The curriculum included some critical content, but mainly fostered a critical process, with critical reflection as the cornerstone, as advocated by Michael Reynolds.[43] I introduced 'critical thinking' and wanted to explore how this transferred back to the NHS culture, conscious that I might be creating dissonance. However, the students talked about how this approach gave them, as developing managers, a stronger voice, and gave them new discursive resources to challenge dominant practices. They reported that learning this new language was a crucial tool for reflection. However, for me, there were some challenges. Several senior practitioners were invited to speak. I hadn't anticipated the impact of the students' increasing critical thinking and concept of 'voice' on those sessions and was soon acutely aware of the 'dangers' of students challenging guest speakers! While I was comfortable, and openly encouraged students to challenge my deliberately controversial content, these senior practitioners ignored or failed to adequately answer their critical questions and I had not predicted such disruptive consequences.

In another example of critical pedagogy, I was the external examiner of an MA in Strategic HR. Aileen Lawless, the program director, introduced a process radical pedagogy with elements of content-radical pedagogy, again with the emphasis on critical reflection. However, on our journey through the evaluation of several cohorts, we witnessed students becoming powerful, but also recognized sometimes their powerlessness in their employing organizations. We began to ask some critical questions.[44] How is HRD talked about as students strive to become a community of critically reflective practitioners, recognizing the role of discourse? What does this analysis reveal about the power and emotion of critical approaches to HRD? What is the political and ethical role of educators in facilitating (or otherwise) a radical pedagogy? We are still struggling with these questions, and the implications for our own HRD practice, and consequences—beautiful or otherwise—for our student-practitioners.

Connecting teaching, research and practice in one final way, I also believe there are some critical aspects of HRD in doctoral supervision. Because of my own emotional rollercoaster and oscillating feelings of power and powerlessness, I have developed an interest in my practice as a doctoral supervisor and mentor of novice supervisors. With Clair Doloriert and Jim Stewart,[45] we suggest supervisors might unconsciously ignore or simply dismiss the issues of power and emotion in doctoral supervision, and their crucial role in this unique, delicate, dynamic, complex relationship. Doctoral supervision is arguably the highest form of teaching, facilitating learning and supporting individual development. Supervisors are in positions with various forms of power, such as reward, expert and legitimate. Yet, students also have power as Grant[46] illustrates in the demand to read numerous draft chapters. The work I've done with Clair and Jim highlights the need to recognize and manage the power dynamics and shifting dependencies within doctoral research. We also need to more carefully consider the extent to which both parties have implicit/explicit expectations and obligations, in the sense of a psychological contract, as I discovered with one of my recent students.[47] Important questions to raise here include: whose research agenda is being addressed? Whose preferred research philosophical orientation is being utilized? Whose intellectual property is acknowledged, for example, through co-authorship?

TO CONCLUDE

I have argued that HRD is critical to help avoid future global corruption and financial crises. I have briefly reviewed the historical and disciplinary roots of critical HRD. I have considered ways of becoming critical and hope I have shared with you evidence of the emergence and cautious accomplishment of critical HRD in teaching, research and practice.

However, I am fully aware of the concept of critical HRD as a target for skepticism. What is the place of such radical, democratic ideals in the context of a performative orientation? I argue that critical HRD has a crucial role in attempting to positively influence the values and behaviors of corporate board members and senior managers to pursue more democratic working practices that provide both profit and meaningful work. However, we need more research here.

I am also aware that critical HRD could be accused of being just another impotent discursive artifact—all talk, and no action. I grappled with that possibility in my own doctorate. It is easy to problematize in theory but how can we act to effect change? This is an ongoing debate in the CMS arena.

I wonder if critical HRD is part of—in tension with—HRD? I do not seek to elevate critical HRD to become the only way of thinking about HRD, but offer it as an alternative. If being critical is signaling a move from orthodoxy, are we in danger of creating/perpetuating 'us' and 'others,' and if so, is this problematic?

Do CHRD people have the power and influence to take this critical agenda forward? Thinking back to my critical teaching interventions, whose vision and goals were we struggling toward? Mine, yours, others, theirs? And what is the focus of our emancipatory efforts—whom are we seeking to emancipate, and why?

Finally, and related to this, is it ethical to pursue such an idealistic agenda in a capitalist economy? Or is it critical? Thank you.

THE AFTERMATH

In this reflective section, I am in the unusual position of not being able to look back and reflect on this professorial lecture as I have yet to present it, but I can look forward and imagine how I might respond to colleagues, here in Bangor Business School, and beyond. Writing this has provided an opportunity to link my own practices of critical HRD with the culture in which I work and is a natural extension of my own auto-ethnographic research.

I wonder how this will go down. I shall certainly be nervous presenting it, as a lone critical voice. Yet, perhaps, that is exactly how critical HRD practitioners might feel in other capitalist work organizations. Do I also risk cultural suicide, as Stephen Brookfield identified? I wonder what effect it might have.

Could I achieve a small win, in a very local context? Might I stimulate colleagues to think of themselves as practitioners of HRD? Could I stir some tiny rumblings of criticality, inspiring colleagues to experiment and open up more democratic and discursive spaces to debate issues of power, values and emotion with students? If so, how responsible should I feel for any possible dark consequences and how supportive should I be of staff and students who find themselves in new perceived positions of power or powerlessness? My intention is not to convert anyone, but to open up possibilities for recognizing and respecting other ways of teaching, researching and practicing HRD, within and without the higher education context. But perhaps with these small, local, micro-emancipatory efforts, this just might build a critical mass.

NOTES

1. Kiran Trehan and Clare Rigg. (2011) 'Theorising critical HRD: A paradox of intricacy and discrepancy,' *Journal of European Industrial Training* 35(3): 276–290, esp. 276.
2. Sally Sambrook. (2004) 'A "critical" time for HRD?' *Journal of European Industrial Training* 28(8/9): 611–624.
3. John Walton. (2003) 'How shall a thing be called? An argumentation on the efficacy of the term *HRD*,' *Human Resource Development Review* 2(3): 310–326.
4. Monica Lee and Tim Hatcher. (2003) 'HRD and the democratic ideal: The conflict of democratic values in undemocratic work systems,' in J. Winterton (ed.), *International, Comparative and Cross-Cultural Dimensions of HRD*, Toulouse.
5. Tony Watson. (2004) "Human resource management and critical social science analysis,' *Journal of Management Studies* 41(3): 447–467.
6. Laura Bierema and Michelle D'Abundo. (2004) 'HRD with a conscience: Practicing socially responsible HRD,' *International Journal of Lifelong Education* 23(5):443–458.
7. Monica Lee. (2001) 'A refusal to define HRD,' *Human Resource Development International* 4: 327–341.
8. Jean Woodall, ed. (2005) 'Convergence and diversity in HRD,' *Human Resource Development International* 8 (1): 1–4.
9. See, for example, Mats Alvesson, and Hugh Willmott. (1996) *Making sense of management: A critical introduction*, London: Sage.
10. Gibson Burrell. (2001) 'Critical dialogues on organization,' *Ephemera* 1(1): 11–29.
11. Carole Elliott and Sharon Turnbull. (2005) 'Critical thinking in human resource development: An introduction,' in Carole Elliott and Sharon Turnbull (eds.), *Critical Thinking in Human Resource Development*, London: Routledge, 1–7, esp. 1.
12. Carole Elliott and Sharon Turnbull. (2002) 'Critical thinking in HRD: A panel led discussion,' *Proceedings of the Annual AHRD Conference*, Honolulu, Hawaii: *Academy of Human Resource Development*: 971–973, esp. 971.
13. Sally Sambrook. (2001) 'HRD as emergent and negotiated evolution,' *Human Resource Development Quarterly* 12(2): 169–193.
14. Kiran Trehan, Clare Rigg and Jim Stewart. (2002) 'A critical turn in HRD,' *Call for Papers for the Critical Management Studies 3 Conference*, available at www.cms3.org. Last accessed July 2002

15. M. Billig. (2000) 'Towards a critique of the critical,' *Discourse and Society* 11(3): 291–292.

16. Clare Rigg, Jim Stewart and Kiran Trehan, eds. (2007) *Critical human resource development: Beyond orthodoxy.* Harlow: Pearson Education FT Prentice Hall, 3–8.

17. Tara Fenwick. (2005) 'Conceptions of critical HRD: Dilemmas for theory and practice,' *Human Resource Development International* 8(3): 225–238, esp. 229.

18. Ibid., 225.

19. Valerie Fournier and Chris Grey. (2000) 'At the critical moment: Conditions and prospects for critical management studies,' *Human Relations* 53(1): 7–32.

20. Claire Valentin. (2006) 'Researching human resource development: Emergence of a critical approach to HRD enquiry,' *International Journal of Training and Development* 10(1): 17–29, esp. 24–25.

21. Ibid.

22. Tara Fenwick. (2004) 'Toward a critical HRD: In theory and practice,' *Adult Education Quarterly* 54(3): 193–209.

23. Russ Vince. (2005) 'Ideas for critical practitioners,' in Carole Elliott and Sharon Turnbull (eds.), *Critical Thinking in Human Resource Development,* London: Routledge, 26–36.

24. Stephen Brookfield. (2001) 'Repositioning ideology critique in a critical theory of adult education,' *Adult Education Quarterly* 52: 7–22.

25. Sally Sambrook. (2000) 'Talking of HRD,' *Human Resource Development International* 3(2): 159–178.

26. Laura Bierema and Maria Cseh. (2003) 'Evaluating AHRD using a feminist research framework,' *Human Resource Development Quarterly* 14: 5–26.

27. Clair Doloriert and Sally Sambrook. (2011) 'Accommodating an autoethnographic PhD: The tale of the thesis, the viva voce, and the traditional business school,' *Journal of Contemporary Ethnography* 40 (5), 582–615

28. Stephen Brookfield. (1994) 'Tales from the dark side: A phenomenography of adult critical reflection,' *International Journal of Lifelong Education* 13(3): 203–216.

29. Kiran Trehan. (2004) 'Who is not sleeping with whom? What's not being talked about in HRD?' *Journal of European Industrial Training* 28(1): 23–38.

30. Clare Rigg. (2005) 'Becoming critical: Can critical management learning develop critical managers,' in Carole Elliott and Sharon Turnbull (eds.), *Critical Thinking in Human Resource Development,* London: Routledge, 37–52.

31. Clare Rigg, Jim Stewart and Kiran Trehan, eds. (2007) *Critical human resource development: Beyond orthodoxy,* Harlow: Pearson Education, FT Prentice Hall, 11.

32. Stephen Brookfield. (1994) 'Tales from the dark side: A phenomenography of adult critical reflection,' *International Journal of Lifelong Education* 13(3): 203–216.

33. Michael Reynolds. (1999) 'Grasping the nettle: Possibilities and pitfalls of a critical management pedagogy,' *British Journal of Management* 9: 171–184, esp. 178.

34. Russ Vince. (2005) 'Ideas for critical practitioners,' in Carole Elliott and Sharon Turnbull (eds.), *Critical Thinking in Human Resource Development,* London: Routledge, 26–36.

35. David O'Donnell, David McGuire and Christine Cross. (2006) 'Critically challenging some assumptions in HRD,' *International Journal of Training and Development* 10(1): 4–16.

36. Allan Ramdhony. (2010) A conceptual expansion of critical human resource development: insights into practice in a healthcare organisation. PhD thesis, Napier University, Edinburgh; Allan Ramdhony. (2011) A Conceptual Expansion of Critical HRD: Towards a Post-Reflective Understanding of HRD? 7th CMS Conference, Naples, July.

37. Mats Alvesson and Hugh Willmott. (1996) *Making sense of management: A critical introduction.* London: Sage.

38. Michael Reynolds. (1999) 'Grasping the nettle: Possibilities and pitfalls of a critical management pedagogy,' *British Journal of Management 9*: 171–184.

39. Jurgen Habermas. (1984) *The theory of communicative action: Reason and the rationalization of society*, vol.1. Cambridge: Polity Press

40. Tara Fenwick. (2004) 'Toward a critical HRD: In theory and practice,' *Adult Education Quarterly* 54(3): 193–209.

41. Tara Fenwick. (2005) 'Conceptions of critical HRD: Dilemmas for theory and practice,' *Human Resource Development International* 8(3): 225–238.

42. Sally Sambrook. (2010) 'Critical pedagogy in a health service management development programme: Can "critically thinking" managers change the NHS management culture?' *Journal of Health Organisation and Management* 23(6): 656–671.

43. Michael Reynolds. (1997) 'Towards a critical pedagogy,' in John Burgoyne and Michael Reynolds (eds.), *Management Learning: Integrating Perspectives in Theory and Practice*, London: Sage, 312–328.

44. Aileen Lawless and Sally Sambrook. (2008) 'Critically reflective practice and peripheral participation: A powerful or a powerless position?' *9th International Conference on HRD and Practice across Europe*. Lille: IESEG.

45. Sally Sambrook, Jim Stewart and Clair Roberts. (2008) 'Doctoral supervision: A view from above, below and the middle,' *Journal of Further and Higher Education* 32(1): 71–84. Clair Doloriert and Sally Sambrook. (2009) 'Ethical confessions of the 'I' of autoethnography: The student's dilemma,' *Journal of Qualitative Research in Organization and Management: An International Journal* 4(1): 27–45.

46. Barbara Grant. (2003) 'Mapping the pleasures and risks of supervision,' *Discourse: Studies in the Cultural Politics of Education* 24(2): 175–190.

47. Delia Wainwright and Sally Sambrook. (2009) 'Working at it: Autoethnographic accounts of the psychological contract between a doctoral supervisor and supervisee,' *4th Annual International* Ethnography Symposium, Liverpool University.

Part II

Location

This part considers how HRD is located within the wider field. To some extent it addresses the situated nature of HRD that is alluded to in the previous part. This part starts in 2003 with Chartchai Na Chiangmai's examination of HRD in Thailand, in which he presents a model of holistic management of human resource development, based around the development philosophy of sufficiency economy. These proposals for national development link both to National HRD examined by Gary Mclean in Chapter 15 and to Chapter 11 in which Chanin Vongkusolkit describes the implementation of many of the ideas raised here. Chapter 7, by Nigel Haworth and Jonathan Winterton, recounts a speech given in 2004, in which they jump the level of NHRD to examine supra-state HRD strategies in the EU and APEC regions. They found that despite fundamental differences in the underlying economic objectives of the two approaches and in the means by which the HRD policies are developed, there were important lessons they could learn from each other. We then move to 2009, and the last two speeches in this part. AAhad Osman-Gani maintains the international focus that emerged in 2004 with the Limerick conference (Chapters 3, 7 and 15) and examines factors affecting international managers' adjustment and performance in overseas assignments. This resonates strongly with the following part, 'Implementation,' and, finally, Sharon Turnbull's examination of the qualities that different cultures bring to the notion of leadership resonates with the fourth part, 'Value'ation.'

6 Challenges and Issues of HRD in Thailand

Seeking Holistic and Sustainable Development

Chartchai Na Chiangmai

This chapter addresses the question of how to manage change in terms of building up capacity to become more holistically economic and social competitiveness for sustainable growth and sustainable human development. In the contexts of new set of assumptions underlying the current economic, social, technological environment, a set of ideas on strategic capabilities for which organizations should strive to build was proposed. New capabilities of Thai organizations and people are identified. A model of holistic management of human resource development, based on the author's research experiences on Thai public and private management development over two decades, is developed to create new organization capabilities. In this management model, a concept of human resource development and the "link and learn" strategy are presented to promote a continuous learning process. Competitive capabilities of Thai organizations and people will not be sustained if the management of change and that of human resource development lack the guidance of a well-defined and powerful management philosophy. A management philosophy based on the philosophy of sufficiency economy bestowed to the Thai people by King RAMA IX, the present monarch of Thailand, is such a philosophy to achieve a holistic and sustainable development.
(2nd Asia International Conference on HRD in Asia, Bangkok, Thailand, 2003)

CONTEXT

This chapter is based on a keynote speech that I gave at the concluding plenary session of the 2nd International Conference on HRD in Asia: National Policy Perspectives, November 30–December 2, 2003, at Rama Gardens Hotel, Bangkok, Thailand. There were 130 participants from nineteen countries. More than 130 persons from the United States, Europe and 10 Asian countries participated. Nearly 100 research papers were presented by HRD practitioners, graduate students and university faculty. Conference keynote speakers included Ms. Yong Ying-I, permanent secretary of the Ministry of Manpower Government of Singapore; Dr. Gary McLean, professor at the University of Minnesota; Sathist Sathirakul, senior manager of the Siam Cement Public Company Ltd., Thailand; Takekazu Kaneko, vice president of human resources for Sumitomo 3M, Japan.

The 2nd International Conference on HRD represented a significant development of cooperation among HRD scholars and practitioners in Asia. For some years I have witnessed the increasing sense of international spirit and partnership which translates cooperation of HRD scholars and professionals across the regions into an important and visible organization in its own right, that is, the Academy of Human Resource Development International. I sincerely believe AHRD has been becoming a successful model of international values of cooperation in action.

As human resource development is a most important key to competitiveness and sustainable growth, AHRD can provide a crucial role in development of the countries and people in the world. In my opinion, AHRD can give ideas to governments, business organizations and civil society organizations about how to better their ways of developing human resource and organizations. I have raised in this chapter some ideas on strategic capabilities for which organizations should strive to build. A model of holistic management of human resource development, based on my research experiences on Thai public and private management development, is presented for consideration and further discussion.

THE PRESENTATION

Challenges of HRD in Thailand

A critical question confronting Thai organizations and Thai people today is not whether to change in response to their swiftly changed environment, but precisely how to manage that change. How do they modify organizational structures and cultures and develop new competencies? How do they develop human resource so as to build up competitive capabilities for sustainable growth of Thailand? Importantly, too, how do they sustain that process of change to avoid the recurrence of another economic crisis? In other words, it is the question of how to manage change in terms of building up capacity to achieve more holistically economic and social competitiveness for sustainable growth and sustainable human development.

I will begin my presentation with a new set of assumptions underlying the current economic, social, technological environment. Under a conception of changing realities, new capabilities of Thai organizations and people will be identified. A key strategy toward a sustainable competitive capability is proposed. I then suggest a model of holistic management of human resource development to create new capabilities. I will end my discussion with the philosophy of sufficiency economy. It is a development philosophy given to the Thai people by King Rama IX to achieve a holistic and sustainable development.

A NEW PARADIGM

In the past two decades, the whole world and Thailand have been undergoing rapid and complex changes. The capacity to respond to the rapid changes and the development of competitive capabilities for sustainable growth have become important policy issues. Development planning in the conventional sense is about to become obsolete. Strategy setting and the effective implementation of strategy are of the utmost importance. Thailand and other countries are moving from the so-called Development Era to the so-called Strategy Era.

A future trend that is rapidly spreading across the world is the increasing number of people who are adopting the rule of free competition. In doing so we need to refer to the behavior of others. Economists used to base their models upon the assumption that people decide independently by themselves. Now many recent studies point out that we are becoming inevitably more interdependent in making decisions and in choosing our course of life. This new conception leads to a change in basic economic and social assumptions.

This new paradigm leads us to realize that development strategies should become more pluralistic with multiple goals in order to reach a balanced development of economy, society and natural resources and environment, and hence move toward sustainable well-being.

The Need for New Capabilities

In this conceptual framework, a knowledge-based economy and society are the fundamental basis for formulation of development strategies, and a model of holistic management of human development. Thai organizations and people are therefore required to possess more capabilities to overcome challenges and operate reasonably well. They should be able to

- conceive and execute complex strategies,
- acquire, share and protect intellectual capital, particularly indigenous wisdom, and

FROM	TO
Economic Independence	Interdependence of people, Communities, nations, and the World
Social fragmentation	Social Networks
Political and Administrative Centralization	Horizontal Linkage and Distributed Governance
Single Objective/ Single purpose	Multiple objectives/ multi-purpose

Figure 6.1   New development paradigm.

- manage the interaction of three main forces in the society, namely, private, public and state.

For policy makers and managers, the task is to sustain current capabilities while building those required for tomorrow's success. To do this, Thai organizations and Thai people must learn to be ambidextrous. Thus, the ability to learn from their existing results and experiences in order to leap forward to new and superior performance is indeed challenging.

WHAT STRATEGY SHOULD WE PUT IN PLACE TO BUILD UP THESE CAPABILITIES?

In 1998, one year after Thailand had an economic crisis resulting from the overheated growth and unbalanced development in the mid 1990s, my colleagues and I suggested a set of strategies for sustainable development of the Thai people. These were as follows.

- Rethink
- Learn continuously
- Networking and partnership
- Shrinking the state's roles
- Contented livelihood
- Thai way of happiness

Link and Learn

In response to the new socio-economic and political paradigm and required competitive capabilities mentioned above, I proposed "link and learn" as a master strategy of human resource development in Thailand. The transformation of Thai society toward a knowledge-based economy and society needs a management strategy that is identical to changes in social, economic and political life. Link and learn is such a strategy.

In fact, management itself is a living system. It is based more on biological principles than physical principles. We should apply our understanding of biological systems to the design of structures and processes of relationships between people, communities and nations. The structure of a biological system is characterized by networks of relationships. They are complex, diverse and interdependent sets of relationships or sub-systems. Each sub-system is capable of self-organizing and adapting to the changing environment. The sub-systems do this by linking to and learning from other sub-systems. We should use this evolutionary biological process to drive our ideas and action in developing people and organizations.

Ladies and gentlemen, to implement this HRD strategy effectively, I here suggest a model of holistic management of human resource development.

From the perspective of managing change and development, the model should include not only structure, but also core competencies, processes and organizational culture. The model includes at least three main components.

1. Organizational architecture
2. Human resource development or learning process
3. The philosophy of sufficiency economy

1. Organizational Architecture

An agile organization able to leap from strength to strength needs a capability to do well in external adaptation and internal integration. To realize this, I suggest a redesign of organizational structure and processes based on a concept of network management and a coordination principle of problem analysis, function integration and empowerment or PFE.

In networked organizations, horizontal linkages are more important and meaningful than vertical relations. Organizations and people are tied together by shared vision, shared purpose and collective commitment. Whereas power and authority flow vertically, information and knowledge flow and grow horizontally. The effectiveness of network management is based on trust and communication. Only when we trust each other do we listen and learn from each other.

Linking people and organizations through structures and processes is not enough to ensure an increase in the speed of learning and level of learning capabilities. We need a coordination principle that not only enhances knowledge management but also facilitates the use of knowledge to improve organizational performance. That principle is the coordination of problem analysis, functional integration and empowerment or PFE. It is a firm ground for effective decisions and self-managed teams, and hence high performance organizations.

Starting with an analysis and appreciation of realities, problems, areas or people, one can see clearly functions or activities or resources that should be integrated into a single whole. With adequate empowerment, people will unleash their potentials and capabilities to work and learn to the fullest. The best guarantee for people development is certainly people empowerment.

2. Human Resource Development

In this management model, a concept of human resource development is presented here to promote a continuous learning process. Human resource development is an interactive process of enhancing and facilitating the development of capabilities and potentials of individuals, organizations and communities, through knowledge management, organizational development and community development, to attain personal goals and organizational as well as communal goals effectively, efficiently and harmoniously.

This definition suggests that a concept of human resource development should contain at least four key elements.

1. Interactive learning through actions to develop capabilities and potentials
2. Learning process should take place within organizational and communal contexts
3. Learning activities should be effective, efficient and harmonious
4. Personal goals as well as those of organizations and communities should be simultaneously attained

The concept suggests one should bear in mind three different perspectives in developing human resource. Human resource development is a holistic and developmental process.

1. It is the process of balancing internal and external views or balancing inside-out and outside-in perspectives.
2. The successful development of human resource in organizations requires both structural interventions and psycho-cultural adaptation.
3. Linkages between three levels of development, that is, the individual, organization and community, should be properly steered and facilitated.

3. The Philosophy of Sufficiency Economy

Competitive capabilities of Thai organizations and people will not be sustained if the management of change and that of human resource development described above lack the guidance of a well-defined and powerful development philosophy. Development in Thailand in the past four decades has been primarily led by theories and concepts of development economics and applied rural sociology without strong ideological or philosophical guidance. Much emphasis has been put into techniques of value-adding while proper social values and attitudes have received little attention. The economic crisis in 1997 gave us a costly lesson that sustainable development cannot be achieved without a crystal clear and powerful philosophy serving as a foundation for knowledge building, righteousness and beauty of development.

A management philosophy based on the philosophy of sufficiency economy bestowed to the Thai people by His Majesty King Rama IX, the present monarch of Thailand, is such a philosophy. The philosophy of sufficiency economy, given to the Thai people over the past thirty years, can be observed and learned through many royal development initiatives and projects. The philosophy was voiced strongly to the Thais again right after the economic clash in 1997. The philosophy of sufficiency economy has its intellectual origins in Buddhism and Asian values and attitudes toward life and the world. It embraces a set of guiding principles toward achieving human security and sustainable human development as well as societal and business development.

Sufficiency economy is a system of morals and values of decent living and righteous behavior for people of all walks of life, from family and community up to the state. Development of the economy and running business should be conducted based on the principle of the middle path to effectively cope with uncertainties and risks. Sufficiency refers to a state of being that adheres to three important attributes, that is, moderation, rationality and immunity. These moral qualities enable individuals and organizations to possess good self-protection systems to withstand any impacts of external and internal changes. In so doing, one must be omniscient or well informed, circumspect and very careful in applying knowledge and sciences to every step of planning and implementation. In the meantime, the morality of the people, especially government officials, theorists, businessmen of every echelon, must be reinforced to have moral consciousness of honesty, patience, perseverance and right-mindedness so as to be ready enough to respond swift global changes.

The philosophy of sufficiency economy is at the heart of Thailand's ninth national economic and social development plan. Public and private organizations as well as community organizations are studying and applying this philosophy to their businesses and situations. Campaigns for proper understanding and applications of the philosophy have been undertaken as a social movement toward a new paradigm of development by the government, business organizations and civil society organizations.

The Siam Cement Group (SCG), a principle-centered organization, has brought the philosophy of sufficiency economy into use in business operations. With strong commitment to a well-established business philosophy, SCG can be considered not only as a high performance organization, but an adaptive and living organization as well. After facing financial problems during the 1997 economic crisis and a few years after, SCG has restructured and regained business leaders' positions in their respective industries. There are some organizational structural and cultural constraints to an application of the model of holistic human resource development management and the concept of human resource development proposed in this chapter. Many organizations in Asia are organized in a highly centralized structure with an inside-out perspective of management and a patronage style of leadership. In these organizations, rules and regulations are rather inflexible and employees demonstrate defensive routines and change resistance. Such organizational structure, management mindset and leadership style do not support the free flow of ideas and information within and between levels of organizational hierarchy. Cross-functional learning and collective or shared experience leading to innovation are less likely to be effective. Many employees whose jobs are relatively secure may feel complacency. They are in their comfort zone and likely to resist changing programs.

As learning and sharing knowledge with other organizations in the business ecology and /or community are increasingly important for human resource development, managers will have much difficulty in facilitating learning and building knowledge in and between organizations in which information and knowledge as well as power and status are distributed asymmetrically. Because competitiveness of an organization is more likely to be determined by the speed of learning, we need more research to give a better knowledge of know-how and know-who that can help make our organizations learn fast in order to stay alive and well in the world of increasing uncertainties and high risks. On this note, you may have my congratulations for the success of this conference and my best wishes for the success of your career and life.

AFTERMATH

I would like to end this chapter with some observations and remarks on the development of human resource development (HRD), as a field of study and a management practice in Thailand since 2003. It is fair to say that HRD with emphasis on a human-focused approach has been a fast-growing field of study and research in the Thai academic community in the past five years. HRD appears as a basic course of study in the bachelor's and master's degree programs in business administration and public administration in most Thai universities. More than five strong universities offer a master's degree program in HRD. And the School of Human Resource Development, National Institute of Development Administration, has just launched a PhD program in HRD. For four consecutive years now the four big universities located in Bangkok—Chulalongkorn University, Thammasat University, Mahidol University and the National Institute of Development Administration—have jointly organized the Annual HRD Seminar. The academic meeting is a big annual event for research collaboration and networking among academics and practitioners in the field of HRD.

Leading issues in human resource in large and small Thai business organizations and public-sector agencies have currently been taken into serious consideration, and fierce competition can lead to two underlying themes of management, that is, human capital accumulation and ethical leadership development. Companies and firms have sought to establish their own moral or philosophical management identity or branding through a variety of activities to become high productive and high performance organizations. The Personnel Management Association of Thailand (PMAT) has launched this year an accreditation program on human resource practice in member organizations. The conceptual basis of the program is a concept of human-focused management. The mass media have been very sensitive to the growing concern of the people-first perspective of management in the country. Besides TV programs and radio programs, the top three high-rating business newspapers, namely, *Manager Weekly, The Nation,* and *Prachachat Weekly*, have regularly spared a space for HRD innovation and discussion. Last but not the least, human-centered development and the philosophy of sufficiency economy have been two core principles of the National Development Plan since 1997. And I am very proud to be a tiny part of this paradigm shift movement of the nation.

7 HRD Policies and the Supra-State

A Comparative Analysis of EU and APEC Experience

Nigel Haworth and Jonathan Winterton

In this chapter, we will compare briefly the HRD strategies in the EU and APEC regions in terms of their substantive content and procedural approaches and offers explanations for similarities and differences between the EU and APEC regions in terms of common drivers and different contexts. Despite fundamental differences in the underlying economic objectives of the two approaches and in the means by which the HRD policies are developed, we will suggest there are important lessons from each that could provide opportunities for transfer of experience between the two regions. The APEC approach can gain from EU-style engagement with the trade unions and the EU approach can benefit from APEC-style flexibility, provided the European Social Model is not jeopardized in the process. (5th International Conference on Human Resource Development across Europe: International, Comparative and Cross-Cultural Dimensions of HRD, Limerick, Ireland, 2004)

CONTEXT

This chapter is based on a keynote speech that we gave at the 5th International Conference on Human Resource Development across Europe: International, Comparative and Cross-Cultural Dimensions of HRD, Limerick, Ireland, in 2004. It was a first collaboration between specialists, respectively, in European Union Labor market policies and development, and in those same issues in the Asia-Pacific region. The collaboration was rooted in the specialists spending time in each other's institutions over fifteen years in a burgeoning international collaboration. It reflected a mutual realization that this was a unique combination of regionally based knowledge, which would add a new dimension to international HRD discussion.

THE PRESENTATION: INTRODUCTION

In this talk, we will compare briefly the HRD strategies in the EU and APEC regions in terms of their substantive content and procedural approaches and offer explanations for similarities and differences between the EU and APEC regions in terms of common drivers and different contexts. Despite fundamental differences in the underlying economic objectives of the two approaches and in the means by which the HRD policies are developed, we will suggest there are important lessons from each that could provide opportunities for transfer of experience between the two regions. The APEC approach can gain from EU-style engagement with the trade unions, and the EU approach can benefit from APEC-style flexibility, provided the European social model is not jeopardized in the process.

The European Union

We believe that the emergence of the European Union (EU) represents one of the major events of the twentieth century, having a defining impact on the geopolitics of the new millennium. The fifteen member states have been the architects of HRD policies of the EU outlined below, and the further enlargement of May 1, 2004, presents the EU with a new challenge of maintaining the twin economic and social objectives that have characterized EU HRD policies. The ten new member states increase the diversity of the EU and hence the complexity of developing integrated HRD policies. At the same time, enlargement makes such policies even more crucial for an economic region that now represents some 450 million people.

HRD policy in the European Union

EU HRD policy is defined first by the imperatives of market integration and economic competitiveness. In this context, the first efforts to coordinate employment policy at the European level were apparent at the Essen European Council in December 1994, which identified priorities for employment policy to be followed up at the national level. The Amsterdam European Council of June 1997 subsequently agreed to introduce an Employment Title (chapter) to the Treaty as part of the revisions, and the Extraordinary Luxembourg European Council on Employment, held in November 1977, introduced the European Employment Strategy (EES).[1]

The EES was reviewed after five years of operation in 2002, and the 2003 version of the EES emphasized three overarching objectives: full employment; quality and productivity at work; and cohesion and an inclusive labor market. The Employment Guidelines were restructured and simplified into ten headings, one of which is 'Investment in human capital and strategies for lifelong learning.'[2]

EU policy to promote lifelong learning is derived from the white paper *Teaching and Learning: Towards the Learning Society*, which reiterated the importance of developing a European framework for continuous learning to promote the competitiveness of European enterprises in line with the earlier white paper (*Growth, Competitiveness and Employment*). Significantly, the *Teaching and Learning* white paper also made reference to the need for learning and development to promote social inclusion and specifically linked lifelong learning to social progress and cohesion.[3]

The Lisbon European Council of March 2000 marked the origins of a new European policy framework for HRD, including VET and lifelong learning, linking these with the European employment strategy, establishing targets and benchmarks against which progress can be assessed and implementing measures to facilitate cooperation. The Lisbon summit also emphasized the role of social dialogue in developing skills.[4]

The Feira European Council of June 2000 called for 'consistent strategies and practical measures to make lifelong learning accessible to all.' The Lisbon summit had called for 'reflection on concrete future objectives of education systems focusing on common concerns and priorities while respecting national diversity.' After consulting member states, the Commission produced a report in January 2001, which identified a degree of convergence between member states and proposed objectives for raising the standard of learning in line with the Lisbon objectives

The Stockholm European Council in March 2001 built on this approach. The draft work program submitted by the European Commission to the Education Council in November 2001 proposed that the instruments for monitoring the implementation of these objectives should be compatible with the policy goals in other areas. The Barcelona European Council in March 2002 subsequently called for annual reporting on progress toward implementing the Lisbon objectives.

In parallel with these developments, actions to increase cooperation in VET were initiated following the agreement reached by the directors-general for VET in their autumn 2001 Bruges meeting. The priorities defined in the Bruges Process were given further impetus by the Copenhagen Declaration in November 2002.

Social Dialogue and the European Social Model

Social dialogue, one of the pillars of the European social model, refers to meetings between the social partners: institutions representing employers (private and public) and employees. At the European level, social dialogue refers to meetings and negotiations between the social partners as defined in Article 118b of the EC Treaty. Three social partner representative organizations are involved: ETUC (European Trade Union Confederation, or *Confédération Européenne des Syndicats*, CES), UNICE/UEAPME (*Union des Industries de la Communauté Européenne/Union Européenne des Ateliers et Petites Moyennes Entreprises*) and CEEP (*Centre Européen de l'Entreprise Publique*).[5]

Social dialogue at EU level has contributed to developing HRD policy since the founding of the EEC, with the social partners making proposals and agreeing action through joint opinions as well as contributing to the development of legally binding measures.[6] Analysis reveals that experience from EU countries does not converge towards a clearly defined role for the social partners.[7] The EC has therefore provided funding to promote convergence through introducing exchanges and generalizing best practice through programs such as Leonardo da Vinci.[8] Differences between national VET systems can be expected to impose constraints on social dialogue, but research suggests that the major determinant of the effectiveness of social dialogue over VET is the quality of local trade union organization.

We believe that, more than ever, the policy context of HRD, VET and lifelong learning demands the active involvement of the social partners. At both EU and member state level, the social partners have played a vital role in policy formulation and, especially within member states, in implementation. It was in this context that, on February 28, 2002, the social partners agreed on a *Framework of Actions for the Lifelong Development of Competencies and Qualifications*.[9]

We note that, in the second CEDEFOP policy report, the *Framework of Actions* is both an annual reporting process, as requested by the Barcelona summit, and autonomous, complementary social dialogue as advocated in the European Commission communication on social dialogue. In both respects, social partner activities under the *Framework of Actions* will depend upon a high standard of reporting involving affiliated institutions, raising the issue of research capacity within social partner organizations in the member states

We also note that the principle of social dialogue in promoting HRD, VET and lifelong learning is fundamental to the European approach, but there are fears that enlargement may reduce its effectiveness and legitimacy owing to the weakness of social partner institutions in some of the new member states.[10]

Asian and Pacific Economy Countries

We now turn to APEC. APEC consists of twenty-one economies ranked on both sides of the Pacific, which together contribute more than 50 percent of global GDP and more than 40 percent of world trade. It is almost wholly inter-governmental, allowing only the regional business community special access to its deliberations via an APEC Business Advisory Council (ABAC). It includes economies as diverse as the US and Papua New Guinea. APEC emerged in 1989 from an extended debate about the prospects for Asia-Pacific regional co-operation.[11] The debate was complex, reflecting Asia's mounting economic performance, a consequent concern about protectionism in the global economy, the effects of the Cold War, regional co-operation measures within Asia and trans-Pacific rivalries, just to name the most important factors. Probably the most significant driver was a concern about economic openness. Asian economies wanted reduced tariff barriers in order to sustain their growth rates. APEC provided a forum which could encourage regional markets to stay open and also promote greater openness globally, particularly in the EU. Inevitably, then, trade issues were important in APEC activities. The conclusion of the Uruguay Round and creation of the WTO in 1994 reinforced APEC's focus on trade significantly, for it offered APEC a global platform on which to encourage trade openness.

APEC's Rationale

In 1994, APEC met in Bogor, Indonesia, and united around what became known as the Bogor Declaration. This committed APEC economies to what has become its trademark activity, the promotion of trade and investment liberalization and facilitation (TILF) and, in principle, a further stream of activities in economic and technical co-operation (ECOTECH). Thus, trade (TILF), always on the agenda, became the driving focus of APEC, in tune with the hopes and expectations lodged in the newly formed WTO.

However, before turning to the ECOTECH agenda within APEC, we want to discuss the differences between the EU and APEC in terms of origins and rationale. APEC's origins share little with those of the EU. Regional circumstances, key drivers and history differ significantly. Geographically, whereas the countries of Europe are adjacent and form a geographical as well as politico-economic bloc, APEC is widely dispersed across both sides of the Pacific. 'Europe' is a term that Europeans recognize and, broadly, understand. The same is not true for the Asia-Pacific region. Indeed, one of the major problems facing APEC is the generation of a popular identity that spans Chile and China. There is no uniting history underpinning APEC. It is trite but true to see the origins of the EU in the complex, often bitter, history that defines Europe over the last two centuries. Whereas there are long histories between many member economies of APEC, there is no single unifying historical process bringing them together. Hence the drivers of regionalization are different. The EU is a product of multiple drivers, but priority rests with a combined political and economic vision for Europe. In the case of APEC, the key drivers are, on the one hand, the need for trade openness to sustain Asian growth and, on the other, a desire on the part of other economies to sustain links with key Asian economies and, in turn, guarantee access to those Asian economies for exports. In sum, the APEC process is a far more limited endeavor.

TILF and ECOTECH.[12]

To understand the role of HRD within the APEC process, we begin with the constant tension between the TILF and ECOTECH agendas. This is a tension inherent in the development of the organization, but it also reflects the *realpolitik* of APEC membership. Some economies were essentially single-issue members of APEC, believing that the only value added by participation in the APEC process was in the trade area. The role played by government officials in trade-related departments and ministries in member economies was particularly important in establishing TILF's priority. Even today, the Committee on Trade and Investment (CTI) is primus inter pares in the APEC institutional structure, a status challenged only by the APEC finance ministers and their semi-autonomous activities.

However, economies such as Japan and Canada were running a more traditional regional development agenda before APEC was created, and they sought to include their perspectives in the APEC process. A home for this agenda was found in the 1995 Osaka Action Agenda (OAA).

The raison d'etre for ECOTECH was separate from the TILF agenda, although supportive thereof. Thus, Part 2 of the OAA defined APEC's economic and technical co-operation activities and became a convenient framework in which two competing views of co-operation were to be found. The one saw any ECOTECH activity undertaken by APEC to be subordinate to the TILF agenda. The other gave ECOTECH a high degree of autonomy from TILF.

The Asian Financial and Economic Crisis, ECOTECH and HRD

The 1997 Asian crisis was a shock to the APEC process. APEC's relevance to the region was widely questioned and for good reason. In the immediate circumstances of the crisis, the TILF agenda appeared to offer little succor to the most affected economies. On the other hand, to the extent that APEC could offer short-term support, the ECOTECH dimension was the most relevant. Hence, APEC undertook significant support work in areas such as defining HRD responses to the crisis. The most prominent intervention was undertaken by the APEC HRD Working Group (see below) in its task force on the HRD dimensions of the crisis. The task force produced case studies of the most affected economies and an overview analysis, the latter subsequently submitted to APEC leaders in their 1998 meeting.

Impasse in the WTO and ECOTECH

ECOTECH benefits from the state of the international trade liberalization debate and the particular effects of regional trade agreements (RTAs) and the WTO Ministerials in Seattle, Doha and Cancun. Those who see a future in the WTO agenda and a role for APEC in supporting the WTO, see ECOTECH in two ways—as a back-up area of activity when the trade debate is in a lull, and in terms of capacity building for the trade effort. Those who believe that the WTO trade agenda will lose impetus see ECOTECH as a freestanding alternative framework in which an alternative regional co-operation might be fashioned.

The Institutional Framework for HRD in APEC

APEC's HRD early agenda, laid down in 1995 in Beijing, was formulated in eight priority areas for work. These were:

- The provision of a quality education for all
- The development of regional labor market analyses
- An increase in the supply and quality of managers, entrepreneurs and training in the areas central to economic growth

- A reduction in skill deficiencies and unemployment by designing appropriate training priority areas and outcomes
- An improvement in the quality of curricula, teaching methods and materials
- An improvement in access to skill acquisition
- The preparation of individuals and organizations for repaid economic and technical change
- Support for the TILF agenda

These priorities are much the same in 2004, with one exception. The seventh priority was, as a result of the active intervention of the Clinton-led US government, subsequently amended to read: [To enhance] 'the quality, productivity, efficiency and equitable development of Labor forces and workplaces in member economies.'

HRD issues in APEC are substantially the responsibility of the APEC Human Resource Development Working Group (WG), which, after 2000, operated three networks—EDNET (primarily education issues); the Labor and Social Protection Network (LSPN—primarily concerned with Labor markets, Labor—management issues and social safety nets) and the Capacity Building Network (CBN—with a focus on management capacity building in public, private and business sectors). The WG meets annually and is generally recognized to be the most dynamic ECOTECH forum in the APEC process.

The networks have developed an array of projects (about forty at any given time) designed to respond to the established priorities. In 2000, it was calculated that the WG undertakes about 50 percent of all APEC HRD work.

An essentially conservative organization, as befits an inter-governmental arrangement, the WG is both technicist and unitarist in operation. It focuses on the technical upgrading HRD practices. It generally eschews involvement in the politics of production and policy making, focusing instead on the functional improvement of education, training and production systems. Put another way, APEC is broadly comfortable with contemporary relations of production in market systems. Its aim is to improve the efficiency of those relations, not to challenge them in any substantive way. This is not surprising. The ethos of APEC is to avoid political controversy whenever possible, a quality with which government officials are most comfortable. APEC is also, through both TILF and ECOTECH, embedded in a worldview predicated on the superiority of market relations. Such consensus as APEC creates holds that view as a central tenet.

This also explains for us the unitarism of APEC's HRD approach.[13] The APEC worldview generally assumes one maximizing mode of economic advancement—regional and global integration. Participants in that process—institutions, social groups and individuals—will rationally share that view. In the APEC process, HRD is configured in tune with that worldview. The key actors in that view are business and government—wealth creators, on one side, and wealth creation facilitators, on the other. Other sectors of society are assumed to depend materially upon the arrangements struck between the two key actors. It is logical for those other sectors to conform to the dominant worldview. Hence, APEC has established a vehicle for business-government discussion—the APEC Business Advisory Council (ABAC), which, apart from channeling the views of business into the APEC process (particularly at the annual Leaders' Meeting) also undertakes an analysis of the extent to which APEC is achieving its goals (that is, supporting or achieving that worldview). In this framework, it is unnecessary for other sectors of society to be represented, for two reasons. First, governments represent their sovereign peoples and do so in APEC. Second, the other sectors have nothing useful to add to a process that already protects their best interests.

CONCLUSIONS

We have argued today that the two regions face common challenges arising from globalization, and both the EU and APEC have identified HRD as an essential component of raising competitiveness. Each region has considerable diversity in terms of the economies of member countries, which gives the global challenges different meanings in different contexts and restricts the development of uniform HRD strategies across the region. Whereas the diversity of the EU15 was much less than that of APEC, enlargement to EU25 and beyond is increasing the diversity and making a homogeneous approach equally difficult. The fact that APEC is attempting such a coordinated HRD policy approach should be a source of encouragement to the EU. These apparent similarities, however, mask fundamental differences in the approaches of the two regions.

The first obvious difference, which strikes us, relates to the organization and underlying objectives. APEC's organization contrasts strongly with that of the EU and reflects significant regional tensions about the scope of regional integration. There is little, is any, desire for an EU-type integration in the Asia-Pacific region. Such integration is seen as impracticable for myriad political and historical reasons. Moreover, an OECD-type structure is broadly unacceptable, particularly to Asian economies. The preferred (and only practicable) model is based on consensual decision making, a requirement particularly sought by the ASEAN economies. In sum, there is little in the APEC process to mirror the political, economic and financial integration that marks the EU. Consensual decision making means that controversial issues can be blocked by any individual economy. In the case of less controversial issues, individual economies may not choose to block measures, but may simply choose not to participate in them, or to participate rhetorically but without substance, an option that is not (or should not be) available to EU member states, although the recent changes in the EES suggest that there is a risk of watering down the Lisbon objectives in the face of the reality of the challenges of enlargement.

The second major difference is in the means by which the HRD policies are developed and implemented. Social dialogue is at the heart of the EU HRD policy approach that combines the economic objectives with the European social model. Whereas there are signs that enlargement threatens to weaken social dialogue, the social partners continue to have a determining influence and will fiercely resist its dissolution. This is far from the case in APEC, where the trade unions play a limited role (US and Canada) and the ICFTU continues to report serious violations of trade union rights. The majority of countries have failed to ratify core ILO labor conventions (including Australia, Japan and the US); anti-union activity is commonplace and often orchestrated by governments (as in Thailand, Indonesia and the Philippines); and, in the Communist economies (China and Viet Nam), the trade unions have no independence. Social dialogue is largely irrelevant to the development of HRD policies (with the notable exceptions of Canada and New Zealand), and HRD plays no part in developing a social model.

Given these differences in objectives and means, it is perhaps surprising that both regions have a common recognition of the virtue and necessity of HRD policies. The European social dimension was conceded in order to win trade union acceptance for the single European market and EU integration, because there were fears that the liberalization agenda would only promote employer interests. Such concessions were won because of the strength of union organization, and there is therefore little likelihood of a similar trajectory in APEC in the foreseeable future. However, the trade unions have subsequently become the strongest advocates of lifelong learning and HRD in the EU and ensured that labor standards are not compromised in the interests of competitiveness. This should not be lost on those shaping APEC's HRD policy because ultimately HRD has a major role to play in guaranteeing social progress.

Equally, the extreme diversity of APEC has demanded a much less directive approach and the pursuit of consensus that may offer lessons for the enlarged EU. To the extent that this can be achieved without allowing deregulation and liberalization to erode the EU social model, such flexibility should be welcomed, but the defense of labor standards and the promotion of social cohesion should, and will, be defended by the trade unions as their basis for cooperation.

Thank you.

AFTERMATH: REFLECTIONS

It is interesting to reflect on events since this speech was first given in 2004. At the level of research activity, the authors have used this speech to build an on-going teaching and research collaboration, currently engaged in a comparative text on EU and APEC HRD strategies. Supra-national regional arrangements have been shown to be an excellent catalyst for international research collaboration.

We have reflected since the speech on the importance of both macro and micro levels of HRD analysis in the comparison we offered. The conference at which this speech was offered involved both foci—specialists in HRD at the level of the firm, and those focusing on the macro-level policy and development dimensions of HRD. Thinking about HRD in the EU and APEC, we think that the focus in both areas on productivity and competitiveness requires an understanding of both levels of HRD activity, in a sense unifying the two levels of analysis. This is something to be considered in greater depth, by us and by others.

The issues that we addressed in the speech have taken on a striking importance in the context of the 2008 global financial crisis. In APEC, the labor market consequences of the crisis have required APEC's HRD activities to focus once again on the mitigation of unemployment and the development of appropriate active labor market settings and social protection measures. In the EU, similar pressures have emerged in a far wider and difficult context in which the very future of the Euro zone and the EU is questioned. In the broad context provided by the rise of China and its centrality in global economic performance and uncertainty about the European regional model, any EU-APEC comparison becomes particularly important, and HRD matters are particularly pressing in that context.

We also suggest, on reflection, that, whereas the traditional comparative method, such as we used in this speech, remains an important method, overarching political economies of HRD in a global economy are also needed. Economic and political integration should promote integrated analysis of HRD dynamics. This is, for us, the most interesting challenge to emerge from the substance of this speech.

NOTES

1. EC. (1994) *Growth, competitiveness, employment: The challenges and ways forward into the 21st century.* Luxembourg: European Commission Publications.
   EC. (1997) *Towards a Europe of knowledge.* Brussels: European Commission DG XX11.
2. EC. (2003) *The future of the European Employment Strategy (EES):* 'A strategy for full employment and better jobs for all.' Brussels: European Commission.
3. EC. (1996) *Teaching and Learning: Towards the Learning Society.* Luxembourg: European Commission Publications Office.
4. EC. (2002) *The European social dialogue: a force for innovation and change: proposal for a Council decision establishing a tripartite social summit for growth and employment.* Luxembourg: European Commission Office of Official Publications of the European Union.

5. ETUC, UNICE/UEAPME and CEEP. (2003) *Framework of actions for the lifelong development of competencies and qualifications: First follow-up report*. Brussels: ETUC, UNICE/UEAPME and CEEP. ETUC, UNICE/UEAPME and CEEP. (2004) *Framework of actions for the lifelong development of competencies and qualifications: Second follow-up report*. Brussels: ETUC, UNICE/UEAPME and CEEP.
David Foden and Jonathan Winterton. (2001) 'The role of trade unions in the European employment strategy,' *Proceedings of the 6th European Industrial Relations Congress, Oslo*, June 25–29.

6. Roland Travitian. (1992) *Vocational training I/1992*. Thessaloniki: CEDEFOP.

7. Helge Halvorsen, (1998) 'Role of social partners in the development of training,' Proceedings of the ETF Seminar, Bucharest, October 2–3.

8. Nick Adnett. (1996) *European labor markets: Analysis and policy*. London: Longman.

9. Winfried Heidemann and Wilfried Kruse. (1998) 'Validation and recognition of competences and qualifications.' *European Discussion Paper for the Social Partners*. Düsseldorf: Hans Böckler Stiftung. Jonathan Winterton and T. Strandberg. (2004) 'European social dialogue: Evaluation and critical assessment,' in *The Unification of Europe: The Role of Social Dialogue in the Enlargement Process of the European Employment Strategy*, Brussels: SALTSA/ETUI.

10. Jonathan Winterton. (2004) 'Improving the effectiveness of social partners' involvement in VET,' Proceedings of the CEDEFOP Agora Conference VET Research: To what end? Thessaloniki, February 16–17.

11. Vinod Aggarwal and Charles Morrison, eds. (1998) *Asia-Pacific crossroads: Regime creation and the future of APEC*. New York: St. Martin's Press.

12. Nigel Haworth. (2003) 'Potential in search of achievement: APEC and human resource development,' in *APEC as an Institution: Multilateral Governance in the Asia Pacific*, Singapore: Institute of South East Asian Studies.

13. Michael Zanko, ed. (2002) *The handbook of human resource management practices in Asia-Pacific economies*, Vol. 1. Cheltenham: Edward Elgar. Michael Zanko and Matt Ngui, eds. (2003) *The handbook of human resource management practices in Asia-Pacific economies*, Vol. 2. Cheltenham: Edward Elgar.

8 Human Resource Development Interventions for Improving International Managers' Performance in Overseas Assignments

A Conceptual Analysis on the Effects of Cultural Intelligence

AAhad M. Osman-Gani

This chapter presents a conceptual framework for conducting empirical investigations to study the effects some relevant factors (e.g. cross-cultural training, expatriates' personality, self efficacy, and social network compositions) on international managers' adjustments and performance in overseas assignments. Developed based on extensive reviews of literature, and empirical findings from prior research, the framework would be useful in developing relevant research agenda. Implications for future research in the new field of cross-cultural HRD have been discussed.
(International Conference on Cross-Cultural Management Practice and Research, held at ICCCR & HRM, University of Jammu, India, February, 6–7, 2009)

CONTEXT

This chapter is based on a keynote speech that I gave at the International Conference on Cross-Cultural Management (CCM) Practice and Research, which was organized by the International Center for Cross Cultural and Human Resource Management Research, at University of Jammu, India, during February 6–7, 2009.

The audience of the conference was academic scholars as well as professionals from various fields of management, HR and other related areas. A large number of graduate/post-graduate students attended the conference. The objective of this first conference on CCM research was to gather scholars and professionals and share their latest research and practice-based thoughts on HR and cross-cultural management issues. I was the only keynote speaker invited to the conference, and the keynote address was expected to set the premise of the conference. The objective of my presentation was to introduce the integrated fields of cross-cultural management and human resource development (HRD) to this audience, who did not have much exposure at that time. During the past ten years, I have been working on the concept of cross-cultural HRD by integrating the theoretical perspectives from the fields of international business management and HRD (an emerging and rapidly growing area). I have been involved in conducting research, teaching at several universities and doing professional practices in the areas of international/cross-cultural management and HRD for the past twenty years. My research interests were mostly focused on developing skills and competencies of international/global managers for their effective performance in overseas assignments in different cultural environments. At this conference, I chose to talk on this issue in order to develop awareness and research interests in this field, and thereby to develop the potentials for collaborative research work with scholars from this part of the world. In the following sections of this chapter, I have attempted to cover the major points of my presentation (with some background information) for the benefit of our readers.

INTRODUCTION

With increasing trends of international assignments in global corporations, developing effective global leaders and expatriate managers is becoming an important human resource development (HRD) issue particularly for multinational enterprises (MNEs). One of the major determinants of today's global managers' performance effectiveness is how well they adjust themselves to function effectively in the host culture.[1] In this regard, international HRD literature addresses the expatriate development issues mostly from cross-cultural training (CCT) and skills development perspectives.[2] Research by Shin, Morgeson and Campion [3] found explicit support in cross-cultural management literature for the fundamental assumption that expatriates need to adjust to new cultural environments by adapting their behavior to fit the host country's cultural norms and values. Similar support comes from meta-analyses done by Bhaskar-Shrinivas, Harrison, Shaffer and Luk and Hechanova, Beehr and Christiansen,[4] which show that expatriate adjustment is an important predictor of performance.

Although some studies were done on expatriate adjustment issues, performance issues of international managers have not been investigated systematically and exhaustively, and several important issues that may help their adjustment and performance have not been addressed. Relatively little research, however, focuses on factors that could improve intercultural encounters .[5] In particular, research on individual capabilities for intercultural effectiveness is sparse and unsystematic, leaving an important gap in our understanding of why some individuals are more effective than others in culturally diverse situations.[6] Expatriate performance issues have not been addressed from individual traits and capabilities perspectives by using relevant theories of intelligence.

Earley and Ang [7] developed the construct of cultural intelligence (CQ) based on contemporary theories of intelligence.[8] Defined as an individual's capability to function and manage effectively in culturally diverse settings, CQ is a multidimensional construct targeted at situations involving cross-cultural interactions arising from differences in race, ethnicity and nationality. To date, research on CQ has focused primarily on conceptual theorizing.[9] Ng and Earley [10] discussed conceptual distinctions between CQ, a culture-free etic construct, and the traditional view of intelligence that is culture-bound and emic. Triandis[11] discussed theoretical relationships between CQ capabilities and forming accurate judgments. Brislin et al.[12] discussed CQ as critical for expecting and addressing the unexpected during intercultural encounters. Earley and Peterson[13] developed a systematic approach to intercultural training that links trainee CQ strengths and weaknesses to training interventions. Janssens and Brett[14] advanced a fusion model of team collaboration for making culturally intelligent, relatively realistic team decisions. The objective of this paper is to present a conceptual analysis of cultural intelligence by describing the features of its four dimensions (four-factor model). Based on the above analyses, I propose a conceptual model that would have significant implications for future research in the fields of cross-cultural management and international HRD, as well as for HRD professional practice.

CULTURAL INTELLIGENCE (CULTURAL QUOTIENT—CQ)

Given the newness of CQ, let me start by reviewing the theoretical conceptualization of the four CQ dimensions. Then a model is proposed that relates specific dimensions of CQ to cognitive, affective and behavioral aspects of intercultural effectiveness, based on the framework introduced by Shaffer et al.[15] Earley and Ang[16] anchored their discussion of the theoretical bases of CQ in contemporary theories of intelligence. I would like to summarize their key arguments here.

Cultural intelligence, defined as an individual's capability to function and manage effectively in culturally diverse settings, is consistent with Schmidt and Hunter's[17] definition of general intelligence as 'the ability to grasp and reason correctly with abstractions (concepts) and solve problems. Although early research tended to view intelligence narrowly as the ability to solve problems in academic settings, there is now increasing consensus that intelligence may be displayed in places other than the classroom.[18]

The growing interest in 'real world' intelligence includes intelligence that focuses on specific content domains such as social intelligence,[19] emotional intelligence[20] and practical intelligence.[21] CQ acknowledges the practical realities of globalization (Earley and Ang, 2003) and focuses on a specific domain—intercultural settings. Thus, following Schmidt and Hunter's (2000) definition of general intelligence, CQ is a specific form of intelligence focused on capabilities to grasp, reason and behave effectively in situations characterized by cultural diversity.

CQ as a Multidimensional Construct

Sternberg's[22] integrative framework proposed different 'loci' of intelligence within the person. Metacognition, cognition and motivation are *mental* capabilities that reside within the head, whereas overt actions are *behavioral* capabilities. Metacognitive intelligence refers to control of cognition: the processes individuals use to acquire and understand knowledge.

Cognitive intelligence refers to knowledge structures and is consistent with Ackerman's[23] intelligence-as-knowledge concept, which argues for the importance of knowledge as part of the intellect. Motivational intelligence refers to the mental capacity to direct and sustain energy on a particular task or situation and recognize that motivational capabilities are critical to 'real world' problem solving.[24] Behavioral intelligence refers to outward manifestations or overt actions: what people do rather than what they think.[25]

Applying Sternberg's multiple loci of intelligence, Earley and Ang (2003) conceptualized CQ as including metacognitive, cognitive, motivational and behavioral dimensions with specific relevance to functioning in culturally diverse settings. Metacognitive CQ reflects mental processes that individuals use to acquire and understand cultural knowledge, including knowledge of and control over individual thought processes[26] relating to culture. Relevant capabilities include planning, monitoring and revising mental models of cultural norms for countries or groups of people. Those with high metacognitive CQ are consciously aware of others' cultural preferences before and during interactions. They also question cultural assumptions and adjust their mental models during and after interactions.[27]

Features of the Four-factor Model of CQ

Whereas metacognitive CQ focuses on higher order cognitive processes, cognitive CQ reflects knowledge of the norms, practices and conventions in different cultures acquired from education and personal experiences. This includes knowledge of the economic, legal and social systems of different cultures and subcultures[28] and knowledge of basic frameworks of cultural values.[29] Those with high cognitive CQ understand similarities and differences across cultures.[30]

Motivational CQ reflects the capability to direct attention and energy toward learning about and functioning in situations characterized by cultural differences. Kanfer and Heggestad[31] argued that such motivational capacities 'provide agentic control of affect, cognition and behavior that facilitate goal accomplishment.' According to the expectancy-value theory of motivation[32], the direction and magnitude of energy channeled toward a particular task involves two elements—expectations of success and value of success. Those with high motivational CQ direct attention and energy toward cross-cultural situations based on intrinsic interest[33] and confidence in their cross-cultural effectiveness.[34]

Behavioral CQ reflects the capability to exhibit appropriate verbal and nonverbal actions when interacting with people from different cultures. As Hall[35] emphasized, mental capabilities for cultural understanding and motivation must be complemented with the ability to exhibit appropriate verbal and nonverbal actions, based on cultural values of specific settings. This includes having a wide and flexible repertoire of behaviors. Those with high behavioral CQ exhibit situationally appropriate behaviors based on their broad range of verbal and nonverbal capabilities, such as exhibiting culturally appropriate words, tones, gestures and facial expressions.[36]

The four dimensions of CQ are qualitatively different facets of the overall capability to function and manage effectively in culturally diverse settings.[37] Like facets of job satisfaction, the dimensions of CQ may or may not correlate with each other. Thus, overall CQ represents an aggregate multidimensional construct, which according to Law et al.[38] includes: (i) dimensions at the same level of conceptualization as the overall construct; and (ii) dimensions making up the overall construct. In sum, metacognitive CQ, cognitive CQ, motivational CQ and behavioral CQ are different capabilities that together form overall CQ.

Conceptual distinctiveness of CQ

To further clarify the nature of CQ, we discuss differences and similarities between CQ and personality and other intelligences, as well as existing intercultural competency models.

Personality

As an individual difference capability, CQ refers to what a person can do to be effective in culturally diverse settings. Thus, it is distinct from stable personality traits which describe what a person typically does across time and across situations.[39] Because temperament influences choice of behaviors and experiences, some personality traits should relate to CQ. Consistent with this, Ang et al.[40] showed discriminant validity of the four dimensions of CQ compared with the big five personality traits and demonstrated meaningful relationships between specific personality characteristics and specific aspects of CQ. Notably, and as expected, openness to experience—the tendency to be creative, imaginative and adventurous (Costa and McCrae, 1992)[41] related to all four dimensions of CQ.

Other Intelligences

Because CQ is grounded in the theory of multiple intelligences,[42] CQ is similar to, yet distinct from, other forms of intelligence. We consider two forms of intelligence commonly investigated in management research to illustrate this point: general mental ability (GMA: Schmidt & Hunter, 2000) and emotional intelligence (EQ).[43] CQ is similar to these other intelligences because it is a set of capabilities, rather than preferred ways of behaving.[44] These constructs differ, however, in the nature of the abilities. General mental ability focuses on cognitive abilities, is not specific to particular types of contexts[45] such as culturally diverse situations and does not include behavioral or motivational aspects of intelligence. Emotional intelligence focuses on the ability to deal with personal emotions. Like CQ, it goes beyond academic and mental intelligence. It differs, however, from CQ because it focuses on the general ability to perceive and manage emotions without consideration of cultural context. Given that emotional cues are symbolically constructed and historically transmitted within culture, the ability to encode and decode emotions in the home culture does not automatically transfer to unfamiliar cultures.[46] Thus, a person with high EQ in one cultural context may not be emotionally intelligent in another culture. In contrast, CQ is culture free and refers to a general set of capabilities with relevance to situations characterized by cultural diversity.

Existing Intercultural Competency Constructs

Although there is a large body of literature on intercultural competencies,[47] this research generally suffers from ambiguous construct definitions and poor integration, resulting in a fragmented list of competencies that lack theoretical coherence.[48] Because CQ is grounded explicitly in the theoretical framework of multiple intelligences,[49] the four dimensions of CQ should provide a systematic rationale for organizing and integrating existing research on intercultural competencies. Examining the intercultural competency scales in Paige's[50] review highlights several gaps that CQ addresses. First, most intercultural competencies scales mix ability and personality.[51] Although personality characteristics are important to cross-cultural adjustment, including stable dispositional traits in competency models muddies the validity and precision of these models. Second, although many scales include items that are similar to CQ, no scale is based explicitly on contemporary theories of intelligence, and no scale systematically assesses the four aspects of intelligence. Third, CQ is not specific to a particular culture. Thus, CQ differs from cultural competency models that focus on country-specific knowledge or ability such as the Culture-Specific Assimilator. In sum, we argue that CQ is conceptually distinct from personality traits, other intelligences and other intercultural competencies. Grounding CQ as a form of intelligence allows precision about the nature of CQ as a set of relatively malleable capabilities that can be enhanced over time.[52]

EXPATRIATE PERFORMANCE

Models of the "criterion space" in international HR suggest that fulfilling specific task requirements, as well as developing and maintaining relationships with host country nationals, are the core facets of expatriate performance. These two facets are fairly consistent with the task/technical and contextual/interpersonal facilitation dimensions that domestic researchers have suggested.[53] Task (role-based) performance refers to successful execution of overseas duties, including attaining specific goals or accomplishing definable projects. It should be more strongly related to work adjustment than to relationship performance. When tracked as a separate criterion dimension, relationship (adaptive/contextual) performance is the effective development or maintenance of ties with members of the host country workplace. Hence, we expect that it will be more strongly related to cultural and interaction adjustment.

Cultural toughness and training rigor have also been identified as factors that may have an impact upon the relationship between CCT and overseas performance.[54] Evidence from meta-analysis conducted by Morris and Robie[55] has provided additional support for the argument that CCT is effective in enhancing the performance of expatriates. Research indicates that (1) social networks and access to information and resources (opportunities), (2) trust and norm of reciprocity (motivation), (3) HCNs' intercultural competencies and reliable task performance (abilities) have direct effects on expatriate performance (Liu and Shaffer, 2005).

Whereas various selection techniques have been used to predict personality and training performance within domestic programs, there is almost no research with regard to their validity in predicting training performance in a cross-cultural context, despite the growing importance of CCT. In the scant research that addresses the effectiveness of CCT, studies show that the impact of such training programs on performance is ambiguous and less positive than previously believed.[56] Some studies have reported that CCT had no effect on performance as measured by expatriate failure rates or early returns from international assignments and adjustment.[57] Furthermore, Mendenhall et al.[58] highlighted that most evaluations of cross-cultural programs are limited by flaws in research design because nearly all measures of adjustment and work performance are single-method, self-reported measures. These problems are exacerbated by the fact that despite investing significant money and time into such training, most companies do not evaluate the effects of CCT at all.[59]

PROPOSED RESEARCH MODEL

Based on the above analyses, I have proposed the following conceptual framework that might be useful in developing a future research agenda in the emerging field of cross-cultural HRD (see Figure 8.1). This model can be used to test the direct and mediation effects of HRD interventions (CCT, OD, CD) on CQ for studying the effects on expatriate performance in overseas assignments.

Conceptual Framework

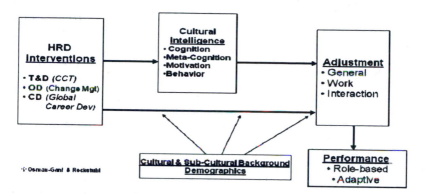

Figure 8.1 Conceptual framework showing the effects of HRD interventions on CQ and expatriate performance.

IMPLICATIONS FOR RESEARCH AND PROFESSIONAL PRACTICE IN HRD

I would like to emphasize the following important implications for intercultural effectiveness and cross-cultural HRD research, as well as for professional practice in relevant areas. First, evidence that CQ is conceptually and empirically distinct from other individual differences, such as EQ and big five personality dimensions, in predicting a range of intercultural effectiveness outcomes suggests the benefits of including CQ when studying culturally diverse situations. Thus, future research on multinational teams, expatriate performance, overseas work assignments, global leadership and cross-cultural negotiation may find that inclusion of CQ improves predictions of effectiveness.

Second, the multidimensional conceptualization of CQ and the differential relationships of the dimensions of CQ with specific intercultural connections is a multidimensional construct, where specific dimensions of CQ have special relevance to different outcomes. For instance, even though research findings show that only metacognitive CQ and behavioral CQ were related to task performance, future research can examine whether cognitive CQ and behavioral CQ are important for other forms of job performance, such as contextual and adaptive performance, where role expectations are less structured and well specified. It also would be important to consider these relationships for different roles, jobs and contexts.

Third, CQ has important implications for intercultural training, which has, to date, focused primarily on knowledge or cognitive training.[60] Cross-cultural training would be one of the most effective interventions in developing the required capabilities in this regard.[61] Because research results highlighted metacognitive CQ and behavioral CQ as fundamental capabilities with relevance to multiple intercultural effectiveness outcomes, training and HRD programs could include modules on both. For example, Earley and Peterson[62] outlined training interventions for CQ dimensions. This included cognitive structure analysis for examining knowledge structures and enhancing awareness and reflection (metacognitive CQ). It also included dramaturgical exercises such as role plays and simulations involving physical, emotional and sensory processes to enhance behavioral flexibility (behavioral CQ).

Finally, based on the findings of recent empirical research,[63] it could be concluded that CQ has predictive capability to identify managers' strengths and shortcomings on certain cultural dimensions that would have effects on their adjustment and performance in international assignments. Before they are sent overseas, appropriate interventions could be recommended after developing and analyzing their CQ profiles on various cultural dimensions. These findings would help corporate leaders and senior executives of MNEs to make more effective decisions about the success of international assignments. International HRD professionals would also be able to use the relevant information for designing and implementing appropriate interventions for improving expatriate performance in overseas assignments. The enhanced performance of international managers will then contribute positively to the organizational performance, thereby helping to sustain competitiveness in today's global business environment.

AFTERMATH: REFLECTIONS ON KEYNOTE SPEECH

As I reflect back on the implications of my speech, I can now see some changes happening among young scholars' and professionals' perspectives of looking at the world of work from a multicultural paradigm. People are now working on several masters 'and doctoral theses with research questions directly and indirectly relating to this new paradigm. In professional practice, HRD and management consultants are increasingly dealing with programs and projects relevant to global and multicultural/cross-cultural management perspectives. Several of us are now working on many international/cross-cultural collaborative research projects, and we already have developed a few global databases relating to the variables of our interests in these areas (HRD, CQ, CCM). It was not easy to convince the academicians and emerging scholars of the significance of these issues for future research. I had to face challenges in presenting these issues to a mixed audience of this conference, but was able to handle the questions effectively. Some of these questions include: theoretical premise, measurement issues (e.g., instrumentation, data collection) and publication opportunities. I am glad that I was prepared and was able to respond to these questions and convince those scholars at the end of the keynote speech. I now feel happy when I receive emails from potential graduate students showing keen interest in doing doctoral research on some issues relating to CQ, CCM and CCHRD. I am also receiving increasing queries about global and cross-cultural training and consulting projects. I hope this keynote speech inspires more HRD scholars and professionals to undertake challenging research and consulting projects in future!

NOTES

1. A.M. Osman-Gani and T. Rocksthul. (2008) 'Antecedents and consequences of social network characteristics for expatriate adjustment and performance in overseas assignments: Implications for HRD,' *Human Resource Development Review* 7(1): 32–57. A.M. Osman-Gani and W-L. Tan. (2005) 'Expatriate development for Asia-Pacific: A study of training contents and methods,' *International Journal of Human Resources Development and Management* 5: 41–56.

2. A.M. Osman-Gani and T. Rocksthul. (2009) 'Cross-cultural training, expatriate self-efficacy, and adjustments to overseas assignments: An empirical investigation of managers in Asia,' *International Journal of Intercultural Relations* 33: 277–290. D.M. Eschbach, G.E. Parker and P.A. Stoeberl. (2001) 'American repatriated employees' retrospective assessments of the effects of cross-cultural training on their adaptation to international assignments,' *International Journal of Human Resource Management* 12: 270–287. A.M. Osman-Gani. (2000) 'Developing expatriates for the Asia Pacific region: A comparative analysis of multinational enterprise managers from three continents,' *Human Resource Development Quarterly* 11: 213–244. J. Stewart Black and H.B. Gregersen. (1999) 'The right way to manage expats,' *Harvard Business Review* 77(2): 52–63. P.C. Early. (1987) 'Intercultural training for managers: a comparison of documentary and interpersonal methods,' *Academy of Management Journal* 30: 685–698. M. Mendenhall and G. Oddou. (1985) 'The dimensions of expatriate acculturation: A review,' *Academy of Management Review* 10: 39–47. D. Landis and R. Brislin. (1983) *Handbook on intercultural training*, Vol. 1. New York: Pergamon. R.L. Tung. (1981) 'Selection and flaming of personnel for overseas assignments,' in M. Wilkinson and M.A. Devanna (eds.), *Columbia Journal of World Business*, 16(1): 68–78.

3. S.J. Shin, F.P. Morgeson and M.A. Campion. (2007) 'What you do depends on where you are: Understanding how domestic and expatriate work requirements depend upon cultural context,' *Journal of International Business Studies* 38: 64–83.

4. P. Bhaskar-Shrinivas, D.A. Harrison, M.A. Shaffer and D.M. Lu. (2005) 'Input-based and time-based models of international adjustment: Meta-analytic evidence and theoretical extensions,' *Academy of Management Journal* 48: 257–281. R. Hechanova, T.A. Beehr and N.D. Christiansen. (2003) 'Antecedents and consequences of employee's adjustment to overseas assignment: A meta-analytic review,' *Applied Psychology: An International Review* 52: 213–236.

5. M.J. Gelfand, M.E. Erez and Z. Aycan. (2007) 'Cross-cultural organizational behavior,' *Annual Review of Psychology* 58: 479–514.

6. S. Ang, L. Van Dyne, C.K.S. Koh, K.Y. Ng, K.J. Templer, C. Tay and N.A. Chandrasekar. (2007) 'Cultural intelligence: Its measurement and effects on cultural judgment and decision making, cultural adaptation, and task performance,' *Management and Organization Review* 3: 335–371.

7. P.C. Earley and S. Ang. (2003) *Cultural intelligence: Individual interactions across cultures.* Palo Alto, CA: Stanford University Press.

8. R.J. Sternberg. (1986) 'A framework for understanding conceptions of intelligence,' in R.J. Sternberg and D.K. Detterman (eds.), *What Is Intelligence?*

Contemporary Viewpoints on Its Nature and Definition, Norwood, NJ: Ablex, 3–15.

9. R.J. Sternberg and E.L. Grigorenko. (2006) 'Cultural intelligence and successful intelligence,' *Group and Organization Management* 31: 27–39.

10. K.Y. Ng and P.C. Earley. (2006) 'Culture and intelligence: Old constructs, new frontiers,' *Group and Organization Management* 31: 4–19.

11. H.C. Triandis. (2006) 'Cultural intelligence in organizations,' *Group and Organization Management* 31: 20–26.

12. R. Brislin, R. Worthley and B. MacNab. (2006) 'Cultural intelligence: Understanding behaviors that serve people's goals,' *Group and Organization Management* 31: 40–55.

13. P.C. Earley and R.S. Peterson. (2004) 'The elusive cultural chameleon: Cultural intelligence as a new approach to intercultural training for the global manager,' *Academy of Management Learning and Education* 3: 100–115.

14. M. Janssens and J.M. Brett. (2006) 'Cultural intelligence in global teams: A fusion model of collaboration,' *Group and Organization Management* 31: 124–153.

15. M.A. Shaffer, D.A. Harrison, H. Gregersen, J.S. Black, J. S. and L.A. Ferzandi. (2006) 'You can take it with you: Individual differences and expatriate effectiveness,' *Journal of Applied Psychology* 91: 109–125.

16. See P.C. Earley and S. Ang. (2003) *Cultural intelligence: Individual interactions across cultures*. Palo Alto: Stanford University Press.

17. F.L. Schmidt and J.E. Hunter. (2000) 'Select on intelligence,' Ii E.A. Locke (ed.), *The Blackwell Handbook of Organizational Principles*, Oxford: Blackwell, 3–14.

18. R.J. Sternberg and D.K. Detterman. (1986) *What is intelligence? Contemporary viewpoints on its nature and definition*. Norwood, NJ: Ablex.

19. R. Thorndike and S. Stein. (1937) 'An evaluation of the attempts to measure social intelligence,' *Psychological Bulletin* 34: 275–285.

20. J.D. Mayer, R.R. Caruso and P. Salovey. (2000) 'Emotional intelligence meets traditional standards for an intelligence,' *Intelligence* 27: 267–298.

21. R.J. Sternberg and E.L. Grigorenko. (2006) 'Cultural intelligence and successful intelligence,' *Group and Organization Management* 31: 27–39.

22. R.J. Sternberg. (1986) A framework for understanding conceptions of intelligence,' in R.J. Sternberg and D.K. Detterman (eds.), *What Is Intelligence? Contemporary Viewpoints on Its Nature and Definition*, Norwood, NJ: Ablex, 3–15.

23. P.L. Ackerman. (1996) 'A theory of adult intellectual development: Process, personality, interests, and knowledge,' *Intelligence* 22: 227–257.

24. S.J. Ceci. (1996) *On intelligence: A bioecological treatise on intellectual development*. Cambridge: Harvard University Press.

25. R.J. Sternberg. (1986) 'A framework for understanding conceptions of intelligence,' Ii R.J. Sternberg and D.K. Detterman (eds.), *What Is Intelligence? Contemporary Viewpoints on Its Nature and Definition*, Norwood, NJ: Ablex, 3–15.

26. J.H. Flavell. (1979) 'Metacognition and cognitive monitoring: A new area of cognitive inquiry,' *American Psychologist* 34: 906–911.

27. R. Brislin, R. Worthley and B. MacNab. (2006) 'Cultural intelligence: Understanding behaviors that serve people's goals,' *Group and Organization Management* 31: 40–55.

28. H.C. Triandis. (1994) *Culture and social behavior*. New York: McGraw Hill.

29. E.g., G. Hofstede. (2001) *Culture's consequences*. Thousand Oaks, CA: Sage.

30. R. Brislin, R. Worthley and B. MacNab. (2006) 'Cultural intelligence: Understanding behaviors that serve people's goals,' *Group and Organization Management* 31: 40–55.

31. R. Kanfer and E.D. Heggestad. (1997) 'Motivational traits and skills: A person-centered approach to work motivation,' *Research in Organizational Behavior* 19: 1–56.
32. A.S. DeNisi and R.D. Pritchard. (2006) 'Performance appraisal, performance management and improving individual performance: A motivational framework,' *Management and Organization Review* 2: 253–277.
33. E.L. Deci and R.M. Ryan. (1985) *Intrinsic motivation and self-determination in human behavior.* New York: Plenum.
34. A. Bandura. (2000) 'Cultivate self-efficacy for personal and organizational effectiveness,' in E. A. Locke (ed.), *Handbook of Principles of Organizational Behavior,* Oxford: Blackwell.
35. E.T. Hall. (1959) *The silent language.* New York: Doubleday.
36. W.B. Gudykunst, S. Ting-Toomey and E. Chua. (1988) *Culture and interpersonal communication.* Newbury Park, CA: Sage.
37. P.C. Earley and S. Ang. (2003) *Cultural intelligence: Individual interactions across cultures.* Palo Alto, CA: Stanford University Press.
38. K.S. Law, C.S. Wong and W.H. Mobley. (1998) 'Toward a taxonomy of multidimensional constructs,' *Academy of Management Review* 23: 741–755.
39. P.T. Costa Jr. and R.R. McCrae. (1992) *Revised NEO personality inventory (NEO PI-R) and new five-factor inventory (NEO FFI) professional manual.* Odessa, FL: Psychological Asses ment Resources.
40. S. Ang, L. Van Dyne and S.K. Koh. (2006) 'Personality correlates of the four-factor model of cultural intelligence,' *Group and Organization Management* 31: 100–123.
41. See P.T. Costa Jr. and R.R. McCrae. (1992) *Revised NEO personality inventory (NEO PI-R) and new five-factor inventory (NEO FFI) professional manual.* Odessa, FL: Psychological Asses ment Resources.
42. R.J. Sternberg and D.K. Detterman. (1986) *What is intelligence? Contemporary viewpoints on its nature and definition.* Norwood, NJ: Ablex.
43. See K.S. Law, C.S. Wong and W.H. Mobley. (1998) 'Toward a taxonomy of multidimensional constructs,' *Academy of Management Review* 23: 741–755. J.D. Mayer, R.R Caruso and P. Salovey. (2000) 'Emotional intelligence meets traditional standards for an intelligence,' *Intelligence* 27: 267–298.
44. See J.D. Mayer, R.R Caruso and P. Salovey. (2000) 'Emotional intelligence meets traditional standards for an intelligence,' *Intelligence* 27: 267–298.
45. F.L. Schmidt and J.E. Hunter. (2000) 'Select on intelligence,' in E.A. Locke (ed.), *The Blackwell Handbook of Organizational Principles,* Oxford: Blackwell, 3–14.
46. See P.C. Earley and S. Ang. (2003) *Cultural intelligence: Individual interactions across cultures.* Palo Alto: Stanford University Press.
47. For a comprehensive review, see R.N. Paige. (2004) 'Instrumentation tin intercultural training,' in D. Landis, J.M. Bennett and M.J. Bennett (eds.), *Handbook of Intercultural Training,* 3rd ed., Thousand Oaks, CA: Sage, 85–128.
48. Y. Yamazaki and D.C. Kayes. (2004) 'An experiential approach to cross-cultural learning: A review and integration of competencies for success expatriate adaptation,' *Academy of Management Learning and Education* 3: 362–379.
49. P.C. Earley and S. Ang. (2003) *Cultural intelligence: Individual interactions across cultures.* Palo Alto: Stanford University Press. R.J. Sternberg, and D.K. Detterman. (1986) *What is intelligence? Contemporary viewpoints on its nature and definition.* Norwood, NJ: Ablex.
50. R.M. Paige. (2004) 'Instrumentation in intercultural training,' in D. Landis, J.M. Bennett and M.J. Bennett (eds.), *Handbook of Intercultural Training,* 3rd ed., Thousand Oaks, CA: Sage, 85–128.

51. E.g., CCAI: Cross-Cultural Adaptability Inventory; CCWM: Cross-Cultural World Mindedness; CSI: Cultural Shock Inventory; ICAPS: Intercultural Adjustment Potential Scale; IDI: Intercultural Development Inventory; MAKSS: Multicultural Awareness-Knowledge-Skills Survey; OAI: Overseas Assignment Inventory; and Prospector.

52. P.C. Earley and R.S. Peterson. (2004) 'The elusive cultural chameleon: Cultural intelligence as a new approach to intercultural training for the global manager,' *Academy of Management Learning and Education* 3: 100–115.

53. Ones, D. S., & Viswesvaran, C. (1999). Relative importance of personality dimensions for expatriate selection: A policy capturing study. Human Performance, 12, 275–294. W.C. Borman and S.J. Motowidlo. (1993) 'Expanding the criterion domain to include elements of contextual performance,' in N. Schmitt and W.C. Borman (eds.), *Personnel Selection in Organizations*, San Francisco: Jossey Bass, 71–98.

54. J. Stewart Black. (1988) 'Work role transitions: A study of American expatriate managers in Japan,' *Journal of International Business Studies* 30(2): 119–134.

55. M.A. Morris and C. Robie. (2001) 'A meta-analysis of the effects of cross-cultural training on expatriate performance and adjustment,' *International Journal of Training and Development* 5(2): 112–125.

56. Mendenhall, M., Stahl, G., Ehnert, I., Oddou, G., Osland, J., & Kühlmann, T. (2004). Evaluation studies of cross-cultural training programs: A review of the literature from 1988–2000. In D Landis, & J Bennett (Eds). The Handbook of Intercultural Training. Thousand Oaks, CA: Sage . M.A. Morris and C. Robie. (2001) 'A meta-analysis of the effects of cross-cultural training on expatriate performance and adjustment,' *International Journal of Training and Development* 5(2): 112–125. L.N. Littrell and E. Salas,. (2005) 'A review of cross-cultural training: Best practices, guidelines, and research needs,'. *Human Resource Development Review* 4(3): 305–334.

57. Selmer, J. (2005) 'Is Bigger Better? Size of the Location and Expatriate Adjustment in China', International Journal of Human Resource Management, 16(7): 1228–42.;

58. M.E. Mendenhall, G.K. Stahl, I. Ehnert, G. Oddou, J.O. Osland and T.M. Kuhlmann. (2002) 'Evaluation studies of cross-cultural training programs,' in D. Landis, J.M. Bennett and M.J. Bennett (eds.), *Handbook of Intercultural Training*, vol. 3, Thousand Oaks, CA: Sage.

59. Mendenhall et al., 2004; L.K. Stroh, J.S. Black, M.E. Mendenhall and H.B. Gregersen. (2005) *International assignments: An integration of strategy, research, and practice*. Mahwah, NJ: Lawrence Erlbaum Associates.

60. P.C. Earley and R.S. Peterson. (2004) 'The elusive cultural chameleon: Cultural intelligence as a new approach to intercultural training for the global manager,' *Academy of Management Learning and Education* 3: 100–115.

61. A.M. Osman-Gani. (2000) 'Developing expatriates for the Asia Pacific region: A comparative analysis of multinational enterprise managers from three continents,' *Human Resource Development Quarterly* 11: 213–244. A.M. Osman-Gani and T. Rocksthul. (2009) 'Cross-cultural training, expatriate self-efficacy, and adjustments to overseas assignments: An empirical investigation of managers in Asia,' *International Journal of Intercultural Relations* 33: 277–290.8.

62. See P.C. Earley and R.S. Peterson. (2004) 'The elusive cultural chameleon: Cultural intelligence as a new approach to intercultural training for the global manager,' *Academy of Management Learning and Education* 3: 100–115.

63. S. Ang, L. Van Dyne, C.K.S. Koh, K.Y. Ng, K.J. Templer, C. Tay and N.A. Chandrasekar. (2007) 'Cultural intelligence: Its measurement and effects on cultural judgment and decision making, cultural adaptation, and task performance,' *Management and Organization Review* 3: 335–371.

9 Worldly Leadership

Uncovering Ancient and Indigenous Leadership Wisdoms for a More Sustainable World

Sharon Turnbull

The majority of leaders across the globe today have been conditioned in some way by western and US-centric leadership theories and methodologies. This thinking has been driven through our global business schools and business cultures, often to the exclusion of non-western traditions and cultures and the valuable insights and wisdom these may have to offer. As western leadership traditions struggle to find answers to major global problems of poverty, sustainability, economic stability and health, Sharon's research at The Leadership Trust has been focusing on uncovering alternative ancient and indigenous leadership wisdoms that might help to address the complex challenges of today's world. The keynote outlines the findings of the research so far, and discusses the HRD implications that these findings imply, and in particular what these findings suggest for the leadership development agenda.
(Inaugural professorial lecture, Worcester University, 19 May 2009)

CONTEXT (WRITTEN BY MONICA LEE)

This chapter is built around the inaugural professorial lecture that Sharon gave on May 19, 2009, to mark her appointment as visiting professor at Worcester University. At the time, Sharon was director of the Centre for Applied Leadership Research at The Leadership Trust, and her audience and focus clearly reflected her multiple roles as academic, researcher and practitioner. She made great use of audio clips and pictures, and the lecture was very well received and remembered. It provided a fascinating insight into alternative forms of leadership, which I hope comes through in this text-limited version.

THE PRESENTATION: WORLDLY LEADERSHIP

How often do you think about leadership of and for the world? I guess you'll probably think about leadership quite often, but perhaps largely about leadership of your businesses, of your organizations. In today's lecture what I'd like to do is to talk about some of the research that we've been doing at the Leadership Trust and to take you through a journey to explore leadership in some new ways, I hope in some ways that you haven't previously thought about. There is a lot of talk at the moment about a crisis of leadership. There's so much going on that makes us worry about our world. Lovelock[1] now has taken to calling global warming global heating, and I don't know about you but I quite like warm but I'm not sure about heat. Of course none of us can have failed to have noticed the global economic crisis that is going on all around us. Thomas Friedman is talking about the flattening of the business world; he's talking about a change in the landscape, a more level playing field, about the growth of new countries in the world economy. He's talking about the rise of China, the rise of India and so on, and all of that makes the world very unpredictable, an unpredictable place for businesses but also a very unpredictable place for the rest of us. Of course much of that change in the business world has come about as a result of the communications revolution. Many of you will know of the rise of India and Bangalore, perhaps through the use of software and call centers. These shifts are often linked to an increasing amount of materialism and greed; to a crisis of ethics, in addition to that crisis of leadership. This afternoon I'd like to talk about the potential crisis of ethics and leadership together.

Maybe all of these problems are not new. This is a photograph I took in India of one of Gandhi's final homes, and I'd just like to read it to you because I think it picks up on some of the problems that I just mentioned. This little plaque is called The Mad Rush, and it says, *'the people who are in the mad rush today increasing their wants senselessly suppose that they are enhancing their importance and real knowledge. A day will come when they will exclaim what have we been doing. One after another many civilizations have risen, flourished, declined and disappeared and in spite of their big boast of human progress I am inclined to ask to what end all this. What's the purpose. Darwin's contemporary Wallace has said that despite the various discoveries and inventions during the past 50 years the moral height of man hasn't increased even an inch. Tolstoy has said the same thing, Jesus, Buddha, Prophet Mohammed, all have said the same thing.'* So here we are in the midst of all of these world crises, and Gandhi was saying some similar messages all those years ago.

Just a few words about how I got onto the research track of what we've been calling worldly leadership. When I got to the Leadership Trust, I had been researching organizational behavior and organizational change and culture, and suddenly I thought well actually if I'm going to work for a leadership organization I suppose I ought to find out something about leadership. So I started to read the literature of leadership and discovered that it was 99.9 percent Anglo-American, and I also discovered that the literature on leadership, although it had made great strides over previous decades, now seemed to be going back on itself and making no real further progress.

Soon after I joined the Leadership Trust I was invited to take up the role of directing the International Masters Program in Practicing Management.

This is a program some of you may be familiar with. It was set up by a professor called Henry Mintzberg,[2] who had the belief that MBAs were really not developing the kind of managers and leaders that we needed, and we really needed a different kind of education for managers. This program was set around the world; six different business schools partner in this program; it's still going and attracting leaders from very many large organizations across the world. And this was the other part of the journey which started me thinking about worldly leadership, where leadership theory was going and what might be missing in terms of the leadership theoretical agenda. As I went round the world I started to explore leadership in other settings.

So my first contention in this lecture today is that leadership theory has for a long time been trapped in Western mindset. Mark Mendenhall,[3] who's written a lot about global leadership, says that the vast majority of empirical leadership research has been undertaken by US and British scholars. That also means that even where research concerns other parts of the world it tends to be viewed through the eyes of Western people, and so it still has that particular Western lens.

Last week I thought for fun I would have a look on Amazon.com to see how many books on leadership there are right now. This was May 14, so I'm sure that there are a few more since then. But at the time there were 326,324 books on leadership, and as I scrolled down the top sellers, guess what, they were all from America, and then I finally found some that had been produced and written in India, but guess what, they were all using Western leadership theory.

Nancy Adler,[4] an American leadership academic, says that most leadership theories are actually domestic theories masquerading as universal theories, and I think when she talks "domestic" there she's talking about US theories masquerading as theories that will work in other places around the world. The other thing about global leadership theory is that it's got very obsessed with attributes, traits and competences, and I don't know if any of you are, I'm sure there are many of you from the corporate world, and you too I'm sure will have lots of interesting attributes, traits and competences. In fact she did a survey and she found that in terms of the research that's been going on, on global leadership, she found exactly fifty-six so-called global leadership competences, which she then distilled into six categories. And then she said: "But how does this help us?" So even after she had done this, she couldn't see much point in these fifty-six categories.

The other thing that's happening, the second point in my contention, is that Western management education is starting to drive out Eastern and Indigenous wisdoms from many societies. The reason that I say that is that about fifteen years ago I was involved in setting up the International Masters Program in Practicing Management,[5] the one that I was then later asked to direct for a few years, and one of the things that Henry Mintzberg wanted to happen was that each business school would teach leadership and management from the perspective of its own culture—through the lens of its own culture, using the business traditions of its own culture and a pedagogy, a teaching method, from its own culture.

So we duly waited for the different schools to produce a module for the program, and guess what, we got two drafts of modules from the Korean business school and the Indian business school crammed full of Harvard and Stamford business cases. And when we wrote back to them and said well this is American pedagogy, why are you designing a module for your country to exemplar your leadership using Harvard case studies, we don't understand, and of course they said well we've been educated, we've been out there, we've come back, we actually don't know any more what you mean by designing a module using the Indian lens or the Korean lens.

The only business school that did know was the one that we used in Japan. Japan designed a truly Japanese module. But at that point it did make me wonder and worry what is happening to the wisdoms in these countries, in these cultures, where the business schools feel obliged to adopt the Western and the American models of leadership and management. And, second, if that's the case, that would be all fine and good as long as leadership was able to resolve those major global problems. But, as I think you were nodding when I said there seems to be a bit of a leadership crisis, we know that, maybe I'm being a bit too dogmatic here, but it certainly seems to me that Western leadership is currently failing to address the critical social environment and economic problems facing the world right now.

So the aims of the research program, as we started to dig into it, were first to uncover from close up those important leadership wisdoms in oral and ancient cultures hitherto either overlooked or hidden by the more dominant Western voices and, second, to rediscover how these ancient, indigenous and Eastern leadership wisdoms can help the world to come through those crises that I was talking about both locally in their own domains and also globally. The 'ancient' refers to those scholarly works that have been written over time; they may be thousands of years old but still endure and still have messages to tell us about leadership. We looked at those as well as those oral traditions that perhaps actually know a lot about leadership but don't write it down and certainly don't get it published in the leadership journals that we all read.

So toward worldly leadership wisdom. Henry Mintzberg has said that worldly mindset is about engaging at close proximity in the many different worlds within worlds that make up our globe and enrich our experience. But, very important, he adds the words "and act." So he's making a call for a leadership which not only is wise and knowledgeable but takes action in the world. He also suggests that to have a worldly lens or a worldly mindset you need to seek to understand particular responses to specific conditions. So we're talking very local, very micro here. A plurality of world views, understanding the richness of the world, and the patchwork that makes up the world.

So this is very much, very different from a homogenous theory of leadership. It values and seeks . . . and therefore the best possible approach to studying leadership would be something that we scholars would call emic and simply means research on the inside. So as opposed to looking from the outside in to actually go inside, inside a culture, inside a tribe, inside a society or a community, and feel and understand what goes on in that community.

WORLDLY LEADERSHIP IN PRACTICE

You're probably thinking well this all sounds a bit theoretical; what does that mean in practice? So let me give you a few examples about how we've been going about researching these ancient, Eastern and indigenous wisdoms. We've basically been trying to combine understanding of ancient literatures, and many of them are still available, with a contemporary anthropological study in Eastern and indigenous cultures. We have set up a network of scholars researching this kind of leadership in different parts of the world and finding a way to connect ourselves together and start to produce knowledge through researchers around the world.

So, first, let's go to the East, both ancient and modern, and the reason I'm going to talk about the two together is that, as we suspected, the ancient wisdoms are still pervasive to a degree in some of those societies, and of course they're being driven out, and Western discourse is very strong also, but our research has been looking for those wisdoms where they might arise in societies around the world.

Indian Forms of leadership

Back to Gandhi; I guess his short statement that many of us have come across before might well on its own help answer a lot of the problems of the world if more people actually followed it. *"There is enough in the world for everybody to need but not enough for everybody's greed."* Many of us know that phrase, but living by it is quite difficult. So one of the bits of research that we started to do was to find out to what extent this kind of wisdom was lived by and followed by everyday Indian leaders. Just a little bit about those principles, Gandhian principles. Some of you might know better about these than me, but let me have a go. The first satyagraha meaning soul-force, and that's, if you remember Gandhi's life, all about the sacrifice of self and leading by example. The second, which is *sarvodaya*, the upliftment of all, is about serving the interests of each and everyone, but of course also to include care of the earth, of animals, forests, rivers and land. Third, self government, *swaraj*, which is about self transformation both at the individual level, self discipline, self restraint, but also about social transformation, small-scale decentralized participatory structures. And finally, and I think we're just about catching up thinking about this in the West, local economy, local production, not transporting things across the world that actually we produce on our doorstep. So many prophetic and important principles there.

Yes, we did find Gandhi alive and well among some of the leaders that we interviewed, some of the Indian leaders in India that we interviewed; just a couple of quotes to give you an example of how Gandhian ideas still come out in India.

This is a modern Indian leader talking about social responsibility and shall I read it" He says: *"I have to make enough money to put bread on my family's table, but I don't have to have Rolls Royce to go around in, as long as I'm mobile I'm okay. And then I will do all this, you know, as though I'm the Prime Minister of my country. I'm not going to wait for the politicians to do what they have to do, I will go within the sphere of my influence and I will do it. I just feel that every little drop that we do, you know, don't wait for the government to do this, or so and so to do this, whatever we can do on our own."* And this is just in a response to an interview which asked him about his leadership and how he makes decisions and what he values, still a quite strong sense of community responsibility.

Another Indian leader talks about and says: *"Some of us are lucky to earn a lot of money, but treat it as pure luck, and what you do with the money is, as Gandhi says, business people are trustees for society, you know. Society has allowed you to make money, so never give that away to your children, that's most damaging. . . . .If I was Prime Minister I would have an inheritance tax of 90%.*. And he was very, very serious about this; he really felt strongly about that social responsibility.

Just before we go on let me say that of course Gandhian leadership is not the only form of leadership in India, and we did find many Western models of leadership there too and also some negative issues. Some of you will be familiar with the ancient scripture, the Bhagavad Gita, which is important to many Hindu Indians. There's some contention about how old it is, but the latest and probably one of the strongest views is that it goes back five thousand years and that it was probably an oral text before it was finally written down. This is a story of Lord Krishna who is actually Vishnu in disguise giving advice to Prince Arjuna. This is a book about humanistic and inclusive leadership. It's about duty, it's about acting with purity, it's about acting in the common good and very important for Indian society too about acting as teacher.

A couple of quotes just to give you a bit of a feel: *perfection is achieved when each attends diligently to his duty; a good leader is one who is incapable of hatred towards any human being, who is kind and compassionate, free from selfishness, without pride, calm in pleasure and in pain and is forgiving.* This is an Indian leader in response to an interview about his leadership. This is taken straight out of the interview and he says: *"Lord Krishna says in our Gita, it's our Gita, however old it is, your job is to work without any expectations with all humility, with sincerity, with full concentration on your work, if you do this you will get your just deserts."* And as we were interviewing these Indian leaders we did find that same recurring theme. So whereas Western leaders would tend to say I'm working hard in order to achieve a specific goal, and the goal is more money or a bigger business or a more successful business or whatever, many Indian leaders that we spoke to said we need to work hard and the rest will be taken care of; we don't have to worry about the outcome, we just have to do our duty and work hard.

This theme of the raj-*rishi* leader as guru and teacher is very strong, or was very strong in the leaders that we spoke to; a couple of examples. "*Give better opportunity to the other person to grow and take that team along with them as family,*" that's one Indian entrepreneur. Another one said: "*So we've got to make everyone understand and sit with them, you know, talk to them, explain things in detail so that, you know, they understand.*" These were both SME leaders. Another ancient Indian text is the Upanishads—and a quote from that: "*O Almighty God, you protect both of us, the teacher and the students together. You bear both of us together, may both earn the shakti (power of learning) together. May our learning be luminous, impressive, may we never bear ill will towards each other*"–. again, emphasizing the importance of that leader-follower relationship and leader as teacher.

Chinese Forms of leadership

What I want to illustrate by moving across three continents in this lecture is both some of the pervading and prevailing themes that apply in all places and also of course differences. Some of you may be familiar with Confucian values. It's been very much underground for many years, as you can imagine, and since China has become a lot more liberalized apparently the Confucian values have started to re-emerge and people are freely talking again about Confucius's influence. So some very similar themes actually to those ancient Indian texts, the values of benevolence and righteousness, and intellect, heart, feelings, courage, faithfulness, altruism. It was interesting that one of the questions that we asked the Indian leaders was if you could give one thing from your leadership knowledge and culture to the West what would it be, and in many instances, totally separate instances, the Indian leaders said it would be emotion. "We feel looking at you in the West there's not enough emotion in your leadership." Interesting here that Confucius also talks about emotion as part of leadership.

There's also a very strong theme of learning. For Confucius, you had to first become the *Junzi* (the refined man) and should never cease learning because your aspiration is to gain perfection, that is the sage, and yet the Chinese character for Junzi also is action. So there's still a sense that action is important in leadership. And the learning journey here in the Confucian values is more about character training than vocational learning. For the Chinese, if you build your character as a leader then the vocational bit will follow.

A couple of quotes, this is from Confucius: "*Man of ethical humanity must also practice what he has learned. When he wishes to establish himself he must at the same time establish the others. When he wishes to be prominent he must also help others to be prominent.*" So very much thinking about that leader-follower relationship, it's from the *Analects*. And another one, which is from a leader interviewed by a Chinese academic, Yunxia Zhu, who's been looking for Confucianism in Chinese leaders: *"Confucius says learning should go hand in hand with thinking and self reflections. So a wise entrepreneur must learn and reflect at the same time, which is also the way towards enterprise and success."*

So you can see that there are some themes emerging here, but there are also some subtle differences in the way these ancient wisdoms have developed over time in these Eastern cultures. Lao-tzu, the father of Taoism, used water many times to explain the nature of leadership as he saw it, and this is a summary of how he saw leadership. He says: *"Leadership is like water, water is altruistic because it supports life, and is modest and humble because it always takes the lowest ground. It is adaptable and flexible because it can stay in a container of any shape, and it is transparent and clear."* And I really feel the sense of the humility that is encapsulated in that metaphor.

I started asked leaders 'What's your definition of leadership, what's your rule of thumb of being a good leader?' and this is what one Korean said, a very senior leader from LG, who'd just left China after working there for a long time, and this was his spontaneous reaction. *"A good leader is defined as acting like the nature of water. The reasons are as follows. Water gets joined together and becomes one. Water flows from up to down interconnected together. Water purifies everything even if any muddiness."* So what we're finding is an ancient wisdom becoming absorbed and infused, apparently unconsciously, because this leader didn't cite Taoism in his response, but nevertheless it was guiding his principles, guiding his leadership practice.

Japanese Forms of leadership

Japan is an island, as you know, and Japan has a very homogenous culture; probably one of the most homogenous cultures that exists with little immigration over the years. They have a very complex culture and a unique approach to leadership. The one facet of Japanese leadership that really interested me a lot is the idea of what they call *ba*. I'm sure I didn't pronounce that right but you get the drift. Ba is the responsibility of a leader to create a shared space for emerging relationships. It's about making and finding, enabling others to find a platform for advancing individual and collective knowledge, and the Japanese have a strong view that if you don't get people together and find a way to create the relationships that enable creativity and innovation to spark, it won't happen. So it's the idea that knowledge creation transcends itself.

African Forms of leadership

Okay, so we've touched a little bit on the Eastern leadership wisdoms. Africa's a huge continent, of course, and so there are many African wisdoms. So let's just touch on one or two. Archbishop Desmond Tutu says: *"Africans have this thing called ubuntu. It's about the essence of being human and is part of the gift that Africa will give the world. It embraces hospitality, caring about others, being able to go the extra mile for the sake of others. We believe that a person is a person through another person, that my humanity is caught up, bound up, inextricably with yours.*" It's very important and I'll show you a clip, if we have time at the end ,of Tutu talking about what leadership is.

This by contrast is a quote from an interview that I recently did with an NGO leader who is working in northern Ghana. Northern Ghana is the poorest part of Ghana, and his role is to try to develop shared leadership among the villages, to help the villagers to sustain leadership in order to sustain their villages. So I asked him 'What is leadership for sustainability to you?' and he had a fantastically interesting and long answer but just a little clip here I think gives you the flavor of it. He says: "*Leadership for sustainability can only be achieved when there is shared leadership.*" He'd not been to a business school by the way anywhere. He'd learned this on the ground through his work with the NGO. "*So we identify the champions and so each champion will have sub-champions so that every turn it's almost like you have a cascade. You have a cascade there in the system.*"

What a wonderful bit of knowledge being shared with me from an African NGO leader on the ground in the middle of nowhere, many, many miles from a business school. He also talked about how he trains the emerging leaders in the village, many of whom are women, and about how he trains those women to deal with what he calls 'the leaders who are leaders by death.' And what he meant was leaders who inherit leadership, and become village elders. He told me the story about how he has to help those emergent leaders not only to learn to lead and to learn to train other people to lead but also to deal with the politics of the village elders. And he talked about how he persuaded them to believe that they had a responsible role, and then actually once they felt that they had a responsible role the emergent leaders would actually take the real responsibility. We never do that in our lives, do we?

Okay, and then on to the Masai, if you have been on safari or visited Kenya you will undoubtedly have met this wonderful tribe. They are known for their responsibility, respect, community, contribution, courage, honesty and wisdom. When one tribal elder was asked "How long will you be chief warrior?" he replied "For as long a time as it takes me to find a better one than me." If only our leaders, business, political and governmental, had that philosophy, how much better a place would our world be!

Masai children are given early responsibility. This little girl was given her first goat to tend at about the age of six. Some of you if you've been in Kenya or any parts of Africa you will see this happening. What these little children learn when they're given their first goat is about responsibility, and they're told: "*In your arms is the future food of our community. Tend it well and we live; let it die and we die with it.*" And they don't need to do more than that. These children look after their goats, they look after the camels, they don't need supervising, they don't get checked, they don't get asked to report on where they've been during the day because they learn responsibility very early. We also have another nice quote, and it's relating to wisdom that a young pair of eyes will spot a lion before an old pair of eyes—thereby recognizing and valuing the wisdom of younger people.

Masai leader (clip)

"How do you become a leader, I think it is like wine, it must mature. You cannot take leadership, you must be given leadership, and leadership is given because of what people have seen is the potential to follow this individual who will reach a certain point. But you cannot take leadership and expect people to say we must embrace him because he has forced himself upon us. But leadership is, first you must have dignity, you must have that kind of value that attracts others to you to say we would like this individual to represent us in whatever avenue of life you belong to, whether in the church, whether in the schools, whether in colleges, whether in just the community level. If you have a personality that has dignity then you can move yourself to become a leader.

You don't need to grab it, you don't need to shout about it but practically people will recognize and say I wish to have this person guide me to such and such a point because I know he will lead us to achieve a certain objective. But many a time today people think leadership is to have wealth. Many have found wealth through dubiousness. That doesn't make you a good leader just because you have abundant wealth. Because people don't seem to look back and say how did he gain this wealth. If you gain wealth through hard work I think it would make sense to lead others to say you need to work hard to achieve this. But you cannot steal and rob banks and accumulate wealth and say you need to work hard to achieve wealth, that's a contradiction completely.

So leadership must mature, we must listen to others, give opportunity to listen to others because life is a never ending education for us. You are educated on a day to day basis, just like the weather has changed over time, even you will change over time, but how you accommodate yourself in society is largely dependent on how you will give others an opportunity to say their minds, listen to them and be listened to, that I think is leadership."

So I think we have a lot to learn—from the tribal, the ancient, the indigenous, the Eastern. Some of the themes are recurring, such as responsibility, humanity, honesty, benevolence, custody of your community and society, and being a trustee of the two; teaching is knowledge and wisdom, contribution, contributing honesty and action.

Rowley[6] talked about wisdom being a combination of knowledge, ethics and action. In the indigenous wisdoms we see all three. When we read about Western leadership theory we see quite a lot about knowledge, we see something about action, but how often do we actually read about the ethics or the purpose of leadership in that theory.

DEVELOPING WORLDLY LEADERSHIP

So you might be thinking, what about *developing* worldly leadership, how would we do that? Well it seems also to me that what all of these cultures have in common is the belief that you can't be a leader without understanding yourself first, and even that little girl with the goat had to learn about responsibility as she was given that goat to tend. And we've been saying that at the Leadership Trust for quite a long time now, okay not as long as some of those ancient scriptures but at least since 1975 that leadership begins with learning to know and control oneself first, and then and only then can we lead and enable others.

But I think also to develop worldly leadership it is about deeply immersing oneself and finding encounters in close proximity with new and alien settings. It's about meeting leaders who themselves exemplify and embody these qualities. So the Ghanaian NGO leader was a great inspiration and taught me a lot about leadership and how you might engender sustainable leadership. It's also about shared reflected sense making, ideally in a culturally rich and diverse group, and it's of course about collaborative translation of ideas into action; it can't be done individually.

This deep emotional connection with worlds within worlds can help all of us, West, Eastern, indigenous, to learn more and to share more knowledge about leadership. I like this quote: "*Leadership is a continuous process that involves living by example, displaying the highest levels of honesty, humble presentation without imposing oneself or intimidating others and being constantly present.*" That was a Japanese leader, and I don't think we would have the same form of words from most Western leaders. I might be wrong, I hope I'm wrong.

So, in conclusion, where have we got to in this research? We're in very early days, there's lots more to learn and we hope that our worldly leadership research will continue over a good number of years together with a wide range of leaders, academics, scholars, practitioners to try and more fully understand that range of all the leadership wisdom, but the conclusion, so far anyway. Worldly leadership goes beyond knowledge; it has to include ethics and action. It has to also emphasize the shared leadership of community at societal levels. It also gives voice to previously unheard voices, either disenfranchised, marginalized or simply people who would not be asked usually. I mean how often have you asked a Masai leader to talk to you about leadership?

So leadership wisdom beyond Western thinking is in our view largely untapped, a largely untapped source of knowledge, and what we want to advocate now is a lot more close-up research that will help shape our understanding of leadership processes and philosophies and practice beyond the Western world.

Thank you very much for your attention, thank you.

AFTERMATH (ADDED BY MONICA LEE)

Sharon's interest in worldly leadership has continued to develop, and she is at present out of communication, expanding her understanding in far-flung places. The aftermath has turned into 'watch this space'!

NOTES

1. James Lovelock. (2000 [1979]) *Gaia: A new look at life on Earth*, 3rd ed. New York: Oxford University Press.
2. Henry Mintzberg. (2004) *Managers, not MBAs: A hard look at the soft practice of managing and management development* San Francisco :Berrett-Koehler.
3. Mark Mendenhall, T. Kuhlmann and G.K. Stahl (2001) *Developing global business leaders: Policies, processes, and innovations.* Westport, CT: Quorum Books.
4. Nancy Adler. (1997) *International dimensions of organizational behavior*, 3rd ed. Cincinnati: South-Western College Publishing.
5. Jonathan Gosling and Henry Mintzberg. (2003) 'The five minds of a manager,' *Harvard Business Review* (November): 54–63.
6. Jennifer Rowley and Frances Slack. (2009) 'Conceptions of wisdom,' *Journal of Information Science* 35(1): 110–119.

Part III

Implementation

The chapters in this part have a particular focus on the practical aspects of 'doing' HRD. This starts more recently than did the previous two parts. It could be that discussions of practice had a shorter influence upon the respondents than did other topics, but I would be surprised if that were the case—particularly as many of the speeches in other parts have a lot to say about implementation, and the speeches I have placed here also tie in closely with other areas. Perhaps this is an interesting anomaly for you, the reader, to ponder. Be that as it may, we start with a speech by Larry Dooley that he gave in 2007, which examines the impact of emerging technologies and e-learning on talent management within organizations. We might expect any speech on technology to be out-of-date within a couple of years, yet his analysis remains valid and pertinent. This is followed by Chanin Vongkusolkit, who, as CEO of Banpu in Thailand, gives a detailed account of corporate social responsibility and governance for sustainable development within his company, which links closely with Chartchai Na Chiang-mai's examination of HRD in Thailand in the previous part. The next chapter follows a similar theme of strategic organizational development within a different cultural context. It recounts a 2009 speech given jointly by Sharon Mavin and Dawn Robinson, who together outline a journey of change within SAGE (where Dawn is head of Learning and Development). This joint presentation, by an academic and a practitioner, represented the strength of the research and practice partnership they had developed. The last chapter in this part is a recent speech by Nicholas Clarke, looking at leadership development in a variety of situations, and from that, positing the need for a multi-level perspective in evaluation and research—which resonates with the threads of leadership and complexity that permeate these speeches.

10 The Impact of Emerging Technologies and E-Learning on Talent Management within Organizations

Larry M. Dooley

Rapid technological advances have greatly impacted traditional E-Learning. The impact of web 2 technologies led to the coining of "ELearning 2" to describe the emerging elearning forms that utilize web 2 technologies. Characteristics of Web 2 technologies include software services, harnessing collective intelligence, and pagerank algorithm.

Uses of emerging technologies has further reinforced the belief that learning is a social activity that occurs during group interactions. The belief that learning comes not from the design of learning content but in how it is used is gaining support. The traditional approach to e-learning focused exclusively on the needs of the company and often revolved around courses, timetables and testing. In contrast, e-learning 2 takes a 'small pieces, loosely joined' approach that combines discrete but complementary tools and web services (blogs, wikis and other social software) to create purposeful learning communities. E-learning 2 also promotes the idea of personal learning environment (PLE), which is a customizable learner centered environment that is comprised of various services that is useful to an individual's learning. It enables an individual to access information at their discretion. (Asian HRD Conference, Beijing, China, 2007)

CONTEXT

The sixth annual Academy of Human Resource Development Asia conference was held November 2–5, 2007, in Beijing, China. The largest Asia conference to date, more than 400 delegates registered. There were more than 300 papers delivered with 157 being delivered in Chinese. This was the first AHRD conference offering simultaneous language translation for all participants. This conference, hosted by the Center for Human Resource Management and Research in the School of Government at Peking University, offered a different look than in the past, with eighteen keynote speakers. After each Chinese speaker, another speaker would offer comments on the address delivered. This conference was held a year prior to the Beijing Olympics, and therefore, China was making a huge effort to emphasize the country's expertise in human resource development. This added extensive pressure to all keynote speakers.

Peking University, under the leadership of Xiao Mingzheng as conference host, involved numerous sponsors; more than twenty media outlets reported this conference nationally across China. Conference delegates were treated to wonderful luncheon buffets and conference dinners. Cultural performances such as a special performance by the Peking Opera were presented. Conference delegates were offered excursions to such renowned locations as the Forbidden City, the Summer Palace and the Great Wall of China.

We are in a rapidly changing world relative to technology. Even technology we used less than a year ago has now changed. Software that drives PDAs and other smart phones is updated at least monthly by vendors. Phone apps (software applications for smart phones) are the new packaging vehicle for most entities. At the time this address was delivered, the world was just beginning the huge technology explosion that has gripped all of us. The following address may seem elementary to us now; however at the time it was delivered, it was a sneak peek into what was expected to be the new technology revolution. Following is the address I delivered.

THE KEYNOTE: INTRODUCTION

In a recent book written by Thomas Friedman, he exclaims that "The World Is Flat!"[1] You would think in the 21st century our educational systems would have taught the scientific evidence that the world is round. This address, though, is not really about science, but about global competitiveness. We realize in this century, to use a slogan once used by a regional telephone company, "reach out and touch someone" now applies to the entire planet and not merely to the next township over. Friedman makes the case that outsourcing jobs and investments through connective technologies has not only shrunk the world, but has flattened it. That is a profound statement and one that human resource development professionals must consider. The notion of global competitiveness stems from the ways in which individuals and companies collaborate and share knowledge. Friedman presents ten "flatteners" of our world.

The first flattener, called 11/9/89 by Friedman, was the fall of the Berlin Wall. If there was ever a concept of suppressing communication, it was the Berlin Wall. The toppling of this wall was the beginning of the process of flattening the world. After the fall of the Wall, information and even economic policies could flow more freely.

The second flattener, called 8/9/95, was when Netscape went public at the price of $28 per share. This basically meant the Internet was now available for everyone from age 5 to 95. No longer was it only available for the early adopters or geeks, it was available for everyone. There were actually two different phases that were implemented. The first was the phase where all like computers on a local network could communicate with one another. However, Apple computers could not talk to Microsoft computers in this phase. The second phase was the Internet browser email phase, which allowed anyone with this technology to talk to each other.

The third flattener was referred to as workflow software. This was a more quiet change that most people did not pay a lot of attention to. It is generally thought to have happened in the mid 1990s and allowed more communication within businesses and continents. This was primarily due to the adoption of standards such as HTTP and HTML. This also meant people with computers could talk to each other without a technician in between.

The fourth flattener is uploading, and it allowed people to put information on the web. This has allowed very complex things to be shared with less hierarchy and money than ever before, especially in terms of digitized and disaggregated work that can be moved to any place in the world where it is better and cheaper. This also introduced Wikipedia, podcasting and blogging.

The fifth flattener is outsourcing, which allowed any call center, business practice or business knowledge that could be digitized to be outsources to any company who could respond.

When a whole company can be sent to another country that is known as off-shoring, which is the sixth flattener, mostly chosen for tax purposes or for the cost of labor. This is not merely moving a business practice or a business unit but an entire factory. Otherwise, it is known as outsourcing.

The seventh flattener is known as supply chaining. This is most accomplished when a company does business with suppliers, retailers and customers horizontally to create value. It is often considered that Walmart is the largest company in the world that sells nothing! The company is essentially an organization that matches retailers with customer, for a small price. Supply chaining has been enabled by a flatter world, but the world is flat in part because of supply chaining.

The eighth flattener is in-sourcing. Or as Friedman said, once the world was flat, small companies could now see around the world! The example Friedman gives is of United Parcel Service (UPS), who contracts with Toshiba to repair computers. When someone calls into Toshiba for a return, the call is routed to UPS who sends the address label to the customer; the computer is shipped to UPS, who repairs the computer and returns it to the customer. The customer never realizes the computer was never shipped to Toshiba, but it was repaired by Toshiba-trained support staff of UPS!

The ninth flattener is informing, which essentially is the work of Google, MSN Web search, Bing and so on. There used to be a popular saying, "Knowledge is power," but in this case, the knowledge is being given away. Anyone with access to a computer and access to the Internet can have access to the world's knowledge.

The last flattener is referred to as steroids because it enhances or strengthens the others. Cell phone use or voiceover IP for videoconferencing is an example.

These ten world flatteners have implications for global HRD professionals. There is indeed convergence of new players throughout the world, like

Taiwan, China, India, Russia, Eastern Europe, Latin America, Central Asia and Brazil, whose economies and political systems have opened up so that their people are free to join the free market. They can also jump into the game without the old technological infrastructure to slow them down. But staying competitive does not just require connectivity. It also requires the ability to successfully design knowledge systems that are accessible across borders of time and place. So, what does eLearning have to do with globalization?

eLearning provides HRD professionals the opportunity to deliver instruction to large numbers of learners who are unable to access residential programs because of time or place restraints. The increased use of computers and the Internet for information delivery has made online instruction possible. eLearning has been defined as the appropriate application of the Internet to support the delivery of learning, skills and knowledge in a holistic approach not limited to any particular course, technologies or infrastructures. Text, graphics, audio, video, animation and interaction are brought together in such a way that instruction can be provided via the Internet right to the desktop of the learner.

Course developers and trainers involved in the delivery of these courses require unique skill-sets that have often been associated with distance education but may be different given the delivery mechanism. The need for documentation of these skill-sets has been articulated in previous studies. In order to better prepare HRD professionals to develop and deliver instruction for delivery via eLearning, clear identification of competencies is critical.

Companies and agencies are turning to eLearning as a means to promote their products; educational institutions are turning to eLearning to deliver courses; and not-for-profits are turning to eLearning to reach clientele. The potential to reach across geographic distances regardless of time is paramount. There is a definite need to prepare professionals that have eLearning skill-sets to help companies keep their employees up-to-date and their companies competitive.

Competency identification and measurement are useful for educational practitioners, clients and potential employers. Determining competencies helps to improve human performance and unify individual capabilities with organizational core competencies. Training programs and certificates which provide an organized means of obtaining identified competencies help individuals become more competent and more effective in their chosen career.

ELEARNING 2 AND WEB 2 AS A 21ST CENTURY SOLUTION

The 21st century has brought technology to our fingertips but also the realization that we have an aging workforce coupled with a critical need to increase the knowledge within our organizations. With communications birthing a wired workforce, with a retirement crisis inevitable and the growing demand for knowledge workers, how can organizations retain corporate knowledge and effectively develop talent?

Marquardt[2] defined organizational learning as "an organization which learns powerfully and collectively and is continually transforming itself to better collect, manage, and use knowledge for corporate success."

It empowers people within and outside the company to learn as they work. Technology is utilized to optimize both learning and productivity."

Karen Watkins and Victoria Marsick[3] proposed six strategies that form the basis for organizational strategies to promote learning: 9(1) create continuous learning opportunities, (2) promote inquiry and dialogue, (3) encourage collaboration and team learning, (4) establish systems to capture and share learning, (5) empower people toward a collective vision and (6) connect the organization to its environment. Organizational learning is clearly the key to organizational effectiveness. How then can organizations capitalize on organizational learning and harness the power of the communication age?

Rapid technological advances have greatly impacted traditional eLearning. The impact of Web 2 technologies led to the coining of the phrase "eLearning 2" used to describe the emerging eLearning forms that utilize Web 2 technologies. Let's take a look at some of the advancements that have been described as web 2 technologies.

The ground-breaking entrance of Google into the communications field cannot be overlooked. Friedman listed the entrance of this tool as his ninth flattener in his book. Google, however, took it a step further when it introduced software that runs on a browser. Google Docs is a great example. It is a free, web-based word processor, spreadsheet and presentation application offered by Google. Documents, spreadsheets and presentations can be created within the application, imported through the web interface or sent by email. Files can be saved to a user's computer in various formats. It supports popular Microsoft Office file types such as doc or xls.

There was a time when companies hunted down employees who used Internet services other than their own and blocked them with firewalls. The thought was that everything had to stay within the organization. Now, the more online users a company has, the more valuable it becomes because of the wealth of knowledge contained within its large online user groups. Harnessing the collective intelligence is the new motto of organizations today. No longer do organizations dictate the specific sites employees only can visit; now the employees are freer to roam as long as the end result leads to performance improvement within the organization.

The barriers to being able to create Internet content have drastically fallen; as a result, more Internet users are creating and sharing personalized contents in various forms with one another. This information is organized and distributed using RSS (Really Simple Syndication) aggregators. RSS allows users to subscribe to a webpage with notification sent to them every time that page changes. The current notion of everyone as publisher is reminiscent of the late 1980s and early 1990s desktop publishing boom, but on a larger scale. Examples include: (1) written information, blogs and wikis; (2) pictures/graphics: flickr; (3) invitations: evite; (4) audios and videos: podcasts and YouTube; (5) social networking applications: MySpace, LinkedIn, Facebook and other similar sites that combine the above four features. Social networking such as Facebook has changed our very existence.

Another huge change in Web 2 technologies is that software is being designed and built as small components that can be plugged into other applications. This kind of composition is often called Mash-up. Most all online training programs utilize "plug-ins" as a way to extend the system without loading the software; it is loaded by the end-user. Another example is the collaboration between Google Maps and Craigslist, whereby maps from Google are linked to real estate listings on Craigslist to direct customers to the property being marketed. Another breakthrough is in the production of cinema or motion pictures. TagLoop is being used to point to images, audio or RSS feeds to link to the film so as not to have to recreate the file. Those items are tagged inside TagLoop where they can be reordered and layered over each other. This amazing concept is transparent to the viewing audience but saves an incredible time and cost in the final production costs of a film.

Harnessing the collective intelligence is the mark of a learning organization. But how can technology be used to accomplish this feat?

Google Page Rank Algorithm

This is a method of using the link structure of the web to provide a more accurate search result. For example, a Google search for Texas A&M University will take you to http://www.tamu.edu because that's the page about Texas A&M University that is most frequently linked to by other websites. This is a web browser that is in fact "learning!"

Amazon

It created competitive advantage by engaging its users and leveraging their input to create better search results. In fact, Amazon began as just a book company but has expanded its business by acting as a search engine for customers' diversified interests and needs. However, Amazon did not stop there, but also became a reseller for goods from other retailers, similar to what Walmart is doing on site in its retail stores. An Amazon search always leads with "most popular," a real-time computation based on sales and other factors.

eBay

Competitive advantage is the critical mass of buyers and sellers. Clearly the most successful auction house online, this site brings buyers and sellers together, for a fee. Beginning as a clearinghouse of independent buyers and sellers, it now also hosts companies looking for an extended market base.

Wikipedia

The online dictionary allows anyone to read, edit and upload content. The only major drawback from this source is that many younger generation students confidently use this site a fact and even have cited it in papers for class as a reliable source for research!

Social Bookmarks

This concept enables Internet users to store, organize, share and search bookmarks of web pages. Some people have called this concept folksonomy, a style of collaborative categorization of sites using freely chosen keywords, often referred to as tags. Tagging allows for the kind of multiple, overlapping association that the brain itself uses, rather than rigid categories. Examples include del.icio.us, Simpy and Connotea.

Collaborative Spam Filtering

This is the concept that a collection of email users' decision about what is spam will provide better spam filtering. Cloudmark SpamNet collects data from every installed copy of SpamNet (more than 900,000 users). According to *PCWorld* Review, it had the lowest false-positive rate of any spam filter it has ever tested; a catch rate of more than 98 percent.

REDEFINING ELEARNING

Uses of emerging technologies have further reinforced the belief that learning is a social activity that occurs during group interactions. The belief that learning comes not from the design of learning content but in how it is used is gaining support. The traditional approach to eLearning which focused exclusively on the needs of the company and often revolved around courses, timetables and testing is disappearing. In contrast, eLearning 2 takes a "small pieces, loosely joined" approach that combines discrete but complementary tools and web services (blogs, wikis and other social software) to create purposeful learning communities. eLearning 2 also promotes the idea of a personal learning environment (PLE). A customizable learner-centered environment is made up of various services that are useful to an individual's learning. This environment enables people to access information at their discretion. Take a look at how eLearning has evolved.

The ownership of the content has moved from a top-down management-owned philosophy to one that is bottom up and learner-driven. Whereas the development of learning content was once very expensive and time extensive, now learners themselves can create their own learning, using development tools that are, in fact, free.

Evolution of eLearning Over Time

	The Beginning (1.0)	First Evolution (1.5)	Current (2.0)
Elements	Courseware, Authoring tools and Learning Management Systems	Learning Content Management System (LCMS); Discussion Groups,	Social Networking, Bookmarking, Add-ins, WIKI, BLOGS, Create your own webpages, etc
Who Manages?	Top-down, instructor-centered "Sage on the Stage"	Mostly management-driven, with some limited collaboration	Learner-centered, peer learning, self-directed, "Guide on the Side"
Development	Long-term, very expensive, created completely outside organization	Quick turn-around, inexpensive, in-house created	Immediate, free, learner created
Relative time to create	One hour	Quarter hour	One minute
Timing of work creation	Prior to the job	In between the job and the work	While at work
Batch	One at a time	In pieces	At any time you need it
Access to content	Through professional learning management system (i.e., WebCT)	Company owned Intranet	Personal web search or RSS feed
Who Creates Content?	Instructional Design team or outsouce	Subject Matter Expert hired by company	End user!

Figure 10.1   Evolution of eLearning over time.

Probably one of the larger advancements in the eLearning 2.0 phase is the "where" this type of learning takes place. As has been previously mentioned, learning was never completed while at work but either took place prior to work or after traveling to a training site; now the learning takes place while at work, using company-owned and -maintained equipment.

Delivery of the content was often in one package or in stages, and now it delivered on demand in any increment the learner requires. Note, it is now delivered whenever *the learner* demands it and not when the supervisor requests it. That is a huge change. Instructional design is also changing from a behaviorist approach to more of a constructivist approach, from instructor-driven to learner-centered.

Access has moved from the company-owned learning management system or intranet to a learner-accessed RSS feed or a search through the many search engines available. And finally the creator of the content has moved from a formal instructional designer or subject matter expert to the individual learners themselves. We have in fact moved from what I call "a sage on the stage to a guide on the side." Development is no longer expensive and time consuming but immediate and free to develop.

RECOMMENDATIONS

Build an eLearning system on the concept of community-based eLearning. Consider how training materials will be disseminated (learner-centered training methods) and explore personal learning environments (ELGG, PebblePad or some form of eLearning portal). Consider how knowledge sharing will take place within the organization. Social software like blogs and wikis can be strategically used for documenting and sharing knowledge as well as facilitating team learning. Explore the use of blogs with their assortment of add-ons for richer organizational news that includes images, audio and video files as well as better feedback options. Promote the use of (RSS/Atom) newsreader as a means of getting the latest information. Consider the use of Facebook which could be a means of quickly identifying and communicating with experts within departments in an organization.

We now know that not everyone communicates the same way. College students today rarely own watches (they use their cell phone clocks) or email. Instead, they communicate via text messaging and social networks. An organization does not need to change its communication mode; it just needs to add other ways for individuals to connect. Do not only send out an email; also post on the organization's webpage, Facebook page and Twitter account. Casting a broad net will catch the most fish!

I visited with a former student who is beginning a start-up company and who said they are devoting all their marketing and advertising to social networks, web pages and Twitter. The future is now!

AFTERMATH: THEN AND NOW!

This was the speech as it was delivered. Times have really changed since the time of the speech. Let's examine the changes that have taken place.

- Diversity. One of the major changes taking place in business today is the diversity issue least recognized by the masses as diversity . . . the impact of the different generations working together and the social and cultural traits that impact their use of technology. The younger generation, especially Generation Y, has grown up with this technology. They are accustomed to sitting at their desks and conducting multiple conversations at once. They are online on social media, Twitter, message boards, chat rooms, playing fantasy sports and websites fairly constantly.
- Social media. In the beginning of social networking, Facebook was for college and university students (in fact you must have had an .edu address to subscribe), and MySpace was use for everyone else. After Facebook was opened to everyone, MySpace lost many of its members; Facebook is now the standard for most people as can be seen by current statistics. Social networking is no longer seen as being used only by the

young; according to *digitalbuzz*,[4] there are currently 500 million users with more than 50 percent logging in on a given day. Now teenagers and 90-year-old grandparents are active users. An average user has 130 "friends," and people spend more than 700 billion minutes per month on Facebook. Created originally in the US, now more than 70 percent of Facebook users are outside the US. Two hundred million users access Facebook from mobile devices and are twice as prone to access the network as are those accessing from a computer. And let's not forget about Twitter. Social media are connecting the new world in ways we never would have thought of at the time this address was delivered in 2005!

- Email, texting and cell phones. The use of differing and multiple devices for communication is becoming a generational issue that is affecting the workplace today. Once in its infancy, email is now the prominent communication venue of business. However, the use of email as the primary communications modality differs with age. Because of factors such as a declining economy and employees desiring to work longer, for the first time in history, there are four generations in the workplace; however the markers for these generations differ by geographic location globally. Some are "marked" by historical events, and some are merely marked by age. In the US, these generations are as follows:

- *The silent generation,* born between 1925 and 1945. Recognized as children of the Great Depression, which had a profound effect on them and their values.

- *Baby boomers,* born between 1946 and 1962. These were the children born after World War II and were born in increasing numbers and made a huge impact simply by population numbers.

- The next generation, known as *Generation X, has* no universally agreed date, but includes those born in the 1960s and 1970s but no later than 1982.

- *Generation Y, or* the Millennial Generation, begins about 1982 and ends around the turn of the century.

- *Generation Z* or the "I" Generation or the Internet Generation, has been known by some to cross over the Y Generation and begin in the 1990s but is strongly characterized by those born with Internet already plugged in.[5]

So, as one can see, the use of email, texting, instant messaging (IM) and cell phones is characterized by the generations they represent. Those born with cell phone usage cannot go a day without their devices; those in earlier generations, who leave their phones at home by mistake, just do without. I read a news article in the paper recently where one person killed another because he thought the person had taken his cell phone! Text messaging, or the need for instant gratification, is the communication mode of choice for the Millennial Generation and Generation Z; a generation also that rarely uses email because it takes too long to complete the communication cycle. The adoption of nation-wide and international calling plans with cell phones continues to flatten our world. In the beginning, cell phone plans had only local service, with distances outside the local calling plan added as long distance. Now, calling plans make it not only easier but a necessity for business.

Voiceover IP is another revolutionary breakthrough. Early videoconferencing was accomplished by either a dedicated T-1 line or by dial-up; in either case, it was very costly and only businesses could afford the cost. With the advance of voiceover IP, companies such as Skype® became a free service that is used globally to connect business executives, university faculty and even family with their children while away from home. Originally only accessible through computers, this technology is now available as an application on some cell phones. The introduction of technology into the workplace has in fact flattened our world and created a linked society.

It is important to remember that despite the ever-changing and rapid advances in technology, and thus the apparent dating of this speech, the core points of adjusting the learning experience to the media remain constant. In any discussion of technology and planning for the future, every question asked in determining the technology to use comes back to the audience intended. As noted in Figure 10.1, the ownership of learning is now learner-centered. We have multiple tools at our disposal that most of us are aware of: Facebook, iTunes, YouTube, Twitter, Flickr, and Skype, but are you aware of these: Vimeo, Behance, Foursquare, Bit.ly?

As we move into a world of managing our cyberspace with our employees, we need to remember that it is quality and not quantity that matters. We must continue to understand our audience and work with this audience to achieve mutual goals. Social connection still matters, and that is what we have been about from the beginning. We must interact with our audience, work smarter and not just harder and above all, use these new media tools to do what we have always done. However, remember, wheels have more than one spoke. That means that we must continue to create our message, but unlike days of old, we must disseminate our message using multiple platforms because our clients are no longer all using the same. We must communicate our message on multiple platforms and all at the same time!

NOTES

1. Thomas Friedman. (2005) *The world is flat*. New York: Farrar, Straus and Giroux.
2. David R. Schwandt and Michael J. Marquardt. (1999) *Organizational learning: From world-class theories to global best practices*. Boca Raton, FL: CRC Press, LLC.
3. Victoria J. Marsick, and Karen E. Watkins. (1999) *Facilitating learning organizations*. Brookfield, VT: Groer.
4. Aden Hepburn. (2011) 'Facebook statistics, stats and facts for 2011,' *Digitalbuzz*, accessed June 17, 2011, at http://www.digitalbuzzblog.com/facebook-statistics-stats-facts-2011.
5. Greg Hammill. (2011) 'Mixing and managing four generations of employees,' *FDU Magazine*, accessed June 17, 2011, at http://www.fdu.edu/news-pubs/magazine/05ws/generations.htm.

11 Corporate Social Responsibility and Corporate Governance for Sustainable Development

Chanin Vongkusolkit

We have a strong belief that an industry will be strong only when it is developed in tandem with CG, social and environmental responsibility, which in turn creates shareholder value at each stage of our development. This sentiment underlies our Sustainable Development Policy and commitment to be a good citizen, being committed to social responsibility, high degree of fairness, integrity and ethical standards to all parties. In every location, we are dedicated to conducting our business responsibly, ethically and lawfully in all matters

Banpu provides equal opportunity to everyone, regardless of race, nationality, language, or gender. Banpu believes in its vision, its strategic goals, and the strong solidarity of bonding under the "Banpu Spirit", which comprise innovation, integrity, care, and synergy. It is our belief that every individual's capability can be developed and enhanced. And it is Banpu's policy to support and provide an opportunity for everyone to maximize their professional growth through self-development, on-the-job training, coaching, training, and job rotation. Banpu have conducted CSR activities both at the corporate and local levels, concentrating on community development, education, environment, and youth development in the areas where businesses have been operating including Thailand, Indonesia, China and Laos. This Key-note examines how these principles and been developed and enacted and their effect upon Banpu, and the societies it operates within.
(7th Asian International Conference on HRD, Bangkok, Thailand, 2008)

CONTEXT

This speech was presented at "The 7th Asian Conference of the Academy of HRD," November 3–6, 2008, Bangkok, Thailand. The participants were from two main groups—academics from the UK, US, Malaysia, South Korea, Belgium, Singapore, Netherlands, India, Australia, Japan, China, Thailand and Saudi Arabia; and people from private-sector organizations such as Bangkok Hospital Medical Center, Coral Beach Resort Sharjah-UAE, Consultants, Betagro Group of Company and Banpu Public Company Limited.

Banpu Public Company Limited ("Banpu") was established in Thailand in 1983 as a coal-mining venture and listed on the Stock Exchange of Thailand in 1989. In the 1990s, the company diversified into power project development in Thailand, coal mining in Indonesia, port operations and industrial minerals. I am one of the founders of Banpu; and have been chief executive officer since the company was first established. I have tried to relate the company's practices to be in line with leading research and development to stimulate innovations and position Banpu as a leading company. Besides, the ideas of corporate governance, corporate social responsibility and sustainable development, have also been central to the company's businesses. Even before I gave this speech in 2008, Banpu had been among the few organizations trying to implement these ideas. As a result, I was delighted with the opportunity to speak to such a select group about our intentions and achievements.

Banpu has committed itself to running a long-term business and creating values to all stakeholders. Being a good corporate citizen with high responsibility to the society, running the business in compliance with rules and regulations as well as business ethics and treating everyone in a fair manner are the core practices which bring sustainability to Banpu. To achieve these goals, we emphasize the importance of corporate governance, corporate social responsibility and sustainability development through different means to all our staff at all levels of operations.

As human resource is one of key drivers in the company's sustainable development, Banpu puts high emphasis on managing its human capital; starting from setting up HR philosophy to implementing HR practices in line with business needs. Banpu provides equal opportunity to everyone regardless of race, nationality, language or gender. The company believes strongly in its vision, its strategic goals and the strong solidarity of bonding within the "Banpu Spirit," consisting of innovation, integrity, care and synergy.

THE PRESENTATION

Historically Banpu's growth in relation to CG and CSR can be defined mainly in two periods: the first period between 1985 and 2000 when we experienced an incremental development of the concepts and practices; and the period of 2000 until the present when we see ourselves moving toward structural and cultural change of policies and practices for CG and CSR. It is also important to emphasize that these policies have been developed alongside the development of Banpu; and their development has contributed to the company's success to date.

As a small business at the start of the 1980s, Banpu grew and became listed on the Stock Exchange of Thailand (SET) in 1989, with policies and practices of CG, as well as human resource management and development (HRM and HRD) as core and central to its activities. In 1999, the quality, safety and environment (QSE) policy was announced, and the company's core values were identified (integrity, team spirit, dedication and openness to criticism). The second period, the period for structural and cultural change toward sustainable practices, started at the same time with our first major business expansion overseas in 2000, when Banpu was becoming among the "SET-50," or one of the fifty largest listed companies in Thailand in terms of market capitalization. As its tradition, CG, HRM and HRD were also recognized as parts of the company's strengths, apart from relying solely on financial performance. Since 2002, a clearer, written CG Policy and Code of Conduct, as well as HRM and HRD policies, have been established. In 2004, the company's core values have become the "Banpu Spirit" (innovation, integrity, care and synergy), which all have since then been central to Banpu's activities in all operations/offices. Our CSR and Sustainable Development Policy have been formalized since 2005 and 2006, respectively.

Being recognized as one of the most respectable companies in these areas has contributed to the success of Banpu over the past years. It has made entering into new geographies easier as we are known to be respectful of our host communities and the environment in every country where we operate. All stakeholders, both internal and external, have trusted us to deliver our promises, which is a key to success in the highly competitive market. In addition, these factors would enable us to encounter any future challenges, for example, the changing mining laws and regulations and the environmental regulations in our countries of operations.

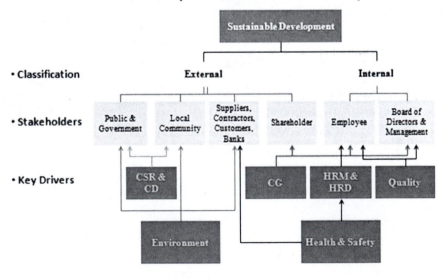

Figure 11.1   Banpu's sustainable development framework.

BANPU SUSTAINABLE DEVELOPMENT

"Banpu Spirit" provides the foundation for our approach to sustainable long -term growth—management of economic, environmental and social risks as well as opportunities. At Banpu, we have a strong belief that an industry will be strong only when it is developed in tandem with social and environmental responsibility, which in turn creates shareholder value at each stage of our development. This sentiment underlies our Sustainable Development Policy, which was established in December 2006; and our commitment to being good citizens, being committed to social responsibility, a high degree of fairness, integrity and ethical standards toward all parties. Stakeholders' concerns and interests are central to our considerations.

Banpu classifies its stakeholders into external and internal parties; with key drivers addressing each particular stakeholder group, to ensure the company's activities sufficiently address their needs/requirements. External stakeholders include public and government, local community, supplies, contractors, customers, banks, as well as our shareholders. The internal stakeholders include our employees, as well as the board of directors and management.

In terms of key drivers supporting each stakeholder group, good environmental management, both business and social aspects, will help to promote a good working relationship with public and government, local community, suppliers, contractors, customers and banks. At the same time, we also believe that corporate social responsibility (CSR) and community development (CD) directly address the needs and concerns of public and government and local community. Health and safety will ensure a good working environment for all external and internal parties. Corporate governance (CG) function reassures high standard of conduct for our shareholders, employees, management and board of directors. Efficient and effective HRM and HRD allow the company to have the required quality and quantity of human resources for sustainability purposes. Last but not least, quality management will help make sure all our employees, management and the board of directors perform their respective tasks with productivity.

A. Environmental Management

We base our environmental management policy and practice on the principle of creating societal value through harmonizing business practice with nature enrichment. In doing so, we ensure that we are socially responsible in all activities from investment, operation, through to mine closure. Banpu's environmental management focuses on three areas:

1. *Environmental concerns lead to the opportunity in renewable energy business*
   Also clean coal technology and coal upgrading
2. *Environmental management system*

Such as environmental impact assessment (EIA), integrated environmental management and mine master plan and ISO14001

3. *Mine closure management*
Such as rehabilitation fund, mine closure management system

B. Corporate Social Responsibility (CSR)

Banpu CSR aims to contribute to the development of society; support the sustainable growth of local communities and encouraging Banpu staff to be good citizens in each country where we operate our businesses. Our CSR vision is to be acknowledged as a socially responsible and environmentally friendly organization; promoting and contributing to the development of society by being a good corporate citizen, committed to safety practices and caring for nature and the environment.

Banpu conducts CSR projects at two levels; corporate and local. The local level is responsible by operating business units through community development programs focusing on community traditions, religions, education, health care, occupations, infrastructure and micro finance that are suitable for community conditions and responding to local needs. We put great emphasis on community engagement, which is done through open dialogues (formal and informal individual and small group discussions) with community members and the Community Consultative Committees (made up of representatives from local administrative offices, community members, NGOs and the company). When conducting or implementing our CSR projects in local areas, we also emphasize standard procedures, transparency, fairness and capacity building, while promoting care and friendly collaboration. Examples of our CSR projects at the local level in Thailand include support for a community bank prototype by Chiang Muan Mine, an annual education sponsorship for local students and support for local tradition. Our local-level CSR programs implemented by our three coal mines in Indonesia (Indominco, Kitadin and Trubaindo) cover irrigation development and water supply, fishery, occupations, medical services, infrastructure development and capability building, to name a few.

At corporate level, our CSR projects are responsible to not only corporate affairs group, but also to other relevant units involved. Our corporate-level CSR projects concentrate on the areas of education, youth and environment, which reflect our "Banpu Spirit" as well as our brand's attributes. This CSR strategy is in line with the government's national development direction as we seek collaboration with endorsements by government and non-government organizations as well as academic institutions when initiating/creating our CSR programs at corporate level. Examples of our CSR projects at corporate level include the education program called "ICT and Education Development for Six Schools in the North" (later renamed "Banpu Education for Sustainability"), teachers' training programs, environmental learning aid "GLOBE Animation VCDs and Bi-lingual Storybooks" for elementary students, environmental science camp "The Power Green Camp" with an approach of envi-science learning through actions, and the "Youth Innovation Market Place" (YIM) that encourages and supports youth groups in running social projects based on their interests and talents. CSR programs at corporate level in Indonesia have been run by our subsidiary (PT. Indotambangraya Megah Tbk), with examples of coal storybooks for children—an educational activity under the "ITM for Education" program, a waste management training program and the rescue operation to support any disasters in Indonesia. In China, we also pay great importance to social responsibility. Our CSR activities in China include support to the Luannan County Banpu Special Education School providing financial support (school uniforms, computers and so on, to disabled students), the Banpu Table Tennis Club (BTTC) at Zhengding City of Hebei Province, and a financial relief fund for victims of natural disaster such as the recent Sichuan earthquake.

To achieve our CSR goal and vision, we believe that key success factors are the involvement and participation from communities and target groups; this is to build a sense of belonging and allow us to achieve continuous capacity building for involved parties and community members.

C. Health and Safety Management

We base health and safety management on the principle of securing business continuation through occupational and managerial risk precaution. A key strategy is to create awareness and embed into ongoing activities that will make sure all the precautions are in place, for example, risk management (via risk management committee and risk profiles/mitigations plan) and OHSAS 18001. This also includes all other activities in the value chain (e.g., contractor management system, CMS).

D. Corporate Governance (CG)

The objectives of Banpu's CG are to create sustainability to the company, deliver fairness to all stakeholders and embed CG culture within our people. CG started as early as 2002 when we began to develop CG policies and Code of Conduct, with the first official edition announced in 2003. This was again updated in 2004; and the official revision of "CG Policy" and "Code of Conduct" (2nd edition) has then been published since 2005. These policies have been developed under the guidance of Banpu's strong culture within the "Banpu Spirit," with emphasis on integrity, dedication, team spirit, discipline and voicing concerns.

The CG implementation covers both internal and external stakeholders, in a variety of means and methods:

Shareholders

This is done by complying with CG best practices and principles under the Stock Exchange of Thailand (SET) CG Principles and Best Practices, as well as the Equitable Treatment to Shareholders by the Securities and Exchange Commission (SEC).

Employees

CG for our employees is carried out by promoting and emphasizing best practices of CG within the organization, for example, the internal journal "Banpu Insight" promoting the story of CG in daily life, as well as establishing a channel to receive CG-related complaints.

Board of Directors

This is done by setting strategic directions and CG policy to strengthen board governance, including duties and responsibilities to shareholders, by emphasizing equitable treatment to shareholders, and board composition by balancing number and roles of independent directors.

Management

Our senior management acts as role models for CG best practices within the organization, with regular sharing sessions from the management to staff on how to carry out CG in practice. Management must also ensure that subordinates comply with the company's Code of Conduct.

Customers

We comply with all terms and conditions agreed on with our customers, and we also set up a system and process where customers can place their complaints, if any.

Trading Partners

We comply with all terms and conditions agreed upon in transactions, provide reliable information and accurate reports and seek mutually acceptable solutions under Banpu CG policy and the Code of Conduct.

Government

We comply with local laws, rules, regulations, customs and traditions of all countries in which we operate.

Public, Community and Society

We are a responsible corporate citizen, which contributes to constructive activities in society and undertakes activities that will cultivate the staff's social consciousness and cause it to become part of our corporate culture.

Because of our CG policy and practice toward all stakeholders, we have received various awards and recognitions from many institutions. For example, we have received the certification of "Distinction in Maintaining Excellent Corporate Governance Report" for the second consecutive year from the Stock Exchange of Thailand (SET) at SET Award 2006, and Board of the Year Award in 2006/2007.

E. Human Resources Management and Development (HRM and HRD)

This is among the most important areas for Banpu to achieve sustainable growth by focusing on preparing highly competent staff to serve our business direction and growth, responding to the needs of our people and equipping our people with a strong spirit of working under cross-cultural environment. Our human resource philosophy has been developed as an essential part of people management to provide equal opportunities to everyone regardless of race, nationality, language or gender. This would ensure strong solidarity of bonding under the "Banpu Spirit" core values, while also prepare our staff to adopt flexibility, adaptability, mobility, positive creativity, in order to embrace true professionalism. This is also to comply with CG policy and the Code of Conduct. The three principles central to our HRM and HRD activities are performance-based system, equitability, and competency-based system.

The performance-based system has been used by the company as a key integral part to HRM and HRD as a whole. In this system, all employees have their own annual performance plan; in the form of agreed key performance indicators (KPIs) and targets to be achieved in a particular year, which in turn will be used to determine their merit increase. In addition, there are also other tools used to drive sustainable performance, including a variable bonus scheme for different staff levels, a production bonus and a discretion bonus.

In terms of equitability, there are a number of practices ensuring our fair treatment to all employees. We carefully consider job responsibility and profession, as well as benchmark it with a job grading system and salary structure of peer comparables and the related industry. In addition, we also promote "Happy Workplace," by both "physical" and "soft" sides. For example, we emphasize the office lighting system, ergonomic work stations, security systems and office equipment to ensure our employees have enough work facility for their jobs. For a softer side, we incorporate the "Banpu Spirit" and code of conduct into employees' normal working life, as well as provide channels to receive complaints to ensure our people can work harmoniously, with productivity. In particular, work-life balance has always been among the top priorities; for example, the company encourages each individual employee to work from home three days per month.

The competency-based system is also another key principle to help ensure that the company achieves sustainable growth through its people.

There are a number of practices to ensure that each employee/management is to be developed in line with the person's respective current and future competencies:

Career management is done by setting up career paths, succession plans and individual development plans (IDP) based on individual competency and future career; "Banpu Leadership Competency," as well as its associated development programs for Banpu's management and staff at all levels, have been established to ensure each employee is properly developed and has a good future career with the company.

Training and development is also a key tool to develop each employee/management in line with their required current and future competency. The company has always allocated at least 5 percent of annual salary as a guideline for training and development budget. The training and development programs not only focus on job-based competency, but also on other competencies necessary for working with the company, e.g., quality and safety program, IT program and so on. There are also several means to carry out the training and development programs, not just by conventional instructor-led training courses; the company also facilitates other self-learning programs such as e-learning courses and knowledge-sharing sessions for both general and technical topics. Training and development medium-term plans are regularly defined, implemented and rolled out every two years, based on each individual's IDP from a competency profile assessment and company's future need.

Banpu Spirit

We believe the "Banpu Spirit" (innovation, integrity, care and synergy) can help the company to achieve business results and sustainable growth in our highly diversified locations of businesses. The Spirit is also seen to support our brand attributes; and to be recognized by all stakeholders. A common practice is for each individual to have a 40 percent behavioral assessment in their annual performance assessment to be in line with behavior from the Banpu Spirit program. There is also the "Innovation Award" encouraging innovation in work systems and procedure to, for example, increase efficiency and/or reduce cost. A "Banpu Spirit Survey" is also conducted every year to understand areas for improvement, which leads to corrective actions. In addition, there are three key activities in implementing the Banpu Spirit:

1. Communicate to all employees on a regular basis, through various means and methods.
2. Turn into practice/behavior by training and education: A lot of activities have been done to promote and encourage all employees to familiarize themselves with Banpu Spirit behavior; for example, Banpu Spirit workshops, role models from key management, success story telling, reward and recognition for behaving in line with the Banpu Spirit.

3. Turn into group habits and norms, then into corporate culture: We see this as a "journey" that never ends but needs to be constantly communicated and implemented all the time to ensure the desired behavior is instilled in the company.

F. Quality Management

This is based on the principle of sustaining competitiveness with operational excellence using the tool of total productive maintenance (TPM) from ISO 9001 as fundamental. For example, our LP2 mine site in Lampang Province in the north of Thailand has been certified with ISO 9001, 9002, EIA, TIS 18001: 2000; and has also received the TPM Excellent Award (World Class Award). At this LP2 mine site, we started implementing quality programs by providing knowledge and training to all staff levels, followed by continuous campaigns and promotions, led by those at the manager level to act as role models for staff, which proved to be very successful. We are in the process of attempting to repeat this success story from LP2 mine at our other mine sites, to ensure that quality management principle is instilled throughout the company.

In conclusion, we firmly believe that such a strong and integrated focus on corporate governance and corporate social responsibility for sustainable development has been a major contributor to the successes achieved by Banpu.

AFTERMATH: WHAT HAS HAPPENED AND CHANGED SINCE THIS KEYNOTE WAS GIVEN IN 2008

In this third section of the chapter I will look at changes in Banpu since the keynote was given and the ideas it described were further enacted, as well as commenting on how this area of interest has changed in the last few years. Within Banpu, the main areas that have changed are:

Social Responsibility

Banpu has been recognized by not only its stakeholders but also by the public in general. Its CSR projects, which emphasize mutual cooperation between all involved parties in the process, yield a fruitful result to the society where the projects have been implemented. Banpu has been recognized for its social responsibility activities in the last couple of years by having been selected as one of the nominees for the Social Responsibility Awards organized by the Stock Exchange of Thailand (SET) for two consecutive years (2008 and 2009). In addition, Banpu has been active in the CSR Club of the Thai Listed Companies Association, aiming at encouraging listed companies to conduct their business with social responsibility. Banpu is one of the CSR club founders.

People

A business expansion has transformed Banpu into a genuinely regional company in the Asia-Pacific region. Banpu today has more than 5,000 staff in four countries, the majority of whom are based in Indonesia, Australia and China. Approximately 5 percent of Banpu's staff are located in Thailand—a dramatic transformation since the early days of the company's formation in the early 1980s.

Integrating people from different cultures and backgrounds; and working in Banpu's core values, is a major challenge. But this is seen among our top priorities going forward. Our growth and success to date are the effort, dedication and conduct of our people. The spirit and quality of our human resources determine our ability to sustain our competitiveness, maximize shareholder value and deal with future challenges and uncertainty.

To sustain our competitiveness and to ensure that further growth does not de-stabilize what we have achieved to date, Banpu has developed a professional and sophisticated human resource development programs and management systems. The main objectives are to ensure a motivated workforce with shared core values, as well as harmonious but innovative interaction between employees: a philosophy of continuous improvement–and a healthy work-life balance.

Banpu Spirit

The Banpu Spirit is the DNA of Banpu people, consisting of the principles of 'integrity,' 'innovation,' 'care' and 'synergy.' In the world of business, trust is everything; and we expect Banpu people to operate with highest 'integrity' and transparency in all their dealings. Banpu staff are encouraged to contribute actively to 'innovation' by submitting new ideas that can improve work and/or life at Banpu. Rewards are given at every stage of the innovation process: when an idea is selected, when the implementation proposal is approved and when ideas are successfully implemented. This system is introduced throughout the company in all countries. For example, in 2009, we introduced the 'Kompak' program from small focus groups discussion in Indonesia. These groups have been established to create and share new ideas—and to discuss implementation. We have also expanded this new system to include an Innovation Contest. In November 2009, three finalists from a total of 361 worthwhile implemented ideas were invited to a final ITM Innovation Convention in Balikpapan.

Banpu people should also show genuine 'care'; and we encourage positive engagement with the local communities where we work. Our corporate social responsibility programs in Thailand, Indonesia and China reflect our care for community development, career development, education, environment and youth. For more than five thousand people working together across four countries, 'synergy' is also a critical element in creating a strong sense of teamwork and fairness. Banpu's culture of collaboration is supported by various Banpu Spirit activities throughout the year.

Leadership

Banpu's culture places great importance on our people's performance and motivation. There are many sources of motivation such as personal drive, creating value for our customers and shareholders or contribution to society. At Banpu, there is also another source of motivation unique to Banpu, which is to follow in the footprints of successful examples set by our senior management in the past decades. Banpu's selected senior management, some of whom have been with the company for long time, have been at the heart of the company's growth and success and are seen as inspiration for many new leaders in the younger generations. As a result, our leadership is expected to also provide inspiration and mentoring to junior staff, be an example, and set a standard as well as promote desired behavior and attitude to which others should aspire.

Human Resources Management

Where applicable, Banpu is run as a matrix organization aiming to optimize efficient systems in countries in which we operate. Going forward, we will accommodate more to local needs while ensuring the implementation of policies, standards and guidelines—and the monitoring of key business performance. The most important aspect of the matrix organization, however, is that Banpu people can share information and expertise more readily in different countries. This benefits our projects and people because it allows for specialization, which increases the depth of knowledge, while facilitating the management of professional development and career progression.

Human Resources Development

Training and development are essential in increasing our people's capabilities for superior performance and are core components of our philosophy of continuous improvement. Our human resources development plan builds leadership and entrepreneurship for senior management, while focusing on advancing the professional knowledge and management skills of our middle management. Technical knowledge and continuous improvement are emphasized for professional and operational staff.

Embracing the Future

Banpu is a dynamic regional energy company. Our primary focus is coal; but as part of our 201–2015 Strategic Plan, Banpu is also actively pursuing investments in the area of new energy that might be a foundation for the world's energy in the future. In the age of global challenges, Banpu is determined to adapt and innovate. Adaptability, innovation and synergy among our people are more important than ever in moving Banpu forward. We invest in our people for their success and the company's success, and engage our people in creating value in line with social well-being, environmental stewardship and economic prosperity of the countries we operate in.

AWARDS AND ACHIEVEMENTS

- "One of the three listed companies in Thailand with the 2009 highest CG score" ranked in the CG Watch Thailand report conducted by the Asian Corporate Governance Association in collaboration with CLSA Asia-Pacific Markets, Asia's leading independent brokerage and investment group.
- One of the "Top Ten Best Public Companies in 2009" (Money & Banking Magazine).
- Ranked sixth on the Best Public Company in 2009 based on an analysis of business information of the top 200 listed companies in the Stock Exchange of Thailand (SET) in terms of market capitalization (excluding listed companies undergoing the rehabilitation) and forty-nine listed companies in the MAI based on the information as of end of year 2008).
- Ranked one of fifty most fabulous companies in the Asia-Pacific region in 2010 or "Asia's Fab 50" by FORBES ASIA, a leading business publication and website in Asia. The company is the only Thai company receiving this regional recognition in 2010. The focus was on each company's five-year track record for revenue, operating earnings and return on capital while recent results, share-price movements and the business outlook were also taken into consideration.
- Ranked in several categories including the Best Managed Company, The Best CEO, The Best CFO, The 2nd Best Corporate Governance, The 3rd best Investor Relations, The 3rd Most Committed to a Strong Dividend Policy, The 4th Best Corporate Social Responsibility (FinanceAsia, a leading financial magazine and website in Asia).

Banpu has been recognized by local and international media as an outstanding corporation with excellent management, in particular, in terms of good management, good corporate governance, as well as social and environmental responsibility. These are the results of the dedication of all Banpu people who commit to take their roles and responsibilities to meet expectations of our stakeholders, aiming at achieving our organization vision to become "an energetic Asian energy provider of quality products

& services and be recognized for its fairness, professionalism and concerns for society and environment."

Because our attempt to show clear linkage between business performances with corporate governance and corporate social responsibility for sustainable development, it is a good sign that many other listed Thai companies have also embarked on the same journey. This will inevitably lead to the practices being more widely adopted and improved, as well as uplifting the standards of the practices in Thailand as a whole.

Over the years Banpu has continued to expand the implementation of its corporate governance and corporate social responsibility policies to all new countries and subsidiaries in line with the company's growth. In addition, Banpu aims at deepening the understanding of these policies among the management and staff through a variety of activities ranging from inter-departmental workshops to the distribution of information through bulletin boards and email. The bottom line here is to ensure that Banpu employees embrace the main governance, social responsibility and conduct principles as part of their everyday decisions and behavior to ensure corporate sustainability.

We are also delighted to be able to demonstrate that such esoteric notions as corporate governance and corporate social responsibility for sustainable development can be put into practice in a way that transforms the company and the life of the people within it.

12 Complexity and Imperfection
HTD Research Alive in Practice

Sharon Mavin and Dawn Robinson

The chapter is co-authored between HRD practitioner, Dawn Robinson, Head of Learning and Development, Sage UK Ltd. and academic, Professor Sharon Mavin, Dean of Newcastle Business School, Northumbria University, UK. Sharon was Chair and host of the 10th International Conference UFHRD & AHRD (10th-12th June 2009), HRD Research and Practice across Europe, Complexity and Imperfection in Practice. The specific format of the conference, reflecting the interests of UFHRD and AHRD and growing research debates, was structured around the practice-theory nexus. Dawn Robinson was a keynote speaker at the conference and Sharon Mavin, was Dawn's academic respondent. Within the chapter Sharon presents the introduction, an academic response to the keynote, and the conclusion of the chapter. Dawn outlines the Sage approach to Strategic HRD and illustrates a particular HRD intervention as a case study. Dawn outlines the exciting 'cultural' journey of change with Sage, with a particular focus on the Enable management development program. Dawn highlights how as Head of Learning and Development she drew upon organizational culture research and diagnostics and Authentic Leader Development theory to underpin the Sage approach. Sharon provides the bridge between research and practice and outlines the Sage HRD journey through the HRD dualisms, offers an additional aspect of the approach, skills and competence of the individual HRD practitioner to the theoretical framework of exploring strategic maturity in HRD and identifies areas for future research in Authentic Leader Development Theory.
(10th International Conference on Human Resource Development Research and Practice across Europe "HRD: Complexity and Inperfection in Practice" Newcastle Business School 10-12 June 2009)

THE CONTEXT

The following chapter is co-authored by HRD practitioner Dawn Robinson, head of Learning and Development, Sage UK Ltd (Sage), and academic, Professor Sharon Mavin, Newcastle Business School, Northumbria

University. As in the actual keynote, Sharon presents the introduction, an academic response to the keynote and the conclusion of the chapter, and Dawn outlines the Sage approach to Strategic HRD (SHRD) and a particular HRD intervention as a case study.

The keynote by Dawn Robinson, which outlined a case study of HRD practice and my academic response, was delivered at the 10th International Conference, HRD Research and Practice across Europe, entitled HRD: Complexity and Imperfection in Practice. The conference was held in the UK, at Newcastle Business School, Northumbria University, June 10–12, 2009. At the time I was vice chair of UFHRD and chair of the Practitioner and Organizational Activities Committee. The specific format of the conference, reflecting the interests of UFHRD and AHRD and growing research debates, was structured around the practice-theory nexus and reflected my own and Newcastle Business School's commitment to advancing business and management practice. The keynote and response discussed here were particularly important because I was the chair and host of the conference and this gave me the opportunity to progress the relationship between Sage and Newcastle Business School.

In developing the keynote and response I was delighted to collaborate with Dawn Robinson, head of Learning and Development, Sage, and engage in discussions about the HRD practice and research nexus within the context of the conference theme: complexity and imperfection in practice. The collaboration with Sage reflected ongoing academic debates[1] concerning the utility and impact of HRD research to organizations, and how to engage practitioners in the communities of UFHRD and AHRD. The keynote outlined a research-informed HRD intervention in Sage, which was of specific relevance as it drew upon the use of Dennison's[2] Organizational Culture Analysis tool, the theoretical frameworks of authentic leadership development,[3] which had limited empirical base at the time, and which focused upon the individual emotional impact of HRD in organization. The particular HRD intervention presented in the keynote was only one part of a holistic approach designed to support the business strategy; therefore I was also interested in exploring how Sage was following a SHRD approach in practice.

DAWN ROBINSON AND SAGE (UK) LTD

Sage is a subsidiary of The Sage Group plc, a leading supplier of business computer software and services, to 6.2 million customers worldwide, which has its headquarters in Newcastle upon Tyne. Formed in 1981 by entrepreneurs, the Group was floated on the stock exchange in 1989 and now employs 14,500 people in its global market, leading companies worldwide. At the time of the keynote, Dawn Robinson was (and still is) head of Learning and Development for Sage, having worked for the company more than over seven years. Dawn's key objectives were: to develop and lead a Learning and Development Strategy to meet the business vision: management and leadership development; policy and people development; succession planning and talent management; process simplification and resource program—brand, tools, development and process.

Dawn's keynote as delivered in 2010 follows; however in providing a context for the keynote case study I have used Sage's own words, from its website, below:

At Sage, we live and breathe business every day. Through our people, business software, services and our partners, we are passionate about helping businesses of all sizes achieve their ambitions by helping them to overcome the day-to-day practicalities of running a business, so that they can do business the way they want to.

Our range of business software and services is continually evolving as we constantly innovate. The range includes software to manage your business' finances, run the payroll, manage customer and supplier relationships, plan the business and support your HR function. In the UK, we provide software and services to over 760,000 small and medium-sized businesses.

Our business is full of people with passion and energy. In the UK alone, Sage employs over 2000 people and this ever-expanding team of highly trained people, which includes industry experts, accountants and entrepreneurs are all passionate about doing the best thing for customers. The collective experience and commitment of our people in answering millions of customer queries means that we more often than not understand the problems our customers face, today and tomorrow.

THE KEYNOTE—DAWN ROBINSON

I am absolutely privileged to be here on behalf of Sage for the tenth anniversary of the HRD conference at Newcastle Business School. I'd like to start by telling you about Sage before I focus upon the learning and development area and in particular 'Enable,' which is a successful management development program we have delivered. Sage operates around the globe in more than twenty countries, which link into the Sage Group via North America, Europe, UK and Ireland, South Africa and Australia. Sage has been around for more than twenty-five years. We have more than 14,500 employees across the world, almost six million customers. Sage reports into Sage Group. Here in Newcastle we have a specific business stream for the small business division, the mid-market division which concentrates on construction and business partners and reselling which is down in Winnersh. The Accountants Division is over in Manchester, whereas central functional areas are focused in Newcastle and cover information systems, HR, Legal and Facilities and Sage Online which is our web shop. We provide a range of business software and services, and this is what makes us different from our competitors because of the after sales service value we also offer. Our revenue in the UK is roughly £200 million, and we have more than 2,000 employees. Newcastle is our headquarters, established since 2004. We then have the other UK sites which are acquisitions and therefore challenges in themselves culturally.

The way it was. . . . It was 2003 when I walked into Sage in HR and General Operations and Paul Stobart was appointed at the same time as the new CEO. Literally that week Graham Wiley left as one of the founding entrepreneurs, (nothing to do with me with my HR hat on by the way), as we'd reached a crossroads in the business. There were only so many bells and whistles you could put on a piece of software. It actually reminded me of my HR days in M&S—they wouldn't have fitting rooms, they wouldn't advertise, etc. and look where they are now. We were the same—we were at the crossroads and we needed to do something different as a business.

So we brought in ATOS KPMG, and they started to talk to us about our command and control leadership that had developed over a number of years because of our growth as an entrepreneurial business, but this command and control culture had stifled us. We didn't have a clear vision or strategy, and we had a group of middle managers that weren't as skilled as we would have liked them to be. So we bravely worked with ATOS KPMG to look at what we call the Dennison[4] Culture Survey. Some of you may be aware of the survey, but here you have a number of different cultural traits to align the performance of your business. If you are a successful business you would start to see certain quartiles being lit up, and the more quartiles you have, the more successful you are in terms of your culture. Here we were in 2003 (not many quartiles 'lit up'), and as you can see it could only get better; there was lots of room for improvement; but the issue was where to begin?

We decided to prioritize setting the vision and mission for the future because if people did not know where we were heading, how would we know when we had got there. The other priority was around our leadership area, and we chose to work on the transformational leadership research by Avolio and Bass[5] because their framework included transactional as well as transformational leadership. Following the development and implementation of HRD, over the course of two years when we went back to revisit the Dennison culture survey we saw some great results and improvements.

Our UK strategy was now clear for everyone to see. We wanted to be the business software company that everyone recommended. We had particular long-term objectives that concentrated on the employer and being a trusted brand; but that was just the start. We then needed to develop the real foundation of what we stood for and we started to concentrate on our shared values. What some people would call the guiding principles, and over the course of two years we started to gradually embed these into our organization. It didn't just happen overnight.

So we were trying to be simple, although we were complex. We were trying to be agile with our customers, and obviously innovation was absolutely key to the software that we produced. We wanted our customers to trust us, and we obviously wanted to be open and transparent in everything that we did, but it wasn't just about the values. We started to work on the brands, too. We moved away from the plain white packaging for the software products, and the plain green, and came into our own with our color palettes and began to use our actual people in the organization to advertise and brand. In fact I am proud to say two of my team are on those pictures. We worked with Uffindell West as external marketers and we brought our brand to life. Over a couple of years we reminded our people at every corporate induction that our people and our customers were important to us, that we lived by our guiding principles. We reminded them of our vision, and we worked on corporate social responsibility. Our guiding principles are simplicity, agility, innovation, trust and integrity.

As far as learning and development (L and D) was concerned it couldn't sit in isolation. It was about attracting, recruiting, retaining and rewarding people. So it had to be completely linked as a full employee cycle. So as far as the business plan was concerned and the business strategy you can see that L and D was actually marked against four key areas. On the talent side in the resourcing program we had our website called Sage.co.uk, where we now have real people from our business who have been filmed talking about their experiences, so if you want to apply for a job one of our people will pop up and tell you about their role and what they actually do. We also worked on consistency around succession planning and talent management materials and career development reviews. On the development side we looked at the management and leadership skills, and in engagement we moved away from the Dennison survey and we worked with ETS as an external supplier to work on our own Sage-ified culture survey, so we could truly look at a return on investment in particular areas in relation to what we had done, and on policy development we supplied the materials to support the policy and change with some of our leaders.

I moved from HRM into L and D in 2007. It was a brand new role for Sage, and I had aligned three key focused areas. One was talent management to try and enhance the current talent pipeline that we had. The other area was around leadership and management development, and I looked at centralizing a learning portal for us, so our people could look at different development needs and be able to find a recommended program to use. Of course everything I needed to do had to be justified. I was in a commercial organization, so I truly needed to look at a return on investment—the statistics and performance measures were vital.

We still had the challenges, though. With Avolio and Bass and transformational leadership we'd worked with 120 of our leaders in the business, but we still wanted further sustainability. We still had reports from the EngageCulture Survey that were telling us we still had a command and control culture. We wanted to work and move away from fixating quarterly targets, and we had many of our managers and leaders who had been promoted because of their technical merits and not because of their people management skills. What we wanted was an ideal program that gave us some consistency with how our leaders would lead their people, to break down those barriers and silos and to increase self-awareness and self-confidence—to create a real and authentic connection—something very different from what we had been used to in the past.

We went out to tender, and we met with BlueSky who became a partner for us to work together in Sage-ifying a bespoke leadership program to engage our staff. In October 2006 they worked with us through the night, literally, with a number of us working together to bring the program alive. We branded it and it was known as *Enable*. We focused on Sage specific examples and values, and we deliberately mixed learning styles and business streams, and men and women, to go on a week-long residential program. We buddied them up in advance before they went along, to learn about each other's area in the business. We had pre and post briefings and people came away with an action plan and personal objectives. The modules in the program had the leadership standard embedded throughout. Similar to the guiding principles I spoke about, we are starting to look at the morals and ethics and behaviors to develop a consistent framework for how we lead our people. So there were five key modules, it was residential, based in Northumberland. We talked about whether it would be non-residential, but we felt that the social networking and the experiences people had outside formal learning time were as important as the program. Paul Stobart our CEO, headed almost every single program from December 2006 when we started to run. We ran for two solid years with a program every month; he was there, all but two programs, and we had people return who had been on the program to talk about what they had put into practice from the tools they had actually used. It was the first time that we started to talk about the differences or not, between management and leadership. We looked at handling conflict, at challenging people, we looked at facilitation and performance management and coaching and giving feedback, but rather than just hear from me I would like to share with you some participant feedback on the *Enable* program.

"I was amazed and I was turned around." "On the surface this program is about leadership and giving you the tools that you need to lead and drive performance. In reality this program is about you." "It's something that happens to you, it's a massive learning journey that you go on." "I'd like to think I'm a confident person but that inner self belief was something I was lacking and that came out in the program as something that I really needed to work on, to believe in myself, the ability I actually have." "The results speak for themselves, from employee engagement survey results right through to targets and they have been achieved but I have got to say there are also less tangible parts to it, from a change in the mindset, real energy, commitment and focus I am now getting from my people." "I see and hear and I almost feel a difference, a difference in style, a difference in skills, a difference in initiative, a real ownership being taken." "They made a point of sharing how you were performing during the sessions and actually about who you were and what they were seeing of that so it was very, very insightful." "You can see that shift, you can see

an improvement in the way people do things and their style and the way they do things, the way they say things and the way they behave."

And the actual results? *Enable* was nominated even within Sage Group as part of our internal innovation awards. It was shortlisted against all the different pieces of software. It was the first time a people program was up there with Sage software. We were also recognized by the Chartered Institute of Personnel and Development. We won the Regional Innovation Award just last year, and as far as the culture survey was concerned, putting the customer first had gone up from 61percent to 80 percent and this was from the Engageculture survey I was talking about, so we could specifically focus on the ROI. Recommending us as a great place to work went from 78 percent to 87 percent.

Operationally absence has gone down, saving us almost £400,000 a year, and call quality in the customer services area had increased. As far as the leadership area was concerned 88 percent of our people agreed that their line manager inspired them to achieve their objectives; that was an 18 percent improvement on 2007, and it went on. . . . It talked about the line manager motivating people to do their job; the line managers actually working by our guiding principles, and 86 percent agreeing that their line manager shows appreciation for the work that they do.

It wasn't just about *Enable*. What I tried to do was pull together a full development journey for Sage. We had lots of good pockets of development ,but it was never in one place, so after a piece of diagnostic work we developed the career framework. This includes the exec, the senior managers and leaders, team managers, skilled, multi-skilled and technical people, and across the business we worked on corporate induction, the customer experience and encouraging secondments to happen. We do a lot on product training, linking in with the learning portal because we have a lot of product upgrades. On the softer side I wanted to show how you could experience different events and programs depending on how long you stayed in Sage. So for example *Aspire* is a brand new program which is a management induction program because we had lots of managers saying we don't know what we don't know, we're suddenly promoted, we come into Sage as a business and it's confusing. Help us put all the tools please into one place.

Inspire was a new modular senior leadership program for the top high potential people we identified through talent management. In Sage 'Group' we are trialling a global development program to look at the consistency of approach around the leadership standard. Also we are focusing on personal leadership & taking responsibility which is where we are trialling a program called PLP. Across the middle we have educational sponsorship, for which we spend more than half a million pounds annually. We are also about to pilot a 360 tool for effective feedback, and I am up-skilling people from the exec right through to our team leaders on how to conduct effective career development reviews. I am quite concerned that we are afl at structure, so we need to try and encourage, as much as we possibly can, lateral moves in our organization; but enough from me. Last, I'd just like to finish with some Enable attendees telling you how they feel about the program.

(Music and film clip followed with further feedback directly from participants on the Enable program, highlighting the emotion and emotional journeys participants had experienced)

PROFESSOR SHARON MAVIN—ACADEMIC RESPONSE

My role is to make sense of Dawn's presentation in terms of the HRD research-practice nexus and the Sage approach to strategic HRD. I am sure you agree that, looking at Sage's journey, why I was so delighted Dawn was prepared to share this with our HRD community and also to illustrate the research impact and value to organizations. Dawn and I have had a number of conversations around the research-practice nexus and have explored how HRD is complex and imperfect but HRD research is *alive* in practice.

One of the issues I was particularly interested in and wanted to explore in relation to the Sage approach is grounded in the work we are doing ourselves in Newcastle Business School, led by my colleague Jane Turner, around ALD. We have several research studies under way and use the philosophy to underpin our executive development and coaching activities. I'm sure it has been noted by you all, how brave it is to see a FTSE 100 company talking about emotion and emotional development. Dawn and I looked at the ALD theory base which appeared around 2005 published in Leadership Quarterly.[6] We

Figure 12.1   HRD dualisms and Sage.

Figure 12.2   Mapping strategic HRD.

discussed the focus of the theory base as being about owning one's own personal experiences, thoughts, emotions, needs, wants, preferences and acting in accordance with one's own 'true self,' expressing what you think and feel and behaving accordingly.[7] We also agreed on ALD as authentic leaders being developed through self-awareness, self-acceptance, authentic actions and relationships, while remaining cognizant of one's own vulnerabilities.[8] In theory this all sounds feasible but in practice how many of us are comfortable enough in our own skins to behave in an authentic way when we lead?

There has been a lack of empirical research underpinning the ALD theory base, and Dawn's presentation has given us the opportunity to actually look at theory in practice and explore the impact of the theory in practice. Some of you will have recognized the words used by the BlueSky facilitator in the film clip, "Why should anyone be led by you?"[9] In our discussions I wanted to know from Dawn how she got to ALD, often seen as theory only. The Avolio and Bass[10] research worked so far for Sage in practice, but it wasn't sustainable and they wanted something more bespoke. It was in looking for a non-traditional leadership program that Sage came to the research base of ALD.

In discussing the HRD research and practice nexus and Sage's SHRD approach, we talked about where the approach sits in the context of HRD dualisms.[11] These dualisms were developed as a result of HRD researchers over many years attempting a definition and exploring differences between SHRD and HRD. It has been argued that the identification of sets of dualisms may help explain what HRD is about and that a dualistic perspective is perhaps more fruitful that attempting neat definitions of HRD.[12] It is clear from Figure 12.1 outlining the Sage HRD approach that they didn't follow one set standard set of dualisms. Their journey jumps around and between the HRD dualisms, highlighting complexity and imperfection in practice. For Sage, it was strategic but it was also operational. It was about change but it was short term. It was about building the brand. It was enabled but it was controlled. It was directly managed but it was a soft approach.

In listening to Dawn's presentation we hear the realities of HRD in practice. In our research base HRD as a concept, model, approach, discourse or set of practices remains unclear. However a number of dimensions [13] help us understand HRD approaches. Mapping Sage's journey against the dimensions of strategic HRD at Figure 12.2 (with Sage noted in circled text) was easy to do.

REFLECTING BACK

In light of the HRD dimensions, reflecting on the Sage approach, an important and impactful issue for me was Sage's commitment to a social, discursive and emotional approach to people development. As Jamie Callahan notes in Chapter 18, of this volume, issues of emotion continue to be on the fringes of academic study but with steady interest and growing critique

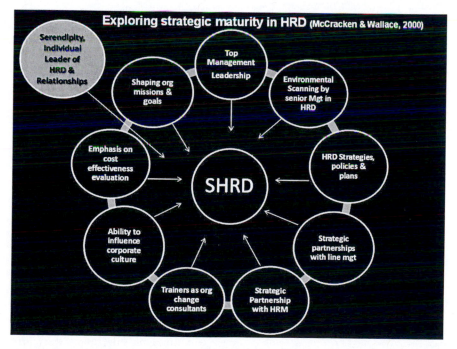

Figure 12.3 Exploring strategic maturity in HRD.

in HRD oriented conferences and journals. The Sage case study enabled an HRD community to see and hear the importance and value of emotion aspects of HRD in practice.

Reflecting on our collaborative discussions in preparing for the keynote and response, we both easily identified the complexity and imperfection of HRD in practice. For example, Dawn and I talked about the interchange and hybrid use of leader-manager labels in Sage which begs the question 'Is it really just in education and business schools that we make the distinction between them?' A further discussion concerned Dawn's job title and whether it was important in establishing the strategic importance and value of HRD in practice and the 'voice' of HRD in Sage. Dawn noted that this was also a complex issue. There had been numerous labels for people development over time in Sage and 'Learning and Development' had the 'best fit' culturally.

In moving to a summary of our discussions, why did Dawn and I think the HRD journey in Sage was so successful? Is it that there was continual CEO involvement? That off the shelf L and D was unsuitable and Sage developed bespoke? Was it that the HRD interventions were research based? Was it that there was a new leadership framework grounded in emotionality and authenticity that had personal and emotional impact? Or is it actually just about Dawn as an individual? Is it actually about Dawn's commercial credibility, her influence and her own research based practice?

Where that took me was looking back at the drivers of SHRD in organization and Harrison's approach,[14] that SHRD is primarily triggered by organizational strategy, external labor market strategies and value systems. I found myself asking the question whether SHRD is actually just serendipitous. Is it about key factors coming together at the same time? Is it about timing? Is it an act of faith or is it individual dependent? Could it be about the commercial credibility and the personality type of the person leading HRD in the organization and their ability to develop relationships with the CEO, the executive team and HRD providers? On discussing this with Dawn, she argues that it's all of the above. However, revisiting a theoretical framework for exploring strategic maturity in HRD[15] (shown at Figure 12.3), one of the key considerations that can be added to the framework from Dawn and my research-practice collaboration, is that (1) we should be researching serendipity and timing in organization, (2) we should be exploring the impact of the individual leader of HRD and (3) we should be researching their skill, competence, their power, their influence and their ability to harness all of this in strategic relationships, because while organizations can develop the elements of strategic HRD frameworks, without the right individual leader of HRD how does this move from theory to practice?

AUTHENTIC LEADER(SHIP) DEVELOPMENT UPDATE

Returning to authentic leader(ship) development, researchers are now challenging the assumption that a leader's self-reference "will automatically be communicated to followers who will experience the leader as authentic."[16] Often a leader's internal sense of self is not readily apparent to observers,[17] and this raises questions of how can a leader's values and integrity, argued to have a positive relationship with follower trust, be made visible and evident to followers? Is authentic leader behavior attainable? How does a leader know when he or she has achieved a level of authenticity? What are the gender issues associated with authentic leadership and how are power and politics in relation to ALD considered by the research base?

There is limited empirical research exploring the attributes and indicators of authentic achievement; however measuring ALD is complex and goes some way to explaining the current lack of empirical work.[18] Furthermore there is a concern that by attempting to 'measure' authentic leaders in practice, this approach could become too prescriptive, with people attempting to become or live up to *an* ideal of an authentic leader. This of course undermines the very nature of ALD through personal exploration. Current studies have considered *how* followers assess leader authenticity through measurable variables such as the amount of time spent with leaders; however, they have not considered *why* followers perceive leaders in particular ways. Personal exploration and meaning attachment through disclosure of leaders life stories not only increase individual leaders' self-awareness but also indicates to followers their level of self-knowledge and the clarity from which followers are able to draw to interpret their leader's authenticity.[19] There is a need for further research to explore the complexity of ALD in practice, to develop our understandings of this concept.

AFTERMATH: THE PRACTICE-RESEARCH COLLABORATION

For Dawn and I our collaborative relationship has continued, evidenced through this chapter and relationships between the two organizations. I have been working with Dawn and Sage director-level colleagues, sharing my research on women's advancement, whereas Dawn is now a member of the Advisory Board of Newcastle Business School, ensuring that our own SHRD research and practice is open to external challenge and to further enable the HRD practice-research nexus.

NOTES

1. Nancy Berger, Marijke Kehrhahn and Martha Summerville. (2004) 'Research to practice: Throwing a rope across the divide,' *Human Resource Development International* 7(3): 403–409.
   Peter Kuchinke. (2004) 'Theorizing and practicing HRD: Extending the dialogue over the roles of scholarship and practice in the field,' *Human Resource Development International* 7(4): 535–540. Sharon Mavin, Phil Wilding, Brenda Stalker, David Simmonds, Chris Rees and Francine Winch. (2007) 'Developing "new commons" between HRD research and practice: Case studies of UK universities,' *Journal of European Industrial Training* 31(1):

4–18. Darren Short. (2004) '2004: A significant year for research-practice links in HRD,' *Human Resource Development International* 7(4): 541–544. Jean Woodall,. (2004) 'Why HRD scholarship runs ahead of HRD practice,' *Human Resource Development International* 7(1): 3–5.

2. Daniel Denison. (1990) *Corporate culture and organizational effectiveness.* New York: Wiley.
   Daniel Denison and A.K. Aneil Mishra. (1995) 'Toward a theory of organizational culture and effectiveness,' *Organization Science* 6(2): 204–223.

3. Bruce Avolio and William Gardner. (2005) 'Authentic leadership development: Getting to the root of positive forms of leadership,' *Leadership Quarterly* 16(3): 315–338. Bruce Avolio, William Gardner, Fred Walumbwa, Fred Luthans and Douglas May. (2004) 'Unlocking the mask: A look at the process by which authentic leaders impact follower attitudes and bahaviors,' *Leadership Quarterly* 15: 801–823. Bruce Avolio and Fred Luthans. (2006) *The high impact leader: Moments matter in accelerating authentic leadership development.* New York: McGraw-Hill. Alice Eagly. (2005) 'Achieving relational authenticity in leadership: Does gender matter?' *Leadership Quarterly* 16(3): 459–474. William Gardner, Bruce Avolio, Fred Luthans, Douglas May and Fred Walumbwas. (2005) 'Can you see the real me? A self based model of authentic leader and follower development,' *Leadership Quarterly* 16(3): 343–372. William Gardner, Dawn Fischer and James Hunt. (2009) "Emotional labour and leadership: A threat to authenticity,' *Leadership Quarterly* 20: 466–482. Remus Ilies, Frederick Morgeson and Jennifer Nahrgang. (2005) 'Authentic leadership and eudaemonic well-being: Understanding leader–follower outcomes,' *Leadership Quarterly* 16: 373–394.
   Todd Pittinsky and Christopher Tyson. (2005) 'Leader authenticity markers: Findings from a study of perceptions of African American political leaders,' in William Gardner, Bruce Avolio and Fred Walumbwa (eds.). *Authentic Leadership Theory and Practice: Origins, Effects, and Development*, Oxford: Elsevier, 253–279. Boas Shamir and Galit Eilam. (2005) 'What's your story' A life-stories approach to authentic leadership development,' *Leadership Quarterly* 16(3): 395–417. Raymond T. Sparrowe. (2005) 'Authentic leadership and the narrative self,' *Leadership Quarterly* 16: 419–439. Fred Walumbwa, Bruce Avolio, William Gardner, Tara Wernsing and Suzanne J. Peterson. (2008) 'Authentic leadership: Development and validation of a theory-based measure,' *Journal of Management* 34(1): 89–126. Fran Yammarino, Shelly Dionne, Chester A. Schriesheim and Fred Dansereau. (2008) 'Authentic leadership and positive organizational behavior: A meso, multilevel perspective,' *Leadership Quarterly* 19(6): 693–707.

4. Daniel R. Denison. (1990) *Corporate culture and organizational effectiveness.* New York: Wiley. Daniel Denison and Aneil Mishra. (1995) 'Toward a theory of organizational culture and effectiveness,' *Organization Science* 6(2): 204–223.

5. Bruce Avolio and Bernard Bass. (1999) 'Re-examining the components of transformational and transactional leadership using the Multifactor Leadership Questionnaire,' *Journal of Occupational and Organizational Psychology* 72(4): 441–462.

6. Bruce Avolio and William Gardner. (2005) 'Authentic leadership development: Getting to the root of positive forms of leadership,' *Leadership Quarterly* 16(3): 315–338. Alice Eagly. (2005) 'Achieving relational authenticity in leadership: Does gender matter? *Leadership Quarterly* 16(3): 459–474. William Gardner, Bruce Avolio, Fred Luthans, Douglas May and Fred Walumbwas. (2005) 'Can you see the real me? A self based model of authentic leader and follower development,' *Leadership Quarterly* 16(3): 343–372.

Remus Ilies, Frederick Morgeson and Jennifer Nahrgang. (20050 'Authentic leadership and eudaemonic well-being: Understanding leader–follower outcomes,' *Leadership Quarterly* 16: 373–394. Boas Shamir and Galit Eilam. (2005) "What's your story' A life-stories approach to authentic leadership development,' *Leadership Quarterly* 16(3): 395–417. Raymond T. Sparrowe. (2005) 'Authentic leadership and the narrative self,' *Leadership Quarterly* 16: 419–439.

7. Kim Cameron, Jane Dutton and Robert Quinn, eds. (2003) *Positive organizational scholarship*. San Francisco: Barrett-Koehler, 241–261.

8. Fred Luthans and Bruce Avolio. (2003) 'Authentic leadership: A positive developmental approach,' in Kim Cameron, Jane Dutton and Robert Quinn (eds.) *Positive Organizational Scholarship*, San Francisco: Barrett-Koehler, 241–261.

9. Rob Goffee and Gareth Jones. (2006) *Why should anyone be led by you? What it takes to be an authentic leader.* Cambridge: Harvard Business School Press.

10. Bruce Avolio and Bernard Bass. (1999) 'Re-examining the components of transformational and transactional leadership using the Multifactor Leadership Questionnaire,' *Journal of Occupational and Organizational Psychology* 72(4): 441–462.

11. Thomas Garavan, Noreen Heraty and Bridie Barnicle. (1999) 'Human resource development literature: Current issues, priorities and dilemmas,' *Journal of European Industrial Training* 23(4/5): 169–179.

12. Jim Stewart and Jim McGoldrick, eds. (1996) *Human resource development: Perspectives, strategies and practice.* London: Pitman.

13. Thomas Garavan, Noreen Heraty and Bridie Barnicle (1999) 'Human resource development literature: Current issues, priorities and dilemmas,' *Journal of European Industrial Training* 23(4/5): 169–179.

14. Rosemary Harrison. (1997) *Employee development.* London: Institute of Personnel and Development (IPD). .

15. Martin McCracken and Mary Wallace. (2000) 'Exploring strategic maturity in HRD—rhetoric, aspiration or reality?' *Journal of European Industrial Training* 24(8): 424–467.

16. Donna Ladkin and Steven Taylor. (2010) 'Enacting the 'true self': Towards a theory of embodied authentic leadership,' *Leadership Quarterly* 21: 64–74.

17. Donna Ladkin and Steven Taylor. (2010) 'Enacting the 'true self': Towards a theory of embodied authentic leadership,' *Leadership Quarterly* 21: 64–74. Todd Pittinsky and Christopher Tyson. (2005) 'Leader authenticity markers: Findings from a study of perceptions of African American political leaders,' in William Gardner, Bruce Avolio and Fred Walumbwa (eds.), *Authentic Leadership Theory and Practice: Origins, Effects, and Development,* Oxford: Elsevier, 253–279

18. William Gardner, Dawn Fischer and James Hunt. (2009) 'Emotional labour and leadership; A threat to authenticity,' *Leadership Quarterly* 20: 466–482.

19. Bruce Avolio, William Gardner, Fred Walumbwa, Fred Luthans and Douglas May. (2004) 'Unlocking the mask: A look at the process by which authentic leaders impact follower attitudes and behaviors,' *Leadership Quarterly* 15: 801–823.

13 New Boundaries in Leadership Development
The Need for a Multi-Level Perspective in Evaluation and Research

Nicholas Clarke

The paper challenges conventional thinking on what to evaluate in leadership development. Drawing upon recent empirical findings in the area of leadership development, as well as developments in our understanding of leadership from relational, team and complexity perspectives, a multi-level model to underpin evaluation research and practice in the area is outlined. This identifies differing evaluative criteria for leadership development at the individual, dyad, team, organizational and community levels with a clear focus on social as well as human capital. The paper concludes with re-iterating the need for the HRD field to adopt far more expansive models to both guide and understand leadership training and development than the traditional, rational-economic approaches that have dominated much of the literature to date.
(12th International Conference on Human Resource Development Research and Practice across Europe, Gloucestershire, 2011)

CONTEXT

This presentation was delivered at the 12th International Conference on HRD Research and Practice across Europe, 2011, in Cheltenham Spa, UK, where the theme was sustainability and social responsibility. I focus on expanding our understanding of leadership development to include community impact and developing broader sets of criteria that include social capital.

THE PRESENTATION: NEW BOUNDARIES IN LEADERSHIP DEVELOPMENT

In my presentation today, I want to draw upon recent developments in our understanding of leadership from relational, team and complexity perspectives in seeking to put forward a multi-level model for guiding evaluation, research and practice in the area of leadership development. Once we start to recognize that leadership is a multilevel phenomenon, social capital as well as human capital development become significant criteria of interest in considering what to evaluate in leadership development, and this of course exposes one of the major limitations of many of the evaluation models in HRD that have failed to consider social capital as a legitimate outcome of HRD efforts in organizations. I think within the field this is now beginning to change, and there have been a few contributions identifying the importance of social capital emerging or developing through HRD;[1] however these ideas are yet to have informed the development of more comprehensive models to guide HRD evaluation. But more than that, I would argue that once we recognize leadership as occurring and looking different depending upon the level we are looking at, then models to guide research and practice in evaluating leadership training and development must identify criteria of interest that integrate our understanding of leadership right through from individual, dyad, team, organizational as well as higher levels including community.

I would argue that the HRD literature falls well short in responding to evolving theory in leadership. Furthermore, current models and approaches to evaluation as well as theoretical development are trailing behind HRD practice in this area. In particular, for well over fifty years now, most approaches to evaluation have been dominated by the KSA formula, focusing on evaluating HRD within the narrow confines of its impact on individuals' knowledge, skills and attitudes. Of course more detailed evaluation models have appeared in the literature. However, these models all suffer from similar limitations when we consider evaluating leadership training and development. Let me outline what I think these are:

The first is that none of these sufficiently address appropriate criteria for evaluating training and development beyond the organizational level, nor do they offer clear theoretical explanations as to how training and development at the individual level impacts the organizational level. This is a major problem that continues to impede progress in HRD theoretical development. This is a particular problem now as increasingly research suggests that wider impacts are now being expected from leadership training and development that is being undertaken in many areas.[2]

The second is that most of these models remain wedded to a deterministic and reductionist conceptualization of training and development that is based upon simplistic cause and effect relationships. This continues despite much evidence suggesting that the impact of HRD at organizational level, let alone beyond, often fails to demonstrate positive effects. This also flies in the face of our understanding of organizations and organizational networks as complex social systems where effects arise through, and are subject to, continuous and interacting feedback loops shaped by many contextual factors.

The third problem I can see is that within our field we have imprisoned ourselves in a mindset dominated by return on investment that is starving us of innovative thinking that can help push us further toward developing far more expansive theoretical models to help potentially explain HRD impacts. These rational-economic-driven models simply ignore developments in our understanding of how decisions are made in organizations, many of which are subject to limitations in our knowledge. More typically research shows that decisions in organizations are more often based on information that we consider "good enough."

THE EVOLVING LANDSCAPE OF LEADERSHIP DEVELOPMENT

The model I would like to present to you draws upon recent research in which I was involved; this examined how leadership training and development varied across ten business sectors, collecting data from leadership academies that were based in these sectors. These leadership academies were primary providers of leadership training and development in their respective business sectors, and we found that there were significant differences in the nature of leadership training and development being undertaken by these academies. Our analysis found that training and development differed along eight specific dimensions, including the goals of leadership development, its level of focus, services and products offered, training/development content and whether there was a behavioral framework underpinning it. So whereas in some business sectors leadership training and development are expected to result in changes to follower attitudes and behaviors, which is an individual level criterion, other sectors expected changes in organizational performance, which is an organizational level outcome. In some sectors improvements in either the health or social well-being of local communities was expected from leadership development. These differences in the expected level of impact were then reflected in the characteristics of the leadership training and development undertaken.

This does make sense from a resource-based view of the firm perspective, because one would expect the planning of leadership training and development to reflect the demands being made on leadership as it responds to the specific needs of its internal and external environments. This of course has also been the basis for a number of calls within the field of leadership to abandon universalistic ideas of effective leadership completely, particularly as relational perspectives on leadership have become more popular, those that recognize that leadership is as much dependent on followers as it is on leaders. But it's not just about followers. We know for example that both organizational structures and cultures can influence the type of leadership styles found in organizations. A transactional style of leadership is often more prevalent where organizations are subject to considerable external regulation whereas more directive styles of leadership often occur during times of financial crisis or major organizational instability.

So we have some evidence, then, that leadership training and development can differ substantially depending upon the level at which one expected it to impact. This prompted the question of how we should go about determining the value of leadership development when viewed from

Level	Summative Criteria	Formative Criteria
INDIVIDUAL Leader	1. Leader Knowledge, Skills and Behaviors (Cognitive Skills, Business Skills, Strategic Skills, Social Skills Emotional Skills 2. Leader Self-Awareness 3. Leader Effectiveness	1. Leader characteristics (Developmental Readiness, Opportunities and Motivation to Lead, Motivation to Perform) 2. Transfer climate 3. Job Developmental Challenge (Working across boundaries, Unfamiliar responsibilities, High level responsibility Creating change, Managing diversity Access to feedback)
INDIVIDUAL Follower	1. Follower Outcomes (Attitudes and Performance)	1. Follower Implicit Leadership Theories
LEADER-FOLLOWER DYAD	1. Leader-Follower Bonding Social Capital	1. Leader-Follower Relationship Quality (Affect, Contribution, Loyalty, Respect)

Figure 13.1   A multilevel model for evaluating leadership training and development: individual and dyad levels.

Level	Summative Criteria	Formative Criteria
TEAM	1.Team Effectiveness (eg team climate, team dynamics) 2. Team Performance 3. Team Bonding Social Capital	1.Team Leadership Processes (Maintenance of team mental models, Monitoring the internal and external environment, Behavioral and performance expectations, Task-focused and Person-focused team behaviors). 2. Team Leader Behaviors (Relational leader behaviors, Citizenship behaviors, Social and Emotional behaviors)
ORGANIZATIONAL	1. Organizational Performance and Effectiveness (Efficiency, Human Capital and Adaptation to environment) 2. Organizational Bridging Social Capital	1. Leadership Culture 2. Indices of Connectivity (eg network collaboration, trust and growth)
COMMUNITY	1. Community Social Capital	1. Integrative Leader Behaviors 2. Shared Leadership 3. Inter-organizational Learning Capability

Figure 13.2   A multilevel model for evaluating leadership training and development: team, organizational and community levels.

a levels-of-analysis perspective. So this is a first attempt at outlining what I think a more comprehensive model for evaluating leadership development might look like. In the model I outline summative and formative criteria that might be used to determine the value of leadership development when it is expected to impact differing levels. A key feature of the model is that I identify how leadership interacts at these differing levels of analysis— something not attempted before within the literature.

You can see from the model shown in Figures 1.1 and 13.2 that I identify five levels of analysis: individual, dyad, team, organizational and community. In talking about this model, I will focus in more depth at the team and community levels of analysis, because these I think represent areas that have to date been unexplored in terms of evaluation or indeed leadership development more generally. But for completeness I will highlight a few salient points in terms of criteria for determining the value of leadership training and development at the other three levels.

EVALUATING LEADERSHIP DEVELOPMENT

Individual and Dyad Perspectives

To begin with then, evaluating leadership training and development at the individual level is obviously the most well known, and there has been considerable research built up over the years that shows leadership development can result in changing the knowledge, skills and attitudes of leaders. But in addition, other summative criteria are included which are leader self-awareness, leader effectiveness and follower outcomes, including attitudes such as commitment and performance. Incorporated here are also formative evaluation criteria. Dimensions such as leader characteristics, transfer climate and developmental challenge many of you will be familiar with; however you will notice that I have also included the formative criteria of follower implicit leadership theories. This recognizes the growing literature showing how followers contribute to leadership outcomes and are far from passive players in determining leadership effectiveness. These implicit leadership theories are perceptions that followers have regarding what is effective leadership; they are shaped by the types of leadership cultures that exist in organizations. The impact of any leader development in terms of expecting an impact on followers is therefore likely to be influenced by the implicit leadership theories that followers have. One can understand how this might become particularly significant when considering cultural differences in what is expected from leadership and how leadership development that is based upon empowerment perspectives, for example, might be less effective when leaders are placed in contexts where followers are used to much higher power distance.

Building on some of the leadership development research that has highlighted the importance of evaluating relationships such as in leadership coaching[3] and research in the area of leader-member exchange,[4] I introduce the idea that determining the impact of relational quality between leader and followers is also important. A number of differing conceptualizations of the LMX construct have appeared in the literature, but more recently there has been some convergence on four indices, which include respect, affect, contribution and loyalty. This of course recognizes leadership as a relational activity rather than a set of behaviors or styles performed by the leader. It is of course a measure of the quality of the relationship between leader and follower and is therefore a dyad and not an individual measure. Its importance here is its significance as a target for formative evaluation because it contributes directly to whether the outcome criterion I have identified here of leader-follower bonding social capital is achieved. Again this is a dyad level measure and one that we have found to contribute to individual level outcomes such as follower citizenship behavior. You will see that I identify social capital as one of the chief evaluative criteria at all levels beyond the individual level. Internal social capital captures the notion that resources are embedded in and obtained through social ties that bond social units. It very much reflects the notion that when talking about leadership development, leadership is seen as a function of social resources within relationships and wider social systems. By contrast, leader development is thought of as more primarily concerned with expanding an individual's potential to occupy leadership roles.

A Team Level Perspective

Moving on in the model, I introduce criteria that might form the targets for evaluating leadership training and development at the team level. It's fairly intriguing that the general trend in recent times, in all sectors of developed economies, has been restructuring to team-based structures. Some research from the US suggests that more than 80 percent of organizations operate using teams. Yet very little has been written about leadership development from a team perspective. Perhaps the assumption has been that the type of leadership associated with team effectiveness or team performance is no different from that which has been found to bring about changes in followers' behavior more generally. However, there is good reason to indicate that such an assumption is far too simplistic and has not taken sufficient regard of the research that has been undertaken looking at the characteristics of leadership in teams. Compared to the fairly voluminous amount of research that has looked at leadership and individual level outcomes, it is fair to say that the literature relating to leadership and team effectiveness is modest, but nonetheless there have been some significant developments that have implications for shaping our thinking regarding what types of outcomes we should expect from leadership development aiming to improve team performance. This suggests we should be measuring or capturing data along differing sets of indices.

In thinking about this I have looked at the empirical literature showing that leadership can be found to influence team effectiveness and team performance, and in the model presented here these are two of the three chief summative evaluative criteria. But what does leadership look like that brings about these team level outcomes? Here there are particular leadership processes and leader behaviors that have been found to influence these team level outcomes. We can see these as important dimensions to evaluate that constitute formative type evaluation criteria. What factors are we aware of that make up the team process of team leadership? Three specific areas have been suggested in the literature.[5] The first is actions that create, maintain and ensure the accuracy of the shared mental models within the team. Many of you will be familiar with the importance of shared mental models as a key component associated with organizational learning, but there is also a significant body of literature that has looked at the importance of shared mental models within the team literature, including areas such as transactional memory. This includes important aspects such as a collective understanding of the team's task and values, as well as key strengths and limitations of team members. Actions and procedures that are designed to monitor the internal and external team environments so as to ensure the team can respond to changes and therefore ensure its adaptability are also important. Finally, the need for actions that track the abilities and any skill limitations within the team is a further team process alongside establishing performance expectations. So we can say that in terms of the type of leadership that seems to be important for bringing about team performance and effectiveness, it is this specific set of leadership actions and behaviors above others that seems to be significant. Leadership training and development designed to improve leadership in teams therefore must focus on designing content that is more closely aligned with improving team leadership capacities in these sorts of areas.

You can also see in the model that I identify a further target for formative evaluation here, which I label as team leader behaviors. I distinguish this from team leader processes because I view the previous category of actions as those that potentially could be carried out by all team members and not necessarily those of the team leader. So leadership in the previous category is very much viewed as a systemic property within the team. This second category of team leader behaviors, however, I highlight as a specific set of behaviors by the team leaders themselves that are associated with the third summative evaluation criterion I include in the model of team bonding social capital. Here I have drawn on more recent research that has shown that relational type leader behaviors can bring about bonding social capital, which refers as I said before to social capital within more tightly configured groups, which is why I think these team leader behaviors may be particularly significant for bringing about social capital within team structures. This is based on recent findings showing that relational leader behaviors, i.e., the type of behavior that brings about strong inter-personal relationships, are associated with developing greater social capital. Other work has also found that altruistic citizenship behaviors were associated with greater network centrality.[6] And of course network centrality is an important feature of connectivity within networks that is a good indication of levels of social capital.

Together, then, this suggests that both relational and altruistic team leader behaviors are likely to be associated with enhanced social capital within teams overall. I should stress that this has yet to be empirically demonstrated in teams, but does seem to be theoretically consistent with what one might expect. What strengthens the argument here is the suggestion that further coordinating mechanisms are also necessary for team effectiveness in addition to team leadership. Two of these are shared mental models and mutual trust. If we look at the literature on social capital, these are precisely the types of antecedents that have been found to give rise to cognitive and relational forms of social capital, respectively. So the idea that specific types of team leader behaviors can bring about social capital in teams appears to make some sense. And following from this, it is these types of behaviors that we should focus on when determining what we should evaluate when looking at the impact of leadership development at the team level.

An Organizational Level Perspective

Now I said earlier that I wouldn't spend too much time discussing organizational level evaluation criteria, because many of you will be familiar with this already. As you can see, this includes organizational performance and organizational effectiveness as two of the chief summative target criteria. Many of you will have examined this yourselves in leadership development initiatives. But I will just briefly mention the two areas I have suggested as important formative criteria in the model, because these represent more recent developments. The first of these is leadership culture. This is based on recent work in the area of leadership development that suggests these development activities bring about improvements in organizational performance through improving the three dimensions of direction, alignment and commitment within organizations.[7] Direction refers to widespread agreement on the organization's goals and mission; alignment as the organization and coordination of both knowledge and work; and commitment as the willingness of members of the organization to work for the greater interests of the organization. Importantly, the impact of leadership development on direction, alignment and commitment is mediated through leadership culture. One of the significant outcomes of leadership development then is its influence on leadership practices and beliefs which are primary elements of a leadership culture. This includes the beliefs of followers about leadership as well as of course leaders. If we return to my earlier argument identifying the importance of follower implicit beliefs as moderating the impact of leadership development at the individual level, then the significance of leadership culture, which is an aggregate measure of beliefs about leadership in the organization, as a moderating variable at the organizational level certainly makes sense.

The second formative evaluation area I have identified again reinforces the significance of social capital as a key outcome we should expect from leadership development. A distinction I make here, though, is that it is bridging forms of social capital in which we are interested, which refers to network ties and relationships between more diverse groupings. Here I highlight indices of connectivity as important evaluative criteria that we should target when looking to determine the value of leadership training and development at the organizational level. I have included three aspects of connectivity in the evaluation model to consider when evaluating at the organizational level. These are (1) the extent of coordination and collaboration that is present among leaders as a result of leadership development; (2) the level of trust that exists prior and subsequent to leadership development; and (3) whether we can find evidence of growth in leadership networks as a result of the leadership development initiatives that are undertaken. This set of indicators can give us a good idea of the levels of social capital that are present, and of course underscore again the importance of social capital as a key outcome of leadership development as opposed to the more limited focus on human capital.

A Community Level Perspective

I carry on with this theme of social capital but expand significantly on this in the model, when I next consider leadership development at the community level. Here you can see that the only summative criterion of interest I identify in this generic model is that of community social capital. That's because I argue here that leadership training and development are essentially being used as part of a coherent strategy for enhancing collaboration between organizations and their leaders, in an effort to solve what we often refer to as 'messy' problems. Often these are the types of intractable and complicated issues that affect the social well-being of local communities such as crime, unemployment, drug and alcohol use, as well as a wide range of health-related issues such as improving mental health, care for the elderly or promoting healthy lifestyles. Here in the model, I try to identify what might form legitimate targets for evaluation criteria when we think about what leadership looks like when we examine the concept at the community level. I draw specifically on the literature on complexity and integrative notions of leadership. If we look at leadership from a complexity perspective, then unpredictability is a natural feature that arises from the interactions between many diverse social systems coming together which give rise to complex feedback systems.[8] An important theme from this perspective is that rather than being about personal influence and heavily dependent on human relation models, leadership instead incorporates wide-ranging processes for managing dynamic systems and interconnectivity between organizational and larger social systems.

After applying this framework, interactive dynamics within such complex social systems leave little room for reductionist or deterministic approaches that are unable to satisfactorily account for their emergent and adaptive properties. It is these emergent and adaptive properties that facilitate innovative and responsive problem solving that is essentially self-organizing. The role of leadership is seen as providing the conditions whereby distributed forms of intelligence can develop spontaneously, and therefore it involves influencing network structures and creating favorable conditions for innovation to flourish. This is sometimes called catalytic leadership; I particularly like term leadership is that "what makes things happen." Leadership from a complexity perspective thus expands leadership beyond just a focus on interpersonal relationships, but also includes novel ideas regarding particular processual as well as structural catalysts that together enhance network adaptability and problem-solving capacities. Structural as well as cultural interventions are therefore also part of a much broader conceptualization of leadership and following from this what we might think of as leadership development.

These ideas are the basis for the thinking behind the four criteria for formative evaluation of leadership development that I have identified in the model as significant at the community level.[9] These I have listed as (1) integrative leader behaviors, (2) network conditions, (3) shared leadership and (4) inter-organizational learning. I want to address these now briefly and explain the rationales for selecting these specific dimensions.

If we examine the first of these targets for formative evaluation, integrative leader behaviors, this draws upon much of the work that has been done in the areas of collaboration, particularly in the public policy arena, and takes as its fundamental principle that individual practices can shape the interactions between processes and structures. There have been a number of important contributions in this area that have identified the types of leader behaviors or practices that appear significant in shaping productive interconnections between organizations. These all share a common theme in emphasizing the types of behaviors considered important for boundary spanning and creating boundary groups: hence the label integrative leadership behaviors. These include capabilities such as communicating and sharing a vision, political and social skills, building work groups and effectively implementing policy decisions. Synthesizing differing contributions from this literature, I have suggested five key integrative leader behaviors in the evaluation model that make up part of our thinking on what might be thought of as leadership at this level of analysis. These are (1) relational behaviors, (2) political skills, (3) visionary behaviors, (4) authenticity and finally (5) systems thinking. So we can see here major differences in the types of leader behaviors that might be significant for evaluation at the community level; these stand in contrast to those at the lower levels I have identified.

But a more expansive model of leadership at the community level also points to the need for us to think about other structural and processual conditions that can bring about or foster the emergent and adaptive qualities of these interconnected social systems. So the second area for formative evaluation identified in the model refers to network conditions. This is very much in keeping with the idea that leadership can also be emergent within interconnected structures, and is both embedded within and shaped by the context and situation. Here I am thinking of how structures and governance within the network interact with practices. So a broad set of interventions that shapes or creates network conditions can be thought of here as constituting leadership development; this includes HRD interventions such as organization development, as well as formal and informal practices that shape collaboration such as developing policies, meeting arrangements and how conflicts are resolved. Of course as well as these processes, structural arrangements such as the creation of boundary spanning groups would also figure as a legitimate component of leadership development. You can see how this really does push our ideas of what might constitute leadership development well beyond traditional notions, once we begin to see leadership as a property of social systems rather than simply as about leader interpersonal influence.

Shared Leadership

The next area that I suggest forms a key focus for evaluation is the extent to which network arrangements give rise to, or support, the notion of shared leadership. This is inconsistent with perceiving leadership as a more distributed, fluid, systemic construct and implies that no individual performs all of the leadership functions. Instead, leadership may result from a process of negotiation between network members. Increasingly, complex organizational environments require effective team working that provides the underpinning for a shared model of leadership associated with the concerted actions of multiple players. From a complexity perspective, shared leadership within the social system is seen as enabling spontaneous boundary experiences which generate shared meaning between differing actors; these experiences are therefore central to knowledge exchange, problem solving and mutual learning. Again leadership within complex systems places an emphasis on spontaneous and self-organizing processes for generating new knowledge, which is the self-evident rationale for my incorporating interorganizational learning as the final target for formative evaluation for leadership development at the community level.

Concluding Thoughts

I would like to conclude by outlining what I think the model offers in taking this specific area of HRD forward. First, this is an initial attempt to outline a more expansive model for thinking about the nature of leadership at five levels of analysis, which integrates more recent theoretical developments from the leadership literature. It considers what this might mean for how we then evaluate leadership development when viewing leadership from these differing perspectives. The multiplicity of goals represents a significant departure from the way in which leadership training and development have been thought of in the past, and suggests practice is evolving far more quickly than theory in this area. This requires more innovative approaches to evaluation and models to underpin leadership development. Next, it explicitly recognizes leadership as a multi-level phenomenon, and as such lends itself for considering what we might be seeking to achieve from leadership development or how we might determine its value, when moving from individual, to team, organizational and community levels. As organizations seek greater returns from their leadership development efforts, the lack of cross-level models to guide HRD therefore become more apparent. This also highlights the limitations of normative perspectives of HRD that fail to recognize that it is often shaped by multiple and at times contradictory goals. The third area I want to emphasize is the more explicit recognition of social capital as a chief outcome we should be looking to achieve from leadership development, which has generally been absent from the traditional approaches that have appeared in the HRD literature for assisting evaluation. Finally, I have stressed both formative and summative evaluative criteria. Part of the rationale for this I have argued is based upon my view that reductionist and straightforward linear cause-effect relationships are less likely to be found, the more we operating in environments of increasing complexity. But it's also about enabling us to expand our thinking about the types of variables even at lower levels of analysis that appear to either moderate or perhaps even mediate the impact of leadership development on various outcomes. Obviously in doing so we open up far greater opportunities for us to determine the value of leadership development, and in so doing we can make a stronger case for the importance of HRD, particularly now as many of the developed economies are entering periods of major fiscal constraints.

THE AFTERMATH

It is early days in terms of the initial development of the model, but it has laid out the basic framework for beginning to understand better the nature of leadership development as we move away from individual level through to team, organizational and community levels of impact. In the short term it is hoped that the model will prompt HR practitioners to consider how to engage in leadership development more broadly and innovatively beyond just individual level sets of competences to also incorporating relational and systemic perspectives. It also highlights the significance of potential moderating factors at a number of levels that can influence the impact of any intervention, and it offers some advice about what to plan for when undertaking an evaluation so as to take account of these factors. The model also suggests some practical guidance to assist HR managers when selecting and/or developing interventions in leadership development that are more likely to target the key outcome criteria they expect . So, for example, investment in personality tests would be most appropriate for enhancing leader self-awareness, whereas investment in organizational development interventions (e.g., team building, strategy workshops, culture change) may be deemed important for enhancing LTD organizational or community effects.

Next stages in research will involve testing some of the propositions put forward in the model, suggesting how leadership interacts at these differing levels of analysis which have yet to be supported empirically or where empirical evidence is minimal. Whereas some of this will be fairly straightforward, such as examining how leadership development targeting specific team leader behaviors contributes to team level social capital, looking for interactions between individual level leader behaviors or team leadership processes and higher level impacts will require more innovative research designs. It is hoped that the model will assist other researchers in the HRD field where the lack of a unifying theory to date that underpins leadership development has hindered our approaches for thinking about the processes by which HRD interventions in this area bring about their effects.

NOTES

1. See, for example, Julia Storberg. (2007) 'Borrowing from others: Appropriating social capital theories for "doing" HRD,' *Advances in Developing Human Resources* 9: 312–340, suggesting that participating in training can promote organizational social capital.
2. See Jay Conger. (1992) *Learning to lead: The art of transforming managers into leaders.* San Francisco: Jossey-Bass; Brandi Collins. (2001) 'Organizational performance: The future focus of leadership development programs,' *Journal of Leadership Studies* 7: 43–54; and recent research by Nicholas Clarke and Malcolm Higgs. (2010) 'Leadership training across business sectors: Report to the University Forum for Human Resource Development,' (UFHRD). Southampton: University of Southampton.
3. See Ely et al. (2010), who presented an integrative framework for evaluating leadership coaching. The focus of assessment also included those factors and conditions considered to bring about positive coaching outcomes such as rapport and trust which are dyad level indices. Katherine Ely, Lisa Boyce, Jonathan Nelson, Stephen Zaccaro, Gina Hernez-Broome and Wynne Whyman. (2010) 'Evaluating leadership coaching: A review and integrated framework,' *Leadership Quarterly* 21: 585–599.
4. See Mary Uhl-Bien. (2006) 'Relational leadership theory: Exploring the social processes of leadership and organizing,' *Leadership Quarterly* 17: 654–676.
5. See Eduardo Salas, Dana Sims and Shawn Burke. (2005) 'Is there a "Big Five" in teamwork?' *Small Group Research* 36: 555–599.
6. See, for example, work by Abraham Carmeli, Batia Ben-Hador, David Waldman and Deborah Rupp. (2009) 'How leaders cultivate social capital and nurture employee vigor: Implications for job performance,' *Journal of Applied Psychology* 94: 1553–1561; and Mian Zhang, Wei Zheng and Jun Wei. (2009. 'Sources of social capital: Effects of altruistic citizenship behavior and job involvement on advice network centrality,' *Human Resource Development Quarterly* 20: 195–217.
7. See Wilfred Drath, Cynthia McCauley, Charles Palus, Ellen Van Velsor, Patricia O'Connor and John McGuire. (2008) 'Direction, alignment, commitment: Toward a more integrative ontology of leadership development,' *Leadership Quarterly* 19: 635–653.
8. Complex leadership involves looking for patterns of interactions and mechanisms that on a basic level offer us some insight into how leadership enables productive networks. See Mary Uhl-Bien and Russ Marion. (2009) 'Complexity leadership in bureaucratic forms of organizing: A meso-model,' *Leadership Quarterly* 20: 631–650.
9. See Sonia Ospina and Erica Foldy. (2010) 'Building bridges from the margins: The work of leadership in social change organizations,' *Leadership Quarterly* 21: 292–307; and Barbara Crosby and John Bryson. (2010) 'Integrative leadership and the creation and maintenance of cross sector collaborations,' *Leadership Quarterly* 21: 211–230.

Part IV

Value'ation

The speeches in this part have a particular focus on the values, emotions and spirit of HRD. The first, Chapter 14, was given in 2001 by David Megginson and examined the notion of spirit in organizations. He grounds this in discussion of coaching and learning communities, thereby resonating with discussions of leadership in other chapters. In 2001 the focus was on the interface between individual and the organization; by 2004, and Gary McLean's speech, it was shifting to a wider screen, looking at the development of nations through HRD (NHRD) and the values associated with that. Development in the practice of HRD was supported in 2005, but the call for the inclusion of humor within our work, was made, in a memorable and humorous manner, by Gene Roth and Darren Short. In the same year, on a different continent, Darlene Russ-Eft was asking us to examine our values as we use evaluation within organizations, emphasizing the challenges of addressing the multi-dimensional values of multiple stakeholders. The last chapter in this part is based on a speech given by Jamie Callaghan in 2008. She examines the emotions of leadership, looking at their management and manipulation from a critical perspective, thereby particularly resonating with Sally Sambrook's work in Chapter 5, and Sharon Turnbull's in Chapter 9, as well as discussions of leadership throughout this book.

14 Cultivating Spirit in Organizations

David Megginson

This chapter spells out an agenda for HRD in addressing issues of spirit on organizations. It recognizes the confusion that spirit causes, with people associating it with religion, but makes a case for spirit which can embrace the secular. It also examines disspiritedness as a contrasting phenomenon which helps to throw light on what spirit might mean. It ends by setting an agenda for learners, helpers, teachers in HE and leaders in organizations for cultivating spirit in organizations.
(Inaugural professorial lecture at Sheffield Hallam University, 28th February 2001)

CONTEXT

This chapter is based on the inaugural lecture given in 2001 to mark my appointment as professor of Human Resource Development at Sheffield Hallam University. As is common in the UK, this speech was open to all, and academics as well as people from other walks of life were invited. My speech was based upon my research into the understanding of consciousness, attempts to define spirit and to explore the idea of spirit consciousness in the context of autonomy and power. At that time these ideas were quite radical, and I grounded them in an exploration of learning strategies and communities.

PROPERTIES OF CONSCIOUSNESS

Consciousness seems to me to be an output of complexity. As systems get more complex they develop processes of reflexivity; they begin to "make sense" of what is happening to them at a lower level. Simple thermostats do this, and more sophisticated air conditioning systems do it taking into account more variables. They, of course, are still rigid, determined systems, where one set of input conditions leads inevitably to one output. But if you go on adding variables or levels of decision making, you soon come to a system resembling sentient behavior. And, it doesn't take too many variables.

I have wondered at the whirling freedom of wading birds flying over a saltmarsh. Computer scientists have found that they can simulate the pattern of the shape and movement of the flocks with just three "decisions" for each simulated bird. And if you change the parameters (twist a knob) for just one of these decisions, then you get the flocking characteristics of a different species of bird. "Keep a minimum of seven inches apart," and you get dunlin; "keep ten inches apart," and you get "knot." Bird watchers, watching these patterns on a screen, would not believe that the programmed blobs, called "boids" by the computer scientists, were not hazy film of actual flocks of birds. And if you add a few layers and a bit of fuzzy logic, then you rapidly encounter behavior that seems distinctly human. Let's not kid ourselves that we are fancier than is the case. Much of what we do has a strongly pre-programmed quality to it, albeit with several layers of automatic adjustment built in. However, we are not just programmed. This is where consciousness appears.

Argyris (1991)[1] suggests that nearly all of us have a program or routine running in our heads that he calls model I, which among other things, suggests that we should:

- minimize negative feelings;
- decide unilaterally not to challenge others' thinking; and
- not create the conditions where our own thinking and assumptions are exposed and opened to challenge.

He says that model II, by contrast, involves:

- opening our own thinking to critique;
- critiquing the thinking of others; and
- sharing thoughts, feelings and impulses to action that are customarily hidden.

In other words, he is for a balance of advocacy and inquiry. In British organizations, we tend to suffer from too much advocacy and not enough inquiry. We need to hold onto the possibility that, however passionately felt or logically argued, our case may be unsustainable. We might be wrong. Such a stance will enlarge consciousness and enable us to develop our capacity for understanding and the likelihood of our being understood. How can we hope to be understood if people only know a carefully edited and selected fraction of what is going on inside us? Because he moved from Yale to Harvard, Argyris has met a few ethologists, whose studies of animal behavior have convinced him that model I is hard-wired into all primates. This is troubling. It is the task of individual and organization development to make possible a challenge to the limiting assumptions of model I. Furthermore, any business "qualification" worthy of the name must spend as much time as it takes to help people learn how to transcend model I.

I remember working with a chief executive in the public sector. His team and its functioning were blocked by the hostility felt by the deputy for the chief and vice versa. The chief was courageous and he agreed to work through the differences. This was model II in action, and it was difficult and painful and involved tears of frustration. But it changed the relationship, and the team's effectiveness. I also remember a start-up team within ICL, where the management realized it didn't have certain key skills needed to build an entrepreneurial business. Management was afraid that telling the rest of the team of its lack would be demotivating. The MD and I advocated telling, and management did this. This candor galvanized the rest of the team and increased the respect for the managers. So, consciousness, according to this line of argument, is about noticing what is going on at the layer below and making a "deliberate" adjustment at the higher layer—challenging taken-for-granted assumptions.

Where does this talk of layers and variables leave us? Are we just automata with attitude? Followers of Steiner suggest that developing a consciousness soul requires moving toward indifference from sympathy and antipathy. This seems strange. Who wants to be indifferent? But in fact it is our sympathies and antipathies that are automatic. As Richard Horobin said, memorably, in an unpublished communication he wrote a long while ago:

> "The significance of feelings Is that they are not truths But instructions My feelings don't tell me What the universe is made for Or whether I'm worthwhile Or what my lover would Be like to live with (Happy ever after?) No! Feelings Tell me What TO DO. That's all And of course Like any other authority They are often wrong."

So, for me, consciousness is that quality of being which creates the possibility of choice. This choice is contrasted with the patterns of feeling (as in Richard's words) or deference or customary thinking which can keep us on fixed rails. Conscious choosing is guided by criteria that can themselves be examined and critiqued.

A DEFINITION

Spirit means life, and both life and livelihood are about living in depth, living with meaning, purpose, joy and a sense of contributing to the greater community. A spirituality of work is about bringing life and livelihood back together again (Fox, 1994). If it sounds a bit high-flown let's try working from its opposite. What is spirit not? Or what is it to be dispirited? I think it may be easy to find a consensus here—we share a sense of what it is to be dispirited, even if we don't agree on what spirit is.

Let me tell you a story about being spirited and being dispirited. One day a few weeks ago two interesting things happened to me. I was standing by the photocopier (a common professorial task) and a charming young woman who was in occupation of the machine asked me if I was a Christian. I gave the usual equivocal quaking answer about being non-doctrinal, but that many of us . . . did this, and others . . . thought that, then I asked her why she had asked. And she said one of the nicest things that I have heard from anyone outside my immediate family; she replied, "Well, you seem to glow." Wow. Thank you. For me, the life of the spirit is about this inner glow. And one observation I have about the glow is that it isn't caused by outside circumstances.

So, perhaps, (in spite of Fox's[2] definition) it is not about joy, but about bliss. (Bliss is commonly differentiated from joy in being uncaused.) I think, insofar as I was experiencing anything that made me glow inwardly, it can't have been caused by what had just happened. Apart from queuing by the photocopier, another exasperating event had hit me an hour or two before. This was that I had a row with a manager in the university. The details don't matter. Not true: of course they matter. But I am not going to tell you about them! Anyway, as a result of this row, for which I was responsible, and which remained some-what unresolved at its conclusion, I felt dispirited. "Oh, what's the point?" I was thinking. "I might as well retire early, eat a packet of halva, get a job as a gardener, become a parish councilor and so on." I suspect we all have our particular escape routes, which we dream about when we get dispirited.

So cultivating spirit in organizations can be seen as not allowing our-selves to get dispirited—balancing the rows with the heartening conversa-tions. As Jack Canfield says, people often complain, "How can I get on when I've got a creep for a boss? It's not fair. This isn't it! It'll be it when I get a boss who isn't creepy." The bad news is that this is it. It is our life, now; and of course the great advantage of having a creepy boss is that we get to learn how to handle creepy bosses. And remember, going back to my own example for a moment, that I was responsible for the row. So, another point from this story is that it is not only my responsibility to keep up my own spirit, but also to ensure that, like the young woman by the copier, I support the spirit of others. My final point from the story is that perhaps my friend in the photocopier room mistook a face flushed by anger, pride, shame and frustration at my row, for one that was glowing from within.

What are the underlying principles at work, in relationships that can enhance spirit? Here is my list:

- Learn to speak one's own truth. As we develop this capacity, we can extend it to speaking truth to power. Once we do this our lives become much more exciting, fulfilling and dangerous. As they should.
- Listen to others' truth—this means everyone's—porters and vice-chancellors, cleaners and MDs. All have their story. And we need to listen to them in an open accepting way that exposes ourselves to the risk of changing our perspective.
- Recognize the routines that enclose our own thinking. Chris Argyris is the most potent advocate I know of the importance of this step. Model I behavior seems reasonable and civilized, but ultimately

thwarts learning. Model II behavior appears wild and irresponsible, reckless and rude, but we need to learn how to do it to flourish in a spirited organization. Argyris suggests that the deep difficulty of organization learning is that model I thinking and action are "self-sealing": in other words, when we are engaged in them, we are blinded from seeing that they are dysfunctional.

- Then we have to take life seriously. Let me explain: I am reporting Evison's research (Evison and Horobin[3]) into the effects of laughter as a life enhancer. She concludes:

Let's take life more seriously
Laugh more to
Learn more and
Love more, and
Live longer!

And if she can persuade the Scottish branch of the British Psychological Society of this then we need to take her seriously indeed!

These principles are often referred to as dialogue processes and are wonderfully described in Nancy Dixon's[4] book Dialogue at Work. Another way of approaching this fascinating area is through social constructionism. My friend Chris Blantern uses the following example of constructionists' concerns.

A and B are in the house together. The phone rings. A says, "That's the phone." What did A mean? It could have been: "The noise we hear comes from the telephone" or, "Answer the phone!" Or, indeed, "I am the person who decides who answers the phone round here!" This is a sharp illustration of levels, of the ambiguities of power, and of the sheer difficulty of ever understanding what is going on. "No, I didn't mean THAT. What's eating you tonight?"

So, spirit, if I can use a Diageo metaphor, is not easily distilled. It emerges from a purging, shriving, expiational approach to examining one's own, and others', truth. This route to discovery may not be fun, but it can be a path of joy, as we reach out to the essence of each other.

SPIRIT CONSCIOUSNESS

Now let's tie the idea of spirit and the phenomenon of consciousness together. According to brain research, spirit consciousness, which gives a widely reported sense of a numinous or mystic vision, comes from waves of energy at 40Hz across the whole brain. These oscillations bind or integrate disparate perceptual or cognitive events. Zohar and Marshall[5] suggest that these are the neural basis for what they call spiritual intelligence.

Whatever the correlates in the brain, the experience here described is one common to mystics of all religious traditions, and is also linked to what Abraham Maslow and Carl Rogers, Martin Buber and Ken Wilber refer to as peak experience, self-actualization, the fully functioning person, the I-thou relationship, unity consciousness. It represents often only a momentary vision, but it is also one that remains with the person so blessed, and provides him or her with an abiding sense of the glory and wonder of the cosmos. It also seems to create a longing, a questioning: "Why can't all life be like this?" Spirit consciousness, for me, then, is a phenomenon that takes place in the individual, but it emerges often in the context of community or, at least, in communion between people. Let's look at the individual side of this equation a bit more first.

AUTONOMY

When I was taking my master's degree at UMIST, my tutor, Dick Ottoway, noticed that I seemed deeply engrossed in issues of my own autonomy. He said, providing a role model for those of us who supervise dissertations, "If that is the big issue for you, then write your dissertation about it." I said, "What? About autonomy in organizations?" And he, bless him, said, "No. About your own autonomy." I was lucky to have a tutor who recognized that learning should be about personal unfolding, but I have since come to the view that pretty well all research (and, especially, all research in social and management sciences) is about this personal unfolding. It is just that, if we have unsympathetic tutors or supervisors, we have to dress up our story in a spurious impersonality.

Autonomy is about the evolution of the self from an external reference point to an internal one: about the emergence of the ego. As I suggested earlier, this process has its dangers, but it is also necessary. The transformation of the Business School in 2001, from a fragile living community, to a sort of store of dismembered parts, illustrates a need for the development of autonomy. The day of the announcement about the Business School's reorganization, I heard some people say, "I must consider my options," or "How can we keep our group together?" or "I'll ring my contact at . . . so and so." Others, sinking into despair, said, "I have no choice," or "I will have to wait and see what HR say to me." Which strategy, do you think, tends to lead to the fulfillment of desire? My view is that the situation is complicated. The pre-autonomous people, who hand their fate over to others, damp down their desires so much that they end up having no hopes that could be disappointed. Having read Kafka's[6] wonderful Collected Aphorisms, I try to emulate the spirit of them from time to time. They seem to capture the complexity and ambiguity of addressing the moral issues that we face in life and work, in a way that the simple nostrums of much management literature do not. Here is one of my aphorisms: If you think you can or you think you can't—you're right. But, if I think that I can't, then a beneficent universe will occasionally give me what I didn't dare dream of. So, thinking that you can't guarantees the experience of a life filled with random kindness and acts of senseless beauty. However, when this happens to us, we are overcome with fear, and tense up, ready for the big foot to come down from the sky and crush us.

So neither fatalism nor autonomous striving is a guarantee of a happy or successful life. However, my work in fostering personal development planning in the insurance industry gave larger scale evidence of the value of personal autonomy.[7] As our program of personal development planning came to an end, the company we had been working in merged with another insurance company. Observers of this merger noticed that those from "our" company were ready for what happened and were not so disabled as their opposite numbers by feelings of fear, anger, remorse, regret and unvoiced wants. My sense now of the place of autonomy is that it is a crucial phase in development, but that it is not the end of development

POWER

One of my intellectual heroes, Illich,[8] in Deschooling Society, talks about enabling structures. Dialogue processes and social constructionist methods update this vision. But what are the limits of the help that we can engage in to empower others? Here is another of my aphorisms: If I make you free, I am simply binding you into my dream of freedom. And by this act of empowerment, I show that my dream is an illusion. However, the alternative, of listening to you complaining about your imaginary chains, seems insufferable.

And here's yet another: I am solely responsible for my own development but once I am alone each path is as good as any other.

These paradoxical and self-conflicting little statements seem to be the only way I have of approaching the great conundrum of power. I have a sense that the primary function of those with power and authority is to create a space to let others perform. D.H. Lawrence said in his book about his journeys in Mexico: The straight course is hacked out in wounds against the way of the world.

As someone who has spent much of his professional life trying not to run "straight courses" I find this remark particularly apposite. Trainers and educators, managers and directors can all use their power, sparingly and with good heart, to liberate the energy, commitment, wisdom and skill of those who work with them. Or not. Why is Friday called "poet's day"? Why do more people die in the hour of the week between 8.00 and 9.00 on Mondays than in any other hour? Why are so many people oppressed by their work? Because of the abuse of power! In the organizations I have worked with as consultant and friend over a number of years, I have seen, felt, smelled, tasted the difference between enabling management and oppressive management. Being an enabling manager is simple, but (as its rarity attests) it is not easy. An enabling use of power requires a quality difficult to manifest in many organizations—this is self-effacement—recognizing that you need others more than they need you.

LEARNING, LEARNING STRATEGIES AND LEARNING COMMUNITIES

What is Learning Anyway?

"What can we learn?" and "Of what does learning consist?" I have spent time with a fascinating group of writers and thinkers over the last couple of years preparing a Declaration on Learning.[9] We saw learning as both process and outcome, as incremental and transformational, as having a moral dimension, but we never, to my satisfaction, agreed why learning that matters in organizations is so frustratingly difficult to achieve. Why do senior managers again and again reorganize, when, with a little more patience, trust and a systemic perspective, they might have allowed the organization to right itself? Why do members of failing organizations put so much energy into saying that things are all right, that the way that they are measured is unfair, that they just don't understand our situation? Why do honest leaders, when they say, "Recovery will take time; the figures are bad but we can put them right—over time," do not get given the time? Instead, decisions are made which mean that any possibility of the figures being improved, within the time set by the people who knew the situation, is lost? You will guess that these questions are not mere abstract speculation for me at the time of writing with a reoranization in the offing.

Organizational learning is about engagement, courage, struggling with ambiguity, multiple stories, competing narratives, advocacy and inquiry. It is

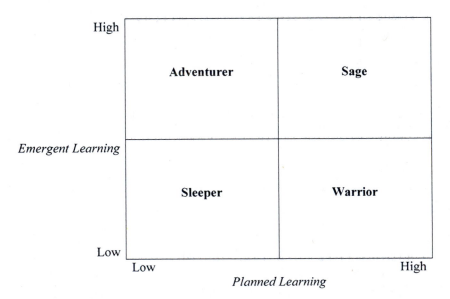

Figure 14.1   Planned and emergent learning strategies.

not fruitful to attempt to reduce this diversity to one account. We may not ever all agree what should be done. If we can all walk away knowing that we have been heard and that our scrap of wisdom added something, however small, to creating the outcome, then we have done some organizational learning.

PLANNED AND EMERGENT LEARNING

I have developed a distinction between planned and emergent learning strategies[10] and in this work, I treat the two strategies as of equal merit, and offer, as a sage ideal, the combination of the focused planning of the warrior and the restless, emergent curiosity of the adventurer.

It is only at the point of meeting between order and chaos that we can learn significantly. It is here that we can embrace complexity. It is here that we can be saved from a life-denying approach to appraisals, quality audits, competency frameworks, strategic HRM and all the sorry panoply of stale routines that Denis Pym of London Business School once memorably described as "paper based employment rituals."

It is only when we are on the very edge of dissolution that we can learn and change. The zone between the frozen order of the warrior-planner and the whirling chaos of the emergent adventurer is the place of possibility. At the wave's edge. At the moment in the Cavatina of Beethoven's late quartet, Opus 130, when the beautiful lyrical flowing theme breaks down, sobbing, and the first violin part is marked beklemmt, oppressed, our hearts stop, and we say, "This is taking me into a space from which I may emerge transformed."

We need in our attempts to change organizations to find this place. In it we can transform the rituals into lively processes which engage us in making things better. And this is not just continuous improvement—it is also about creating the possibility of radical change (if you continuously improve a dispatch rider, you don't end up with a fax machine!). So perhaps the university authorities have done us a favor by dissolving the Business School. Complexity theory, great art and all the stories of the triumph of the human spirit tell us that this is where we can learn. But to do so, we need friends.

LEARNING COMMUNITIES

We find these friends in our learning communities. In developing my understanding of communities, I tried to get enthusiastic about communitarianism. It hasn't worked. I have felt oppressed by its rectitude, by its certainty, by its injunctions. Of course we need communities. Of course Margaret Thatcher was a fool when she said that "There is no such thing as Society."

Another of my aphorisms is: Development only makes sense in the context of a community, and all communities are simply prisons, where the prisoners prevent each other's escape. If we do not enroll in a prison, we will starve, alone, in the desert. When we go into the desert for long enough, there we will see the truth. Returning with this truth, we will be thrown into prison for sedition.

I don't think it is in the spirit of the genre to explain aphorisms. However, this one leaves my argument more open than even I am comfortable with. All worthwhile endeavors in business, in learning, in development come (to borrow an old phrase from the 17th century English revolution), "in the knot of one another's labor." Let me give you some examples from my own practice. I have developed

- a change process in the national park authority over three years .The National Park officer involved every staff member in developing the organization's vision, their values and their ventures;
- a process for company-wide self-development with my friends in a major technology company;
- an international step change in development in PwC Central and Eastern Europe;
- an understanding of how men can relate fearlessly and vulnerably within the Men Consultants Self-development Group—meeting once a month for the last twenty-three years;
- units on the MSc in HRD on managing learning processes where successive groups of students have created their own self-regulating, enquiring community;
- insights about peer mentoring with Mentoring for Export group of busy volunteer MDs of SMEs in both the UK and the Republic of Ireland.

These schemes represent a fascinating story of community, by the way. Don't you public sector people get tempted to talk of "selfish, greedy business people, only in it for the money?" These MDs do it first to support other businesses, second because they have been helped themselves, third because they care passionately about their industry's future, or fourth because they are driven by that generativity which leads people at a certain age to want to pass on their wisdom.

All these learning communities are characterized by:

- voluntarism;
- self-responsibility;
- sharing of time for exploring our own stories; and
- a growing openness to ourselves and to each other.

In summary, learning takes place in the spaces between us. It doesn't belong, even in the lives of most geniuses, to the solitary, heroic individual. I shall frame my conclusions in the form of more questions. I have chosen the questions that work and work on me: that undermine my defenses and that challenge my complacency.

Questions for Learners

We are all learners; there is no such person as a "non-learner," whatever the Secretary of State for Education and Employment might say in his speeches. Some of us learn things that mostly do others and ourselves harm. Some of us pursue "good" learning, but writ small and narrow—the search for qualifications, for competences, for what is prescribed by others. To this last group I address the following questions:

- How much complexity can you embrace? How much ambiguity can you tolerate? Where can you find a place, and the support you need, to live and to learn adventurously on the wave's edge?
- How can you become conscious of your own routines and step up a layer so that you can examine them?

Questions for Helpers

Having been one of these helpers all my working life, I am conscious of the limits of our art. I also have a sense of the wonderful gift of being with people just at the point where they are ready to make a real difference in their own lives and in the lives of others:

- How can you act in the service of the learner's agenda? How can you start with the learner's dream? How can you create space for him or her to unfold?
- How can you prevent your skills giving you power to distort, subvert and subtly transform this agenda?
- How can you prevent yourself from waiting till people are about to learn something for themselves, and then tell them what it will be?

Questions for Teachers in Business Education

I have been influenced by the arguments of Illich and Jacques in critiquing the role and modus operandi of higher education. Jacques[11] offers two powerful questions:

1. "How would the university have to be transformed to produce the ability to learn, rather than static knowledge, as the product by which it is legitimated in society?" and
2. "How could the academic be rewarded for learning, rather than knowing?"

To these I would add two questions of my own:

1. How long can we go on peddling answers, when there are pretty well only questions, and the answers that there are don't lie in the university

but on the razor edge of reflective practice—in the space between individual soul, meaningful work and conceptual illumination?

2. How can you transform teaching by numbers and other quality processes from a numbing, bureaucratic routine to a journey of discovery and a path toward a deeply engaged learning community addressing what matters to them with passionate advocacy and open inquiry?

Here are some questions for the rest of us:

- Why don't you spend twice as much effort on helping your people learn, and half as much on controlling?
- Why don't you policy makers for learning liberate the fantastic energy of people in this city, in this region, in this country and throughout the world to work and play together, by creating a context of asking, not of telling, of sharing, not of shaping?
- If we are losing money, why not engage all our efforts in making more or saving costs? You think that you have . . . but listen to the talk in your corridors and car parks.

If we all did that, I would expect to see productivity mushroom and costs plummet. But, more important, we would go some way to making workplaces fit to house the human spirit

AFTERMATH: WHAT HAPPENED NEXT?

This chapter, which is based on my inaugural lecture, was warmly received at the time it was given in 2001, and it has provided a touchstone for my practice since that date. It has led me to consider questions of what to do and how to do it. These ideas have not pushed me toward working with particular kinds of organizations. The lecture directly led me to doing some interesting and inspiriting work with an Anglican diocese, but it has also, indirectly, led me to working with directors in a global investment bank. What I have found is that in organizations from many different sectors and countries there are individual managers, including those at the very top, who are preoccupied with issues of purpose and identity. Investment bankers are notoriously unpopular following the credit crunch, but one of the bankers I have coached has had as a goal. 'I want to become a half-decent person.' You may have your prejudices challenged to hear that he has more than adequately achieved this goal and is moving on from there, while bringing thinking outlined in this chapter to his future work in the bank. Other coachees have heard about what he is doing and have said to me that they would like some of this, too. So the opportunity to formulate these ideas has had a pervasive impact on my practice and has touched many of the people I have worked with over the last decade.

Has it had a wider impact? I would not wish to make any grandiose claims for my drawing together of these ideas. Since the lecture, I have had a regular trickle of requests from people—some consultants and coaches, others senior managers in public, private and voluntary sectors—for copies of the lecture. Talking with these people, I find that they cite a wide range of contacts who put them onto this piece, and, often movingly, they talk about the yearning for an orientation to work and life of the kind spelled out in this chapter.

I have brought some of these ideas to bodies such as the European Mentoring and Coaching Council and Quakers in Business, and they have woven the ideas into their own thinking. But has there been a wider take-up than my personal and modest sphere of influence? I find it hard to judge. There has been a stream of books about spirituality that predates the lecture and has continued, I would judge, with about the same frequency as before. The overwhelming majority of these texts, however, offer something different from this chapter. They offer homilies and nostrums or systematic presentations of some spiritual practice or set of beliefs. What this chapter does is to explore a process—a way of finding one's own path—rather than following another's. Krishnamurti[12] suggests that nobody can teach you the way. He enjoins us to find out for ourselves and stand by what we find out. And this way is a perennial philosophy that was established before my lecture and will continue long after.

NOTES

1. Chris Argyris. (1991) 'Teaching smart people how to learn,' *Harvard Business Review*: 99–109.
2. Matthew Fox. (1994) *The reinvention of work: A new vision of livelihood in our time.* San Francisco, New York: Harper.
3. Rose Evison and Richard Horobin. (2000). The Therapeutic Uses of Laughter: Research, Theory and Applications, British Psychological Society Scottish Branch, scientific meeting, October 14.
4. Nancy Dixon. (1998) *Dialogue at work.* London: Lemos and Crane.
5. Danah Zohar, and Ian Marshall. (2000) *SQ—spiritual intelligence: The ultimate intelligence.* London: Bloomsbury.
6. Franz Kafka. (1994) *The collected aphorisms*, trans. Malcolm Pasley. London: Syrens.
7. Stephen Gibb and David Megginson. (2001) 'Employee development,' in Tom Redman and Adrian Wilkinson (eds.), 2001 *Contemporary Human Resource Management*, London: FT/Pearson, chap. 5.
8. Ivan Illich. (1971) *Deschooling society.* Harmondsworth: Penguin.
9. Margaret Attwood, Tom Boydell, John Burgoyne, David Clutterbuck, Ian Cunningham, Bob Garratt, Peter Honey, Andrew Mayo, David Megginson, Alan Mumford, Michael Pearn, Mike Pedler and Robin Wood. (2000) *A declaration on learning: A call to action.* Maidenhead: Peter Honey.
10. David Megginson. (1996) 'Planned and emergent learning: Consequences for development,' *Management Learning* 27(4): 411–428.
11. Roy Jacques. (1996) *Manufacturing the employee.* London: Sage.
12. Jiddu Krishnamurti. (1999) *This light in oneself: True meditation.* Boston: Shambhala.

15 National HRD
What in the World Is It?

Gary N. Mclean

This presentation was made at the 5th International Conference on Human Resource Development across Europe, Limerick, Ireland. While not my first presentation on NHRD, it was significant in establishing NHRD as a legitimate research focus.

Following a review of an expanded definition of HRD, a beginning definition of NHRD is offered. The importance of this topic follows, with a focus on how the concept has the potential for helping countries. Some research has suggested one set of emerging models of NHRD, and how some countries have defined and developed NHRD is described. Countries have included different components in their implementations as they attempt to overcome existing inefficiencies of HRD at the country level when an integrated NHRD system is not used. Then, barriers, attributes, and outcomes of excellent NHRD are suggested. I conclude that NHRD is a professional imperative.

Since the presentation, there has been considerably more attention to NHRD, both by me and by others in the field. Specifically, it has led to two issues of ADHR, a debate/exchange in HRDR, and numerous research articles conducted around the world. Some additional updates are also suggested.

(5th International Conference on Human Resource Development across Europe, Limerick, 2004)

CONTEXT

This speech was originally presented in 2004 at the 5th International Conference on Human Resource Development across Europe, Limerick, Ireland. The concept of National HRD was captured in 1964 in Harbison and Myers's definition of HRD.[1] This definition presented an economic development perspective of HRD: As early as 1986, India renamed its Ministry of Education the Ministry of Education and Human Resource Development. The Republic of Korea followed suit in 2001. Thus, the concept, when presented in this keynote, was not a new idea. Rather, the impetus for moving the concept more toward the center of HRD came from the research reported by McLean and McLean, which broadened the scope of HRD and emphasized HRD beyond that of the corporate organization alone.[2]

If I were to make this presentation today, I would make many changes in it, including a definition of NHRD and some possible emerging models. Nevertheless, consistent with the objective of this book, the following represents what was presented, including its flaws!!

THE PRESENTATION

To date, there has been no definition offered for National HRD (NHRD), and, in fact, it may not ever be possible to come up with one definition for NHRD. After all, we have struggled for a long time to find a definition for HRD, but we haven't succeeded with that, and I hope we never come up with the one, right definition for HRD. I expect the same will be true for NHRD.

In the McLean and McLean definition of HRD, we proposed a paradigm shift in outcomes away from the unitary performance or learning paradigms that dominated HRD prior to this definition. Furthermore, until this time, the primary outcomes of HRD were at the individual, group or team and organizational levels. Our 2001 definition expanded outcomes to include, in addition, work processes, community, nation and region.

Because each country has its own culture, politics, economies and stage of development, we expect that there won't be one common definition of NHRD that fits every country.[3] Therefore, each nation or each region must define NHRD for itself, and there should be no expectation that there will be a common definition across countries or regions.

SO, WHY IS THIS TOPIC IMPORTANT?

There are many reasons why HRD needs to keep the topic of NHRD at the center of our discourses about HRD and its meaning. For many countries, human resources are their primary resource. As such, developing the population, in whatever ways necessary, must be a primary responsibility for that country. In addition, human resources are critical for national and local stability. Equally important, and in part connected to the need for stability, if we are ever to break the cycles of welfare, poverty, violence, unemployment, illiteracy and socially undesirable employment (human trafficking, prostitution, drug dealing and so on), we must provide integrated and coordinated mechanisms for people to develop. Beyond economics, HRD has the potential to improve individuals' quality of work life. Furthermore, there is increased need to deal with the ambiguity of global coopetition (cooperation and competition simultaneously).

There are other reasons why this topic is so important, not only to HRD, but also to developed and developing countries. The demographics of most developed countries suggest a potential labor scarcity (fewer younger workers with an aging workforce supporting a much larger aging population). We see this in many countries, but especially in Italy, Japan, Korea and even China, including Taiwan. The US is so far escaping this phenomenon, because immigrant and minority populations maintain high birth rates relative to the low birth rates of the, barely majority, white population. In developing countries, on the other hand, HIV/AIDS continues to have a significant impact on the workforce, especially among younger workers, potentially damaging present and future workforces.

Within the globally competitive environment that most countries face, there is increased pressure on productivity in most countries. NHRD has the potential for helping countries meet their growth and productivity goals. Dynamic changes in technology also keep pressure on the upgrading of all human resources. We see this in the rush by many countries to establish themselves as technology dominant in the world.

In spite of the obvious importance of the concept of NHRD for countries, academia has lagged far behind in its documentation of the experiences countries have had with NHRD and the emerging theories that need to be in place for academia to be more helpful to nations in exploiting the benefits from NHRD. There is a start at this in the upcoming issue of *Advances in Developing Human Resources*.[4] But, even with this initial undertaking, we have not heard the voices of many in the government sector who have been responsible for implementing NHRD policies and plans in their countries. This voice is needed!

We find some interesting quotes about the importance of NHRD, although not labeled as such at the time, from economists interested in the economic development and well-being of countries. For example, Marshall stated: "Developed, educated, motivated people are an unlimited resource . . . [while] undeveloped, uneducated, unmotivated people are a monumental drag on an economy in the internationalized information era" of contemporary times.[5] Briggs, another economist, concluded: "While economists in general and policymakers in particular have focused upon physical capital as the explanation for long-term economic growth, it has actually been human resource development that has been the major contributor."[6]

Clearly, any country that sees its human resources as important (and those few that don't tend to be autocratic and oppressive will find National HRD important for all of the reasons outlined above, plus more that I may have overlooked).

DOES NHRD FIT WITHIN HRD?

There are some who will see the inclusion of National HRD within the scope of HRD as an unjustified and unwarranted expansion of the meaning of HRD. People who see HRD as situated only within the confines of organizations, and often for-profit corporations only, will have difficulty seeing the need for the field to expand its understanding of its goals and foci. Yet, as a field that has access to so many positive and powerful tools and understandings, why should we limit ourselves to such a small segment of our society? Furthermore, as a field that embraces change in our theories and practices, shouldn't we also be embracing change in the scope of our work and in the theoretical frames that we bring to that work?

Out of the debates about the meaning of HRD, and recognizing the ethnocentricities of prevalent definitions as being situated primarily in the US, and secondarily in the UK and India, I was convinced that we needed to look more broadly at how the definition of HRD was evolving around the world. Out of that research, in thirteen countries, we offered the following expanded definition of HRD:

> "Human Resource Development is any process or activity that, either initially or over the long term, has the potential to develop work-based knowledge, expertise, productivity and satisfaction, whether for personal or group/team gain, or for the benefit of an organization, community, nation, or ultimately, the whole of humanity."[7]

We have been accused of being too idealistic in this definition, especially in the last phrase, "the whole of humanity." If so, what's wrong with being idealistic? Perhaps that's the only hope the world has of survival. And if we, in HRD, can contribute to that survival, don't we have a moral imperative to do so? Furthermore, I still remember vividly a poem that I studied and memorized in high school, *Andrea del Sarto*, by Robert Browning: "A man's reach should exceed his grasp, else what's a heaven for?" In a similar vein, Don Quixote's song in *The Man of La Mancha* echoes the same theme:

> "To dream the impossible dream. . . .
> This is my quest
> to follow that star,
> no matter how hopeless,
> no matter how far."

While we are dreaming about accomplishing the impossible, we can fantasize our presence in Harry Potter's world[8] and ask, where are the wizards and witches to help HRD accomplish this dream for humanity? Without assuming a unitary cause, who will bring us the *Patronus* to drive away the *dementors* of poverty; unemployment and family and community violence caused by economic instability, illiteracy, wars, job dissatisfaction, child labor, prostitution, illegal immigration and other economic woes?

Many nations are at a fork in the road. They must decide if they are going to continue on the path that leads to poverty, conflict, huge deficits in budgets, increasing gaps between the haves and the have-nots and continuing moral decay, or w make the commitment to turn things around and create a national policy that truly affirms the worth of their human

resources and integrates those components of their society that are necessary to provide their inhabitants with well-being and promise for the
future. And, if they make the right choice, how will they proceed in developing an NHRD approach?

EMERGING MODELS OF NHRD

Based on our summary of the cases contained in Cho and McLean,[3] we were
able to identify five models or approaches to NHRD. We do not believe that
only these five models exist for NHRD world-wide. We believe, however,
that it is a beginning. We hope that this type of research will continue as we
attempt to identify the census of such models. The models emerging from
this beginning attempt to describe examples of NHRD include:

- Centralized Model (in which planning is done by the central
  government)
- Transitional Model (in which planning is done in a tripartite way,
  with the involvement of unions, central government and employers,
  usually in the process of moving away from the centralized model)
- Government-Initiated Model toward Standardization (in which met-
  rics are established, usually by business and industry, at the initiative
  of the central government)
- Decentralized/Free Market Model (in which there is no involvement
  of the central government as the market, which is presumed to be free,
  establishes the plans and processes otherwise associated with NHRD)
- Small-Nations Model (in which small countries, such as in the South
  Pacific Islands or the Caribbean, join together to develop and accomplish their plans)

Country Specific Applications of NHRD

What follows are examples of how a few countries have approached, or are
approaching, the application of NHRD.

The Republic of Korea (South Korea) is an example of a country that
has elected to use a centralized model for NHRD. It is interesting to me to
note that, even in a country that has formally decided to adopt an NHRD
policy, including renaming its Ministry of Education the Ministry of Education and Human Resource Development [note: this has subsequently
changed], there is no agreement on what NHRD actually means.

The Korean Education Development Institute referred to NHRD as
"The national effort to maximize social efficiency for and publicize human
resources."[9] The Korean Research Institute for Vocational Education and
Training identified NHRD as all efforts by society to have efficient development and utilization of national human resources required for increasing the
quality of life and strengthening national competitiveness for a knowledge-

based 21ˢᵗ-century society. These efforts are composed of individual, social and cultural dimensions. Kim (2000) defined NHRD as "A process of creating values in which human resources are formed and utilized strategically at a national level."[10] And, finally, The Commission for Education and Human Resource Policies defined NHRD as "The total efforts by a nation to strengthen national competitiveness by facilitating creation, utilization, and expansion of knowledge through developing and efficiently managing human and social capital."[11]

A couple of examples of a *small nations* model are available, both in the Asia-Pacific region. The *South Pacific Islands* represent the small nations model, having formed a consortium of twenty-two islands and territories and five foreign governments still involved in the region that are, in themselves, considered too small to support their own NHRD policy and programs.

Rodgers defined HRD as "a holistic concept, incorporating intrinsically Pacific social, cultural and spiritual dimensions to build capacity and empower people."[12] The Secretariat of the Pacific Community (SPC) defined HRD as equipping people with relevant skills to have a healthy and satisfying life. Lifelong learning within the cultural contexts is also emphasized by the SPC.[13]

In the *broader Asia-Pacific region*, "education and training issues that are cast very widely to include basic education, industrial training, productivity and equity in labour forces and workplaces, creation of comparable labour market data, lifelong learning and management development."[14]

South Africa's emerging definition of NHRD reflects an example of a transitioning model. Lynham and Cunningham have suggested the following emerging definition for South Africa: "A process or processes of organized capability and competency-based learning experiences undertaken by employees within a specified period of time to bring about individual and organizational performance improvement, and to enhance national economic, cultural, and social growth."[15]

In spite of the model that a nation adopts, all nations appear to have a common goal of attempting to predict future labor demands in an effort to provide the appropriate supply of labor, i.e., they strive to develop labor market equilibrium.

ONE GOAL OF NHRD: STRIVING FOR LABOR MARKET EQUILIBRIUM

The tasks of NHRD are difficult. Perhaps the most difficult is to match a heterogeneous labor supply with a heterogeneous labor demand: "The labor market is composed of widely differing types of labor demand . . . and of a labor supply that consists of individuals with widely differing aspirations, talents, skills, locational preferences, and educational experiences."[16]

Many countries attempt to address this need by trying to determine what occupations are emerging in demand, in order to prepare a supply that is adequately trained for the emerging demand. These often show up in five-year plans. While this sounds like a reasonable approach to creating labor force stability, the fact is that no one can predict the future. So, even when lists of the fastest growing occupations are provided to students entering universities, those predictions are based solely on past trends. We are not capable of predicting the future. When there was a shortfall of IT professionals in the US, India was prepared to fill the gap. But others, all over the world, quickly decided that they needed to become specialist providers of IT professionals, meaning, then, that there was an over-supply of IT professionals. Not only is this difficult for countries to predict, it is also difficult for individuals and for educational institutions.

Efficiencies in NHRD

Some have argued that the costs of doing National HRD are too high . . . but consider that, in the US there are more than 125 different federal agencies providing some form of overlapping HRD, not even considering the number of programs at state, county and city levels. In Korea, more than twenty federal ministries are involved in some form of overlapping HRD. This situation is surely not unique to these two countries!

If the US, for example, spends hundreds of billions of dollars for a war in Iraq, and other countries continue to allocate large sums for defense, surely we must find greater efficiencies in what we do in HRD through unified national approaches to HRD! This will be difficult in the US where states' rights are strongly defended over centralized government involvement.

Components of NHRD

The complexity of NHRD can be displayed as in Figure 15.1. And this depiction is suggestive of examples, only. There are many more components that could be added. The fact that this figure contains so many components and yet is incomplete underscores the complexity of attempting to define NHRD. In fact, there is no agreement across nations or among authors writing about NHRD as to the components of NHRD. This adds to the difficulty of attempting to create a theory of NHRD and of understanding how to develop or how to research the concept of NHRD. While this is one barrier to establishing NHRD, there are many others, as explored in the following section.

BARRIERS TO ESTABLISHING NHRD

While the concept of NHRD is attractive, there are reasons why the concept has not taken hold in more countries. There are, in reality, many barriers that stand in the way of implementing NHRD. Some of the extensive barriers are described in this section.

As indicated earlier, the labor market is imperfect and unpredictable. We cannot know what skills and competencies will be needed in the future,

Figure 15.1   Example components of NHRD.

greatly inhibiting our ability to create a perfect demand/supply labor market. Likewise, based on this concept, and as suggested earlier, everyone tries to do the same thing, e.g., the IT and customer service labor markets ultimately led to a glut in the labor market. Still related to labor markets, the mobility of labor can upset the best of government plans. So long as labor can move out of a country or into a country, people will make their own decisions about how to respond to the labor market, rather than waiting for the government to determine this. Freedom of choice may impede governmental action, e.g., the limitation on the number of higher education institutions, the number of people earning degrees for which there is no demand and so on. When I was working in Krygyzstan, I found that a very large portion of the population was studying American Studies. When I inquired what they would do with a degree in American Studies, I was told that there was little demand. So why should such a large portion of the university population major in American Studies? The answer, not surprisingly, is that American Studies majors are required to learn English, for which there is high demand in Kyrgzstan. But, if they studied English as a Foreign Language (EFL), they would have to pay tuition. However, they could major in American Studies without paying tuition because scholarships were provided by the US government, in an effort to influence student attitudes toward the US.

There are also ideological objections to NHRD. NHRD sounds too much like communism, socialism or centralized planning. Is NHRD simply the wolf of the five-year plans in sheep's clothing? In the US (and other countries), there is great suspicion of anything that smacks of centralization or more control or power in the hands of the government, whether centralized or decentralized. Some academics, as indicated earlier, are opposed to any expansion of HRD beyond the tradition roles within corporations.

Another barrier to NHRD is the serious social problems (e.g., wars, HIV/AIDS, internal violence and so on) that impede NHRD. Whereas one could argue that these are, in fact, arguments for having NHRD, others see NHRD as a distraction from focusing on solving these explicit problems.

Perhaps the most serious barrier to NHRD is that it is ambiguous. Lots of politicians, bureaucrats and even academics, surprisingly, are uncomfortable with the concept of ambiguity. They want to see concrete concepts with specific practices laid out for them. For such people, NHRD will not likely ever be a reality.

ATTRIBUTES OF EXCELLENT NHRD

As we consider the attributes or characteristics of excellent NHRD, the first principle to affirm is that it will vary from country to country based on country characteristics. In fact, based on the country culture, development, economy and so on, it will also provide a shifting balance between central, regional and local planning.

Excellent NHRD will be flexible, allowing for quick responses to changes in the world-wide, regional, national, and local economies and labor markets. This is especially important for those countries using five-year or similar plans. If these are not flexible, the country stands the possibility of quickly getting obsolete. To achieve this flexibility, NHRD plans must be short-term, while remaining visionary, i.e., no rigid five-year plans!—but consider possible scenarios for at least twenty years ahead. The purpose of scenario planning like this is to help keep the leadership attuned to the need for flexibility.

There is also a social responsibility dimension that must be incorporated into NHRD. It cannot be just about economic growth and development for the country. For example, when individuals lose jobs through no fault of their own, Excellent NHRD will provide training and re-training, education and re-education, re-location and compensation. It will dynamically encourage rather than mandate, e.g., the elimination of overlap in higher education institutions, attracting students to needed fields of study and away from those with excess, providing incentives to pay higher salaries in areas where labor is needed and so on. It is important in this social responsibility that it be non-discriminatory, being designed for everyone! No country can be successful if it privileges one ethnic group or one religion over others. Other factors reflecting social responsibility include encouraging work-life balance with family friendly policies, and social factors must be addressed (e.g., poverty, health, education, political oppression, discrimination, illegal activities and so on).

In excellent NHRD, there will be a clear statement of mission for government agencies, to eliminate any duplication of government services in HRD. Furthermore, the role of the political system and its components will be well-defined.

Excellent NHRD will emphasize coopetition with other countries in the region, and perhaps even with any country willing to partner. This is a tricky concept; it is a combination of cooperation and competition. A good example of the need for coopetition occurs within the Caribbean region. The islands are too small to do extensive advertising on their own. Through coopetition, they can cooperate in getting tourists to see the Caribbean as a destination and then compete to get them to come to their island.

The leadership for excellent NHRD must be interdisciplinary. No one field holds all of the information necessary to implement an excellent NHRD approach. It does not belong solely to education, or science and technology, or labor or any other typical government ministry. All must work together for the betterment of their country's benefit. Furthermore, leadership must consist of the *very best minds available*; they must not be limited to cronies or political friends or politicians or civil servants, and not necessarily even to citizens of the country, *unless* they are truly the best minds available.

Excellent NHRD objectives will be established based on the capabilities of the system, not on wishes, desires and needs. Too often countries (and companies) set their goals on what they want rather than what they are capable of achieving. Such an unrealistic approach to objectives is destructive rather than motivational or helpful.

Other factors that will likely be reflected in excellent NHRD, while not exhaustive, include:

- It will not be constrained by the culture of the country, while still considering country culture.
- It will be heavily biased toward research and theory, while remaining thoroughly practical.
- Evaluations will include both qualitative and quantitative measures.
- Desired outcome measures will be both quality and quantity.
- Budgets to support NHRD will increase dramatically annually, gradually replacing social welfare and defense budgets.
- Tax incentives will encourage the use of quality HRD.

If all of these factors, and more, are implemented well, we should expect to see the following outcomes, among others.

OUTCOMES OF EXCELLENT NHRD

Because NHRD will look different from country to country, it is not clear what the outcomes will be for a specific country. This will depend heavily on the objectives set by the country (or region) for its NHRD policies and practices. However, some of the possible outcomes include:

- Functional illiteracy will be eliminated.
- Employment in socially undesirable occupations (prostitution, drug dealing, illegal activities and terrorism) will steadily decline because

of the availability of attractive, alternative employment in a socially supportive environment.

- There will no longer be a need for child labor; all children will receive adequate education while having their physical needs met, along with those of their families.
- The right mix of people will emerge from excellent NHRD. Creative approaches will be needed to attract people to occupations and preparation programs that are not deemed to be socially acceptable, e.g., plumbers, construction workers, hotel workers, etc.
- The quality of primary and secondary education will improve and be more comprehensive in its curriculum.
- The quality of higher education institutions will improve as their quantity decreases, and they will become more sensitive to the labor market.
- Less money will be spent in traditional forms of HRD, while increasing funds will be available in non-traditional forms of HRD.
- There will be increased legal and encouraged flow of labor across national boundaries to seek labor market equilibrium.
- There will be zero or negative population growth, except for immigration.
- There will be progress toward full employment without underemployment.
- Improvement in the health situation will occur, in spite of cultural and religious restrictions.

As suggested,

> If human resources are truly 'the wealth of nations,' their development carries with it the parallel responsibility to recognize that their contribution to the economy must enhance the quality of life on this planet and not lead to its enslavement, impoverishment or extinction.[17]

C'MON, MCLEAN, GET SERIOUS!

OK, I admit it; I may have my head in the clouds! I'm talking about Utopia! But isn't that who we are as HRD professionals? We dream of developing individuals to have a better life. We dream of developing organizations that are productive, safe, supportive, nurturing, successful, competitive, financially secure and profitable. Aren't these also pie-in-the-sky goals?

Why should we dream of less than this for our communities, our nations, our regions and our common humanity than what we dream for individuals and organizations? NHRD won't be perfect; but it can and should move us along on our pathway to improved humanity. I am suggesting that NHRD is HRD's professional imperative! Can any country choose to do less than develop NHRD? As HRD professionals, can we choose to do less than to encourage the development of NHRD and to participate in it?

The path will not be easy.
There are many unanswered questions.
But this journey must become our home.

THE AFTERMATH

This presentation, while not the first one I made on NHRD, was significant in establishing NHRD as a truly legitimate research focus for the field and has led to considerably more attention, both by me and by others in the field. Specifically, it has led to two issues of *Advances in Developing Human Resources,*[18] a debate/exchange in *Human Resource Development Review*[19] and numerous research articles conducted around the world. Research based on the concepts associated with NHRD has also evolved into Regional HRD[20] and community development.[21]

Subsequent to this presentation, I have also proposed a definition of NHRD—not as a definitive answer to "What is NHRD?" but as an opportunity to dialogue and discuss in efforts to come to a better understanding of what NHRD might be and how it fits within the broader field of HRD:

> *National Human Resource Development (NHRD) is an undertaking at the top level of government and throughout the country's society that coordinates all activities related to human development (HD) to create greater efficiency, effectiveness, competitiveness, satisfaction, productivity, knowledge, spirituality and well-being of its residents. It includes education, health, safety, training, economic development, culture, science and technology and any factors influencing HD.*[22]

I look forward to the ongoing discussion about NHRD with the optimism that HRD will be proactive in contributing to the theory, research and practice of NHRD.

NOTES

1. Frederick H. Harbison and Charles A. Meyers. (1964) *Education, manpower, and economic growth: Strategies of human resource development.* New York: McGraw-Hill.
2. Gary N. McLean and Laird D. McLean. 'If we can't define HRD in one country, how can we define it in an international context?' *Journal of Human Resource Development* 4: 313–326.
3. Eunsang Cho and Gary N. McLean. (2004) 'What we discovered about NHRD and what it means for HRD,' *Advances in Developing Human Resources* 6: 382–393.
4. Now published as Gary N. McLean, AAhad M. Osman-Gani and Eunsang Cho, eds. (2004) Human Resource Development as National Policy,' *Advances in Developing Human Resources* 6(3). Thousand Oaks, CA: Sage.
5. R. Marshall. (1986) The Role of Apprenticeship in an Internationalized Information World, Conference on Learning by Doing Sponsored by The

International Union of Operating Engineers, the U.S. Department of Labor, and Cornell University, Albany, NY, April 6: 1.

6. Vernon N. Briggs, Jr. (1987) 'Human resource development and the formulation of national economic policy,' *Journal of Economic Issues* 21: 12–36.

7. Gary N. McLean and Laird D. McLean. (2001) 'If we can't define HRD in one country, how can we define it in an international ontext?' *Human Resource Development International* 4: 322.

8. Joanne K. Rowling. (2003) *Harry Potter and the Order of the Phoenix*. New York: Scholastic.

9. Korean Education Development Institute. (2000) *The direction and tasks of national human resource development*. Seoul: Author. (Korean)

10. Jang-Ho Kim (2000) *Major policy diagnosis, analysis, and development of national human resource development*. Korean Research Institute for Vocational Education and Training. Seoul: Author. (Korean)

11. The Commission for Education and Human Resource Policies. (2001) *National human resource development policy report to initiate 21st century knowledge state*. Seoul: Author. (Korean)

12. Jimmie Rodgers. (2001) 'Human resource development: A crucial challenge for the Pacific Island,' presented at the Second Meeting of the Conference of the Pacific Community. Noumea, New Caledonia: 2.

13. Secretariat of the Pacific Community. (2001) *Population and development planning in the Pacific*. Noumea, New Caledonia: Author.

14. Michael Zanko and Matt Ngui. (2003) 'The implications of supra-national regionalism for human resource management in the Asia-Pacific region,' in Michael Zanko and Matt Ngui (eds.), *The Handbook of Human Resource Management Policies and Practices in Asia-Pacific Economies*, vols. I and II, Cheltenham, UK: Edward Elgar, 2003): 5–22, esp. 13.

15. Susan A. Lynham and Peter W. Cunningham. (2004) 'Human resource development as national policy and practice—The South African case,' *Advances in Developing Human Resources* 6: 319.

16. Vernon N. Briggs, Jr. (1987) 'Human resource development and the formulation of national economic policy,' *Journal of Economic Issues* 21: 1210.

17. Vernon N. Briggs, Jr. (1987) 'Human resource development and the formulation of national economic policy,' *Journal of Economic Issues* 21: 1236.

18. Susan A. Lynham, Kenneth E. Paprock and Peter W. Cunningham, eds. (2006) *Advances in developing human resources 8(4): National human resource development in transitioning societies in the developing world*. Thousand Oaks, CA: Sage. Gary N. McLean, AAhad M. Osman-Gani and Eunsang Cho, eds. (2004) 'Human resource development as national policy,' *Advances in Developing Human Resources* 6(3). Thousand Oaks, CA: Sage.

19. Gary N. McLean, Susan A. Lynham, Ross E. Azevedo, John E.S. Lawrence and Frederick Nafukho. (2008) 'A response to Wang and Swanson's article on National HRD and Theory Development,' *Human Resource Development Review* 7: 241–258.

20. Ahn Young-sik and Gary N. McLean. (2006) 'Regional human resource development: The case of Busan City, Korea,' *Human Resource Development International* 9: 261–270.

21. Siriporn Yamnill and Gary N. McLean. (2010) 'The application of action research model in community development: The case of Lumpaya Village, Thailand,' *Human Resource Development International* 13: 541–556.

22. Gary N. McLean. (2008, April 5) 'National HRD: Challenges and implications,' keynote presentation at the Texas A&M University Chautauqua Roundup, College Station, TX, Slide 5.

16 Get Up There and Start with a Joke
Humor in HRD

Gene L. Roth and Darren Short

Humor exists in workplaces in many forms and it is purposefully used by a variety of types of workers. It is rarely neutral in the workplace, often it is used by workers or supervisors as means to an end. Although humor is pervasive in the workplace, it has received scant attention in the HRD literature. In particular, connections are rarely made between the rich literature base of humor and the practices of HRD in work settings. This chapter offers a discussion between an HRD professional who has a great passion for connecting HRD theory and practice, and a university professor who has a passion for examining humor in the workplace. Given that they each share a questionable sense of humor, the intent of the chapter will be to use forms of humor to provoke new insights about humor applications in the workplace, and to foster scholarship that links HRD practice and humor literature.
(12th AHRD Conference, Estes Park, Colorado, USA, 2005)

CONTEXT

This chapter represents a dialogue between a professor and a scholarly practitioner who share a common passion—humor. They are both critically acclaimed for their many futile attempts at it. Gene Roth is a stuffy old professor who not only makes his students wretch from his humor in the classroom, but he also enjoys digging into the research behind what makes humor work—or not. Darren Short is a practitioner in the broad field of human resource development (HRD). His mere presence in the profession is due to a failed attempt at humor in the early 1990s when he delivered a major government press announcement with a hand puppet. Between them, Darren and Gene have participated in more successful and failed humor than anyone, so they have become the experts. They share another passion—the Academy of Human Resource Development (AHRD). The AHRD is a global professional association with the mission of leading the field of HRD through research. Gene is a past-president of the AHRD and Darren is president from 2012 to 2014. Several years ago, they facilitated a workshop on humor and workplace learning at one of the AHRD annual conferences (12th AHRD Conference, Estes Park, Colorado, US, 2005). Given that they are both prone to memory lapses, this chapter offers their best efforts to reenact what may have actually taken place during the workshop. Anyone who actually attended the workshop should turn away now.

JOKING CULTURE IN THE WORKPLACE

DARREN

Gene, let me try to kick things off on a light note with my two favorite jokes. I would attempt my humorous animal impressions, but they just won't work on the written page (note to readers: if Darren ever asks to show you his impression of a pigeon coming back from the library, you would be wise to decline rapidly). *There are two goldfish in a tank, and one turns to the other and asks, "Do you know how to drive this thing?"* That's a groaner—I apologize. Let me try with my second favorite joke: If you ever stared at a can of orange juice because it said 'Concentrate' on the side, then you might be a redneck. (A well-deserved callout goes to Jeff Foxworthy.)

No? Okay. Perhaps humor in writing is elusive and is confined to such greats as Dave Barry, Spike Milligan and those who write on bathroom stalls after a few too many drinks. It is therefore a real challenge to write about humor without its becoming as dry as a cheap sherry. Indeed, humor may be like that little speck in your eye, the one that drifts around at the edges of your vision, and the moment you try to focus on it, it moves even further away. Humor could just be that speck. Gene, our challenge is: Can we discuss humor in HRD without its becoming the least humorous book chapter ever written?

GENE

Darren, I have read some of your previous book chapters, so I am confident that this chapter will not be the least humorous one ever written. However, putting my rubber chicken down for one moment, and focusing on the task at hand, may I suggest a good starting place is to explore how humor is experienced in HRD, and then we can move on to how theory and research help us to understand humor applications. Of course, that wasn't a very humorous comment, and so perhaps it helps to explain that the whole paragraph was typed while I was wearing a clown nose.

DARREN

In an attempt to explore the connection between humor and HRD, I have kept a personal journal for the last few months to record when and where I have seen humor in HRD practice, and its impact. Let me share just a few reflections and illustrations from my journal, and then let's consider how this relates to theory and research. You know, it's interesting that the vast majority of my accounts of humor in HRD practice are positive. I have seen humor used to:

- Ease the tension at the start of a training course—to quickly relax a group, and position the participants for more quickly getting into content that may be challenging for them.
- Transition between topics, as a segue as it were, to wrap up an intense topic and help students to let go of that phase of a training course and be prepared to move into the next phase.
- Aid a coaching session by finding the humor in a role-play performance and help students to feel unthreatened by the experience and to try more challenging scenarios.
- Help people cope with bad news, as in "gallows humor" at the time of downsizing.

As I witnessed these incidents, it was clear to me that those involved in the humor were walking a fine line. Excessive humor (i.e., too much, too intense or too frequent) could easily have derailed the training and generated a negative impact. The same caveat would apply to humor that attacked or threatened recipients, which would have resulted in them closing down rather than opening up. However, those delivering the humor in the preceding situations knew where that line was, and walked down it with grace. Which, for me, illustrates the competence issues with humor—if you are good at it, then it is a key tool in the HRD arsenal; but if you lack the competence, then it will take you down like a bad joke at a funeral (and, yes, I speak from personal experience on that one, and I apologize to David for that joke at Uncle Orville's wake!).

So, how does all of this relate to humor research?

GENE

Darren, I believe that several constructs in the humor literature can be aligned with aspects of human resource development. The work of HRD practitioners is deeply rooted in the context of the work setting. In any work setting, humor resides. It can be found in a variety of forms and it is applied to serve a variety of purposes.

As a starting point, I have found the research conducted by Gary Fine and Michaela De Soucey[1] to have relevance for HRD practitioners. They talk about a joking culture that exists within organizations, and this joking culture is a component of a larger organization culture. The joking culture can be described as the way that humor has taken place, how it has evolved and how it is woven into the fabric of the organization. Fine and De Soucey explain that the joking culture is historicized and referential. That is, humorous incidents become part of the organization's folklore; they become part of organization's history; and they are referred to by workers. For example, it is the story of when Ralph superglued Clem's work boots to the floor and Clem had to use the power chisel to break them loose. Clem lost his sole that day. Or, the times when William would throw a cup of water over the bathroom stall when Larry would visit his porcelain throne at precisely 9:37a.m. each morning. In the joking culture of a workplace, workers will refer back to these critical incidents as a way of conveying their positions within the history of the organization. The stories demarcate status, tenure and an understanding of the evolution of the organization. Have you worked in organizations, or worked with clients, in which a certain type of joking culture could be found?

DARREN
Yes, I have worked in such places. When I discuss those experiences, people generally assume that they were environments that were low-performing. That is, there is often an assumption that people are unwilling to state openly that seriousness equals performance, and that humor equals suboptimal performance. Interestingly, in my experience, I have found little correlation between the presence of joking culture and performance. Perhaps a dissertation topic resides among those variables for someone. Where I have seen a positive impact, the joking culture generates team cohesion, and the jokes are part of the bonding experience and form part of the fabric of a team. When that has happened, teams have been high-performing yet fun places, and my mind here immediately goes to the stereotypical fast-growing start-up company. Of course, joining such a team can be somewhat daunting, especially if the newcomer has not worked in such an environment before. Even for someone who has, there are challenges in understanding the "inside jokes" of the team, and also understanding where the line is that shouldn't be crossed. A good example is when people misread the boundary of acceptable humor and only find out where that boundary is when they say something that they consider humorous, only to see the look of surprise or shock on the faces of those around them. Before you ask, Gene, as I know you will, I have also been that person leaping blindly across the boundary of decency.

HUMOR AS A PARADOX

GENE
That observation takes us on nicely to the work of an important scholar in the humor literature, Rod Martin.

DARREN
He's not Steve Martin's brother is he?

GENE
I don't believe so, but he has traveled via planes, trains and automobiles. But more to the point, Rod Martin wrote the seminal textbook, *The Psychology of Humor: An Integrative Approach*.[2] He helps us understand the ways in

which humor is a paradox, in that it can be used for one purpose or the opposite of that purpose. For example, if you want to smooth interactions among workers, humor can be used for that purpose. On the other hand, put-down humor and aggressive humor can be used to ruffle feathers and create tension among people. For another set of purposes, humor can be used to bring people together and let workers know that they belong to a group through the use of insider jokes and humorous stories. Or conversely, humor can be used the opposite way to let workers know that they do not belong to a clique and the jokes are not intended for their understanding and consumption. From another vantage point of humor as a paradox, self-deprecating humor can be used by managers to let workers know that managers are human beings who want to reduce the power distance between workers and management. Or for the opposite purpose, managers can use aggressive humor to keep workers in their place and put them down with insulting humor. Perhaps the worse work situation is the manager who has a form of "humor bi-polarity;" that is to say, a manager who is apt to use humor for competing purposes and the workers struggle to interpret the intentions behind the humor. At one moment the manager might be joking about teamwork, and the next minute the manager is demeaning workers with aggressive humor. Workers face the uncertainties of not knowing what to expect from the manager's humor style. This type of situation is aligned with Chris Argyris's writing about managers who have "espoused theories" and "theories in action." In other words, a boss might use rhetoric in the workplace that espouses empowering workers, and try to use jokes to portray such a management style; however, the boss may feel threatened by the potential loss of power, and his/her theories in action would be to use aggressive humor in an autocratic manner. The ability of humor to be used for competing purposes has led several authors to describe it as a double-edge sword. Because humor is such a paradox, as noted by Martin, making definitive claims about it in research and practice is a challenge. Do you have personal experiences with some of these applications of humor?

DARREN

As you describe the double-edged sword of humor, I find myself agreeing with it in principle, and yet I struggle to identify a situation where I have seen it happen. Perhaps I have just been lucky with where I have worked, or those I have worked alongside. Even so, the fact that your description resonated with me makes me believe that I have seen it more than I'm immediately aware of. Those situations I have experienced include where people use humor on a regular basis, and so people are not always clear if something is intended to be funny when they are suddenly serious. I recall laughing at someone once, only to find that they were making a serious point. "Oh, your dog really did die! I thought you were making a funny analogy. I take back the furry throw-rug joke."

From an HRD perspective, especially in the training room, I think that HRD practitioners need to be particularly wary of the double-edge sword of humor: both in their own use, and in that of their trainees. When considering their own use, imagine the impact on a training course where the instructor's humor is unpredictable, inconsistent, difficult to interpret and sometimes intended to be negative. When considering the use by trainees, this could have an equally devastating impact on the learning environment in the room, and HRD practitioners need to be quick to spot it and stamp it out. In my experience, laughing along in the hope that a trainee's ill-advised humor will pass unnoticed is only likely to send a message to the other students that it is not only tolerated but that it is completely acceptable. In that respect, the HRD practitioner needs to be the role-model for acceptable humor use in the classroom and, at times, the guardian of the boundary of acceptability that should not be crossed.

HUMOR AS A MEANS TO AN END

GENE
One of my favorite articles was written by Leide Porcu in *Humor: The International Journal of Humor Studies*.[3]

DARREN
My gosh, Gene, this is starting to sound like you know your literature on the subject. Tread carefully. So, tell me about Porcu.

GENE
Well, by now you should realize that I don't have much of a life if I spend it reading humor research. And, I will openly admit that I enjoyed reading Porcu's ethnographic account of humor use in a Sardinian fish market.

DARREN
A Sardinian fish market? Are you sure you're not making this up?

GENE
If you think that HRD practitioners work on a slippery slope, compare it to working in a Sardinian fish market! Porcu's rich description of this unusual context delineates patterns of humor use that are prevalent with the working-class men of the market. Her accounts of this work context reminded me of the rural factories where I worked earlier in my career. She describes how the humor is embedded in the history of the market, and humor is applied purposefully by the stakeholders of the market. That is to say, humor is used to serve one's needs, whether it is to gain status among other workers, smooth interactions with a customer or cope with the drudgery and unpleasantness of the work. The central message that I gleaned from Porcu's article is that workplace humor is purposeful. I might use it to establish my wittiness, or to gain status over another worker or to suck up to a boss. Porcu provides a vivid account of how the stakeholders of the fish market strategically used humor to their advantage. Her ethnographic

account of this specific workplace caused me to wonder about how HRD practitioners might serve their purposes through applications of humor. And if there is merit in systemically infusing humor into one's interactions with others, then it leads me to believe that HRD practitioners would be well served to refine their skills at interpreting and applying humor is the workplace. What are your thoughts on these observations?

DARREN

What a wonderful observation. It certainly matches my experiences. I find that humor is rarely without purpose within the workplace. Of course, the purpose may not be obvious to those observing; however, that obscurity does not mean that no purpose exists. I see it in the gallows humor that surrounds those left behind following a workforce reduction. The humor eases the stress and uncertainty, and it also helps people to cope with the mixed feelings of guilt and relief from surviving the reduction. Similarly, I see it in the way jokes and humorous stories are shared about a particularly awful boss as a way of coping and easing the pain, and also as a way of checking out whether one person's reactions to a situation are shared by another—if the other person laughs at the story, perhaps he or she is a supporter (a joke shared is a problem halved).

I could continue with more examples, but I see the word count going up and see Gene's eyelids getting heavy at my stories. Suffice it to say, HRD practitioners should view humor as a tool they can use—by no means the only tool, or even one they use frequently, but a tool nevertheless. To not have that tool leaves HRD practitioners one tool shy in their toolbox, and who wants to be missing a tool? Also, the HRD practitioner needs to be an educated interpreter of humor—after all, many a true word is said in jest; so, if you hear the jest, can you find the true word that is the intention of the humor?

THE JESTER IN THE WORKPLACE

GENE

I can relate to your metaphor. On more than one occasion I have been referenced as not being the sharpest tool in the shed. But on another note, let's continue to examine humor as a communication tool. Humor can be used in a way that allows people to say things in jest that they would not ordinarily say because of power relationships in the workplace. Jean-Louis Barsoux[4] has written about the importance of corporate insolence within organizations. An example of such insolence is workers using humor as a means to illuminate the self-delusion of those in power. In other words, you probably should not come right out and say that the boss's idea is as useless as teats on a boar, but you can jokingly comment about the ineptness of the idea. Humor can be used to attack the actions and strategies of those in power in a circuitous or indirect way. The initiator of the humor has an escape door if or when the ire of the boss is raised: "Oh, I was just kidding. I wasn't serious." But underneath the joking façade lies the resistance of workers. Humor can be used to pick away at the ignorance, stupid decisions, arrogance and other flaws that they see in the higher-ups of the organization. Whether or not these forms of resistance are openly flaunted says a lot about the culture of the organization. Most organizations have one or more informal jesters who use humor to question the assumptions made by those in power. The degree to which the actions of jesters are embraced or scorned by organizational leaders can vary greatly. Some leaders might welcome the divergent thinking offered by the jesters, whereas others might feel threatened by anyone who questions the judgments of those in power. Barsoux explains that often times the role of the jester is played by certain types of workers. They may be advanced in their careers and not worried about the typical progression up the career ladder. They may be more secure in their roles and not worried too much about the repercussions of their strategic humor. Barsoux poses an intriguing suggestion for leaders to legitimize the role—establishing a type of ombudsman-humor-role that is immune from retaliation. In such a way, a leader can be made wary of dissident viewpoints and faulty assumptions. Darren, from your base of practice, what are your thoughts on this notion of the workplace jester?

DARREN

I'm intrigued as it sounds like you're describing me. I'd never considered myself a jester, but perhaps I am just that person who brings humor to tough situations so that others can find themselves more comfortable. As I dwell on that, I'm reflecting back on where I've worked before and who has played the jester role and you're right—they were typically people in positions where they'd reached a plateau in their career who had less to lose from annoying those in power and had less to gain from toeing the official party line. Of course, I don't like to think that's me, but perhaps reluctance to owning up to such a role is common among most jesters. I also seem to think that most jesters I've met are male. What do you think, Gene, is there a male/female distinction here?

GENE

Gender is a fascinating topic in the humor literature, but the breadth and depth of the topic extend far beyond the limits of this chapter. Helga Kotthoff provides an excellent overview with her article 'Gender and Humor: The State of the Art.'[5] From my own examination of the literature, the connection of gender and humor has been traditionally linked by considering the initiators and receivers of humor. In heterogenic romantic relationships, for example, males have been depicted as humor initiators and females have been the receivers. The use of humor is akin to the other tactics found in nature by which males flaunt their wares to attract the attention of females. Perhaps contemporary men use humor around women because they have somehow lost their peacock feathers through centuries of evolution. However, this simplistic view of humor and gender has its critics. Kotthoff cautions us that the stereotype of the "actively joking man" and the "receptively smiling woman" has decreased as a humor model in the literature. She explains that the relevance of gender differences and humor varies from one context to another. Given her assertion, how might the boundaries for humor use differ for women compared to men in the workplace? We have already described how humor use is purposeful in the workplace. Do social norms of the workplace affect how women apply humor? Stephanie Schnurr[6] provided an interesting case study on how women supervisors applied humor in a male-dominated technology work context. These female leaders had to walk the tightrope of asserting their leadership and yet keeping their femininity in a "man cave" of technology. Schnurr's research delineates the challenges of "doing leadership" and highlighting the gender-specific challenges of a male-dominated workplace. These women leaders used humor not only as a tool for leadership, but also to demarcate gender identity with their work roles.

DARREN

Hang on. Did you really just use the term "man cave of technology"? That must be a first for me. Putting aside any caves, whether male or female, I'm reflecting on my own experience of gender and humor within the world of HRD practice. Talking based solely on my own experience, and being careful not to generalize outside that, I've experienced men in HRD practice to be a little more audacious in their use of humor when compared with a lower key approach from the women I've worked with. Of course, my experience may be dissimilar from anyone else's, but I've certainly seen men take more risks in their use of humor. They have been more likely to push the humor envelope in a training room and, consequently, have been more likely to crash and burn from the failed humor or humor that crosses a line into the unacceptable. When I reflect on the use of humor by many of my female colleagues, it has been more subtle, and so more likely to help fine-tune the climate in a training room than to make a major shift. I wonder whether others have noticed these kinds of gender differences in humor usage? I also wonder why such differences exist. For example, is the work environment more accepting of risk taking in male humor? Or, are men more oblivious to the risk of using humor? Are men slower to realize that joking about the boss's personal hygiene is not a good idea? Yet again in our chapter, we have identified a possible research dissertation for a PhD student who otherwise would be left studying the impact of a lowly variable on a population of Psych101 students.

So, if that was humor and gender, Gene, what about humor and other human differences?

GENE

Several researchers have explored how humor is associated with different types of people. Unfortunately, one of the central themes in the literature is how humor can be used to attack all areas of difference—race, gender, age, physical limitations, class, religion, weight, height, power, etc. In Elliott Oring's book *Engaging Humor*[7] he has an informative yet disturbing chapter on hate humor. His message is clear. If you can think of a way that a group of people is different from you, you can craft humor that attacks and belittles that group in some way. Politically incorrect humor is a form of aggressive humor that can occur many ways in the workplace. Aggressive humor is linked to superiority theory—a strand of humor theory that can be traced back to Thomas Hobbes. Incidents happen in the workplace that make you scratch your head and wonder, "What were they thinking?" Harassment of various forms continues to occur in the workplace, and in the majority of cases, humor has been a part of it. Sometimes reports of these situations appear in media such as newspapers or news reports, but more often than not they end up in the human resource director's file cabinet. The worst cases spiral toward the courtroom and can result in huge damages to a company—both in terms of reputation and monetary losses. Years ago all employees of a university where I worked were required to attend sexual harassment training. Although I thought the training was conducted professionally, I was disappointed in how the topic of humor was handled. I knew from the literature that humor was involved in the majority of sexual harassment cases, yet the only caveat the trainer provided was to not use inappropriate humor in the workplace. It left me to wonder, what exactly is inappropriate humor? What separates the borders between appropriateness and inappropriateness? Who determines the borders? Are the boundaries clear? There lies the rub. Appropriateness of humor varies greatly from one individual to the next. Workplaces are at risk if organizational leaders merely rely on workers to use common sense to guide their judgments regarding offensive humor. Their sense is not common. Workers do not have a universally shared understanding of appropriate humor. If there was a clear demarcation about appropriate versus inappropriate humor perhaps we would make better progress in extinguishing the various forms of harassment that continue to plague our workplaces.

CONCLUDING THOUGHTS ON HUMOR AND HRD

DARREN
Well, all good things must come to an end and, so must other things, just like this chapter. It feels like we have just scratched the surface on humor: if humor is the rash, then this chapter is the quick scratch. However, it would be good to consider longer term solutions, akin to a strong antiseptic or even a change in behavior that keeps us away from rash-inducing activities. I therefore wonder what advice we can share with our researcher and practitioner colleagues. I'll start by reflecting on some advice for HRD scholar-practitioners. As I've described elsewhere:

> "HRD scholar-practitioners operate as a bridge between HRD research and HRD practice to improve the understanding and practice of HRD. They ground their practice in research and theory, they are champions

of research and theory in the workplace and in professional associations, they conduct research, and they disseminate findings from their
own research and practice. In doing these, they are partners with academics and practitioners alike."[8]

In light of this, I recommend the following to scholar-practitioners:

- Ground your HRD practice in humor research and theory. Review a
  few of the references in this chapter and look beyond these to better
  understand the theoretical frameworks for humor, and then use these
  to analyze your own use of humor. Consider how changing your own
  humor usage could make you a better practitioner, and increase your
  impact and consider how humor could become an additional tool in
  your HRD toolbox.
- Champion research and theory in the workplace and in professional associations. Once you have a better understanding of humor
  research and theory and have used that to improve your own practice,
  then look beyond yourself to others. Share this information with your
  work colleagues and customers, and find ways of engaging their interest in improving their use of humor in the workplace.
- Conduct research, and disseminate findings from your own research
  and practice; partner with academics and practitioners alike. As you
  have seen from this chapter, we have a lot of unknowns in the arena
  of humor in HRD. This observation means that there are a lot of
  potential research areas, and many internal practitioners have access
  to organizations that can act as the research sites for those studies. So,
  either partner with a researcher on a humor-based study, or design
  your own. Some of the topics you may want to consider include: the
  relationship between humor and learning in the training room; how
  male and female HRD practitioners make different use of humor in
  their work; the impact of student humor on other students in a training course; and the impact of humor on employees' receptiveness to
  change. And those are just four ideas generated without the benefit of
  caffeine this morning, so your own ideas will be even better.

AFTERMATH

(By Monica Lee: you must have realized I couldn't stay quiet for long.)

This session was well attended and much talked about, being so different
from the normal conference fare. It has gone down in the annals of history
as a 'good experiment'—and very much the sort of thing you would expect
from Gene and Darren. It changed people's thinking at the time, and is still
remembered fondly. Has it changed practice? I don't know—hmm—is this
a call for more research on humor in HRD, I wonder? Perhaps I will let
Gene have the last word after all:

GENE

The preceding recommendations are right on target for HRD scholarly-practitioners. We hope that those who are still reading this chapter and have not dozed off yet will consider one more suggestion. I encourage you to aggressively seek out more humor in life and put it to your good use. Chuckling at the absurdities of life can provide a healthy dose of humor to help you get through each day.

NOTES

1. Gary Fine and Michaela De Soucey. (2005) 'Joking cultures: Humor themes as social regulation in group life,' *International Journal of Humor Research* 1 (1): 1–22.
   Cecily Cooper. (2008) 'Elucidating the bonds of workplace humor: A relational process model,' *Human Relations* 61(8): 1087–1115.
2. Rod Martin. (2007) *The psychology of humor: An integrative approach.* Burlington, MA: Elsevier.
3. Leide Porcu. (2005) 'Fishy business: Humor in a Sardinian fish market,' *Humor: International Journal of Humor Research* 18(1): 69–102.
4. Jean-Louis Barsoux. (1996) 'Why organizations need humour,' *European Management Journal* 14(5): 500–508.
5. Helga Kotthoff. (2006) 'Gender and humor: The state of the art,' *Journal of Pragmatics* 38: 4–25.
6. Stephanie Schnurr. (2008) 'Surviving in a man's world with a sense of humour: An analysis of women leaders' use of humour at work,' *Leadership* 4(3): 299–319.
7. Elliott Oring. (2003) *Engaging humor.* Urbana: University of Illinois Press.
8. Darren Short and Thomas Shindell. (2009) 'Defining HRD scholar-practitioners,' *Advances in Developing Human Resources* 11(4): 472.

17 Evaluation within Organizations
So, What Are the Values?

Darlene Russ-Eft

Evaluations of programs, processes, and products take place within for-profit and not-for-profit organizations. One important aspect of an evaluation is to determine the merit, worth, or value of the evaluand. Merit represents an intrinsic form of *value*, while worth represents an extrinsic form of *value*. Furthermore, evaluations within organizations take place within a system. As such, they contribute to decision-making and strategic planning, and they take place within a political context. These characteristics point to other forms of *values*. These value forms emerge from the views and perspectives of various stakeholders in the evaluation, such as the evaluator and evaluation team values, executive and management values, HRD specialists and program staff values, and trainee values. Beyond the immediate organization, however, are the consumers or customers of that organization, and the values that they hold can influence the evaluand and the evaluation. One final *value* form involves the values held by the larger society. This presentation discusses the influence of these various value forms and identifies how these value forms can enrich and add value to the evaluation and the organization.
(6th International Conference on HRD Research and Practice across Europe Human Resource Development: Addressing the Value; Leeds Metropolitan University, UK, 25-27 May, 2005)

CONTEXT

The keynote was presented at the Sixth International Conference on HRD Research and Practice across Europe (May 26–27, 2005). It was sponsored by the University Forum for HRD (UFHRD) and the Academy of Human Resource Development (AHRD). The conference theme in 2005 was "Human Resource Development: Addressing the Value." This conference represented one of the largest gatherings of European HRD researchers and practitioners and drew presenters and attendees from Asia and the US. As a current academic and a former practitioner for many years, my intention was to examine the state of HRD evaluation and to consider some of the values that are represented in both HRD and in the field of evaluation.

In 2005 and continuing somewhat today, many HRD practitioners understood evaluation to be represented by the end-of-the-session reactionnaire or possibly by the Kirkpatrick[1] four-level taxonomy. Such a representation failed to consider alternative conceptualizations, purposes and approaches to evaluation. But, even more important, it ignored the value issues involved in any evaluation. In particular, such evaluations fail to identify and to address the views, values and information needs of the various stakeholders affected by the evaluation.

THE KEYNOTE ADDRESS

I'd like to begin my talk today with a short vignette and problem for all of you. . . .

You have been asked to undertake an evaluation of a basic skills training program designed to help the chronically unemployed to obtain and maintain employment. After several meetings with the vice president of Human Resources, the manager in charge of overseeing the program and the local government officials providing funding for the program, all of the stakeholders agree to have you undertake a formative evaluation.

After all, the program has only been in operation for about one year. The vice president, manager and funding agency feel that it is important to focus on what aspects of the program could be improved. After the program had been operating for several years, they had planned to undertake an evaluation to determine the outcomes and impacts of the program. During the past several months, you have been gathering data through a variety of sources. You have reviewed documents available on the program. You have conducted some interviews and observed some of the training. One day the vice president calls you with some excitement and asks to meet with you as soon as possible in order to discuss a wonderful opportunity. You wonder what might be going on, but you agree to the meeting.

When you arrive, the vice president tells you that a potential foundation funding source has been identified. A meeting with foundation staff confirms that they are extremely interested in the program and may be able to provide some needed financial support. As part of the proposal, they would like to see some of the evaluation results, highlighting the outcomes of the program. You immediately say that the focus of the evaluation has been on areas needing improvement. The vice president says, "Yes, I know that that is what we agreed, but I'm sure that you have some evidence as to the good work of this program." You say, "We have just begun to analyze the data, and we have been primarily concerned with identifying areas needing improvement. In addition, we have only been collecting data for a couple months on a program that has only been functioning for a year. How can we say that any of the positive outcomes resulted from the program?" The vice president says, "Yes, I know that you have a reputation for good and thorough and fair work, but this is such an opportunity! The funding will allow us to strengthen and expand the program ... in particular, we will be able to make those improvements that you recommend. I'm counting on your good work to help us with this effort."

I'd like you to turn to your neighbor to discuss what you, as the evaluator, should do in this situation. Spend about five minutes on this discussion.

WHAT IS ILLUSTRATED IN THIS SHORT VIGNETTE IS A CLASH OF VALUES

Evaluation is a value-laden field. Indeed the word "evaluation" means "to determine or fix the value" or "to determine the significance, worth, or condition."[2] Michael Scriven[3] used similar words to define evaluation by stating that "valuation refers to the process of determining the merit, worth, or value or something, or the product of that process." He proceeded to define each of these main concepts. Merit involves intrinsic value. Worth is defined as the value to an institution or a group. Thus, the merit of an HRD researcher might be found in his or her creativity, whereas the worth to the university or the organization comes from the grants or fame that the researcher brings to the institution. Similarly, like the previous vignette, the merit of the program rests with the ways in which it improves the lives of the workers. The worth of the program for the organization arises with the reduction in turnover, the improvement in productivity and the possibility of obtaining outside funding for the program. When finally coming to the value of the program, a judgment must be made that extends to all claims of merit and worth, or to all claims of intrinsic or extrinsic value.

Based, then, on this definition of evaluation, I would like to explore with you today the various facets of what is meant by value or values in evaluation. I will begin by examining the issue of extrinsic or intrinsic value. Then I will introduce a systems model for evaluation. Using that model I will explore the extrinsic and intrinsic values of the various stakeholders suggested by the model. I will then conclude with some suggestions for identifying the multi-dimensional values of the multiple stakeholders.

WORTH AND MERIT (OR EXTRINSIC AND INTRINSIC VALUES)

The distinction between extrinsic and intrinsic factors arises in a variety of arenas related to HRD. For example, Lyle Spencer's work in competencies[4] recognized the distinction between extrinsic and intrinsic competencies. Specifically, he presented "the iceberg model," stating that certain competencies were hidden whereas others were easily observed. He described the former as being 'intrinsic drives to act in the absence of environmental pressures or rewards' and the later as 'conscious beliefs or value drives formed by early social reinforcement.' He continued with:

> *The iceberg model has implications for the design of competency-based human resource applications. Competencies differ in the extent to which they can be taught. Content knowledge and behavioural skills are easiest to teach, and attitudes and values are harder. (Spencer, 1997: 7)*

Thus, within the domain of competencies, there is a recognition that extrinsic and intrinsic competencies, traits or values exist. Robert Sternberg's work on intelligence[5] also suggests a difference between the explicit and the implicit. On the one hand, there is knowledge or intelligence that can be measured with the typical paper-and-pencil test. Sternberg and colleagues call this "formal academic knowledge." It is knowledge that is taught, is extrinsic and is made explicit. In contrast is "tacit knowledge."

> *Tacit knowledge is typically implied rather than stated explicitly. . . . Tacit knowledge is intimately related to action. It takes the form of "knowing how" rather than "knowing that." . . . Tacit knowledge is practically useful. Tacit knowledge is instrumental to the attainment of goals people value. The more highly valued a goal is, and the more directly the knowledge supports the attainment of the goal the more useful is the knowledge. (Sternberg et al., 1995: 917–17)*

Sternberg proceeds to describe tacit knowledge indicating that it differentiates among people and leads to success. Note that he later examined such knowledge in a variety of cultures and settings.

Finally, within HRD, there is a recognition of extrinsic and intrinsic values in the work of Argyris and Schon.[6] They describe the types of mental maps that individuals possess and that guide actions. These theorists describe and discuss the differences between the two types of mental maps, specifically 'espoused theory' and 'theory in use.' Espoused theory is what is one uses to describe people's behavior to others. In contrast, theory in use tends to be tacit or implicit, but it is what leads to certain actions.

> *When someone is asked how he would behave under certain circumstances, the answer he usually gives is his espoused theory of action for that situation. This is the theory of action to which he gives allegiance, and which, upon request, he communicates to others. However, the theory that actually governs his actions is this theory-in-use. (Argyris and Schön, 1974: 6–7)*

We can, however, turn directly to the research on values. Kluckhohn[7] defined values as:

> *A value is a conception, explicit or implicit, distinctive of an individual or characteristic of a group, of the desirable which influences the selection from available modes, means and ends of actions. (Kluckhohn, 1957: 395)*

Thus, within various fields, including research on competencies, intelligence, organizational and systems theory and values, we find the distinction made between concepts that are considered extrinsic, explicit and visible and those that are intrinsic, implicit and hidden.

A SYSTEMS MODEL OF EVALUATION

The systems model, shown in Figure 17.1, was introduced by Preskill and Russ-Eft[8] and has been explicated in subsequent work. The model suggests that there are multiple factors and stakeholders that can influence an evaluation. These exist within the evaluation process and the organization, as well as being external to the evaluation and organization.

The model begins by recognizing that the evaluation processes influence the evaluation and the organization. These processes include focusing the evaluation, determining the evaluation's design and data collection methods,

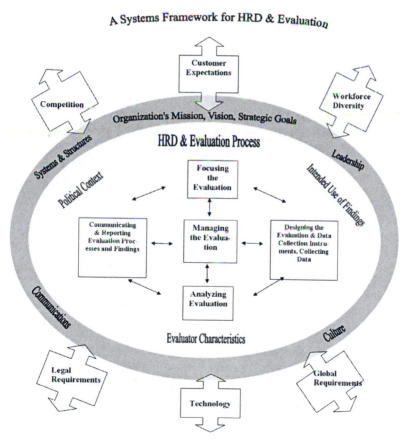

Figure 17.1   Systems view of evaluation.[9]

collecting data, analyzing the data and communicating and reporting evaluation processes and findings. The internal processes of planning, managing and budgeting take place throughout the evaluation. It must be recognized that the evaluator and the evaluation team can be considered the primary stakeholders for, and influencers on, these processes.

Still related to the evaluation itself, but involving those outside the evaluation team, are three other variables that are critical. These include the political context in which the evaluation is being conducted, stakeholders' reasons for conducting the evaluation (their intended use of the findings) and the evaluator's characteristics. The political aspects typically are influenced by those in positions of power, and thus, these people tend to be the executives and the funders of the program. The reasons for the evaluation can tend to emanate from such stakeholders as the executives and those managing and implementing the program. The last factor recognizes the effects of such evaluator characteristics as competence and expertise and the evaluator's relationship to the organization and the program or process being evaluated, for example, whether the evaluator is internal or external.

For an evaluation (or in fact any intervention) to succeed, it must be aligned with the organization's mission, vision and strategic plan. In addition, the organization's infrastructure oftentimes dictates how well the evaluation can be implemented and whether the findings are used.[10] Thus, the organizational culture can determine the level of participation and even the honesty displayed. As with most organizational interventions, supportive leadership lends credibility to the evaluation effort and points toward evaluation findings that will be used. The organization's systems and structures can facilitate data collection and help to ensure participation. Finally, the communication system can provide effective methods for disseminating the findings. Such communication and reporting have been shown to be a critical factor leading to decision making and action. Furthermore, such communication systems provide support for future evaluation efforts.[11]

Finally, the model recognizes that any organizational evaluation is influenced by the external environment, including such factors as competition, customer expectations, workforce diversity, legal requirements, technology and global context. These variables often can affect the extrinsic and intrinsic needs and values of the organizational stakeholders.

VALUES AND THE SYSTEMS MODEL

The systems model indicates the variety of factors and stakeholders that can influence an evaluation. This next section reviews the various factors and examines the extrinsic and intrinsic values associated with each stakeholder group. Extrinsic values can be identified by public statements whereas intrinsic values must be derived and hypothesized. For this presentation, I will adopt the self-interest model prevalent in social psychology.[12] As stated by Tyler:[13]

The traditional explanation for why people care about justice can perhaps best be described as an effort tempered with realism to pursue self interest. . . . This tempering is an effort to maximize their long term self interesting acquiring desired resources, which benefits from ongoing social relationships. (Tyler, 1994: 858)

Evaluator Values

Using the systems model, we can see that the evaluator's values enter the system in key decisions regarding the evaluation process itself. In addition, the evaluator's characteristics and background play a part affect the evaluation.

The evaluation profession throughout the world recognizes that evaluators need to follow certain ethical standards or values.[14] An analysis of the various guidelines shows some of the underlying themes.[15] These include:

- Professional foundations and competence
- Professional responsibility, integrity, accountability
- Respect for people
- Social responsibility

It should be noted, however, that this last theme appears less frequently and appears to be a less widely held value. We might from this analysis conclude then that four sets of values represent the explicitly held values. We might, however, contemplate what would be the implicit values that are being expressed through these explicit statements. Frankly, it appears that an important implicit value involves that of maintaining the credibility of the profession, one's own credibility within the profession and one's own connection to future clients and the profession. As a result, those in evaluation tend to promote certain types of evaluation approaches, such as theory-driven evaluation, goal-free evaluation and utilization-focused evaluation.[16]

Executive and Management Values

Executives and managers are extrinsically concerned with the health and well-being of the organization or their particular function within the organization. Such a perspective can be seen from the work of Garavan and Russ-Eft.[17] Garavan, for example, reported that the values expressed by executives and managers focus on such issues as increased worker productivity, increased worker flexibility, and creation and promotion of certain values of change, innovativeness, teamwork, and quality (among executives) and elimination of skill gaps increased skill performance (among managers). Similarly, Russ-Eft reported that in strategically driven HRD, executives lead the initiative with an orientation toward changing the organization, whereas managers tend to focus on skill development and the links to organizational strategy.

If we then examine what might be the intrinsic values being expressed, we observe that all of the values and issues identified by executives and managers are tied directly to their own success and longevity within the organization. If an executive does not demonstrate improved organization performance, then that person tends to be eliminated from the organization. Similarly, a line manager must show evidence of effective unit or division performance.

With both explicit and implicit values directed toward organizational or unit success, it is no wonder that executives and managers tend to be the ones asking for evaluations that examine the impacts, outcomes or return-on-investment of the HRD intervention. Executives would tend to request such evaluations, particularly if they are focused at the organizational level. In contrast, line managers would be most interested in the ways in which the evaluation shows improved performance of workers within their own particular unit or department or division.

HRD Specialists and Program Staff Values

According to Garavan, HRD specialists express a concern with having credibility and status with other organizational members and view key evaluation criteria in terms of meeting specified objectives and providing quality and relevance in their efforts. Among these individuals, some key evaluation criteria consist of number of employees trained and categories of employees trained along with improving individual performance. These concerns track closely with the developmental focus of HRD interventions described by Russ-Eft.

The implicit values expressed by HRD specialists and program staff members tend to focus on their own job performance and on being recognized for the quality and credibility of their own efforts. Certainly, the ubiquitous use of reaction forms at the end of training points toward the importance for these professionals of receiving good ratings for their performance skills, with less attention to the impacts that the training intervention might have. In addition, in order to achieve credibility with their efforts but to avoid criticisms based on the outcomes or impacts of their work, these professionals tend to embrace formative evaluations. The results of an evaluation can then be used to make whatever improvements might be needed.

Trainee Values

The trainees are individuals who participate in the training either voluntarily or involuntarily. According to Garavan, these individuals expressed values in advancing their own labor mobility and promotability and achieving certification

In this case, the extrinsic and intrinsic values seem to merge. Self-interest for these trainees leads to a concern for individual growth in order to obtain a more secure, better paying or more highly regarded position. In other words, the trainees hope to advance their own careers and, thereby gain more power and control over their work. This concern appears to relate directly to empowerment evaluation in which there appears 'the use of evaluation concepts, techniques, and findings to foster improvement and self-determination' (Fetterman, 2001: 3). It should be noted that this approach has a bias for the disenfranchised, and we may find it problematic to view trainees in that light. Still, the notion that HRD intervention and even the evaluation process should lead to trainee improvement and self-determination would mesh with the extrinsic and intrinsic values or promotability.

Consumer, Customer or Client Values

One group of stakeholders that tends to be overlooked in many organizational evaluations, but does appear in the Preskill and Russ-Eft systems model discussed earlier, is the group of customers or clients of the organization. Presumably, if an HRD intervention is effective at the organization, divisional and individual levels, there would be some effects experienced by customers. Certainly, the development of competency models for customer service personnel[18] is undertaken in order to provide the basis for training that will enhance the service for customers.

The Russ-Eft study used a critical incident method to identify needed strategies and competencies. Of the major strategies and competencies emerging from the study, the one described most frequently by customers was 'Render timely, accurate, and thorough service.' The results show that customers are interested in having their own service needs fulfilled.

Turning to the evaluation literature, we can identify at least one evaluation approach that would serve customers. Scriven[19] has advocated an approach labeled consumer-oriented evaluation that focuses on the consumers' needs. Such a method suggests that the views and values of customers and consumers may differ somewhat from those within the organization.

SIFTING THROUGH THE VALUES

The previous sections have described evaluation as determining worth (or extrinsic values) and merit (or intrinsic values). Within a systems model, factors influencing the evaluation were identified along with some associated stakeholders. Using a self-interest model to examine these stakeholders, I identified various extrinsic and intrinsic values and associated them with alternative evaluation approaches. The chapter now turns to an examination of methods for determining these various values.

Mark, Henry and Julnes (2000) refer to values inquiry as involving the use of systematic methods to 'identify the values relevant to social programs and policies and to infuse them into evaluations' (Mark, Henry and Julnes, 2000: 40). What is being suggested in the present chapter is that HRD evaluations undertaken within an organizational setting must involve the identifications of values relevant to the HRD programs and policies and the associated stakeholders.

Renger and Bourdeau[20] presented an exploratory case study that described the methods used for such a values inquiry. The method that they discussed is called the ATM model—A: Antecedent Conditions; T: Target Antecedent Conditions; M: Measurement Issues. The method, then, begins with the development of a visual map of the antecedent conditions and their linkages to the 'problem.' Through stakeholder judgments and research evidence, decisions were made as to specific antecedent conditions that were targeted by the program or programs. A final value judgment involved determining which of the antecedent conditions could be measured.

An alternative approach to this ATM model involves the use of logic models.[21] A logic model 'is the basis for a convincing story of the program's expected performance' (McLaughlin and Jordan, 1999: 66). As with the ATM approach, a logic model provides a visual map showing the linkages from the antecedents and resources, through the various program activities, to the short-term and long-term outcomes and to the final impacts. As described by Russ-Eft and Preskill, the development of a logic model should involve the various stakeholder groups. From the standpoint of clarifying values, it is critical to have all the relevant stakeholders given reasonable sufficient time and political power to be able to express their extrinsic and intrinsic values.

CONCLUSIONS AND RECOMMENDATIONS

As stated by Renger and Boudreau (2004: 39) 'one limitation in using values inquiry is that its methods are not as extensive or as highly evolved as other aspects of evaluation method.' This, then, represents a call to action. Within HRD evaluation, there is a need to develop and then use values inquiry methods. This must begin by determining all of the relevant stakeholders in an evaluation—those internal to the evaluation, program and organization, and those external to the evaluation, program and organization. As HRD researchers, we might ask: What are the best methods for identifying all of the relevant stakeholders?

After identifying these stakeholders, methods must be developed and used for involving the various stakeholder groups. Beyond simple involvement, however, methods must protect any vulnerable populations while enabling their voices to be heard and influencing the evaluation. Again, as HRD researchers, we might ask: What methods might be considered best for involving stakeholder groups and using their values to guide the evaluation?

As discussed here, the values of the various stakeholders can point to different evaluation approaches. This suggests that any particular evaluation should draw upon a variety of evaluation approaches. Several research questions emerge here. To what extent do HRD evaluations employ these various evaluation approaches? If not, what are the reasons? Also, what are the results of those evaluations in terms of stakeholder satisfaction and use? If multiple approaches are employed, what are the results of those evaluations?

AFTERMATH: WHAT HAS HAPPENED SINCE 2005?

Since the time of this keynote, there has been an increasing recognition of the importance of the various stakeholders involved in an HRD initiative. Chanin's chapter in the present book, as one example, uses the frameworks of corporate social responsibility (CSR) and sustainability and recognizes the different stakeholders. Furthermore, that chapter recognizes society and the local and national governments as stakeholders. This recognition represents an excellent extension and expansion of the ideas included in the present chapter. Finally, the ideas included with CSR and sustainability encompass ethical concerns and issues, which represent a major focus of the present chapter. Some of these issues were described in my most recent address titled "HRD Human Resource Development, Evaluation, and Sustainability: Are These Concepts and Activities Incompatible or Compatible?" delivered at the 12th HRD across Europe conference in Cheltenham, England.

Another development, since 2005, has been the work of the International Board of Standards for Training, Performance, and Instruction (ibstpi™). Ibstpi is a non-profit organization that develops and validates competencies related to various HRD arenas. After having developed and validated competency sets for instructors, instructional designers and training managers, the ibstpi directors recognized the need for competencies for evaluators working within organizational settings. The initial work began with a review of various standards provided by national evaluation associations (as mentioned in the present chapter). Russ-Eft et al. (2008) then presented the results of that development and validation effort. Five of the fourteen competencies dealt with the issues raised in the present chapter. These are listed below using their designated numbers:

4. Observe ethical and legal standards.
5. Demonstrate awareness of the politics of evaluation (part of which involves clarifying stakeholder values).
6. Develop an effective evaluation plan (including identifying and collaborating with stakeholders).
12. Disseminate and follow up the findings and recommendations (which involve discussion with and interpretation for stakeholders).
14. Work effectively with personnel and stakeholders (by keeping stakeholders informed and engaged).

The results of this work have been presented and discussed at the AHRD conference and the HRD across Europe conference, as well as the meeting of the American Evaluation Association and the American Educational Research Association.

So, both HRD researchers and evaluation practitioners have greater awareness of the value issues and the need to pay attention to all of the stakeholders for an evaluation. Nevertheless, current HRD practice still tends to have a rather simplistic focus, and more attention is needed to transform HRD practitioner evaluation work.

NOTES

1. D.L. Kirkpatrick. (1994) *Evaluating training programs: The four levels*. San Francisco: BerrettKoehier.
2. Merriam-Webster Online Dictionary. (n.d.) Retrieved May 1, 2005, from http://www.m-w.com/cgi-bin/dictionary?book=Dictionary&va=evaluation&x=17&y=15.
3. M. Scriven. (1991) *Evaluation thesaurus*, 4th ed. Thousand Oaks, CA: Sage.
4. L.M. Spencer Jr. (1997) 'Competency assessment methods,' in L.J. Bassi and D. Russ-Eft (eds.), *What Works: Assessment, Development, and Measurement*, Alexandria, VA: ASTD, 1–36. L.M. Spencer Jr. and S.M. Spencer. (1993. *Competence at work: Models for superior performance*. New York: Wiley.
5. R.J. Sternberg. (1985) 'Implicit theories of intelligence, creativity, and wisdom,' *Journal of Personality and Social Psychology* 49: 607–627. R.J. Sternberg. (1997) *Successful intelligence*. New York: Plume. R.J. Sternberg. (2004) 'Culture and intelligence,' *American Psychologist* 59: 325–338. R.J. Sternberg, R.K. Wagner, W.M. Williams and J.A. Horvath. (1995) 'Testing common sense,' *American Psychologist* 50(11): 912–927.
6. M.Argyris and D. Schön. (1974) Theory in practice. Increasing professional effectiveness. San Francisco: Jossey-Bass.
7. C. Kluckhohn. (1967) 'Values and value-orientations in the theory of action: An exploration in definition and classification,' in T. Parsons and E.A. Shils (eds.), *Toward a General Theory of Action*, Cambridge: Harvard University Press, 388–433. (Original work published 1951.)
8. H. Preskill and D. Russ-Eft. (2001) 'A systems model for evaluating learning performance,' in D. H. Redmann (ed.), *Academy of Human Resource Development: Defining the Cutting Edge*, Baton Rouge, LA: Academy of Human Resource Development, 57–63. H. Preskill and D. Russ-Eft. (2003) 'A framework for reframing HRD evaluation practice and research,' in A.M. Gilley, L. Bierema and J. Callahan (eds.), *Critical Issues in HRD*, (Cambridge, MA: Perseus, 199–257. H. Preskill and D. Russ-Eft. (2005) *Building evaluation capacity: 72 activities for teaching and training*. Thousand Oaks, CA: Sage. D. Russ-Eft and H. Preskill. (2001) *Evaluation in organizations: A systematic approach to enhancing learning, performance, and change*. Cambridge, MA: Perseus. D. Russ-Eft and H. Preskill. (2005) 'In search of the holy grail: ROI in ROI evaluation in HRD,' *Advances in Developing Human Resources*: 71–85. D. Russ-Eft and H. Preskill. (2009) *Evaluation in organizations: A systematic approach to enhancing learning, performance, and change*, 2nd ed. New York: Basic Books.
9. H. Preskill and D. Russ-Eft. (2005); an earlier version of this figure can be found in H. Preskill and D. Russ-Eft. (2003. 'A framework for reframing HRD evaluation practice and research,' in A. Gilley, J. Callahan and L. Bierema. (eds.), *Critical Issues in HRD: A New Agenda for the Twenty-first Century*. Cambridge, MA: Perseus.
10. H. Preskill and R.T. Torres. (1999) *Evaluative inquiry for learning in organizations*. Thousand Oaks, CA: Sage. H. Preskill and D. Russ-Eft. (2003) 'A framework for reframing HRD evaluation practice and research,' in A.M. Gilley, L. Bierema and J. Callahan (eds.), *Critical Issues in HRD*, Cambridge, MA: Perseus, 199–257.

11. R.T. Torres, H. Preskill and M. Piontek. (2005) *Evaluation strategies for communicating and reporting: Enhancing learning in organizations,* 2nd ed. Thousand Oaks, CA: Sage.

12. E. Walster, G.W. Walster and E. Berscheid. (1978) *Equity theory and research.* Boston: Allyn & Bacon.

13. T.R. Tyler. (1994) 'Psychological models of the justice motive: Antecedents of distributive and procedural justice,' *Journal of Personality and Social Psychology* 67: 850–863.

14. African Evaluation Association. (2002) *The African Evaluation Guidelines: 2002,* retrieved January 11, 2005, from http://66.165.73.167/afrea/content/index.cfm?navID=5&itemID=204. American Evaluation Association. (2004, July) *Guiding Principles for Evaluators,* retrieved January 11, 2005, from http://www.eval.org/Guiding%20Principles.htm. Canadian Evaluation Society. (n.d.) *CES guidelines for ethical conduct,* retrieved May 6, 2003, from http://www.evaluationcanada.ca/site.cgi?s=5&ss+4&_lang=an. Deutsche Gesellschaft für Evaluation (DeGEval). (2001, October 4) *Standards für evaluation,* retrieved May 6, 2003, from http://www.degeval.de/standards/standards.htm. Joint Committee on Standards for Educational Evaluation. (1994) *The program evaluation standards,* 2nd ed. Thousand Oaks, CA: Sage.

15. D. Russ-Eft. (2004) 'Ethics in a global world: An oxymoron?' *Evaluation and Program Planning* 27: 349–356. D. Russ-Eft, D. (2005, May) 'In search of evaluator competencies. Human resource development across Europe,' [Abstract] *Abstracts of the Sixth AUHRD/AHRD Conference,* 81. Leeds, England: University of Leeds.

16. H.T. Chen. (1990) *Theory-driven evaluation.* Newbury Park, CA: Sage. H.T. Chen. (1994) 'Current trends and future directions in program evaluation,' *Evaluation Practice* 15(3): 229–238. M.Q. Patton. (1997) *Utilization-focused evaluation: A new century text.* Thousand Oaks, CA: Sage. M.Q. Patton. (2008) *Utilization-focused evaluation,* 4th ed. Thousand Oaks, CA: Sage. M. Scriven. (1973) 'Goal-free evaluation,' in E.R. House (ed.), *School Evaluation,* Berkeley: McCutchan Publishing.

17. T.N. Garavan. (1995) 'HRD stakeholders: Their philosophies, values, expectations and evaluation criteria,' *Journal of European Industrial Training* 19(10): 17–30. D. Russ-Eft. (1997) 'Looking through a different lens: Views of human resource development,' in H. Preskill and L. Dilworth (eds.), *AHRD in Transition: Finding the Cutting Edge,* International Society for Performance Improvement and the Academy of Human Resource Development, 107–114.

18. D. Russ-Eft. (2004) 'Customer service competencies: A global look,' *Human Resource Development International* 7: 211–231.

19. M. Scriven. (1974) *Standards for the evaluation of Educational Products and programs' in G.D Borich (Ed) Evaluating educational programs and products. Englewood Cliffs, NJ: Educational Technology Publications* M. Scriven. (1994) 'Product evaluation—The state of the art,' *Evaluation Practice* 15(1): 45–62.

20. R. Rengerand B. Bourdeau. (2004) 'Strategies for values inquiry: An exploratory case study,' *American Journal of Evaluation* 25(1): 39–49.

21. D. Russ-Eft. (1986) 'Evaluability assessment of the Adult Education Program (AEP),' *Evaluation and Program Planning* 9: 39–47. D. Russ-Eft and H. Preskill. (2005) 'In search of the holy grail: ROI in ROI evaluation in HRD,' *Advances in Developing Human Resources:* 71–85. R.E. Schmidt, J.W. Scanlon and J.B. Bell. (1979, November) *Evaluability assessment: Making public programs work better.* Human Services Monograph Series, No. 14. J. Wholey. (1979) *Evaluation: Promise and performance,* Washington, DC: Urban Institute. J.S. Wholey. (1994) 'Assessing the feasibility and likely usefulness of evaluation,, in J.S. Wholey, H.P. Hatry and K.E. Newcomer (eds.), *Handbook of Practical Program Evaluation,* San Francisco, CA: Jossey-Bass, 15–39.

18 Management or Manipulation?
Emotions within the Context of Leadership

Jamie L. Callahan

This chapter explores the ways in which leaders both manage emotions of themselves and their followers, and also manipulate the emotions of their followers to achieve personal and organizational goals. To depict these phenomena, I present a model of the leadership process of working with follower emotions. I conclude with conceptual implications for the interconnection of leadership and emotion, emphasizing the irony of the masculinized concept of leadership linked with the feminized concept of emotion.
(9th International Conference on Human Resource Development across Europe, Lille, France, 2008)

THE CONTEXT

This speech was delivered in 2008 at the 9th International Conference on Human Resource Development: Research and Practice across Europe, held in Lille, the third largest city in France. The conference was held at the IESEG School of Management, one of the country's top business schools. The conference was sponsored by the University Forum for Human Resource Development (UFHRD) in partnership with the Academy of Human Resource Development (AHRD) in the US. Because the Forum is primarily made up of institutional-level memberships, the audience is dominated by academics and graduate students, largely from HRD programs in the UK and Europe. The nature of the field, though, is such that many of the graduate students are also full-time HRD practitioners. Because of the dynamic of the audience, this keynote had an emphasis on critical theory perspectives of emotion and leadership.

This keynote was particularly important to me because it combined my two main areas of research interest—leadership and the sociology of emotion—under the umbrella of a critical perspective. As I prepared this keynote, I realized that leadership had often been a subject of human resource development discourse, that emotion had only a small voice (very often in the form of job satisfaction or emotional intelligence) and that critical theory had only recently begun to make the most tentative of footholds of discourse within the field. Indeed, that foothold of critical theory discourse was found almost exclusively among UK authors.

I also wanted to enact some of the very concepts that I knew I would be discussing in the keynote. Most notably, I wanted to do something that was different, that would engage the audience and that would stimulate different types of emotions, in other words, the 'deviance' component of the model I will present here. So I began and concluded the presentation by playing music. While it is difficult to recreate the feel of pulsing, rousing rhythms from the start of the presentation or the quirky, catchy tune from the end of the presentation, I have presented those lyrics here to take you back to the 1980s or to break out your iPods so you can use your imagination to relive what it might have felt like to be sitting in the auditorium when I delivered this keynote.

THE KEYNOTE

Risin' up, back on the street
Did my time, took my chances
Went the distance, now I'm back on my feet
Just a man and his will to survive
So many times, it happens too fast
You change your passion for glory
Don't lose your grip on the dreams of the past
You must fight just to keep them alive
It's the eye of the tiger, it's the thrill of the fight
Risin' up to the challenge of our rival
And the last known survivor stalks his prey in the night
And he's watchin' us all in the eye of the tiger

("Eye of the Tiger" by Survivor)[1]

Since 1982, the theme song to *Rocky III* has been almost a standard at pep rallies, town hall meetings in organizations and other events designed to motivate and inspire individuals. Regardless of how one perceives the strategy of playing music to shift the mood of a crowd, it would be hard to deny that the pulsing backbeat and charging lyrics cause many of us to tap our toes or bounce in our seats. This strategy fits with arguments that suggest the role of leaders is to engage, rouse and inspire.[2] Thus, I contend that the strategy employed by symbolic displays such as this is the management, or manipulation, of emotions within the context of leadership. In what follows, I explore those efforts at managing the emotions of (potential) followers and challenge the hegemonic belief that such management is a natural, and somehow good, aspect of leadership. I will first provide some background on leadership as a body of theory and set of practices, then I will describe the role of emotion within leadership, then I offer a model that describes how leaders manage (or manipulate) the emotions of followers and I conclude with some implications of leadership and emotion in organizational contexts.

Leadership

The body of literature about leadership is enormous. Yet, even a brief exploration reveals a thread of emotion-laden behaviors and characteristics that are used to define the essence of leadership. Words such as charismatic, vitality, cheerfulness, inspirational, comfort and more can be found in leadership treatises.[3] These emotionally laden words can be found throughout the history of leadership theorizing, even though it was not popular to raise in one breath the idea of 'emotion' and 'leadership' until the late 20th century.

Early approaches to leadership focused on the traits, characteristics and attributes of the individual that appeared to be responsible for his success as a leader.[4] And, yes, these theories generally assumed that the leader was male, so much so that they are often dubbed 'Great Man' theories of leadership. These leader-focused theories include traits—such as those described by Lao-tzu or Machiavelli, skills approaches popularized by Katz[5] and Mumford,[6] styles as popularized by Blake and Mouton's (1964) Managerial Grid,[7] and the classic conceptions of power[8] ascribed to those in leadership positions.

Later theories began to look more at the context that influenced leadership.[9] These theories, under the umbrella label of 'situational' theories of leadership, suggested that leadership was more than just the traits, skills, style and what-not of the leader. Somehow, leadership seemed to be different depending on the situation in which the leader found himself. And, yes, again, these theories were largely about, and studied among, men. Contingency theory[10] looked at how leaders should be matched to the nature of situations; Situational Leadership Theory[11] looked at how leaders should shift *their* strategies to match situations; path-goal theory[12] was also about how leaders needed to shape their behavior and strategies to match whatever context they encountered. Whereas followers were mentioned as part of the context, they did not figure heavily into understanding leadership.

The next wave of leadership theories *did* look at followers, though. Social-dynamic theories tried to take into account the leader, the context *and* the followers.[13] Once again, these theories were mostly about and for men, but women were starting to gain recognition as part of these theories because studies[14] began to suggest that women excelled at these social-dynamic approaches to leadership. Transformational leadership[15] is grounded in the idea of influencing, or transforming, followers through leader behaviors and characteristics applied mindfully in varying contexts. Leader-member exchange [16] is more psychological and focuses on the nature of relationships formed between leaders and followers. These theories were more explicit in their inclusion of emotional components and even celebrated the importance of emotion-laden concepts, such as charisma.

But it was not until the late 20th century that alternative leadership theories were more explicitly feminized and, in the process, included more emotion-laden realities of leadership. These approaches sought to capitalize on the relational, emotional strengths of earlier theories and, to a certain extent, create theories that were more relevant for women.[17] Whereas some of these theories (e.g., distributed leadership) had been around for a long time, they were generally subsumed in favor of more 'heroic' forms of leadership—like transformational leadership theory. This new wave of ideas about leadership included feminist, postheroic,[18] democratic and distributed theories of leaders and leadership. Now, there are some inherent problems with this feminization of leadership,[19] but that is a subject for another conversation. What seems to differentiate current thought is that the essence of leadership might well be emotion and the ability to manage the emotions of self and other more effectively.[20]

Emotions and Leadership

Even in the earliest, most 'command and control'-oriented theories of leadership, traces of emotion can be found. As much as we wanted to see leaders as 'heroes' who were somehow different from the rest of us, leaders were still people who had emotions, and, in their interactions with other people, they brought out emotions in others. Their ability to work with their own and others' emotions contributed to their success as leaders. So, leadership has at its heart the management, and sometimes the manipulation, of the emotions of followers.

Leaders *have* emotion in that they serve as "a container of the emotions of his or her followers."[21] We've all heard the phrase, "It's lonely at the top." Leaders also might fear losing power or letting down followers; they might envy others for not having the burden of leadership or for appearing to be more successful; they might feel sadness about having reached the pinnacle of success without knowing what comes next. Leaders also *create* emotions because "leadership is the creation of desire."[22] Leaders inspire and motivate their followers. They use charisma to enable followers to envision future possibilities, to empower followers and to energize their followers toward action. Finally, leaders *manage* or *manipulate* their own emotions and the emotions of others. Emotion in leadership is more than just having or creating emotion; emotions serve as a means to an end for leaders. Leadership is the "ability to address the many through the use of charisma, symbols, and other strongly emotional devices, the ambition being to arouse and encourage people to embark upon organizational projects."[23]

So, if leadership is about using emotionally symbolic devices to arouse and encourage followers, let's think back to the opening of this piece and *The Eye of the Tiger*. Sharon Turnbull[24] highlights the cynicism that followers feel as a result of this type of symbolic attempt by leaders to facilitate enthusiasm toward a (their) desired goal(s)—they *feel* it as manipulation and respond according the negative connotation of the word. Kiefer and Van Maanen and Kunda,[25] as examples on the other hand, note how such symbolism may indeed generate enthusiasm (albeit perhaps fleeting and false); are these individuals merely dupes of leader manipulation? Or is there more to it? When is it 'management' and when is it 'manipulation'? I suggest that there is a dynamic interplay between the emotional context and the choices that leaders make within that context. As Heidigger said, "Nothing is anything without a context."[26]

That emotional context today is what Stjepan Mestrovic (1997) calls 'postemotionalism.' Leaders today operate in a society that is devoid of authentic emotions, in which the emotions we experience and express are simply masks of what are perceived to be proper emotions. The task of leaders is to try to generate *authentic* emotions, in themselves and in their followers, in order to create a collective effervescence that will fill the emotional void. The risk in this process, though, is that if the leader is not successful, followers may become alienated and disengaged.

Managing and Manipulating Emotions: The Leadership Process

My colleague, Jenny Sandlin, and I have spent a number of years looking at how social movement groups use emotion management to influence audiences, with the hope of getting supporters to resist anything from Nike to Starbucks to McDonald's and more. We created a model of the process of managing and manipulating follower emotions in order to effect change. I realized that leaders do much the same thing in trying to get followers to engage in organizational change efforts; thus, Figure 18.1 represents the adaptation of the social movement approach to the leadership process of working with follower emotions.

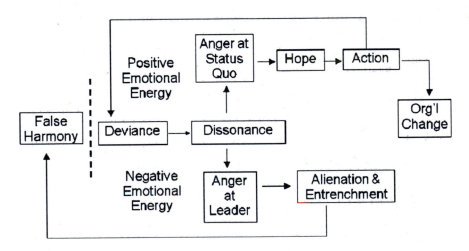

Figure 18.1   Emotion management and manipulation process.

Our context of postemotionalism causes us to exist in a state of false harmony; we aren't even aware that we are really not 'feeling.' In order to break this pattern, leaders need to display otherwise 'deviant' emotional behavior (like rocking out to *Eye of the Tiger* at the start of an organizational retreat, perhaps!). This behavior by the leader causes dissonance in the followers who react to what they perceive as either positive or negative emotional energy from the leader.[27].

Positive emotional energy can be derived in one of two ways. A narcissistic leader generates the illusion of positive energy by 'sucking' power from followers in order to bolster positive feelings for him- or herself. This fits well within the context of postemotionalism because the emotion generated toward the followers is inauthentic and, therefore, is not likely to be perceived as positive by those followers (which means it short-circuits the cycle of emotion management depicted in Figure 18.1). The other way of creating positive emotional energy is by spurring collective effervescence. Tina Kiefer (2002) describes the happy energy that can be generated toward organizational change efforts that are usually associated with fear and anger when a leader inspires collective effervescence. Positive emotional energy leads to anger at the status quo and a hope for change that leads to action and renewed authenticity of emotion.

Negative emotional energy is simply when followers perceive that their energy is being sucked away; they feel manipulated. There is no illusion of positive emotional energy here; it's just a raw power grab to get people to do what the leader wants them to do. Negative emotional energy leads to anger at the leader, and the follower is more likely to internalize the anger and retreat to a state of entrenchment and alienation.[28] So, instead of hope toward change, the system gets stuck in the false harmony of postemotionalism, and cynicism toward leaders' attempts to manipulate emotion ensues.[29]

Implications and Conclusion

There are some things we need to be cautious of, though, when we consider the model I've shared here. The first relates to false dichotomies, the second to feminization and the third to positivistic interpretation.

First, the study of emotion has been plagued with the persistence of dichotomy (principally between emotion and cognition). The model I have presented here is depicted in such a way that there is a danger of a dichotomous interpretation of negative and positive emotional energy as poles of 'masculine' and 'feminine.' Some might assume that the positive emotional energy which includes such a strong relational component would be the realm of the feminine; and, yet, research suggests that women must more often deal with the consequences of absorbing negative emotional energy based on their subordinate position in society.[30] So, whereas emotion has been gendered, to ascribe gender to the ability to generate positive versus negative emotional energy creates a 'false dichotomy' that limits our understanding of how emotion and leadership interconnect.

This issue of feminization with respect to managing emotion is also connected to critiques of leadership theories. Some, like Calas and Smircich (1991), argue that to 'feminize' leadership is inherently flawed because leadership is, by its very nature, masculinized. Organizational systems and structures are inhospitable to this idea of feminine notions of leadership, and, so, truly feminine conceptions of 'leadership' cannot get a foothold in the organization because of normed power structures.

The model also risks further reliance on positivist notions of leadership instead of the more organic, constructivist interpretations of leadership that I believe are more representative of the nature of leadership. First, the structure of the model also implies more of a causal relationship than I believe actually exists. Also, the notion of 'hope' may create a vision that someone (presumably a heroic leader) will save the day, absolving the followers of responsibility toward helping change happen.

These implications might seem to lead us to despair that leadership is inherently and irredeemably inauthentic, manipulative, and masculinized. Nevertheless, I will leave you on a note of either hopefulness that all is not lost, that special individuals who have a skill for dealing with the emotions of others will be able to generate authentic emotion and energy toward positive change. Or, I will leave the cynics among us with a shallow attempt to lull you into complacency and a false sense of happiness:

> Here's a little song I wrote
> You might want to sing it note for note
> Don't Worry—Be Happy
> In every life we have some trouble
> But when you worry you make it Double
> Don't Worry—Be Happy
> Ain't got no place to lay your head,
> somebody came and took your bed
> Don't Worry, Be Happy
> The landlord say your rent is late,
> he may have to litigate
> Don't Worry—Be Happy
> Ain't got no cash, ain't got no style,
> ain't got no gal to make you smile
> Don't Worry—Be Happy
> Cause when you worry your face will frown
> and that will bring everybody down
> Don't Worry—Be Happy
> *Bobby McFerrin, "Don't Worry, Be Happy"*[31]

AFTERMATH: UPDATE

Since this keynote was originally presented, I have had the opportunity to conduct empirical research with colleagues to test the model I proposed in Lille in a leadership context. Our findings suggested a slightly different construction of the model than what Jenny Sandlin and I found when looking at activities of social movement groups engaged in consumer resistance. The original work suggested that negative and positive emotional energy generated by the social movement group (or 'leader') led to different reactions by the (potential) followers. Namely, positive emotional energy generated anger at the status quo and a desire to change the context, whereas negative emotional energy generated anger at the social movement group (or 'leader') and an entrenchment in false harmony. Whereas this model may hold in social movement contexts, subsequent empirical research (Callahan, Kissack and Minnis, under review) suggests that, at least within online communities, *both* negative and positive emotional energy leads followers to react with anger at the status quo and a desire to change the context. The first study dealt with individuals who either currently belonged to the social movement group or stood as audience members when the group staged a resistance event. The second study dealt with individuals who self-selected to be part of the online community. So, what is of interest to me now as a result of these differing findings is how context might influence not just *leader* behavior, but also *follower* reaction to leader behavior within a critical framework.

Whereas the content of the presentation has been affected by research conducted since the original keynote, the context of the presentation has also changed in these few short years. The once tenuous foothold of critical theory within the HRD discourse has begun to strengthen, even in the US. Whereas the European HRD conference, co-sponsored by UFHRD and AHRD, has had a track dedicated to critical theory perspectives for a number of years, the AHRD has since approved both a track for critically oriented conference papers and a special interest group dedicated to critical and social justice perspectives. Leadership and leadership development continue to be highly popular areas of study within the field of HRD. Issues of emotion continue to be fringe areas of study, but with steady interest if one includes satisfaction, commitment and emotional intelligence as 'emotion'-oriented foci of research. And critical perspectives of all manner of topics—from leadership, to LGBT issues, to emotion, to training and development and more—are popping up at conferences and in HRD-oriented journals. Was my keynote the *cause* of this shift? Surely not. But did my keynote contribute to the growing interest in two fringe areas of HRD study—critical perspectives and emotion? I would hope so!

NOTES

1. "Eye of the Tiger" by Survivor, written by Frankie Sullivan and Jim Peterik, recorded 1981, released 1982.
2. Martin Wood. (2005) 'The fallacy of misplaced leadership,' *Journal of Management Studies* 42: 1101–1121.
3. References to 'charisma' can be found in a wide variety of works about leadership, including Kets de Vries (1997) Tiryakian (1995), and Sveningsson

and Larsson (2006). Bass and Avolio (1994) discuss both charismatic and inspirational leaders. Barnard (1938) refers to leaders having 'vitality.' Alvesson and Sveningsson (2003) refer to cheerfulness and comfort. See Edward A. Tiryakian. (1995) 'Collective effervescence, social change and charisma: Durkheim, Weber, and 1989,' *International Sociology* 10: 269–281. Stefan Sveningsson and M. Larsson. (2006) 'Fantasies of leadership: Identity work,' *Leadership* 2: 21. Bernard M. Bass and Bruce J. Avolio. (1994) 'Shatter the glass ceiling: Women may make better managers,' *Human Resource Management* 33: 549–560. Chester I. Barnard. (1938) *Functions of the executive.* Cambridge: Harvard University Press.

4. Jamie L. Callahan, J. Kori Whitener and Jennifer A. Sandlin. (2007) 'The art of creating leaders: Popular culture artifacts as pathways for development,' *Advances in Developing Human Resources* 9: 19.

5. Robert L. Katz. (1955) 'Skills of an effective administrator,' *Harvard Business Review* 33: 33–42.

6. Michael D. Mumford, Stephen J. Zaccaro, Francis D. Harding, T. Owen Jacobs and Edwin A. Fleishman. (2000) 'Leadership skills for a changing world: Solving complex social problems,' *Leadership Quarterly* 11: 11–35.

7. Robert R. Blake and Jane Mouton. (1964) *The managerial grid.* Houston: Gulf Publishing Company.

8. J.R. French and B. Raven. (1959) 'The bases of social power,' in D. Cartwright (ed.), *Studies in Social Power*, Ann Arbor: University of Michigan Press.

9. Callahan et al. (2007).

10. Fred E. Fiedler. (1964) 'A contingency model of leadership effectiveness,' In L. Berkowitz (ed.), *Advances in Experimental Social Psychology*, vol. 1, New York: Academic Press.

11. Paul Hersey and Ken H. Blanchard. (1969) 'Life-cycle theory of leadership,' *Training and Development Journal* 23: 26–34.

12. Robert J. House. (1971) 'A path-goal theory of leader effectiveness,' *Administrative Science Quarterly* 16: 321–328.

13. (Callahan et al. 2007).

14. E.g., Bernard M. Bass and Bruce J. Avolio. (1994) *Improving organizational effectiveness through transformational leadership.* Thousand Oaks, CA: Sage.

15. Marshall Sashkin. (2004) 'Transformational leadership approaches: A review and synthesis,'in A.T.C.J. Antonakis and R.J. Sternberg (eds.), *The Nature of Leadership*, Thousand Oaks, CA: Sage, 171–196. Bernard M. Bass. (1985) *Leadership and performance beyond expectations.* New York: Free Press.

16. George B. Graen and Mary Uhl-Bien. (1995) 'Development of leader-member exchange (LMX) theory of leadership over 25 years: Applying a multi-level-multi-domain perspective,' *Leadership Quarterly* 6: 28.

17. Ann Rippin. (2007) 'Stitching up the leader: Empirically based reflections on leadership and gender,' *Journal of Organizational Change Management* 20: 209–226.

18. Monica Lee. (1999) 'Text, Gender and Future Realities,' in Richard Goodman, (ed.), *Modern Organisations and Emerging Conundrums: Exploring the Post-Industrial Sub-culture of the Third Millennium*. Lanham, MD: Lexington Books, 109–125.

19. Marta B. Calas and Linda Smircich. (1991) 'Voicing seduction to silence leadership,' *Organization Studies* 12: 567–602.

20. Mats Alvesson and Stefan Sveningsson. (2003) 'The great disappearing act: Difficulties in doing 'leadership,' *Leadership Quarterly* 14: 22.

Brigid Carroll and Lester Levy. (2008) 'Defaulting to management: Leadership defined by what it is not,' *Organization* 15: 21.

21. Manfred R.F. Kets de Vries. (1994) 'The leadership mystique,' *Academy of Management Executive* 8: 73–92, esp. 75.

22. Calas and Smircich (1991), 575.

23. Alvesson and Sveningsson (2003), 1435–1436.

24. Sharon. Turnbull. (1999) 'Emotional labour in corporate change programmes: The effects of organizational feeling rules on middle managers,' *Human Resource Development International* 2: 21.

25. Tina Kiefer. (2002) 'Understanding the emotional experience of organizational change: Evidence from a merger,' *Advances in Developing Human Resources* 4: 39–61. Stjepan Mestrovic. (1997) *Postemotional society.* Thousand Oaks, CA: Sage. John Van Maanen and Gideon Kunda. (1989) '"Real feelings": Emotional expression and organizational culture,' *Research in Organizational Behavior* 11: 43–103.

26. John Van Maanen. ('1985) 'Spinning on symbolism: Disquisition,' *Journal of Management* 11: 119–120, citing Heidegger.

27. Randall Collins. (1993) 'Emotional energy as the common denominator of rational action,' *Rationality and Society* 5: 27.
Erika Summers-Effler. (2002) 'The micro potential for social change: Emotion, consciousness, and social movement formation,' *Sociological Theory* 20: 19.

28. Gary Gemmill and Judith Oakley. (1992) 'Leadership: An alienating social myth,' *Human Relations* 45: 16.

29. Sharon Turnbull. (2002) 'The planned and unintended emotions generated by a corporate change program,' *Advances in Developing Human Resources* 4: 16.

30. Summers-Effler (2002).

31. Bobby McFerrin, (1988) 'Don't Worry, Be Happy,' album. New York: Simple Pleasures EMI.

Part V

Visualization

The chapters in this section have a particular focus on the values, emotions and spirit of HRD. They start in 2002 with Gary Mclean speaking at the first conference of the Asian Network about his view of future trends in HRD from a global perspective. Have these trends been realized nearly ten years later? With a focus on the individual, similar to David Megginson in Chapter 14, Rob Poell, speaking a year later, puts forward the vision that are organizations should be there to make people happy. He examines this notion, and proposes areas for further study. In contrast, Monica Lee, in 2004, adopts a macroscopic view and argues that HRD cannot be cocooned from global changes such as those in the climate, technology and population. Finally, both for this section and the speeches in the book, K. Peter Kuchinke brings together the twin threads of human flourishing and global trends that have woven through each section, in his speech in 2010.

19 Human Resource Development
Trends from a Global Perspective

Gary McLean

This chapter contains the keynote which began with asking several questions about what the field of HRD, globally, might look like in five years (of course, this timeframe has now passed). This was followed with discussion about the ongoing process of exploring the definition of HRD and the factors, globally, that seem to influence how it is defined differentially in different parts of the globe. A process was then outlined for how one might approach answering the questions related to a future of HRD. A future search conference held sponsored by AHRD and ASTD, with the intent of describing HRD in 2005, was described and critiqued. Finally, some guesses were offered about the "future" (now the past) in the following areas: Organizational Leadership; Public Responsibility and Citizenship; Work Systems; Employee Education, Training, and Development and; Employee Well-being and Satisfaction. Trying to foretell the future is always a dangerous game, especially when revisiting it 2-3 years after that future was to have happened. This keynote began a number of keynote explorations in which the "predictions" have been updated and trends explored.
(1st Asian HRD conference, Bangalore, India, 2002)

CONTEXT

The first Asian conference of the Academy of Human Resource Development, held in Bangalore, India, October 27, 2002, was the setting for this presentation. For some reason that I do not understand, the topic of "HRD Trends" has proved to be a very popular request for me in Asia. Perhaps this is a reflection of the relative immaturity of the field in Asia. Perhaps it is an effort to apply to services what Asia has shown to be very effective within manufacturing–taking ideas or products developed elsewhere and improving on them.

It has also struck me as strange that this request comes to me, as an inhabitant of the Americas, to tell Asians what trends are within their continent. This particular presentation differs from others in that the request was for me to focus on global trends, not just trends in Asia. And, perhaps anecdotally,

I have been well positioned to respond to such a focus given my extensive involvement in HRD around the globe. I have argued elsewhere[1] that there is a need for more focus on indigenizing HRD theory, research and practice. While this cannot be done in a vacuum, I believe strongly that there is a need for cultures (or countries, as the case may be) need to focus on their context. They need to do this in today's world in a global context, but they cannot simply copy what others are doing and expect that to make them successful.

Clearly, there are significant problems in writing an article on trends and possible futures when written nine years later. But perhaps this article can serve as an indicator of how well trends can (or cannot) predict futures, or, perhaps more accurately, how well I was able to rely on trends to predict what was then the future but is now the present.

THE PRESENTATION

When I was asked to make this presentation, the premise presented to me was to look at global trends in human resource development (HRD) and to project from those trends to the future. There are, however, two problems I faced in working with this premise. First, there is an assumption in the premise that what works and may be appropriate globally may not apply in any specific organization or even a specific country. Second, we live in a dynamic world in which change does not occur in a linear fashion. So, the challenge for today is, how am I going to move from what I see as current trends in global HRD to future scenarios when the past may no longer predict the future? Working with these limitations, my next task was to ask myself, what questions would I like to know the answers to looking five years out? And here is what I came up with:

- Will HRD exist as a discipline?
- What will HRD look like?
- What roles will it play?
- Will there be greater alignment between HRD and organizational strategy?
- What will be the technological impact on HRD?
- What expectations will exist of HRD professionals?
- Are we facing accreditation, certification and even licensure in the field?

Many of these questions are not likely to be answerable from current trends. A favorite quote of mine, source unknown, states: "The secret of forecasting the future . . . is to keep one's feet on the ground and one's head in the clouds." And that was my challenge.

In this presentation, then, I will organize my projections about how current trends will influence HRD's future by focusing on clusters of activities in which we typically find HRD involved.

WHAT IS HRD?

The definitional question of what constitutes HRD has been with us almost since we have started talking about HRD as a field. The purpose of this presentation is not to explore this question in depth—that belongs to another presentation—but, at least in the US, Weinberger contributed to the discussion by gathering major definitions currently in use.[2] Earlier, McLagan, under the sponsorship of ASTD (the American Society for Training and Development), had developed a model allocating the three major areas of Training and Development, Organization Development, and Career Development to HRD.[3]

This model and Weinberger's summary, however, did not resolve the apparent tension between HRD for performance and HRD for learning, a dichotomy that appeared to exist in Weinberger's summary of definitions. Another problem with the discourse on the definition of HRD is that most of the discussion was from a US-centric perspective. In an attempt to resolve both of these problems, we (McLean and McLean) undertook research in countries around the globe to identify how HRD was perceived in those countries, with the intent of creating a cross-national definition, as follows:

> "Human resource development is any process or activity that, either initially or over the long term, has the potential to develop . . . work-based knowledge, expertise, productivity and satisfaction, whether for personal or group/team gain, or for the benefit of an organization, community, nation, or, ultimately, the whole of humanity."[4]

Not only did this research provide input into an emerging definition of HRD that applied globally, but it also suggested that there were identified factors suggesting how definitions emerged within specific contexts to differ from other definitions. Such factors might include scope of activities covered in the definition, audience for whom the definition is intended, beneficiaries and providers of the HRD services, the economy in which HRD is taking place, government and legislative influences on HRD practices and the influence of HRD practices in other countries. These factors, of course, will influence not only how we define HRD, but also how we view its trends and predict its future, varying, as it will, from context to context.

HOW DID I IDENTIFY THE TRENDS AND FUTURE SCENARIOS?

As a member of the audience, you surely will want to know where I came up with my evidence to support my statements of trends and prognoses for the future. (As my eight-year-old granddaughter has already learned, the important question isn't "Why?" but "How do you know?") In a research article, I would label this section "Methods."

So, as with any research study, the first thing that I did was to look at the literature, both what I had available in hard copy and what I could locate online using "trends," "future," and "HRD" in conjunction. Because production time takes so long, published materials were not the most useful to me; they tended not to be very current. What I found to be most useful, however, was to send email requests to consulting, practitioner and academic friends around the world, asking them what they saw as being "not," or generating the most interest right at that member. This wasn't a systematic study, but it did provide current, dynamic information. I also asked them to guess about possible scenarios for the future and attempted to determine if there was a connection between the trends and the scenarios. I had my students brainstorm their ideas from their own experiences domestically and internationally. And, finally, I applied my own creative and cognitive processes to my own experiences to complete my lists.

Just a few years ago, ASTD and the Academy of HRD (AHRD) co-sponsored a future search conference.[5] The objective of the conference was to identify what HRD would be like in 2015. As a participant, I saw obvious differences in perspectives, especially between practitioners and academics, and also across countries. Nevertheless, the following common ground draft summary statements of what the participants expected (or wanted) HRD to be like in 2015 emerged:

- Create synergy between research and practice
- Leverage technology, but maintain human touch
- Strike healthy life balance
- Strive for humane workplaces
- Affirm intellectual capital
- Develop sense of social responsibility
- Embrace globalization/diversity
- Foster lifelong learning
- Manage knowledge and learning
- Develop partnerships and collaboration
- Develop critical and continuous learners

As mentioned earlier, it is extremely difficult to project the future. My own reactions during these sessions was that what emerged was more a statement of HRD values than it was a projection of what HRD was likely to have achieved by 2015. So, recognizing that a group of global experts could not project the future, nevertheless I will attempt to accomplish what this group could not do!! I need, then, to be clear that these are my own personal expectations of what the future is likely to be like for HRD, rather than representing what follows as based on a secret formula (or a crystal ball) for predicting the future.

ORGANIZATIONAL LEADERSHIP

One of the popular clinches of management and HRD is the concept of leadership. Yet, as I read research on leadership, the authors almost never make a clear distinction between leadership and management. I expect that, in the future, we will do a better job of distinguishing between leadership and management. If we do this, then we will see much less research that claims to be about leadership that focuses on the top tier of the organization. Rather, we will see affirmation of the concept that *leadership exists throughout the organization*, leading, then, to a much broader-based focus on leadership as existing throughout the organization, and, in practice, seeing leadership shared more broadly.

The growing popularity of scenario planning is a result, I believe, of management's seeing the need for *quick change and ongoing visioning*. In a dynamic world, the traditional approach to strategic planning (with one-, three-, and five-year plans that often find their way to the bookshelf, not to be reviewed again until the next year's planning cycle), does not serve organizations well. Leadership throughout the organization will need to respond quickly to changes in the environment.

We are familiar with the concepts of competition and cooperation. Increasingly, I see organizations needing to participate in co-creation or, a word that I find increasingly inspiring, *coopetition*, in which organizations cooperate when necessary, while continuing to compete with each other. This will require leadership that thinks more creatively than we usually find in organizations today.

Conflict is often seen as undesirable, and it is when the conflict is focused on the individual, and not on ideas. This leads to the widespread use of the label "conflict resolution" for the intervention to reduce conflict. Yet, conflict that is focused on ideas is actually desirable. In fact, it is idea *conflict that often leads to innovation,* a term that is being used more and more within organizations. Thus, leadership will focus on conflict management, rather than conflict resolution, growing innovation within the organization.

Ever since 1990, with the publication of "The Fifth Discipline,"[6] leaders were reminded of the importance of *systems thinking*, something that is much easier to write about than to do. The same is true of the urging of leaders to produce a *learning organization*, another concept that appears to be self-evident in writing, but for which it is almost impossible to point to a successful implementation. For organizations to continue to succeed in the future, their leaders will need to practice both concepts.

Global citizenship is not easy for many leaders. It requires broad experience in multiple cultures, and it requires leaders to give up their ethnocentric perspectives, at least as much as is possible. We are all outcomes of our culture, and it is not easy to set this perspective aside to become global citizens. Yet, in a world that is shrinking continuously, organizations whose leadership throughout the organization can think and act globally are more likely to be effective in a global economy than organizations with ethnocentric leaders.

Closely related is the *globalization of business*. While not a new concept (global trading, for example, has existed for thousands of years), it is clearly growing in the impact that it has, basically, on all organizations, both for-profit and not-for-profit organizations.[7] Organizations that embrace a global concept—for sales and for procurement—are likely to succeed in ways that those who continue to see their organization as limited in geographic scope are not.

Diversity has been a focus of HRD for some decades now, but, in general, we have not done a very good job of creating a truly diverse organization. And the degree to which we have succeeded depends on the diversity variable and on the country context. India, for example, still struggles with issues related to class (with castes still impacting one's life), gender and religion. In the US, we have continuing issues related to age and sexual orientation, and, strangely, given the laws in place, gender. Illegal immigration also causes emotionally negative responses. Many countries in Europe are struggling with racism resulting from immigration and the mobility of labor across borders. Those countries that are most able to incorporate true diversity across many variables are likely to have companies that are more successful than they would be without diversity. The movement toward such expanded diversity must come from leadership throughout the organization.

The time is coming, because of economic demands and demographic shifts in countries, when we will likely see extensive *delayering of management*. Middle managers, in particular, are likely to become targets for elimination. Supervisors, too, may become a target if Deming's counsel for supervisors to become coaches and trainers, rather than controllers,[8] is not followed.

Out of the growing attention to knowledge management, I expect that we will see leaders in organizations *leveraging intellectual capital*, with real-time capture of knowledge. Given the aging populations in many countries, this will be especially important as baby boomers approach retirement. Traditionally, these people retire with no record of what they know and have learned in their position pre-retirement. When this happens, and this knowledge is not passed on, those left behind will have to rediscover what their elders discovered earlier—a very inefficient way to learn about subjects that have been acquired by earlier workers. This process will go beyond IT capturing information, but it will incorporate general systems thinking, including creation, storage, retrieving, sharing and using information stored.[9]

Finally, leaders in organizations, but also in government, will need to have a shift in value structures; economic growth has been the dominant, and often only, metric for the well-being of a country and its economy. But this cannot continue indefinitely, especially if humanitarian concerns dominate so that the earth's resources are more evenly spread across the globe. Furthermore, with concerns about the environment and global warning, *economic growth*, as we have known it, *can no longer be required (or expected) for success*. I once worked with a CEO whose yearly strategic plan was simple—grow the company by 30 percent—and this was repeated year after year after year. I tried to suggest that such a goal could not be continued indefinitely. Mathematically, this metric would quickly lead to impossibly large numbers and eventually approach infinity. But this CEO did not want to hear this. Sure enough, just a year after my advice was given, the company hit the top and began a rapid decline. It has never quite recovered to the point it was at when it had a choice of looking at its goals in a different way. I don't know what the new exact metric might become—maybe it will be measured in terms of societal development or the happiness of its population. But, whatever it is, it will be a major change for organizations and countries to make. This observation leads naturally to the next section.

PUBLIC RESPONSIBILITY AND CITIZENSHIP

As mentioned in the previous section, organizations are increasingly under pressure to participate in the movement of the *greening of the environment*. As we become increasingly aware globally of how business and industry are negatively impacting the environment, there are increasing expectations among customers and the public, generally, that organizations must participate actively in turning around the negative impact of business practices on the environment in reducing the carbon footprint and reducing the use of non-renewable resources. Sustainability has become an important value within HRD as we provide leadership in our organizations. It may be difficult for HRD to respond to this challenge, however, unless we step up to the strategic table of our organizations where we can have an impact on decisions influencing sustainability.

Beyond their impact on the environment, businesses have been under attack for the many high-visibility incidents of highly unethical behavior. Such behaviors have caused highly emotional responses from the public. As a result, it is hoped that businesses will learn that *ethical behavior* can become a business strategy to improve market share and to attract highly talented employees.

However, because of the violations of public trust that have occurred so frequently, businesses are experiencing increasing *public scrutiny*. Even the appearance of unethical behavior can be detrimental to the reputation of an organization, with the potential of having a negative impact on the business itself. Again, the role of HRD in this process will be negligible unless HRD has established itself as meaningful in the strategies and practices of the organization.

A cynic might conclude that the recent emphasis on *corporate social responsibility (CSR)* has occurred as a counter-balance to the potentially negative impact of less than acceptable ethical behaviors. Furthermore, a cynical response is that organizations use CSR as a marketing tool. For example, Target Corporation, a major discount retailer in the United States, donates 5 percent of its pre-tax profits to community organizations. When you walk into a Target store, there is a large banner announcing this practice. Is the company really committed to helping the organization, or does it hope that more people will shop at the stores if customers know that a percentage of what they spend will go to their community? If this is not the case, then the ethics of such behaviors may be called into question by stockholders of the organization.[10] For whatever reason, it is anticipated the CSR will increasingly create mutually shared community partnerships between for-profit companies and not-for-profit community organizations.

Strangely, in some ways, there is increasing conversation about *spirituality in the business setting*. We might think about this as the "Coming of the Spiritual Age." In the US, this is a difficult concept because of the clear separation of church and state. So those writing about spirituality in the workplace make a real effort to distinguish between religion and spirituality. Such spirituality might be reflected in providing time for yoga,[11] reflection,[12] meaningful work and work-life balance,[13] among others.

WORK SYSTEMS AND PROCESSES

Many of the definitions of HRD include a focus on processes or work systems, and process improvement is a major organization development intervention. This section, then, will focus on work systems or work processes.

The difference in what top executives are paid and what entry-level employees are paid is a major indication of how employees are viewed and valued in an organization. The greater the pay gap, the less valued employees are in the organization. The US, in contrast to some other countries, like Japan, has enormous pay gaps, and they are continuing to increase. If productivity is to continue to grow, and if employees are going to feel valued, then this *pay gap must be reduced*. I would argue, back to an earlier point, that the enormous pay gap that exists in the US is one more example of unethical business practices. I hope that we will begin to see a movement in this direction.

In countries with low power distance,[14] there tends to be *minimal distinction between workers and managers*. However, in mid- to high-power distance cultures, there is considerable distinction between workers and managers, not only in pay, but also in prestige, recognition, power, input into decision making and so many other ways. However, as Deming indicated,[8] the people who know the most about the work systems are those who are working on those systems, the entry-level workers. Thus, it is likely that the fewer the distinctions between workers and managers, the safer and more productive the work environment is likely to be.

In efforts to equalize relationships within an organization, it is expected that there will be greater *sharing of risk-taking and rewards* through programs such as profit sharing or gainsharing.[15] Organizational learning[6] encourages employees to take reasonable risks; when the results are less than desired, employees are then encouraged to learn from those failures. Employees, under this premise, should be rewarded rather than blamed for failures if they learn from those failures. On the other hand, when they succeed, employees should share in the benefit that accrues to the organization.

When such organizational learning is implemented, in order for employees to share in the risks, *employee-empowered decisions* must be possible. Thus, supervisors and managers will need to become more effective at delegating the decision-making process to those employees who are in the best position and who have the greatest knowledge to make good decisions.

Just as employees need to be empowered in their decision making, so also must units within the organization be empowered. This will result in a greater number of *small, autonomous business units* within the broader organization. This argues for decentralization, a long-standing debate within organizational studies. However, because of the need for greater flexibility and speedy decision making, in my consulting experience, I am seeing more and more organizations making this decision, in spite of then giving up some efficiencies that come from the standardization of processes that comes from centralization.

Just as I projected delayering in the management levels, I also see a *reduction in the workforce.* There are a couple of reasons for this. First, the demographics of many countries, as suggested earlier, is resulting in more older citizens and fewer and fewer new workers, because of declining birth rates in many countries. Second, there continues to be a bias in preference of investing in technology rather than in people. I remember in my graduate working reading Buckminster Fuller's[16] and B. F. Skinner's[17] works, both of which suggested that much of our society is based on make-work; if society chose, we could have equal productivity with only 5 percent of our adult population working, as we currently define work. If this is accurate, and it well may be, than we could experience significant reduction in the workforce without sacrificing productivity. As we know, however, society is not likely to accept a 95 percent unemployment rate, even if an equitable economic plan could be developed.

In spite of the continuing interest in the use of competencies for the selection of employees, and the continuing preference in many countries for selecting employees from university programs perceived to be highly rated (or from the university from which the interviewers or management graduated), I expect that there will be increasing reliance on *employee selection based on inherent characteristics.* The need is to have employees who can continuously retool and can acquire new skills quickly as processes or conditions change quickly.

Intellectual capital will grow in importance in recognition of the losses of high numbers of retirees. As a result, there will be a *continuing, emerging understanding and importance of knowledge management.* We still do not know how to do knowledge management very well. The most difficult aspect of knowledge management has been getting people to be willing to share the knowledge that they have. We also have not yet figured out well how to transfer tacit knowledge. These will continue to challenge us in the future.

Brainpower industries (now known as the knowledge economy) will demand that *countries improve their educational systems* and increase the number of students acquiring higher and technical education. Many countries, even the so-called developed countries, have significant problems with their educational systems, and many who need a high quality of education do not receive it. Furthermore, there are many discrepancies between the education needed in the market and the education acquired. In many developing countries, it is not yet common to find students graduating from secondary school, and the quality of the education received is poor. This situation must change for the welfare of individual students, emerging workers and the country itself.

In spite of the emotional response to immigration, often tied to racism, we will find greater *mobility of work and workers*. We already see this in, for example, the European Union where there is freedom of movement for the purposes of work. But we also see it in the extensive illegal immigration that occurs globally. As for the mobility of work, we see the extent to which this is happening through outsourcing, and, when there has been dissatisfaction with the outsourcing, insourcing. Initially, this happened primarily in the IT and call center industries. But it has now evolved to include higher education and medical care, as examples of some industries with high pay and high educational expectations.

With the economic crisis of 1997, especially in Asia, we saw a marked move toward less *long-term employment and more contract workers*. Because of the flexibility that this provides to business, it is probable that we will see this trend continuing. Job security, as expected in some industries and in some countries, is likely to continue to disappear. Unions, which are already on the decline in many countries, will continue to lose their power and may, in fact, even disappear.

Finally, in the face of continuing emphasis on capturing and documenting processes, for the purposes of standardization and training, we will need to have *employees who can accept ambiguity and chaos*. We live in a world that is ambiguous.[18] The dynamism of the business community and the globalization of business all call for employees who are able to make decisions themselves, without having to be told exactly how to respond or how to perform their jobs. In this sometimes chaotic world, we need employees who can operate effectively in ambiguous situations.

EMPLOYEE EDUCATION, TRAINING AND DEVELOPMENT

How do we develop employees to meet the criteria suggested previously in this presentation? Training and development have always been the primary function within HRD. As a result, it should not be surprising that they take one of the major sections for my focus.

One way to improve the educational system, as mentioned previously, would be to *improve academic-business partnerships*. If businesses can do a better job of communicating their needs to the academic community, suggest ways to develop the necessary skills, provide the technology on which potential employees need to be trained and provide internship opportunities to students, it is reasonable to assume that businesses would acquire better prepared employees and would need to spend less time and fewer resources in training employees as they come on board. It is also possible to assume that academic institutions can take more responsibility for continuing education to meet the needs faced by employees with outdated skills.

Another change that we can expect is increased *pressure for self-development*, forcing employees to use their own time, not work time, to develop and upgrade their skills. Businesses have increasingly looked to self-development as technology (the next point) has evolved to support such self-development.

Technology will become the primary method for training, greatly increasing the expectation of self-development. E-learning will also save money for businesses in reducing travel time to training sites, reducing the costs for training centers and providing training only for those who need the specific training.[19] While there remain questions about the effectiveness of online training, there seems to be no way its growth will be slowed.

Another impact of technology and self-development is that we will be in a better position to *customize training* to meet learner needs. When we offer training in a classroom site or even online and require everyone to complete the training, we are not doing a very good job at meeting individual needs of learners. Rather, we treat them as if they all have the same level of skills and need the same level of skills. The reality, however, is that each learner starts at a different place and needs to emerge from the training with different knowledge and skills. Customizing the training will be more effective and more efficient, benefitting both learners and the organization.

In spite of the great difficulty we have in evaluating training and development,[20] it seems inevitable that *the pressure for accountability will grow*. Calls for return-on-investment (ROI) continue to increase, in spite of the fact that it is impossible to establish cause and effect relationships to determine ROI. We will need to continue to work at establishing better systems-wide evaluation systems to meet the demands of management for having better evaluation systems.

EMPLOYEE WELL-BEING AND SATISFACTION

HRD has, as one of its objectives, to create a corporate culture that is supportive of employees' well-being and creates job satisfaction. As for future employment circumstances, we are likely to make some gains but also experience some losses.

Advances are likely to occur in telecommuting or telework.[21] What we know is that working in the home actually increases productivity; some estimates put the increase at as much as 50 percent. In addition, it adds to the greening of the environment by reducing commuting and the pollution that is caused by such transportation. Furthermore, it is particularly advantageous for parents with child care responsibilities. With continuing developments in technology, working off-site is becoming increasingly viable.

Benefits packages will become more complex and individualized. Given the diversity of the workforce, the needs of individuals are often vastly different. Having one set of benefits that apply to all employees can be inefficient and not meet the needs of employees very well. The growing popularity of cafeteria approaches to benefits is likely to continue to grow, giving employees much more freedom to select benefits that meet their needs, while keeping the cost of benefits the same for each employee.

As the employee base in a company decreases, and as intellectual capital becomes more important to organizations, there will be greater *recognition that humans are the organization's most valuable resource*. Once this recognition occurs, it is reasonable to expect that organizational cultures will change to reflect this value that businesses assign to employees.

One way to reflect this greater recognition of employee value is to find ways to *share company ownership with employees*. This was suggested earlier with profit-sharing or gainsharing opportunities for employees. But there can be more aggressive forms of ownership offered to employees through stock ownership.

In part, because employees are more valued, but also because of the complexity of the workplace and the competitive environment globally, there will be real efforts to provide *creative, innovative and challenging work*. Not only will this create a more satisfying work environment for employees, but it will also result in competitive advantage for the organization.

On the downside, there are likely to be fewer employees working longer hours. Because organizations will have a difficult time finding the expertise needed for their business, they will maintain a smaller employee base, but they will want these employees to work longer hours. For those who are fortunate to be employed, this could be an advantage because the extra hours can result in higher incomes. But, as there will be *fewer opportunities for those who are technologically and functionally illiterate*, the overall unemployment rate will be higher in communities and in the nation. This is likely to be an ongoing situation that will not improve. Our expectation of relatively low unemployment rates is probably outdated.

As business become more global, there will be *opportunities, and even expectations, of global mobility*. For those who seek international experiences, this will be a positive thing. But, for those who are not wanting instability in living situations, or for those in dual career relationships, this could be a very difficult expectation.

As one way of meeting the reduced needs for a workforce, there is likely to be a *reduction in retirement age*; yet, because of increased life expectations, *people will work for more years*. (This is one that I got very wrong. Because of budget problems and reduced entries into the workforce, retirement ages are actually increasing.) In the US, today, 70 percent of those who have reached retirement age continue to work in some sort of job, although often at much lower pay than before they retired.

Employees will take charge of their own career development. I'm not sure how new this really is. Career development is one aspect of the traditional triumvirate of HRD that we have not done very well, and businesses have typically spent little time and few resources on assisting employees in their career development. Nevertheless, it is becoming more explicit that businesses expect employees to take charge of their own careers. This is a little contradictory in relation to the increasing emphasis that businesses are placing on mentoring and coaching, two common career development interventions.

RETROSPECTION

It is interesting, almost ten years after making this presentation, to consider the accuracy of the projections that were made. Surprisingly, at least to me, many of those conditions I anticipated have, in fact, occurred. And those that have not occurred seem to be reasonable expectations of what is still likely to happen at some time in the future. But perhaps that's just wishful thinking, as a reflection of my own values and hopes for the future of HRD. This exercise makes evident the difficulty of separating objectivity from subjectivity, if those words even have meaning in such an undertaking.

What is obvious, and cannot be argued, is that the future is inevitable; what that future will be is, at least in part, dependent on how well we lead the development of the human resources that will be affected by that future.

NOTES

1. Gary N. McLean. (2010) 'The need for indigenous theory and practice in human resource development in Thailand,' *NIDA HROD Journal* 1–19 (Thailand).
2. Lisa Weinberger. (1998) 'Commonly held theories of human resource development,' *Human Resource Development International* 1: 75–79.
3. Patricia A. McLagan. (1989) *Models for HRD practice: The models.* Alexandria, VA: American Society for Training and Development.
4. Gary N. McLean and Laird D. McLean. (2001:322) 'If we can't define HRD in one country, how can we define it in an international context?' *Human Resource Development International* 4:(3) 313–326
5. Joe Willmore. (1999) 'Four HRD scenarios of the future,' *Training and Development* 53(12): 38–41.
6. Peter M. Senge. (1990) *The fifth discipline: The art and practice of the learning organization.* New York: Currency/Doubleday.
7. Thomas M. Friedman. (2000) *The Lexus and the olive tree.* New York: Anchor Books.
8. W. Edwards Deming. (1986) *Out of the crisis.* Boston: MIT Press
9. Ikujiro Nonaka. (2001) 'The knowledge-creating company,' *Harvard Business Review* (November–December): 96–104.

10. Max B.E. Clarkson. (1995) 'A stakeholder framework for analyzing and evaluating corporate social performance,' *Academy of Management Review* 20: 92–117.
11. S.K. Chakraborty. (1986) 'The will-to-yoga: Key to better quality of work life,' *Vikalpa*: 113–124.
12. Donald Schön. (1983) The reflective practitioner: How professionals think in action. London: Temple Smith.
13. Reid A. Bates, Timothy Hatcher, Elwood E. Holton III and Neal Chalofsky. (2001) 'Redefining human resource development: An integration of the learning, performance, and spirituality of work perspectives,' in Oscar A. Aliaga (ed.), *Academy of Human Resource Development Conference Proceedings*, Baton Rouge, LA: AHRD.
14. Geert Hofstede. (2001) *Culture's consequences: Comparing values, behaviors, institutions, and organizations across nations.* San Francisco: Sage.
15. Eunsang Cho and Gary N. McLean. (1998) 'Gainsharing plan for the 21st century Korean economy,' *Human Resource Development International* 1: 189–206.
16. Buckminster Fuller. (1973) *Operating manual for spaceship Earth.* New York: Penguin.
17. B.F. Skinner. (1948) *Walden two.* Indianapolis: Hackett.
18. Paul Tillich. (1965) *Systematic theology, vol. III: Life and the spirit, history and the kingdom of God.* Chicago: University of Chicago Press.
19. Allison Rossett and Ken Sheldon. (2001) *Beyond the podium: Delivering training and performance to a digital world.* San Francisco: Jossey-Bass/Pfeiffer.
20. Gary N. McLean. (2005) 'Examining approaches to HR evaluation: The strengths and weaknesses of popular measurement methods,' *Strategic HR Review* 4(2): 24–27.
21. Susan Madsen. (2001) The Effects of Home-based Teleworking on Work and Family Conflict. Unpublished doctoral dissertation, University of Minnesota, St. Paul.

20 Toward a Self-Conscious, Self-Critical and Open-Minded Discipline of HRD

Rob Poell

Are people there to make organizations happy or are organizations there to make people happy? Some authors in the field of human resource development (HRD) seem to argue for the former. This chapter puts forward the proposition that the latter is especially true, which has implications for what HRD should be about. HRD refers to organizing individual and collective learning processes aimed at the development of both employees and the organization as a whole.

The workplace is a crucial, albeit not the only, context for such learning processes to be produced. HRD thus conceived can lead to sustainable competitive advantage, as employees who are facilitated by their organization to engage in personal and professional development both on and off the job will be better able to contribute to organizational success. In other words, happy people can make organizations happy as well.

The chapter also looks at the academic status of HRD and at the relationship between HRD and HRM. In order to bring forward the research base of HRD, especially the knowledge about employee development in different organizational contexts, the chapter proposes three topics for further systematic study: 1) employee learning paths, 2) learning structures in the workplace, and 3) actor learning strategies.
(4th International Conference on Human Resource Development across Europe, 2003)

CONTEXT

The ideas expressed in this chapter originate from a keynote lecture held at the "National HRD Debate," organized in April 2003 by the Dutch Association for HRD Professionals (NVvO, currently named NVO2). An earlier (and much shorter) version of the chapter appeared as a guest editorial in the journal *Human Resource Development International*.[1]
At the time, the HRD community (well, at least the academic HRD community) was trying to recover from Monica Lee's "refusal to define HRD"[2] and from McLean and McLean's rhetorical question "If we can't define

HRD in one country, how can we define it in an international context?"[3] In other words, the questions of what is HRD and can/should HRD be defined at all were high on everyone's agenda—at least in the academic world.

I had always been intrigued by the notion that key leaders in the field were not able or willing to define what that field was. It somehow seemed a contradiction in terms. This is not to say that I had all the easy answers—on the contrary. It did however spark my interest in thinking about the essence of this thing we call HRD. And it led me to articulate my own vision of the field, which is the core of what my speech dealt with.

WHAT IS HRD ABOUT?

Are people there to make organizations happy or are organizations there to make people happy? Some authors in the field of HRD seem to argue for the former. I'd like to think, however, that the latter is especially true. An important, if not the most important, reason for organizations to exist and remain in existence is providing people with a purpose, with meaning, with development opportunities.

This has implications for what I believe HRD should be about. Learning is central to HRD. Whereas "organizing learning" is the shortest fitting description of what I think HRD is, in my somewhat more elaborate definition HRD refers to organizing individual and collective learning processes aimed at the development of both employees and the organization as a whole. Both 'learning' and 'organizing' need to be understood in a very broad sense.

'Learning' is a process of gaining experiences that contribute to expanding one's action repertoire. Some of these experiences are designed specifically for certain types of learning to occur; for example, the ones created by HRD practitioners during training courses or education programs. Most learning-relevant experiences, however, occur naturally and unintended.[4] The workplace is a crucial, albeit certainly not the only, context for such learning processes to be produced.

'Organizing' is bringing a certain coherence to activities taking place. It does not necessarily involve formalizing, structuring or systematizing those activities. There is a tendency in (especially larger) organizations to do the latter—think, for example, of the popularity of competence management systems. However, for people to be able to make sense of their work and their environment, helping them bring some more coherence to their activities often works better than forcing them into a formal structure or system that someone else has created. Organizing is something that people can usually do quite well themselves, and what constitutes 'coherence' should not be defined by others either.

HRD can therefore be conceived as organizing individual and collective learning processes aimed at the development of both employees and the organization as a whole. This can lead to sustainable competitive advantage, as employees who are facilitated by their organization to engage in personal and professional development both on and off the job will be better able (and willing) to contribute to organizational success. In other words, happy people can make organizations happy as well.

HRD AND HRM

My vision of HRD is closer to the learning paradigm than to the performance paradigm in the eternal debate about learning versus performance as main goal of HRD, although I like Yorks's pragmatic stance as well, where he argued that both goals are valid and presuppose one another.[5] My emancipatory stance has been informed by a background in (adult) education, although my current affiliation with a department of Human Resource Studies has done little to reduce the focus on organizations as providers of learning and development opportunities to people.

I have nevertheless been amazed at the high walls that seem to separate the academic HRD discipline from a related field, namely, Human Resource Management (HRM). In my view, HRD is complementary to HRM, which focuses on positioning employees in the right place, whereas HRD emphasizes developing both the employees and their organizational context. The practical fields of HRD and HRM, again, presuppose each other in their perspectives on the employment relationship and should be studied accordingly. In academia, however, the two disciplines remain highly separated in almost all respects. HRD and HRM have different journals, different conferences, different gurus, different textbooks and so forth. Let us have a look at what Dutch, British and American HRM textbooks have to say about HRD and the other way around.[6] The first conclusion must be that most HRD textbooks make hardly any reference to HRM, with the exception of some British authors. The second conclusion is that most HRM textbooks still limit HRD (a seldom-used term) to training and development, presenting the knowledge developed in the 1980s about training needs assessment, design, delivery and evaluation without much reference to insights developed since about learning organizations, workplace learning, communities of practice and so forth. I do think this situation is now improving, but there definitely remains a wide gap between the two academic disciplines.

This rather unfruitful divide between HRD and HRM prevents an integrated understanding (and furthering) of employee development as facilitated by the organization of work, the organization of learning and the organization of people management in companies and institutions.[7] The learning and development aspect of management and organization will only become more important in future, which makes rigorous HRD research crucial within the larger HR domain. HRD could do a better job at learning from insights developed in the HRM discipline and integrating those into its own thinking.

THE ACADEMIC STATUS OF HRD

If the HRD discipline is to help organizations make people happy, what is its current academic status? With all major HRD journals still pursuing SSCI accreditation, one wonders whether they are qualitatively different from more general (HR) management and organization journals that publish HRD articles. A few years ago, with two colleagues I presented a state of the art within the HRD discipline based on a content analysis of 268 studies conducted since 1990.[8] HRD articles published in what I consider to be the two main HRD journals (*Human Resource Development Quarterly* and *Human Resource Development International*) were compared to HRD articles published in twelve mainstream management and organization journals (including *Administrative Science Quarterly, Academy of Management Journal, Human Resource Management, Journal of Applied Psychology, Organization Science, Journal of Management Studies, International Journal of Human Resource Management* and *Journal of Organizational Behavior*).

The authors found few differences in theoretical perspectives and methodological practices between these two groups. The main differences found were between articles published in US and European journals, with the former focusing more than the latter on the individual level, on performance as an outcome of HRD and on the universalistic treatment of theory. In terms of methodology, HRD articles in US journals were much more often quantitative than qualitative, the opposite being true of the European ones. Interestingly, quantitative studies in HRD journals were on average less rigorous than those in mainstream journals, whereas qualitative studies in mainstream journals were less rigorous than those in HRD journals. The analysis showed an image of HRD as a young academic discipline working on theory development, mostly through qualitative research and not-too-advanced quantitative studies, with a concern for the practical application as well as context dependency of theoretical frameworks.

THREE MAIN TOPICS FOR RESEARCH

At the outset of this speech, I made it clear that employee development is a crucial focus and highly worthwhile goal in itself for organizations. I feel strengthened in saying this by authors and good colleagues in the field who seem to share similar ideas, for instance, Victoria Marsick, Karen Watkins,[9] Lyle Yorks,[10] Laura Bierema,[11] Tara Fenwick,[12] Stephen Billett,[13] Joseph Kessels[14] and Ferd Van der Krogt.[15] My stance is informed partly by idealistic or emancipatory motives and partly by strategic or economical reasons. I am convinced that organizations failing to offer ample opportunities for development, to invite the innovation potential of their employees and to capitalize on their knowledge productivity, in the long run will miss out on major competitive advantage. Moreover, in my experience it becomes much easier to understand and explain such phenomena as, for instance, 'resistance' to organizational change, 'dysfunctional' organization processes, 'lack of commitment' on the shop floor and 'unmotivated' employees using a framework that takes into account (primarily) the ideas and interests of employees in learning and development processes. There is, however, a great need for more and better research in this relatively under-addressed area.

In order to bring forward the research base of HRD, especially the knowledge about employee development in different organizational contexts, I propose three topics for further systematic study: (1) employee learning paths, (2) learning structures in the workplace and (3) actor learning strategies.

Employee Learning Paths

Those who want to focus on employee development should at least gain insight into the learning activities they undertake in (and outside!) organizational contexts. The concept of a learning path was introduced by Van der Krogt to indicate the combination of learning-relevant experiences gained by an individual employee in relation to his or her organization. The learning path is that part of the complete learning career that takes place in an organization and is relevant to the employee's professional development. It is a continuous process mostly created by employees themselves, albeit usually far from explicit. Crucial in the definition of the learning path is the meaning attributed by the employees themselves, not by what

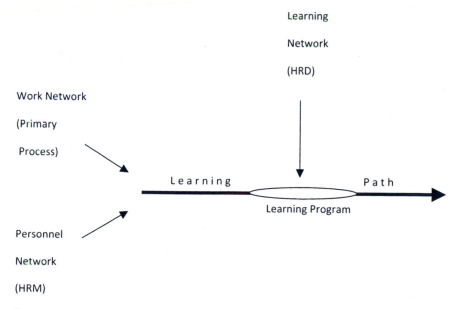

Figure 20.1 The learning path of an employee influenced by three types of network.

the organization, managers, HRD or HRM deem important (although the former will almost never be completely dissociated from the latter).

With Van der Krogt I stipulate that every employee creates and follows his or her own learning path, a specific combination of a learning theme with particular learning activities, in specific learning contexts using certain learning facilities. Qualitative research among nurses showed, for instance, that one nurse sought new knowledge about patients with respiratory problems by finding the latest literature on the subject and translating it in new protocols for the nursing ward together with a subject matter expert; another nurse discussed the question of how to help family members deal with terminal patients together with her direct ward colleagues. Nurses' learning paths in a sample of approximately 100 were found to be independent of departmental or organizational characteristics and clustered around four types: the self-directed, formal-external, social-emotional, and information-oriented learning paths.[16]

Van der Krogt shows that an employee's learning path is influenced by (at least) three organizational networks: the work network (where the primary process of the organization takes place), the personnel network (where employees flow through specific jobs from entering to leaving the organization: HRM) and the learning network (where employee learning is organized: HRD); see Figure 20.1.[17]

The work network has a major impact on the learning path of an employee, because the content and organization of his or her work determine in large part the learning and development potential of the job. The personnel network can also exert substantial influence on a learning path, for example, by offering (or withholding) particular learning facilities, by creating career paths, by rewarding specific behaviors or by performance management systems. The only way, however, in which the learning network can affect a learning path is by offering learning programs that the employee may wish to take part in as part of the learning path. This will occur when an employee consciously decides to learn with others about the theme of the learning path for a certain period. . If this is not the case, or if the quality of the learning program is unsatisfactory to the employee, then he or she will most likely view the learning program (e.g., a training course) as an unwelcome disruption of the learning path.

Research among HRD practitioners showed that they barely take into account the learning paths of employees participating in their learning programs, even though this is an important pre-requisite to their effectiveness.[18] It can be expected that managers, who are made more and more responsible for coaching their employees' learning processes, will find it even harder than HRD practitioners do to take into account the learning paths of individual employees. This makes research into the characteristics, outcomes and supporting of learning paths highly relevant. Key research questions around learning paths include:

1. How do employees create their learning paths?

2. In what ways do employees' learning paths differ?
3. How do learning paths differ among work types and among occupations?
4. What is the relative influence of the work, personnel and learning networks on employees' learning paths?
5. How do employees (implicitly) use the three networks to create their learning paths according to their own action theories?

Learning Structures in the Workplace

A second major topic for future research is the learning structures that exist within an organization. Learning structures are the relatively stable characteristics of the learning network that emerge from learning-relevant processes organized by several actors over time (as indicated in the upper right-hand part of Figure 20.2).[19] They consist, for example, of the material facilities for education and training, the tasks and responsibilities around learning and employees' opportunities for social support in the organization.

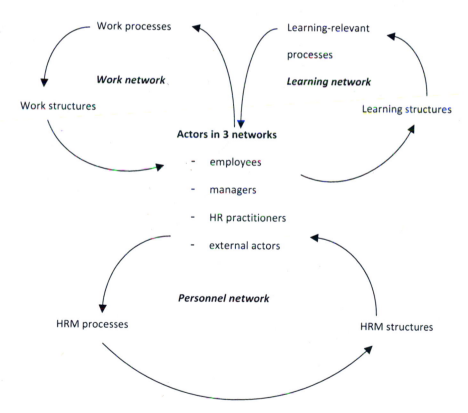

Figure 20.2 The learning-network theory: actors organize three processes from three networks.[20]

Learning structures represent a considerable part of the context in which employees create their individual learning paths; they constitute the explicit learning opportunities offered to them by their organization, besides the more implicit development and growth potential provided by the primary work and HRM processes (see the upper left-hand and lower parts of Figure 20.2, respectively).

What Figure 20.2 shows is that all three networks are organized by actors (in different constellations) and can influence one another. Structural characteristics coming out of one process (e.g., task divisions that have emerged from the work process, or a competence management system out of the personnel process) can, through the actors involved in several networks, impact upon processes in another network (e.g., the learning activities that an employee wants to engage in together with some team members). Although in my view employees are central to the organization when it comes to HRD, the impact they themselves can exert on the three networks varies and depends on their relationships with other relevant actors. Figure 20.2 presents an analytical framework intended to get a grip on these concepts and their relations, not only for theoretically driven researchers but also for employees and other actors in organizational practice wanting to strengthen the underpinnings of their HRD strategies.

Together with several groups of students, over the last few years I have worked on the validation of a questionnaire instrument to measure workplace learning structures (WLSQ), developed on the basis of the learning-network theory.[21] This instrument can be used by employees, managers

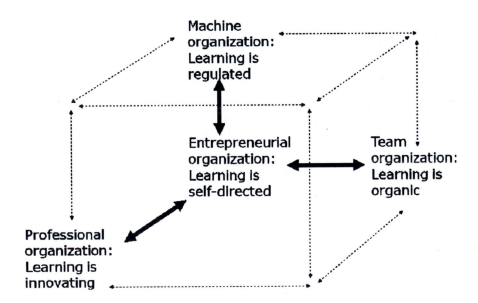

Figure 20.3   Four ideal-typical organizations and their dominant way of learning.[22]

and HRD practitioners to gain more insight into the learning potential offered by the workplace. The first results have shown empirical evidence for relationships between workplace learning structures, on the one hand, and the nature of work (e.g., high versus low autonomy), type of organization (e.g., machine versus professional bureaucracy), role conceptions of HRD practitioners (traditional versus modern), perceived opportunities for growth offered to employees, their motives to engage in learning activities and actual learning activities conducted, on the other hand.[23] The relationships found, however, were not always in line with expectation and in some cases otherwise hard to interpret. Further research into these areas is therefore much needed.

Figure 20.3 visually supports the expectation derived from the learning-network theory that each organization has a unique learning network, which can be described by its position on three dimensions (vertical, horizontal and external). The vertical dimension indicates the relationships between employees and management, the extent to which learning is organized hierarchically. The horizontal dimension concerns the relationships among employees themselves, the extent to which their learning relationships are tight. The external dimension stands for the relationships between employees and external actors, the extent to which employees are integrated within their profession (e.g., taking part in continuing education programs offered by their professional association).

Depending on its position on these three dimensions, the specific learning network of an organization will be located (relatively stably) somewhere within the three-dimensional space presented in Figure 20.3. Also, four ideal-typical learning networks can be distinguished, which will never be found as such in organizational practice but do enable a diagnosis of which learning-network type (or combination of types) is dominant in a specific organization. As the theoretical models of the learning-network theory and their empirical applications have already been well documented in literature,[24] I will not elaborate on them here.

More insight into the structural characteristics of learning networks can help organizations better attune their learning processes to the workforce; individual employees can benefit as it helps them reflect on the context of their learning paths and brings alternative options into view.

Key research questions around learning structures include:

1. In what ways do learning structures differ across organizations (and types of organization)?
2. How do learning processes organized by actors over time lead to learning structures, and to what extent do these in turn impact upon the learning processes (especially learning paths) undertaken by them?
3. How do the work and personnel networks impact upon the learning structures of an organization and upon the learning paths conducted by employees?

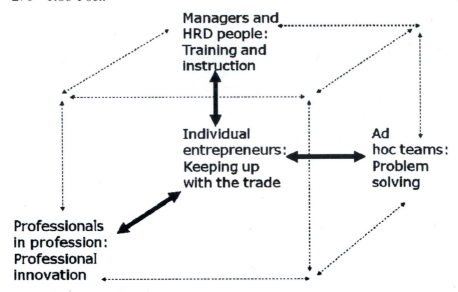

Figure 20.4   Dominant actors and ways of learning in four ideal types.[25]

Actor Learning Strategies

The third key theme I should like to put forward for future research is the strategies employed by employees, managers and HRD practitioners to organize learning processes in different work types and occupations. One of the core ideas in thinking about learning networks is that employees, managers, HR practitioners and other (external) actors each have their own interests, positions and beliefs on the basis of which they act strategically so as to change the existing learning network in the direction they desire. The organization, especially the three networks visualized in Figure 20.1, is therefore regarded as an arena where different actors fight, cooperate and negotiate to acquire scarcely available (learning) resources. Each of the four ideal-typical organizations and learning networks in Figure 20.3 has a specific dominant actor; given the immediate context of the work and personnel networks, the dominant actor has apparently been able to place a major emphasis on the learning network in the organization (see Figure 20.4).

In machine organizations, management is the dominant actor, employing staff departments (e.g., HRD) to translate its policies to learning programs (especially through training and instruction programs). Team-based organizations have teams as dominant actors; learning and working are integrated in these collective entities through problem solving. The dominant actor in professional organizations is the profession itself, through its professionals working in the organization; by participating in professional innovation these professionals learn and adapt their work to newly developed academic insights. In entrepreneurial organizations the individual employee is the dominant actor, responsible as such for organizing his or her own work, learning and career. This typology also has been widely published before;[26] therefore I will not go into detail any further here.

Earlier research had already shown that in the "arena" interactions among actors, managers preferred to use strategies taking the learning network in the direction of the vertical ideal type; employees were found to prioritize strategies consistent with the professional learning network (allowing them to develop competencies that are independent of the organization where they happen to work); HRD practitioners, perhaps on the basis of their own professional expertise, espoused a preference for the problem-solving types of learning prevalent in the team-based organization; however, they claimed the only way to get a foot in the door with management was to conform to their machine-organization-oriented strategy and hence propose neatly defined training and instruction approaches; once they had a green light from management, the HRD practitioners started introducing some of the problem-solving elements they deemed much more effective.[27]

Important research questions around actor strategies are:

1. Which strategies exactly do different actors use to shape the learning network in accordance with their interests, positions and beliefs?
2. To what extent do these strategies differ across organizations (and types of organization).
3. How exactly do the interactions among actors (fight, cooperate, negotiate, et cetera) around learning play out, and what determines who gets to play the dominant role?
4. To what extent do these interactions differ across organizations (and types of organizations)?
5. What impact do the work and personnel networks have on the actor strategies and their interactions in the learning network?

THE EMANCIPATORY IDEAL OF HRD

The body of knowledge to be developed around these four themes is ultimately intended to help organizations make people happy. So why do I think HRD is a (perhaps even *the*) discipline that can fulfill this emancipatory ideal? First, there is continuous debate in the field; there is no fear of critical reflection on the nature of the field. Second, perspectives from very diverse authors, backgrounds, countries and parts of the world are welcomed in the field. And third, many authors seem to care deeply about making organizations happier places as well as making people happier employees.

Why, however, has the emancipatory ideal not been realized yet? There are lots of reasons for that; please allow me to be self-critical of HRD above all (another healthy characteristic of the field, incidentally). First, some debates in the field deal with *either-or* questions (e.g., learning or performance, theory or practice) rather than appreciating the *and-and* nature of such dichotomies. Second, we could do a better job at systematically building on previously developed HRD knowledge, including HRD-relevant knowledge from other fields, for instance, HRM, organizational anthropology, organizational behavior, organizational sociology, political sciences, et cetera. And third, the HRD field often suffers from a severe lack of self-confidence, apparently feeling the need to emulate more established and appreciated disciplines. There certainly is no need for complacency; however, it is much more fruitful to systematically keep building our research and knowledge base than to complain about not being taken seriously by the outside world.

THE AFTERMATH: HOW HAS THE FIELD DEVELOPED SINCE?

In the final part of this chapter, I'd like to reflect on the speech recounted above. The "National HRD Debate," where these ideas originated, started a debate in the Netherlands about the status of HRD and its relationship to HRM, which have traditionally been separated disciplines in the Netherlands. It culminated in a thematic issue of the Dutch-language quarterly HRD magazine *Develop* (Poell, 2006). Most authors agreed that HRD and HRM should move in each other's direction, which could of course be primarily another sign of how far the two disciplines are still apart. Unfortunately the number of HRD academics in the Netherlands has since further decreased (dangerously close to being extinct, actually), and not much progress has been made nationally as a result.

Internationally, fortunately HRD is a flourishing discipline, with its own Academy, four journals (beside a number of related ones that do not have HRD in the title), a rapidly increasing number of scholars reaching full professor positions, a good (and also growing) number of authoritative textbooks and so forth. There are also, however, continuing and strong pressures on HRD as a field, mainly within the universities where HRD scholars work: HRD departments having to merge with (more or less) related departments, an increasing emphasis from deans and administrators to publish only in SSCI journals (still largely meaning: non-HRD journals, although HRDQ was accredited in early 2011) and lack of opportunities for promising young HRD scholars to get to influential positions (implying the average age of HRD academics keeps getting higher).

The basic debate on the nature and boundaries of this thing called HRD nevertheless continues, although to my impression not quite as fiercely as, say, a decade ago. Perhaps this is a result of the greater self-confidence within the HRD community itself that comes with the positive developments mentioned just now. So where are we now as a field? It is my belief that, if HRD manages to stay at least as open-minded as it is now, and to grow some more in terms of being self-conscious and self-critical, its future looks bright. At the same time, there still is a large need for much more and better research on the three topics presented in my speech: (1) employee learning paths, (2) learning structures in the workplace, and (3) actor learning strategies. If the emancipatory ideal that I think HRD should strive for is to be brought any nearer in the years to come, these three topics appear to be a useful—and crucial—place to start.

NOTES

1. Rob Poell. (2007) 'W(h)ither HRD? Towards a self-conscious, self-critical, and open-minded discipline,' *Human Resource Development International* 10(4): 361–363.
2. Monica Lee. (2001) 'A refusal to define HRD,' *Human Resource Development International* 4(1): 327–341.
3. Gary McLean and Laird McLean. (2001) 'If we can't define HRD in one country, how can we define it in an international context?' *Human Resource Development International* 4(3): 313–326.
4. Victoria Marsick and Karen Watkins. (1990) *Informal and incidental learning in the workplace.* London: Routledge.
5. Lyle Yorks. (2005) *Strategic human resource development.* Mason, OH: Thomson South-Western.
6. Rob Poell. (2006, December 15) 'Personeelsontwikkeling in ontwikkeling: Naar een werknemersperspectief op Human Resource Development' [Developing human resource development: Towards an employee perspective on HRD], inaugural lecture as Professor of HRD, Tilburg University, Netherlands, Rotterdam: Performa.
7. Based on Rob Poell and Ferd Van der Krogt. (2010) 'Individual learning paths of employees in the context of social networks,' in Stephen Billett (ed.), *Learning through Practice: Models, Traditions, Orientations and Approaches,* Dordrecht: Springer, 197–221.
8. Arzu Wasti, Rob Poell and Nigar Çakar. (2008) 'Oceans and notions apart? An analysis of the U.S. and European human resource development literature,' *International Journal of Human Resource Management* 19(12): 2155–2170.
9. See Victoria Marsick and Karen Watkins (1990).
10. See Lyle Yorks (2005).
11. Laura Bierema. (1996) 'Development of the individual leads to more productive workplaces,' in Robert Rowden (ed.), *Workplace Learning: Debating Five Critical Questions of Theory and Practice,* New Directions for Adult and Continuing Education 72: 21–30. San Francisco: Jossey-Bass.
12. Tara Fenwick. (2003) *Learning through experience: Troubling assumptions and intersecting questions,* Malabar, FL: Krieger.
13. Stephen Billett. (2001) *Learning in the workplace: Strategies for effective practice.* Crows Nest, Australia: Allen & Unwin.
14. Joseph Kessels and Rob Poell. (2004) 'Andragogy, social capital theory, and implications for human resource development,' *Advances in Developing Human Resources* 6(2): 146–157.

15. See Rob Poell and Ferd Van der Krogt (2010).

16. Rob Poell and Ferd Van der Krogt. (2009, February 19–22) 'An empirical typology of hospital nurses' individual learning paths,' in Jennifer Calvin and Shani Carter (eds.), *Top Ten Best Papers from the Academy of HRD International Research Conference Held in Panama City, FL, USA,* Bowling Green, OH: AHRD.

17. Rob Based on Poell and Ferd Van der Krogt. (2003) 'Learning-program creation in work organizations,' *Human Resource Development Review* 2(3): 252–272.

18. Rob Poell and Ferd Van der Krogt. (2007) 'Tailoring learning programmes to every-day employee learning: Customisation strategies of HRD practitioners in health care,' in Sally Sambrook and Jim Stewart (eds.), *Human Resource Development in the Public Sector: The Case of Health and Social Care,* London: Routledge, 239–252.

19. See Rob Poell and Ferd Van der Krogt (2010).

20. See Rob Poell and Ferd Van der Krogt (2010).

21. Rob Poell, Ferd Van der Krogt and Marjolein Berings. (in preparation) *Development and validation of the Workplace Learning Structures Questionnaire (WLSQ).*

22. Based on Rob Poell, Geoff Chivers, Ferd Van der Krogt and Danny Wildemeersch. (2000). 'Learning-network theory: Organizing the dynamic relationships between learning and work,' *Management Learning* 31(1): 25–49.

23. For an overview, see Rob Poell (2006).

24. For instance, see Rob Poell, Geoff Chivers, Ferd Van der Krogt, Ferd and Danny Wildemeersch (2000).

25. See Rob Poell, Geoff Chivers, Ferd Van der Krogt, Ferd and Danny Wildemeersch (2000); see also Rob Poell and Ferd Van der Krogt. (2006) 'Workplace learning reviewed: Confronting the rhetoric with empirical research,' in Jan Streumer (ed.), *Work-related Learning,* (Dordrecht: Springer, 71–94.

26. See Rob Poell, Geoff Chivers, Ferd Van der Krogt, Ferd and Danny Wildemeersch (2000); and Rob Poell and Ferd Van der Krogt (2006).

27. Rob Poell. (1998) Organizing Work-related Learning Projects: A Network Approach. Doctoral thesis, University of Nijmegen, the Netherlands.

21 HRD
Looking to the Future

Monica Lee

This chapter looks at three areas of global change (climate, technological and population) arguing that these are interconnected and will alter all of our lives. It explores the way in which boundaries are collapsing, leading to the delimitation of the geographic, national, economic, social and personal. I suggest that as the world changes so does the nature of organizations and thus of HRD. This chapter examines the implications of this for the future of HRD and suggests that in an increasing complex world, we need to adopt a holistic perspective through which we can examine the inter-relatedness of the global and local; the economic and the social; the individual and the community. From this I suggest that we also need to consider the need to guard and enhance notions of identity; the development of ethical approaches, and; the role of professional bodies.
(3rd Asian HRD Conference, Seoul, Korea, 2004)

THE CONTEXT

This keynote speech was given at the 3rd Asian Conference of the Academy of HRD: HRD in Asia: Harmony and Partnership, Seoul, Korea, 2004. The Asian conferences were becoming well established and very well attended—particularly by participants from the Asian and American networks. Ever since I first established Human Resource Development International in 1998, it has concerned me that our conception of HRD, of our own practice and of the theories we adopt, is bounded by what we know and are comfortable with. At the time, climate change was seen as a fringe concern in the UK, and potentially 'un-American' in the US. Very few people were bothered about it, and the common conception of HRD was as divorced from it as it was from other potential global changes. Of course, these issues are now well known, and I would write it differently, were I doing it now—but remember—this was 2004. In this account of the presentation I have removed the slides with 2001 climate change data as they are superseded by more recent events and no longer add to the argument—other than to show how scarily accurate some of the early predictions were.

THE PRESENTATION: HRD: LOOKING TO THE FUTURE

Hello. My initial question is 'what does the future hold?'–and what are the implications of this for us? I shall lay out my thoughts from a Western perspective, and would be very interested to know whether an Asian perspective leads to the same conclusions. I see three main areas of change in our lives: climate change, technological change and population change, which taken together, send a message about the future of HR. I will examine each area of change separately, before building a picture of what I think they jointly imply.

1) Climate Change

The Intergovernmental Panel on Climate Change (IPCC)[1] was established in 1988 to assess the scientific, technical and socio-economic information relevant to understanding the scientific basis of risk of human-induced climate change, its potential impacts and options for adaptation and mitigation. The panel states that 'most of the warming observed over the last 50 years is attributable to human activities,' and that 'human influences will continue to change atmospheric composition [of greenhouse gasses] throughout the 21st centaury.' It reports that under business as usual assumptions the global average surface temperature is projected to increase by 1.4 to 5.8 degrees C over the period 1990 to 2100. To place these expected changes in context, the difference in average temperature between the last Ice Age and the present warm period is only between five and seven degrees Celsius (EAE), and such changes occurred over the span of many centuries. Climate change will not necessarily be detrimental to all—some might benefit. For example in Canada, should sea ice thin in the Northwest Passage to the extent that its use by commercial shipping becomes practical, then there could be increased movement of goods and people through Canada's Arctic leading to economic and population growth in the northern communities. It has also been predicted that the area in which I live, cold and windy Lancashire, is likely to either become more like Spain, or if we lose the Gulf Stream, to become like Greenland!

Although the macro movements are well established, the micro predictions based upon them are more speculative Natural variations of climate, such as drought over continental areas and severe cyclonic storms, are likely to increase in frequency, magnitude and extent, thus increasing the exposure of people to such risks in the coming years.[2]. In the case of Central America, there is evidence that hurricane frequency is increasing,[3] which begs the question of whether poor nations can recover sufficiently before the next hurricane occurs. In addition, changes in the spatial distribution of extreme weather events and other adverse climatic conditions are also possible, meaning that human communities that historically have not experienced them may do so in coming years. For example, there is evidence that in the past two decades the occurrence of tropical storms abruptly increased in the northern parts of the traditional Atlantic hurricane region.[4] The IPCC states that changes in precipitation patterns over many continental areas—increased frequency of droughts and intense rain and snowfalls—appear likely to occur in coming decades. As with tropical storms, these changes may be expected to vary both spatially and temporally. Such changes also lead to rapid changes in the ability to produce crops and feed livestock, and in patterns of disease.

Political implications of managing a global issue like this are enormous, including deliberations on who is responsible, and how it should be managed.[5] Whether or not we believe human activity is responsible for the change, we have to accept that it is changing, and quickly, that current changes will have a profound effect on us and; that as these changes intensify, so will their effects.

Climate Change and Migration

Vulnerability to climate change is a function of both degree of exposure to climatic conditions and the adaptive capacity of the population at risk.[6] In some cases whole communities are at risk. For example, current projections of sea level rise and increased tropical cyclone intensity may make many small island states uninhabitable.[7] In others, households within the same community can vary, in relation to attributes such as wealth, gender, age and ethnic origins.[8] Consequently, the risks of migrations occurring as a result of extreme weather events, droughts and changing climate conditions are growing. The rich and those with natural resources can adapt. More often, however, countries lack the social and technical ingenuity needed to adapt successfully to the shortages they face. Many vulnerable populations (especially in developing countries that lack the capacity to cope with recurrent droughts and associated food shortages) will be left with little option but to adopt migration as their adaptive strategy.[9]

For example, regional climate change scenarios for China in the decade beginning 2020 suggest that climate change would result in decreased precipitation across northcentral and northeastern China.[10] Combined with an expected increase in average temperatures, this would lead to drier soil conditions and reduced crop yields, especially where crops cannot be irrigated. Such conditions, should they materialize, would have adverse effects on agriculture and increase pressure on rural dwellers to migrate to other areas in search of economic opportunity, thereby magnifying the existing flow of migrants from the countryside to Chinas cities and lead to socio-political unrest. In northwestern China, where unrest currently exists between Han migrants and predominantly Muslim Uighurs, regional climate models suggest that average precipitation and soil moisture availability may actually increase in coming decades. Such conditions would have a positive effect on average crop yields and likely increase the attractiveness of this region for new migrations of Han Chinese farmers.

This would in turn increase the potential for conflict between the traditional Uighur population and Han migrants.

The IPCC discusses detailed scenarios for other nations, and it is well worth having a look at this web site. My point here, however, is that where national governments can provide minimal assistance to rural populations during hard times, and where technologies such as groundwater irrigation are not possible or beyond the means of most farmers, migration will continue to be used as an adaptive strategy so long as remaining in situ during times of drought and crop failure brings the risk of starvation upon families.

The typical demographic characteristics of those most adversely affected by the conditions in the source area—landless people, rural poor, the sick or elderly, those with little family support are not the typical migrants—these are most often young males. For an intact nuclear family to undertake migration, particularly over long distances, requires access to money, family networks and/or some other form of assistance or capital of above-average education.[11] In other words, it is the most vulnerable that get left behind.

Climate Change and Conflict

All large-scale predictions of the effects of climate change involve scarcity and shift in renewable resources such as water, fertile land, wood for fuel and fish stocks.[12] Such scarcities may act to strengthen group identities based on ethnic, class or religious differences, most notably by intensifying competition among groups for ever-dwindling resources. At the same time, they can work to undermine the legitimacy of the state and its capacity to meet challenges. As the balance of power gradually shifts from the state to the challenging groups, the prospects for violence increase. Such violence tends to be subnational, diffuse and persistent.

2) Technological Change

We are in a time of unprecedented technological growth.[13] Key areas of advance seem to be biotechnology, nanotechnology and new intelligence technologies. Biotechnology and nanotechnology offer the prospect of new ways to enhance our living conditions and longevity (a point I shall return to later), and to add to the adaptive strategies that can be employed in climate change by those who possess such technological advances. I shall, however, focus more on new intelligence technologies here, and particularly upon data management and communications technology. These areas have revolutionized the Western world. Not only can we handle, make sense of and store more and more information, we can also structure it differently. It is no longer necessary to have long chains of command. In theory, anyone in an organization can have access to senior management, and vice versa.

Technological change is leading to increasing open access—with concomitant need for extra security of 'hidden' data.

Similarly, communications are opening up relationships across the world. The web, email and messaging are available to any with access to the systems. Information, facts, data and knowledge are available to any who know how to look for them. With wireless technology , alongside reductions in size of equipment and increase in battery power and with alternative energy sources, we able to work from anywhere and at any time.

Communications are not just about one to one. We have also seen rapid change in mass media with television and video phones revolutionizing how we see the world. Small cameras and live data feed mean that we can have minute by minute exposes of 'world news.' We are in the middle of conflict and catastrophe as it happens—and the fight for ratings means that news has also to be entertaining. The news and our information sources have become economic and political tools in which the news has become a form of live soap opera, played around sound bites. We learn to ignore the bits that don't interest us, and we become hardened to the many tales of woe and the plight of other communities. To some extent, in having to be so selective, we also become more, rather than less, biased in the face of so much information.

Media can distort 'reality' as can we. We no longer need to be 'ourselves' but can adopt alternate personalities—aliases—as in chat rooms, etc. What is 'real' becomes distorted. For example, my son is cycling on his own around Europe for four months, and he explained that he had been so long on the road that he was unsure what reality was—but *at least he has email to keep him in touch with real life.*' There is, of course, a more sinister side to 'reality' and aliases—from spam to illicit transactions to national security issues. Thus mobility and technological change bring us face to face with issues of reality and representation; personal freedom and traceability; Individual rights versus public safety.

Social Division

Large parts of the population do not have access to technology and have far greater concerns than communicating with friends in a chat room—and even if they did have the equipment they would not be able to power it, and probably would not be able to use it—we the privileged assume world-wide literacy. Although I have concentrated on information technology here, the situation is the same with biotechnology and nanotechnology. The technological elite can benefit from the enhanced lifestyle and longevity that goes hand in hand with innovations in these areas. The technologically impoverished cannot. These factors mean that the divide between the technologically elite and others is increasing steadily as technology advances. The technologically elite have the world in their hands—virtually crossing geographical and national boundaries as much as they wish. Their world and that of the technologically poor are separating at a tremendous and accelerating rate—and this difference is around every aspect of the nature of their existence.

3) Population Growth and Decline

I shall now turn to the third main area of change—that of population growth and decline.[14] The 1998 projection for the population of the world in 2150 was nearly 10 billion, but 2002 figures have revised that estimate, such that in the best case scenario (as of Sweden) it will be just over 5 billion, and thus below our current population of 6 billion, and in the worst case scenario (as of Italy) it will drop to just over 3 billion. It has been said that Europeans are drifting toward collective national suicide by the end of the 21st century.'[15] The US presents an anomaly because in 1999 although the fertility rate of non-Hispanic whites was slightly over 1.8 (and thus less than the 2.1 needed for stability) it has a high migrant population, and the Hispanic fertility rate was nearly 3.0 (which is expected to have a compounding effect in future years). Therefore US total population rate is expected to continue to grow, but the nature of the population is expected to change. The difference in immigration rates and fertility rates between Europe and the US shows up dramatically in the forecast age distribution. The current median age in the US is 35.5 years and 37.7 years in Europe. In the year 2050 this will be 36.2 in America and 52.7 in Europe.[16]

Pearce[17] argues persuasively that within the technologically rich world population trends are linked to the cultural diffusion of ideas influencing caregiving and career progression. On the farm even young children are an asset, minding the animals and helping with the harvest. In cities it's a different story: children are more likely to be an economic liability. They need looking after and educating; the spread of TV has opened many women's eyes to wider aspirations and modern birth control methods have increasingly liberated women from the home and child rearing. Not having children has become a statement of modernity and emancipation. Countries such as Sweden that have managed to stabilize their birth rates have done so because of their supportive child care policies, About half the jobs held by Swedish women are part-time, crèches are near universal and paid parental leave lasts for a year. All this is unheard of in Italy, where only 12 percent of paid women have part-time jobs, and in Eastern Europe, where fertility rates have plunged since the collapse of communism wrecked state-funded support services for families. If Pearce is right, and our population in 2150 will be somewhere between 5 and 3 billion, depending whether the Swedish or Italian model comes to the fore, then the decisions that are made now about how best to support those that care for dependents will have a long-term and fundamental effect upon humanity, as well as upon the future of each nation.

Most of this focuses on the technologically rich world, but it is worth noting that high child mortality and the probability that a man will die early act to lower the age at which women would choose to marry: those in occupations with high probabilities of dying young marry earlier than those with a lower likelihood of dying young, and higher expected child mortality encourages earlier marriage.[18] By 2025, only two of the industrialized democracies will be among the twenty most populated countries in the world. Nigeria will be more populous than the US, Iran more populous than Japan, Ethiopia's population twice that of France.

The population is declining sharply in most of the technologically rich world. It is also growing older as people delay having children. The figures for the US indicate slight variation from this, linked to high immigration figures. The reasons for the ageing population appear to be enhanced expectations of longevity and a stable environment. Those nations that have social support systems that enable caregivers to maintain employment are maintaining a low but steady birthrate. In contrast, in the technologically poor world, high child and male parent mortality are linked to early marriage and many children.

The changes I have described each hold strong implications for the way in which we construe the world in the future when considered individually—taken together we can build a picture of what that might be like

THE EFFECTS OF CHANGE

Shifting Boundaries

Perhaps the most striking change will be on boundaries. Geographical boundaries, such as shorelines, flood plains, and in some instances such as the Pacific Islands disappearing, whole areas, are going to shift with climate change. Maps will need to be redrawn. Similarly, as populations shift location national identity will be challenged. In some cases this will lead to conflict in support of maintaining such boundaries. More often, however, the shift is likely to be part of a political process as 'nations' absorb immigrants, who bring their own cultures with them. The ageing population means that skilled migrants will be welcome in many countries, which, otherwise, will not be able to maintain a sufficiently large workforce to support the children and those too old to work.

Changes in technology also mean that, at least for the technologically rich, the world becomes a smaller place—friends and work colleagues can be based in other continents and be just as close as if they were next door or were seen every day. There are few boundaries in the cyber world. This, also, erodes national boundaries, as people relate more freely across them. The boundary-less cyber world is also part of a different form of erosion of national boundaries—the economic one. Global environmental changes and associated negotiations over global resources, responsibilities and population shifts are going to require global political and economic responses, which in turn can already be seen to be eroding the legislative, political and economic boundaries of nation states. Similarly, the power and economic influence of large multinationals challenge those of some nation states, and ignore national boundaries.

As boundaries become eroded, so ownership and identity can become contested. These factors lead to the anticipation of increased conflict that is likely to arise—between the haves and have-nots, between residents and immigrants—within nations and between nations for power, resources and around local, national and global issues; and between governments and multinational bodies, and also between governments and dissatisfied populations.

Shifting Nature of Organizations

It used to be said that an employee of a Japanese organization had a job for life—yet, increasingly, what was meant by 'organization' in this case, was the composite of the senior management who would not be sacked. The many other parts of the organization (insofar as they contributed to the goals of the organization) were outsourced, and thus did not count. This pattern can, in fact, be seen in all organizations, in which the boundary of membership is usually arbitrarily drawn to include those on the core payroll, yet includes many individuals and satellite businesses that contribute to the organization's viability. As boundaries become more uncertain, so the nature of the traditional organization becomes eroded. Large bureaucracies are being replaced by cross-national organizations with a wide net of satellite organizations providing outsourcing.

Many manufacturing industries, including the computer industry, have seen large increases in productivity growth rates and have experienced a reduction in average establishment size.[19] Technological change means that outsourcing is likely to become the norm, with many more, smaller, innovative, entwined organizations that work for one another providing goods and services to whoever may want them across the world.[20] As such they will not have all the separate functional areas usual for traditional organizations, but in association with the flattening effect technology has upon communication and the chain of command, individuals and offices within such organizations are likely to be multi-functional—or internal portfolio workers.

Technology both eliminates jobs and creates jobs. Generally it destroys lower wage, lower productivity jobs, while it creates jobs that are more productive, high skill and better paid. Historically, the income-generating effects of new technologies have proved more powerful than the labor-displacing effects: technological progress has been accompanied not only by higher output and productivity, but also by higher overall employment.[21] Therefore the focus in these firms will be on skilled work, and the need to upskill workers. Those without the skills will increasingly fall by the wayside. The pattern of work will also change, with high flyers being particularly mobile—in a UK survey, 40 percent said they intended to leave their employer within two years and only 7 percent expected to stay more than five years.[22] The focus will be, increasingly, on how to manage high turnover, attract skilled staff and retain those already employed.

Retaining Skilled Staff

Low pay is a dissatisfier, but high pay won't keep people around by itself. The best people don't stay for the money alone. They stay because they are engaged and challenged by work that makes them better at what they do, and they will stay if they have a good relationship and communication with their immediate boss. Having a supportive supervisor is significantly related to increased schedule flexibility, higher job satisfaction, fewer serious problems with child care, reduced work to home interface and reduced stress.[23] Both tenure and productivity are determined by their relationship with the immediate supervisor. 40 percent of those who rated their supervisor as 'poor' were likely to quit versus 11 percent who rated their supervisor as 'excellent.' Such findings bring a challenge to managers concerned with their 'bottom line.' Turnover is expensive and sensitive supervisors would appear to be a key.

Flexible Working

One of the main employee benefits identified by Coyne, Coyne and Lee was the ability to offer flexible work patterns. This will become increasingly important as the population ages, leading to a greater need for care and thus more flexible work conditions for caregivers. By 2050 the European population over the age of 65 is projected to be equivalent to 60 percent of its working age population (40 percent in the US). Therefore Europeans will face an urgent need to care for the elderly whereas the US is more likely to be focused on child care activities. In either case, however, flexible working patterns will be needed to support the care of dependents.

Flexible working is also helped by technological advances, particularly those linked to the ability to handle complex information more easily and at a distance. Organizations are now able to manage their internal statistics and systems more fluidly, such those of keeping track of flexible working, and a wide system of varied benefits no longer presents the logistical problem that it used to do. Similarly, because of advances in technology, organizations are now able to offer many of their employees the opportunity to work from home, for at least part of the time. In this way the home computer becomes the equivalent to a workplace terminal, and the interface between the two becomes transparent. It becomes a flexible package that lends itself to use by non-caregivers as well as caregivers. Flexible scheduling is among the most appreciated benefits because employers don't 'own' their employees' time, and the availability of such practices is expected to expand.[24]

Virtual Migration

Flexible working and technological advance also mean that 'home' can be a mobile concept, and parts of the 'organization' can be located across the world—as, for example, the rise of call centers in Bangalore which operate transparently, such that a person making a local call to a company in the UK does not realize that the call is actually being answered and managed by someone in India. This fundamentally changes the traditional notions of work and organization. Wherever they are located, skilled individuals can work for several organizations from across the world at the same time, and similarly, wherever they are located, adept organizations can call upon the services of skilled individuals from across the world.

Skilled workers need be no longer bounded by geography or loyalty—they can sell their human capital to those who offer the best packages of pay and benefits. Human capital can be seen as the knowledge that individuals acquire during their life and use to produce goods, services or ideas in market or non-market circumstances. Organizations, however, have been slow to realize the value of human capital, and slow to develop the skills to be able to evaluate it.[25] Human capital can be seen as an intangible asset of the organization, and is one that can be poached by other organizations and needs support and development to flourish.

We are moving into an era of physical migration and immigration (as people move to chase jobs and organizations attract employees from other countries) and also *virtual* migration and immigration. The social and political consequences of this have only just started to impact upon nations and have yet to be fully faced. There are also economic challenges. The state needs to find ways to tax and manage a highly mobile workforce that works, as needed, in other countries and that includes work from non-nationals on a piecemeal and irregular basis. Parts of such work, especially the technology-related parts, might also be hard to trace. Work-based contributions to the national wealth such as employment tax might well be hard to administer.

IMPLICATIONS FOR HRD: HARMONY AND PARTNERSHIP

HRD is at the core of the future, but needs to accept a wider role than its traditional 'function' of training and development. I have presented a picture a world with less clear boundaries, a kaleidoscope of cultures and skills, similar to that which I have touched upon previously, in which HRD is the glue of processes and relationships that holds the myriad perspectives together.[26] This is a world of movement, tension, conflict and lack, balanced by rewards for the small, skilled, flexible and technologically aware organizations that succeed by working in harmony and partnership with a wide and shifting selection of other organizations from across the world.

In this final section I shall look at what this might mean for HRD as we know it.

HRD as an Enabler

Technology enables workers to share knowledge and experience without limiting them to one location or time frame. It also enables the organization to manage the financial and scheduling data associated with the employees' work lives in a way that would not have been feasible twenty years ago. The logistical and financial challenges of managing employees with unusual work patterns can be minimized by the use of appropriate systems. Technology also helps each organization develop beneficial partnerships with others. Technology, therefore, helps establish the structures in which we work, but it is HRD that helps establish the harmonious relationships between employees (who might be spread across the world) and the organization, and between different organizations.

HRD needs to become a central part of the organization's strategy if it is to play a crucial balancing role in meeting the needs of the organization and the employees in the uncertain and flexible organization. For example, as the nature of work changes and becomes more fluid, so job descriptions which play an excellent part in a stable and more traditional organizational environment become outdated such that the job description can become an instrument of job limitation. The role of HR in negotiating different forms of job description that allow flexibility in the timing, location and nature of the work that is undertaken, while also protecting the needs and rights of each of the stakeholders, will be vital and challenging.

HRD needs to be at the center of creating an organizational environment that stimulates and values workers, that meets their needs such that it retains them in a marketplace where workplace benefits—including a nice supervisor—can outweigh the lure of a higher wage.

Future Skills

It is the highly skilled and technologically aware who will particularly benefit in the future. As the nature of work changes so HRD's core role in establishing the qualities and abilities required in successful employees and in promoting, developing and assessing these becomes essential.[27] Some of these skills will be job specific. Others will reflect the key role HRD has in helping develop the attitudes and values, commitment, motivation and involvement, without which the organization will be disjointed and inflexible. In other words, the organization's culture, from the CEO to the lowest worker, needs to reflect and support the notion of flexible working: '

HRD will also increasingly need to pay attention to areas such as cross-cultural awareness, diversity and conflict resolution. These areas will be needed both in terms of managing these within organizations and also as key skills that employees will need as they work flexibly across a range of situations as they seek harmony and partnership.

Individual and Ethical Aspects

In a world full of conflict, HRD practitioners and the organizations and people that work with come face to face with hard choices on a daily basis and within their own spheres of operation. For example, Tim Hatcher and I have spent some time exploring the dilemma at the core of HRD[28] in which HRD espouses and promotes democratic values in organizations that are, in essence, non-democratic. Therefore, merely by fulfilling their role HRD professionals are likely to come into conflict with others who are fulfilling the non-democratic managerial role assigned to them. HRD Professionals, therefore, need to be able to appreciate otherness, and to act politically and strategically—they also need to be able to act ethically and morally.

I have written elsewhere about the problems of working ethically as an HRD professional—despite the existence of ethical codes of conduct.[29] Such codes offer guidelines and suggested ways of working in a general sense, but are not written (and cannot be written) in a way that prescribes for every event. Furthermore, as the traditional form of organization, with its predictable environment and associated minimization of ethical challenge becomes replaced by flexible working, so the associated ethical challenge will increase. This increase will affect HRD professionals on an individual day-to-day basis, and it will also affect HRD as a profession.

HRD needs to engage with the personal side of its work, and to appreciate the belief systems that underlie it. It also, increasingly, will be asked to take a collective view on world events—for example, should HRD (as a profession, and HRD professionals individually) be encouraging nations and organizations to engage in protocols established by the Kyoto Treaty in the knowledge of the tremendous harm that will happen if this is not done? Large-scale interventions such as the adoption of political and ethical stances like this call for the involvement of the professional bodies.

The Rise of Professional Bodies

As geographical and organizational boundaries lose their rigidity, people are increasingly turning to their professional bodies to enhance their sense of identity at work and provide a sense of permanence. After all, individuals are likely to be members of one or more professional bodies all their working life, but may only be with a single organization for a few years. It is their profession that stays with them as they move from organization to organization; role to role and nation to nation. Professional bodies, therefore, are likely to become a more vocal champion of their members' needs and rights. They are also in a position to collaborate with, or act as mediator, between the organization, the individual and the state. Perhaps it is the profession, also, who is able to adopt the broader view—to express concerns about those who fail to leap the increasing skills and technology gap. Perhaps it is the professions who can foster ways of helping those who lack the resources or are less able to adapt to change.

There is another area in which the professions can play a vital role. As the workforce becomes more mobile and the nature of work more flexible, there will be an increasing need for benchmarking and being able to make sound judgments about the comparability of qualifications, attainment and provision. For example, with the help of all stakeholders, including the professional bodies, the UK has developed national systems of vocational and non vocational qualifications[30] and systems of rating higher and further educational provision, and in this way, qualifications become portable benefits—in principle the individual is not tied to company-specific training and the organization knows the exact standards the individual has achieved. If migrants can demonstrate that they have achieved the targets set, employers know their suitability for employment.

CONCLUSION

The University Forum for HRD played a role in establishing these ratings within the UK, and, along with many other bodies, is in the process of looking at comparative standards and ways of measuring these across Europe. This will be a long and complicated process—systems of education and assessment and their underlying philosophies vary considerably across Europe, but until such harmony is developed, and a common root of understanding is achieved, organizations will struggle to establish the foundations of their multiple partnerships.

I suggest that the same principle holds globally. As we develop systems of flexible interrelated organizations that can draw employees from across the globe, we need to establish some global understanding of what we expect such employees to be able to do. As with my discussion of HRD's role in facilitating organizations as they become more in tune with flexible working, so I suggest that we need to foster harmonious systems of expectation and ability. We then need to act as enablers—where possible helping those who might otherwise fall on the wrong side of the skills and technological divide to play their part in a world that is less predictable and has translucent boundaries, but which is, essentially, based around partnership.

One area that I have barely touched upon is the implications this scenario has for governments and policy makers. How do you govern such shifting populations? What of security, civic responsibility, taxation, social support and so on? HRD has a role to play in these as well.

What is certain to me, and it is something that I have expounded for many years—and was core to my founding of the journal *Human Resource Development International*, is that HRD encompasses considerably more than training and development. If HRD is to be an active and ethical agent in this new world in which the divide between the rich and the poor grows increasingly large, then HRD has to engage in areas such as politics and policy; law and economics; strategy and structures; philosophy and morality; and so on. HRD, itself, has to become a partner in the struggles of the world in order to promote its core aspirations of harmony.

THE AFTERMATH

Immediately after the speech there were lots of questions and everyone was quite engaged. Some people who had experience with developing nations identified with what I was trying to say, and recounted personal stories of their own. Despite this, it felt as if the majority of the audience didn't really know what to make of it. It was well received, but I wasn't sure I had got my message across. I had help, however. In 2006 I met some of my US colleagues again and they were now very enthusiastic about what I had said. . . . The documentary film *An Inconvenient Truth* by former US Vice-President Al Gore had been released and had taken the US by storm. As one person said—he hadn't really understood my speech until he had seen the film, and then it all made sense. HRD has a wider remit and we had to do something. Indeed—I had the idea for this book following that conversation—so much of what we say or do gets lost if it can't be captured in the normal format of the academic paper.

Since then, I have been asked to contribute to publications along similar lines.[31] I have also been invited to give keynotes at several conferences recently, spread around the globe, which focus on sustainability and responsible development. I have extended this speech with updated information, but also, my thoughts have shifted to pay greater consideration to interconnectedness and the nature of boundaries and their implications for HRD.[32] Toward the end of the speech, as given in 2004 and here, I focused on harmony and partnership because that was the aim of the conference, but I suspect the picture I painted even then was much more one of trying to find a path through dissention and conflict. Despite my Cassandra-like approach, I had not really expected the predicted changes to start happening so quickly. Since 2004 we have had several global emergencies—economic downturns; volcanoes, earthquakes and tsunami; droughts and floods; civil unrest and migration; the spread of illnesses and the need to manage changing demographics— each of these has started locally yet had global impact.

As the predictions made by bodies such as the IPCC come to hold true, even over such a short timescale, I remain concerned about our ability to meet the challenges ahead. I am pleased to see that these things are now being discussed—although I don't claim responsibility for this. Certainly, as far as climate change is concerned, Al Gore and the increasingly violent variations in the climate itself are much more powerful media than I! I do, however, like to think I have had some involvement in a greater widening and questioning of the way in which HRD and its responsibilities is perceived. 'Sustainable' seems to be the concept of the decade. This popularity holds a danger, in that it seems to me that at times people are now really talking about longevity: how can we manipulate the environment to make this company last longer?—thereby forgetting the wider picture; forgetting that the environment needs to last longer as well! Perhaps as more bodies such as CASSE[33] are established, the debate will become more encompassing. Until then we must be beware of reification—such that by labeling it we then no longer need to do anything about it!

NOTES

1. IPCC. (2001) '*Intergovernmental panel on climate change: Summary for policy makers*,' Available at www.ipcc.ch. (accessed 1stst September 2004)
2. These are already increasing—see WMO. (2003, July 2) 'World Meteorological Organisation press release,'available at www.wmo.ch. (accessed 1stst September 2004)
3. James McCarthy, Ozvaldo Canzani, Neil Leary, David Dokken and Kasey White. (2001) 'Climate change 2001: Impacts, adaptation and vulnerability,' Intergovernmental Panel on Climate Change, Geneva, Section 14.1.21.5.
4. Thomas Karl and David Easterling. (1999) 'Climate extremes: Selected review and future research directions,'*Climate Change* 42(1): 309–325.
5. Annie Petonsk, Daniel Dudek and Joseph Goffman. (2001) 'Market mechanisms and global climate change: An analysis of policy instruments,' in *Transatlantic Dialogues on Market Mechanisms*, Arlington,VA: Pew Centre on Global Climate Change. Lawrence Goulder. (2004) 'Induced technological change and climate policy,' Arlington,VA: Pew Centre for Global Climate Change.
6. Barry Smit and Olga Pilifosova. (2001) 'Adaptation to climate change in the context of sustainable development and equity,' in James J. McCarthy, Osvaldo F. Canziani, Neil A. Leary, Neil A., David J. Dokken and Kasey S. White, eds., 'Climate change 2001: Impacts, adaptation and vulnerability, IPCC Working Group II, Cambridge: Cambridge University Press, 877–912.
7. John Hay and Martin Beniston. (2001) Available at www.climatechange.gc.ca. (accessed 1stst September 2004)
8. George Clark, Suzanne Moser, Samual Ratick, Kirstin Dow, William Meyer, Srinivas Emani, Weigen Jin, Jeanne Kasperson, Roger Kasperson and Harry Schwarz. (1998) 'Assessing the vulnerability of costal communities to extreme storms: The case of Revere, MA, USA,' *Migration and Adaptation Strategies for Global Change* 3(1): 59–82. Susan Cutter, Jerry Mitchell and Michael Scott. (2000) 'Revealing the vulnerability of people and places: A case study of Georgetown County, South Carolina,' *Annals of the Association of American Geographers* 90(4): 713–737.
9. Norman Myers. (2002), available at *www.climatechange.gc.ca.* (accessed 1stst September 2004)

10. Barry Smit and Yunlong Cai. (1996) 'Climate change and agriculture in China,' *Global Environmental Climate Change* 6(3): 205–214. Fulu Tao, Masayuki Yokozawa, Yousay Hayashi and Erda Lin. (2003) 'Future climate change, the agricultural water cycle and agricultural production in China,' *Agriculture, Ecosystems and Environment* 95(1): 203–215. Panmao Zhai, Anjian Sun, Fumin Ren, Xiaonin Lui, Bo Gao and Qiang Zhang. (1999) 'Changes in climate extremes in China,' *Climatic Change* 42: 203–218.

11. James Gregory. (1989) *American exodus: The dust bowl migration and Okie culture in California.* New York: Oxford University Press.

12. Berel Rodel. (1994) 'The environment and changing concepts of security,' *Canadian Security Intelligence Publication*: Commentary no. 47. Robert McLeman and Barry Smit. (2004) 'Climate change, migration and security,' *Canadian Security Intelligence Publication*: Commentary no. 86. Fred Pearce. (2004) 'Climate change heralds thirsty times ahead for most,' *New Scientist* 2448: 16–17.

13. Joel Mokyr. (2002) *The gifts of Athena: Historical origins of the knowledge economy.* Princeton and Oxford: Princeton. University Press. Ronald Bailey.(2004) 'Why technology will be the defining battle of the 21st century,' available at *http://reason.com/rb/rb081303.shtml.* (accessed 1stst September 2004)

14. B. Coyne, Ed Coyne and Monica Lee. (2003) *Human resources, care giving, career progression and gender.* London: Routledge.

15. Peter Drucker. (1999) *Management challenges for the 21st. century.* New York: Harper-Collins Publishers, 44.

16. Ellen Hale. (2000, December 22) 'The greying of Europe has economies in jeopardy,' *USA Today*, p. 14A.

17. Fred Pearce. (2002July 20) 'Mamma Mia,' *New Scientist*: 38–41.

18. Berel Rodel. (1994) 'The environment and changing concepts of security,' *Canadian Security Intelligence Publication*: Commentary no. 47.

19. Matthew Mitchell. (2002) 'Technological change and the scale of production,' *Review of Economic Dynamics* 5(2): 477–488(12).

20. Michael Kelleher. (1996) 'New forms of work organisation and HRD,' in Jim Stewart and Jim McGoldrick (eds.), *Human Resource Development: Perspectives, Strategies and Practice*, London: Pitman.

21. William J. Baumol and Edward N. Wolff. (1998) 'Side effects of progress: How technological change increases the duration of unemployment," *Public Policy Brief No. 41*, Jerome Levy Economics Institute of Bard College, 7–30.

22. Andrea Poe. (2000, July) 'The baby blues,' *HR Magazine* 45(7), Alexandria, VA: Society for Human Resource Management, 78–84. Les Worrell and Cary Cooper. (1999) *Quality of Life: 1999 survey of managers' changing experience.* London: Institute of Management.

23. Chris Bourg and Mady Segal. (1999, summer) 'The impact of family supportive policies and practices on organizational commitment to the Army,' *Armed Forces and Society, New Brunswick* 25(4): 633–652.

24. Ken Lizotte. (2001, March) 'Are balance benefits for real?' *Journal of Business Strategy* 22(2): 32.

25. Duncan Brown. (2002) *Evaluating human capital.* London: Chartered Institute of Personnel and Development.

26. Monica Lee. (2003) 'The complex roots of HRD,' in *HRD in a Complex World*, ed. M. Lee, London: Routledge, 7–24.
    Monica Lee. (2004) 'Complex archetypal structures that underlie the "human condition,"' *Organisational Transformation and Social Change* 2(2): 49–70.

27. Jeff Watkins and Lynn Drury.(1999) 'New organisational structures: Skill implications for professionals,' *Human Resource Development International* 2(3): 181–204.
   Monica Lee. (1996) 'Competence and the new manager,' in Monica Lee, Hugo Letiche, Robert Crawshaw and Michael Thomas (eds.), *Management Education in the New Europe: Boundaries and Complexity*, London: Routledge, 101–117.
28. Monica Lee and Tim Hatcher. (2003) 'HRD and the democratic ideal: The conflict of democratic values in undemocratic work systems,' in J. Winterton (ed.), *International, Comparative and Cross-Cultural Dimensions of HRD*, ESC Toulouse: Toulouse,. ISBN 1–86220–149–8
29. Monica Lee. (2003) 'On codes of ethics: The individual and performance,' *Performance Improvement Quarterly* 16(2): 72–89.
30. Monica Lee. (2004) 'National human resource development in the United Kingdom,' *Advances in Developing Human Resources* 6(3): 334–345.
31. Monica Lee. (2007, June 27 and 29) HRD from a holistic perspective,' in David McGuire, Thomas Garavan, Sandra Watson and David O'Donnell (eds.), *Perspectives on Human Resource Development*, Special Issue of *Advances in HRD* 9(1): 150–168. Monica Lee. (2007) 'Locating HRD from a holistic perspective,' keynote speech, 8th International Conference on Human Resource Development Research and Practice across Europe, GLO-BALISATION versus GLOCALISATION: Implications for HRD? Oxford.
32. Monica Lee. (2010) 'Shifting boundaries: The role Of HRD in a changing world,' in *Advances in Developing Human Resources,* Thomas Garavan and Dave McGuire (eds.),. 12(5): 524–535. Monica Lee . (2010) 'Some thoughts on the diffusion of boundaries and borders,' academic response to keynote HRD Strategies in a European Borderless Postal Market: A Hungarian Perspective,' Ildikó Szűts, CEO, Magyar Posta Zrt, *11th International Conference on HRD Research and Practice across Europe*, June 2010, University of Pécs.
33. CASSE: Centre for the Advancement of the Steady State Economy, available at http://steadystate.org/. (accessed 1stst September 2004)

22 Human Flourishing as a Core Value for HRD in the Age of Global Mobility

K. Peter Kuchinke

Brief description: The question over the moral and ethical justification and grounding for human resource development practice and research is moving into sharper relief as the field is broadening its range to include development at the regional, national, and transnational levels. This presentation will provide a historical account of the increase in scope of the field from a) business support to strategic and b) from functional to human development-focused in a variety of settings. This will be followed by a discussion of the contributions of value ethics and, specifically, the notion of human flourishing, which has taken center stage in the literature on human development by scholars such as Amartya Sen, John Finnis, and Sabina Alkire. Drawing on a range of HRD research projects, the central claim of this lecture is that HRD research and practice has, over the past ten years, moved deep into human development 'territory'. Therefore the moral and ethical grounding that is so well expressed in the human development literature extends to human resource development. The lecture closes with a discussion of the implications of the thesis for theory, research, and practice, and points to several areas in need of further conceptual and research-focused development as the field continues to broaden its influence in the age of global connectedness, global organizational reach, and global mobility of labor.
(11th International Conference on HRD Research and Practice across Europe, 2-4 June, Pecs, Hungary, 2010)

CONTEXT

This keynote was given at the 11th International Conference on HRD Research and Practice across Europe (June 2–4, 2010, in Pecs, Hungary). It is among the most recently delivered speeches in this volume, and its occasion marks a special place in the history of HRD conferences, namely, the first international conference held in Eastern Europe. After a decade of alternating the location of the annual European conference between the British Isles and Ireland and the western part of the European continent (primarily the Netherlands and France), the location of the 2010 conference in the heart of Eastern Europe provided the opportunity to expand our collegial network and broaden our understanding of the specific challenges and opportunities in this country and region. At the time of the conference, the global recession and economic contraction had run its two-year course, and there were small but hopeful signs of economic recovery in Europe and North America. Still, unemployment in many parts of the world, including Eastern Europe, remained stubbornly high, and the search for work led many to migrate to other countries, often, however, without a guarantee of finding adequate work. At the same time, the push for global expansion in many multi-national enterprises but also in not-for-profit and non-governmental organizations has brought with it a rapid increase in short-term or long-term work assignments overseas or abroad. In this context, the increased impact and broader responsibility of enterprises on individuals, families, communities and regions around the world has come into relief and has given rise to growing interest in the scholarly and practitioner literatures on the topic of corporate social responsibility, a topic that heretofore had not received adequate attention in our field. Whereas the related scholarship on national HRD, or perhaps better, on HRD as public policy, was a small but influential part of our field, I took the opportunity in this keynote to speak to the broader professional responsibility of HRD in the context of the growing influence of organizations on the welfare of individuals and communities around the world.

THE PRESENTATION

Introduction

I have always been keenly interested in the evolution of our field and the many alternative understandings and shades of meaning that underlie the scholarly discourse and professional practice in our field. This attempt to articulate the shifting meaning of the field is, in no small part, a search for its foundations, foundations in moral and ethical terms that can serve as the bedrock for our field. Whereas our post-modern colleagues may prejudge this search to be futile at best and sinister at worst, it has sustained my interest over the years, has sparked many heated discussions in my work in strategic and management development contexts and is intended here as an invitation to explore a direction previously not adequately addressed. So the intent of this address is to propose and suggest, to invite discussion and alternative points of view and certainly not to expound ex cathedra truths!

The structure of this talk is as follows: I will briefly sketch the importance of values in an age of global mobility—treating it as a context and backdrop against which to discuss the subsequent sections. Following this cursory treatment, I will offer some observations about the role of values: values in the professions in general and values in HRD specifically. Whereas orga-nizations are often portrayed as technical/rational instruments governed by face-less markets and focused on efficient goal achievement, moral and ethical dimensions are, in fact, core to any social organizations, and thus values matter; values are deliberately chosen and pursued (or deliberately ignored or eschewed). In the second section of this address I will talk about human development and its ethical and moral commitments to human flourishing. This will be based on the central arguments by the philosopher John Finnis and economist and Nobel Memorial Prize winner Armatya Sen, who have developed a clear set of values for human development based on reciprocal obligations between social institutions and individuals. The core argument of this address is that human resource development should be viewed as a special instance of human development with a similar, although not identical set of value commitments. I will make the case not on principled but on empirical arguments, showing that in much of HRD research, applied projects,, and in the value stance of HRD scholars and practitioners the commitment to human flourishing is, if not explicit, then at least implicit and implied. The key arguments are (1) that human flour-ishing can and should be the guiding value of human resource development, (2) that human resource development can and should be viewed as a spe-cial case of the broader notion of human development and (3) that human resource development research and applied projects already, although per-haps unknowingly, follow the logic of human development. I thus propose a conceptual shift of our field from the short-term tactical and instrumental to the principled and moral—based on the long-standing, well-developed and deep ethical and economic foundations of human development—and an increased focus on the goals of human development through our pro-fession. In the final section, I will address some of the implications of this value stance for teaching, research and practice.

GLOBAL MOBILITY

Let me link, if only in a cursory manner, the topic of this keynote to the general theme of this conference, HRD in an era of global mobility. The focus on human development seems central to the conference theme given the rise in labor movement across geographic boundaries, whether in terms of outward or inward labor migration, short-term expatriate stays or the use of communication technology that makes it possible to work anywhere and at any time across the globe. While by no means a recent phenomenon, the scope of global mobility and its rate of growth result in an ever larger percentage of individuals affected by and partici-pating in working beyond the confines of time and geographic location. In virtually all cases, the context for the mobility of individuals is an institution: a corporation establishing customer bases or supply chains in other countries, a governmental agency operating overseas or a non-governmental organization implementing a program in another country. Global mobility, thus, unfolds through institutions and organizations, and their provisions, policies, procedures and programs affect employees, customers and communities world-wide. The character and culture of institutions and organization are in no small amount shaped by human resource development—through workforce training, professional and leadership development, organizational change, knowledge management, business partnerships and similar arrangements—and thus our field plays an important role in the process of globalization. The opportunity to shape global organizations entails a responsibility for broader political, social and economic goals and the impact on individuals and communities around the world. In short, just as organizations are wrestling with their role in a global market economy—this discussion is core to the business ethics and corporate social responsibility literatures—so must HRD formulate and refine its own understanding of what it means to develop individuals in the context of work in global organizations and institutions. This involves, as George Copa, retired professor of vocational education at the University of Minnesota, has argued in the context of vocational education,[1] questions about meanings, ends and means—considerations of what goals are worth pursuing, how ends and means of human work activity are related and what the responsibilities are of those who educate, train, coach and mentor in work settings.

The consideration of what HRD *should* aim for takes us into the field of philosophy and, more specifically, ethics and moral philosophy—areas of inquiry that, on first blush appear far removed from the pragmatic concerns of everyday business activity. Over the past thirty years, however, the scholarly and practitioner interests in business ethics, environmental sustainability and corporate social responsibility have flourished, and particularly so in light of the corporate accounting scandals, governmental and military abuse abroad, industrial and environmental disasters and the many instances of personal misuse of power by political and business leaders over the past decade. There has also been an increase in the interest among management scholars in classic humanistic themes such as meaning of work, caring and compassionate organizations and, more broadly, positive organizational scholarship.

VALUES IN THE PROFESSIONS AND IN HRD

The history of the professions informs us that these occupational areas are not value-neutral technologies, but that values play a central role in fields as disparate as medicine, law, engineering and accounting. In order to be granted professional status, an occupational field is required to have expert knowledge, domain boundaries and control over admission, but also a commitment to serving the public good. [2,3] Violations of this commitment, for example, using client-confidential information for personal gain, often lead to disbarment and loss of membership in the profession. A similar demand to serve the public good is placed upon the trades, and this control can be traced back to the craft guilds of Medieval Europe. Public interest provisions do not preclude members of a profession from pursuing private or organization-based gain and interest, but these pursuits must be reconciled in some fashion with the welfare of community and society. The rum runners of old and the drug smugglers and human traffickers in contemporary times may indeed have expertise, tight control over their membership and clearly defined domains of activity, but these are not recognized as professions in the accepted sense precisely because the public interest provision is missing and personal gain the primary motive.

The professions, many trades and indeed many organizations, articulate their commitment to furthering the public good through codes of ethics that outline standards for behavior in the conduct of the professional activity. These codes are intended to keep members of the profession from incurring moral hazard, to provide norms for professional courtesy and to identify provisions to serve the public. [4] Whereas there is public dissatisfaction and even cynicism regarding the efficacy of professional standards, professions and organizations expand considerable effort in developing, revising and making them public. Society demands the formalization of professional behavior to serve the public good, and infractions are routinely made public and condemned in the media. Beyond the values expressed in professional codes of ethics, broader value-based frameworks exist. These include the broader discourse on business ethics and corporate social responsibility, [5] the positive organizational scholarship movement [6] and the International Labor Organization's program on decent work, including fundamental principles and rights at work, international labor standards, employment and income opportunities, social protection and security and social dialogue. [7] These frameworks, and others which could be reviewed, are explicitly value-based and derive their legitimacy not on empirical grounds but on the force of the moral argument. Thus no matter how many instances of unethical behavior in, for example, business may occur, the underlying principles of ethical behavior remain valid and are, in some instances, even strengthened as the public becomes aware of the dangers and damage incurred when ethical standards are violated. Or using a more mundane example: whereas all of us may from time to time speed on the highway or silently pocket extra change given at the cash register of the local supermarket, we endorse the validity and necessity of prohibitions to reckless driving and petty theft.

In the HRD literature, the topic has not received coverage commensurate with its importance. The Academy of HRD (AHRD) published a Standards document a decade ago [8] with the rather vague language concerning the public good (for example: regarding social responsibility: "HRD professional are aware of their professional responsibilities

. . . [and] work to minimize adverse effects on individuals, groups, organizations, societies, and the environment," p. 3). Shortly following its publication, two editorials issued calls for greater awareness of ethical issues and dilemmas in research, practice and publication and the inclusion in course work and leadership development. [9,10] Hatcher published a textbook on HRD and ethics[11] as well as an important discussion of the risk of ethnocentrism in promoting professional codes of ethics in other cultures.[12] In the more recent past a few important contributions have appeared: Fenwick and Bierema concluded in a qualitative study of HRD managers in eight large North American firms committed to corporate social responsibility (CSR)[13] that "HRD appeared to be only marginally involved or interested in the firms' CSR activities" (p. 24). Becker, Carbo and Langella published a conceptual paper on CSR, supply chain management and HRD,[14] and Ardichvili, Jondle and Kowske reported on the results of a multi-country study involving some 23,000 managers in thirteen countries contrasting country and country cluster-level similarities and differences of perceptions of ethics business practices.[15] Whereas these are important contributions, the volume of theoretical and empirical research on the topic of values and ethics is small, judging by the importance of these issues and their far more extensive coverage in the general business and management literature. Moreover, a solid philosophical and ethical framework that might provide guidance to the profession has not been articulated, and herein lies the promise of the human development literature and its conceptual and theoretical foundations.

HUMAN DEVELOPMENT

I would like to turn now to human development, a term that points to a broad, multi-faceted and global set of projects, initiatives and goals in the public domain promoted by national and local governments, non-governmental organizations and international agencies aimed at improving health, education, welfare, security and social justice around the world. Examples include the World Health Organization's (WHO) millennium development goals for global health, the International Labor Organization's declaration of rights at work, the United Nations Development agency's efforts at combating illiteracy and many others. Human development is explicit about its ethical foundation. As Lee Jong-wook, the WHO's director general underscored: "Global health work must be guided by an ethical vision. . . . [t]echnical excellence and political commitment have no value unless they have an ethically sound purpose" (in Alkire and Chen, 2004: 1069).[16] Developing and justifying its ethical purpose, moral philosophy serves an eminently practical purpose, namely, to guide policy choices, shape how programs and initiatives are undertaken and set standards for evaluating their effectiveness.

Alkire, a theologian and economist and currently director of the Oxford Poverty and Human Development Initiative, summarizes four major schools of moral thought that provide a justification for human development: humanitarianism, utilitarianism, equity and human rights, with the last two of particular emphasis on the mutuality of obligation between those sponsoring or providing development initiatives and those receiving them. Development, thus, is not an indulgence but a responsibility, but this responsibility puts obligations on both giver and recipient. Increasing individuals' capability for good health or productive work through development, for example, entails the moral obligation to maintain good health and put one's skills to good use. The objective of development, then, is to expand and equalize the capability of each individual to enjoy those activities, ways of living and general 'functionings' that he or she chooses as a mature and self-directing human being in the context of his or her social, political, economic and psychological context.[17]

Recent literature on human development is also based on the philosopher John Finnis's work; he identifies as the goal of human development the ideal of human flourishing, described in relations to all life domains as "well-being and living well in matters public and private, economic and social, political and spiritual."[18] Its dimensions have been defined by Finnis (1993)[19] as:

- Life, health and safety
- Knowledge and aesthetic experience
- Excellence in work and play
- Friendship
- Self-integration
- Self-expression and practical reasonableness
- Religion and spirituality

These dimensions are viewed as basic reasons for human action out of which "people act in seeking 'wholeness' or 'wellbeing,' in pursuing 'human development.' Thus they may be . . . considered as dimensions of human development."[20] Finnis likens these dimensions to primary colors that can be combined in an infinite variety as basic human values that are incommensurable, irreducible and non-hierarchical.

Given this arguable cursory description of the philosophical framework to justify human development through Sen's capability approach and Finnis's notion of human flourishing and the dimensions of development, we now turn to the question of the relevance of these notions for human resource development. This will be done not by force of philosophical analysis but by calling on circumstantial evidence from a variety of types: first conceptually, by calling upon the previously described AHRD standards, domain definition and graduate students' motivation to enter HRD as a profession; second, by reviewing examples of HRD research and practice in the public sphere; and third, by briefly describing HRD activities in not-for-profit and for-profit organizations. These examples will not be exhaustive but suggest evidence that the ideal of human flourishing from the development literature is not incommensurable with our understanding of HRD theory and practice, can serve to provide a solid philosophical foundation for our field and challenge scholars and practitioners alike to clarify our understanding of the contribution to the public good of our profession.

HUMAN FLOURISHING AND HRD STANDARDS, DEFINITIONS AND STUDENT MOTIVATION

Whereas numerous goals are included in the AHRD Standards document, the preface includes language supportive of Sen's capabilities approach, namely, the "central goal . . . of AHRD professional activities to broaden understanding of the complex activities involved in assisting individuals or organizations to improve their ability to develop themselves" (p. ii). The general principles of the document also refer to rights-based guidelines for development, specifically the "fundamental right, dignity, and worth of all people" and the rights of individuals to privacy, confidentiality, self-determination, and autonomy" (p. 2). These rights, however, are not further specified, and the list is incomplete compared to, for example, the United Nations Declaration of Human Rights from 1948,[21] and furthermore falls far short of Finnis's list of dimensions of human development[22] or, for that matter, other lists of human values, such as Schwartz's.[23] These omissions ought to give rise to vigorous debate within the scholarly community and to a better understanding of the reasons why the document is not receiving increased attention in the literature and at our scholarly conferences. On the other hand, however, it can be argued that a limited set of goals of human development is acknowledged, and the full set would not appear incompatible with the standards.

A second argument for the kinship of human development to our field is in the definitional area. After several years of foundational debates, a conference presentation and subsequent article by McLean[24] appears to have put the discussion to rest by proposing a broad and inclusive definition, namely, HRD in service of "personal or group/team gain, or for the benefit of an organization, community, nation, or, ultimately, the whole of humanity" (p. 322). This definition, widely accepted in the scholarly community, clearly addresses the societal dimension of HRD and places it in the context of the public good without, however, clarifying the relationship between the multiple levels of beneficiaries of HRD activities. In other words, HRD for the sole gain of the personal, team or organization is permissible, whether or not wider public benefits ensue. In this respect, McLean does not specify reciprocity of obligation, and development may be used as a private good by individuals or organizations, whereas Sen's capabilities approach and certainly Finnis's notion of human flourishing demand that at least a part of the gain obtained through development be put in service of the public good and development not solely be considered private consumption.

A third argument linking human development and our field is made by referencing research on the motivation of HRD scholars and practitioners. In 2004, I conducted case study research on three prominent HRD programs in the US[25] and included, among institutional and curricular features, the motivation of graduate students to enter the program and field. There was widespread agreement that HRD courses—which in the US are offered primarily in colleges of education—offered an alternative to the often narrowly profit-driven orientation in business schools, that the role of learning and development was central to the sustainable growth of business enterprises, and that a humanistic value orientation was congruent with students' own philosophical stance. Thus without explicitly referring to human development or human flourishing, these students envisioned their university education and future professional responsibilities to build socially responsible institutions and organizations and stay true to the obligation of our profession with respect to the public good.

HUMAN DEVELOPMENT AND HRD IN THE PUBLIC SPHERE

One of the frame-breaking and surprising developments in HRD is the broadening of the focus of the profession beyond the individual, organizational or work process levels and the inclusion of the development of communities, societies, nations and the world under the auspices of our field. The focus on development at the national and supranational levels (for example: European Union, MERCOSUL, International Labour Organization) is now an accepted and quite vigorous area of scholarship and application (for example: McLean, Osman-Gani and Cho, 2004,[26] Lynham, Paprock and Cunningham. 2006).[27] Taking the field in the realm of public policy implies, almost by definition, the need to broaden the range of desired outcomes or values. As McLean states: "[national human resource development] goes beyond employment and preparation for employment issues to include health, culture, safety, community and a host of other considerations that have not typically been perceived as manpower planning or human capital investment."[28] Specific applied examples of HRD in the public sphere from my own experience include a project to integrate Turkish immigrants in Berlin into German society and to stem the cycle of poverty, violence and crime; educational and economic development in Busan, Korea, to stem the flight of educated and talented professionals to the capital city of Seoul; and the formation of an educational consortium between US and Brazilian universities to foster global talent development capacity among scientists in sustainable agriculture and bio energy fields. Select dissertation projects conducted at my home university also indicated students' interest in public policy: one recent completed dissertation centered on improving performance management and accountability in a UN-sponsored reforestation program in Sub-Saharan Africa, while a dissertation proposal addresses the need for school reform in Kenya to promote entrepreneurship among young high school graduates. It appears evident from these examples, and many others that may be cited from the literature, conference presentations and applied projects, that the field has moved into public policy territory. Here, the whole range of goals for human development should be considered and where the whole range of dimensions of human development and its goal of human flourishing are of central value.

HUMAN FLOURISHING AND HRD AT THE ORGANIZATIONAL LEVEL

The case for the importance of considering the full range of dimensions of human development is equally apparent when considering HRD in not-for-profit or public organizations that are founded and exist to serve a set of public needs. Several examples from my own community involvement will illustrate the point. Each summer, the Park District of the City of Champaign hires some 250 high school students as volunteers to maintain the public gardens, flowerbeds, playgrounds and woodlands. Comprehensive training, mentoring, performance feedback and evaluation programs are in place to ensure that benefits incur to the students and the city, and because of the quality of the HRD provisions the program is successful and in demand. While focusing on work skills, program supervisors encourage intellectual, moral and cognitive development through discussions, group work and problem-solving activities. Mentoring often surfaces and addresses concerns about future education, career goals, personal health and safety, relationships and other areas of personal concern to high school seniors. In this example, it can be argued, many, if not most dimensions of Finnis's notion of human development are apparent, and the opportunity is taken up by the program leaders to address and foster flourishing related to work and non-work related domains of students' lives. A second example might be taken from the City of Urbana's English-as-Second Language program that is free to new immigrants to the area. In this setting, language training is the primary focus, but when speaking to the instructors and observing class sessions, it soon becomes evident that the program serves as a central resource point for all manner of questions related to settling in a new community, such as finding work, overcoming perceived and real discrimination, obtaining housing, finding good schools for the children, studying for the driving test and dealing with many unfamiliar bureaucratic hurdles. Here again, a set of developmental needs exists, is acknowledged by program staff and is fulfilled to some extent or another by different teachers. As with the parks example, the opportunity for expanding immigrants' capability along a wide spectrum of dimensions is present, and the potential for development related to language and many other areas exists and is at least partially, fulfilled.

Two doctoral research projects will briefly be described to illustrate the importance of developing a wide range of human dimensions beyond the obvious work skill area. For two semesters, an HRD doctoral student in my department has worked with the Southern Illinois University School of Medicine as an intern; she is now fulfilling her dissertation research requirements focused on the development of curriculum to improve the mentoring abilities of senior physicians charged with supervising the clinical training of future surgeons. This on first blush seemingly simple instructional design task turned into a deep investigation of social hierarchies in medicine, generational differences in understanding of professional work and commitment, communicative abilities of experts, issues of trust and psychological safety, professional identity and deeply held beliefs and norms about the nature of teaching and learning. The second dissertation example revolves around leadership development of bishops in a Black Baptist church in the United States where core issues of professional calling, spiritual development and balancing between administration and care for the congregations have moved into the center of the research for this population. Both examples illustrate, once again, that in actual HRD practice in these organizational and institutional settings, a range of dimensions of human development is addressed, some explicit and overt, some implied and seemingly accidental, but all of them important to clients and responded to by the providers.

Last, let's consider the role of human development as defined by Sen and Finnis in for-profit organizations, a setting that is conceptually and theoretically the most interesting and also the most difficult.

Let's begin by pointing to the fact that large corporations already offer a suite of developmental provisions far beyond those for immediate or even future job requirements. One example includes the investment in fostering networking and development among under-represented employee groups, for example, Abbott's initiative to link up women in leadership positions in the company to foster their advancement and promotion. Other examples of developmental provisions offered by many large corporations in the US and abroad include the provision of basic health screening, smoking cessation, weight loss, or general fitness, the sponsoring of foreign language clubs, offering of nutrition, investment, and retirement counseling and sponsorship for social events for employees and their families. Without glorifying the motives of such corporate welfare provisions—Barley and Kunda provide a succinct historical treatise on the topic[29]—they illustrate the point that there exists a range of developmental opportunities in corporations that can be characterized as opportunities for human development broadly and go beyond the development required for simple job performance.

The broader question of the responsibility of for-profit organizations for the welfare of their employees and the community is, of course, a central topic in the management literature. The strategic human resource management literature provides models and theoretical justification, be it in the form of contingency models (see Lepak and Snell's HR architecture)[30] or in the form of universal models, such as Pfeffer and Veiga.[31] The business ethics literature provides philosophical justification, be this in the form of the libertarian, free market argumentation such as Friedman (1971)[32] or along Kantian lines of thought, as articulated by Bowie.[33] The *Academy of Management Review,* a top-rated theory journal, has issued a call for papers for a special topic forum on caring and compassion in organizations,[34] and the topic is also at the core of the corporate sustainability and responsibility movement with a recent world guide to five geographic regions and some sixty individual country profiles published in 2010[35], and so I would hope that the debate and discussion over a broader understanding of the role and function of organizations in development can also be reinvigorated in the scholarly and practitioner communities in human resource development.

THE AFTERMATH

In this keynote I tried to connect two literatures that have up to this point existed in isolation: human development with its clearly articulated ethical and moral justification and comprehensive set of dimensions of development, and human resource development with its published standard but limited literature articulating its stance toward development. After a brief review of the core tenets of human development, we looked at examples from research and practice with the aim of showing that, in actual practice, broader sets of developmental goals are pursued than is articulated or acknowledged in much of the domain literature. Whereas the examples from national HRD, not-for-profits and for-profit settings were, of course, deliberately chosen to support the central argument, they do, I think, lend support for the thesis of theoretical kinship and proximity between human development and HRD. The examples also suggest that the broader range of human development dimensions, with its goal of human flourishing, ought to be acknowledged, considered and debated in HRD theorizing and applications. The justification for this can be made from both pragmatic and moral points of view.

Last, much work remains to be done to articulate the position. Human development and human resource development, while arguably related, are not identical, and their differences need to be articulated. Empirical work on development in work contexts must support the theoretical arguments, and this includes, among other tasks, the development of measures for the various dimensions of development. Important as these tasks are, I hope to make a reasonable case for the importance of increased scholarly attention to the moral and ethical dimensionality of our field of professional commitment, to the potential usefulness of the human development construct and its associated literature and the need for further scholarly dialogue on these critical issues.

NOTES

1. George H. Copa. (1984) 'Organizing knowledge for use: A basis for expanding the focus of research in vocational education,' *Journal of Vocational Education Research* 9(4): 1–7.
2. Andrew Abbott. (1988) *The system of professions: An essay on the division of expert labor.* Chicago: University of Chicago Press.
3. Elliot Freidson. (1988) *Professional powers: A study of the institutionalization of formal knowledge.* Chicago: University of Chicago Press.
4. Karim Jamal and Norm E. Bowie. (1995) 'Theoretical considerations for a meaningful code of professional ethics,' *Journal of Business Ethics* 14: 703–714.
5. For example: Ruth V. Aguilera, Deborah E. Rupp, Cynthia A. Williams and Jyoti Ganapathi. (2007) "Putting the S back in corporate social responsibility: A multilevel theory of social change in organizations,' *Academy of Management Review* 32(3): 836–863.
6. For example: Kim S. Cameron, Jane E. Dutton and Robert E. Quinn. (2003) *Positive organizational scholarship: Foundations of a new discipline.* San Francisco: Berrett-Koehler.
7. For example: International Labour Organization. (2010) *Decent work for all,* retrieved online on August 12, 2010, at http://www.ilo.org/global/About_the_ILO/Mainpillars/WhatisDecentWork/lang—en/index.htm.
8. Academy of Human Resource Development. (1999) *Standards on ethics and integrity.* Baton Rouge, LA: Author.
9. Gary N. McLean. (2001) 'Ethical dilemmas and the many hats of HRD,' *Human Resource Development Quarterly,* 12(3): 219–221.
10. Darlene Russ-Eft. (2003) 'Corporate ethics: A learning and performance problem for leaders?' *Human Resource Development Quarterly,* 14(1): 1–3.
11. Timothy Hatcher. (2002) *Ethics and HRD. A new approach to leading responsible organizations.* Cambridge, MA: Basic Books.
12. Darlene Russ-Eft and Timothy Hatcher. (2003) 'The issue of international values and beliefs: The debate for a global HRD Code Of Ethics,' *Advances in Developing Human Resources* 5(3): 296–307.
13. Tara Fenwick and Laura Bierema. (2008) 'Corporate social responsibility: Issues for human resource development professionals,' *International Journal of Training and Development* 12(1): 24–35.
14. Wendy S. Becker, Jerry A. Carbo II and Ian M. Langella. (2010) 'Beyond self-interest: Integrating social responsibility and supply chain management with human resource development,' *Human Resource Development Review* 9(2): 144–168.
15. Alexandre Ardichvili, Douglas Jondle and Brian Kowske. (2010) 'Dimensions of ethical business cultures: Comparing data from 13 counties of Europe, Asia, and the Americas,' *Human Resource Development International* 13(3): 299–315.
16. Sabina Alkire and L. Chen. (2004, September 18) 'Global health and moral values,' *The Lancet* 364: 1069–1074.

17. On Amartya Sen's capabilities approach to human development, see Sabina Alkire. (2002) *Valuing freedoms: Sen's capability approach and poverty reduction*. Oxford: Oxford University Press.
18. Sabina Alkire. (2002) 'Dimensions of human development,' *World Development* 30(2): 181–205, esp. 182.
19. John Finnis. (1993) *Natural law and natural rights*. Oxford: Clarendon.
20. Sabina Alkire. (2002) *Valuing freedoms: Sen's capability approach and poverty reduction*. Oxford: Oxford University Press, 186; single quotation marks in the original.
21. United Nations. (2010) *The universal declaration of human rights*, retrieved online on August 20, 2010, at http://www.un.org/en/documents/udhr/index. shtml.
22. John Finnis. (1993) *Natural law and natural rights*. Oxford: Clarendon.
23. Sabina Alkire. (2002) 'Dimensions of human development,' *World Development* 30(2): 181–205.
24. Gary N. McLean and Laird McLean. (2001) "If we can't define HRD in one country, how can we define it in an international context?' *Human Resource Development International* 4(3): 313–326.
25. K. Peter Kuchinke. (2004) 'Contested domains: Human resource development programs in colleges of education,' *Workforce Education Forum* 3(1): 43–60.
26. Gary N. McLean, Aahad. M. Osman-Gani and Eunsang Cho, eds. *Advances in developing human resources 6(3): Human resource development as national policy*. Thousand Oaks, CA: Sage.
27. Susan A. Lynham, Kenneth E. Paprock and Peter W. Cunningham, eds. (2006) *Advances in developing human resources 8(1): National human resource development in transitioning societies in the developing world*. Thousand Oaks, CA: Sage.
28. Gary N. McLean. (2004) 'National human resource development: What in the world is it?' in Gary N. McLean, A.M. Osman-Gani and E. Cho (eds.), *Human Resource Development as National Policy*, Advances in Developing Human Resources 6(3): 269–275, esp. 269.
29. Stephen R. Barley and Gideon Kunda. (1992) 'Design and devotion: Surges of rational and normative ideologies of control in managerial discourses,'" *Administrative Science Quarterly*, 37(3): 363–399.
30. David. P. Lepak and Scott A. Snell. (1999) 'The human resource architecture: Toward a theory of human capital allocation and development,' *Academy of Management Review*, 24(1): 31–48.
31. Jeffrey Pfeffer and John F. Veiga. (1999) 'Putting people first for organizational success,' *Academy of Management Executive* 13(2): 37–48.
32. Milton Friedman. (1970, September 30) 'The social responsibility of business is to increase its profits,' *The New York Times Magazine*.
33. Norman E. Bowie. (1998) 'A Kantian theory of capitalism,' The Ruffin Series of the Society for Business Ethics 1998:37–60
34. *Academy of Management Review*. (2010) 'Special topic forum call for papers: Understanding and creating caring and compassionate organizations,' *Academy of Management Review* 53(1): 199–200.
35. Wayne Visser and Nick Tolhurst, eds. (2010) *The World Guide to CSR: A country-by-country analysis of corporate sustainability and responsibility*. Ogdensburg, NY: Greenleaf.

Summary

Monica Lee

I am delighted to have so many excellent speeches recorded here side by side, and I have found the aftermaths (the reflections provided by each contributor on the effects of his or her presentation) to be highly illuminating ... but how can I summarize such a diverse and powerful collection? Each of us will see this from our own lens, but there is a central core—these speeches were chosen by HRD people, and were included here because of the impact they had. Collectively, they do represent HRD as WE know it.

In the introduction I explained why I grouped the chapters according to whether they particularly focused on the conceptualization of HRD; where HRD was located; how it was implemented; the values contained within it; or visions of how the future might play out. Each chapter, however, is much more than this. The very nature of a memorable speech is that it covers a lot of ground and pulls together multiple and disparate threads, weaving them into a seemingly simple cloth. In addition, because of the author's reflections, each chapter provides us with an up-to-date view on how each particular patch of the woven cloth has developed.

One thing that did surprise me was in the compilation of the references. I pulled these together in one collection as a useful resource for readers and as a way of accessing what WE consider to be sources of information for our endeavors—and I thought it would be a relatively easy task. By their nature most of the speeches were light on references, and I had assumed that there would be quite a bit of overlap between the chapters. There was very little overlap. Despite core themes meandering through the book, such as leadership, contributors built their cases on wide foundations. While there was some cross-referencing, only 15 of about 450 references was used by more than one person, with Gary and Laird Mclean's' 2001 paper being most popular and referenced by five contributors[1] (and now, is referenced by this summary also!).

I suspect this reflects how we pick our keynote speakers. As I pointed out in Yvonna Lincoln's contribution (Chapter 2), the memorable speeches seem to be those that have brought in information and/or people from outside our common conception of the area—they are the ones that challenge us, and the field would be much poorer without such mixing. So perhaps we should expect that in this instance the references should be spread wide and far.

One thing that almost all the authors agree on is the complex and situated nature of HRD. It seems to me that the early speeches across each of the sections were trying to establish in some way a more complex view of their area than was current at the time; for example, see what I say in Chapter 1, and Tom Garavan's analysis of multiple stakeholders in Chapter 3 and Darlene Russ-Eft's call for the inclusion of multiple stakeholder values in evaluation in Chapter 17. The sub-text in the later speeches assumes the situated nature of what is being examined (see Nicholas Clarke, Chapter 13). Authors of more recent speeches have felt that there is less need to make the case that things are different depending upon where and when you are, and more need to explore what those differences might be.

Similarly, it seems to me that over time, the nature of the HRD focus has shifted from embodied concepts, such as 'the individual,' 'the organization' and so on, to relative concepts, such as the relationship between the two, and the social context. Both Paul Iles, Chapter 4, looking at talent management in China, and Larry Dooley, Chapter 10, looking at the socializing influence of emerging technologies, make this point.

This shift can also be seen in the way in which we make sense of things. The speeches given in the early 90s assumed that a quantitative approach was the norm—to adopt anything else was unusual and challenging—see Yvonna Lincoln in Chapter 2. More recent chapters (such as Sally Sambrook, Chapter 5) assume that interpretative methodologies are alive and well. Authors show an easier and greater freedom of choice about which way of working is most appropriate for what they want to achieve.

There are some very interesting threads that cut across the sections. Gary McLean (in Chapter 19) and Monica Lee (in Chapter 21) both take a wide stance and explicitly address global trends. They adopt different perspectives, but the message is the same—HRD is much more than (just) training and development. A different but associated trend is around the large-scale use of HRD in social development—National HRD being a prime example. Gary McLean offers a wide exploration of this in Chapter 15, which harmonizes well with Chapter 6, by Chartchai Na Chiangmai, who talks of establishing the philosophy and way of working necessary for the health of Thailand. This is mirrored by the company perspective by Chanin Vongkusolkit, in Chapter 11, who is talking about the implementation of this approach in Banpu. A practical example of company development in the West is provided by Sharon Mavin and Dawn Robinson, in Chapter 12.

The differences and similarities between Eastern and Western approaches is examined directly by Nigel Haworth and Jonathan Winterton in Chapter 7, in which they contend that large supra state regions with very different approaches can learn from each other. This notion of shared knowledge is adopted by AAhad Osman-Gani in Chapter 8 as he looks at cultural intelligence; and also by Sharon Turnbull in her exploration of different forms of leadership in Chapter 9.

Conceptions of leadership permeate this book, as do explorations of the emotional sides of the topic under discussion at the time. Jamie Callaghan addresses this directly in Chapter 18, which links to Chapter 20 by Rob Poell, who argues that organizations are there to make people happy. These also link to Chapter 16 by Gene Roth and Darren Short, who address the use of humor more directly.

There is a similar focus on ethical and spiritual aspects of HRD that threads through most chapters, and some contributors address these explicitly. See, for example, an early speech by David Megginson in Chapter 14, in which he talks of the role of the leader as cultivating spirit which is complemented by a later speech by K. Peter Kuchinke who talks of human flourishing.

One thing that is clear throughout these chapters is that, as far as these speakers and the HRD people that recommended them for the book are concerned, HRD from across the world has moved a long way from its original nationally bound institutional roots in training and development.

NOTES

1. Gary N. McLean and Laird D. McLean. (2001) 'If we can't define HRD in one country, how can we define it in an international context?' *Human Resource Development International* 4: 313–326.

Contributors

Jamie L. Callahan is an Associate Professor in the Adult Educational and Human Resource Development Program at Texas A&M University. She has held multiple positions in the Academy of Human Resource Development, including being a member of the Board of Directors. Her primary research interests focus on emotion management and its relationship to a variety of organizational phenomena. Her work has appeared in journals such as *Human Resource Development Quarterly, Human Resource Development International, Human Relations* and *Organization Studies*; she has also co-edited a book entitled *Critical Issues in HRD: A New Agenda for the Twenty-First Century*. She is currently Editor of *Human Resource Development Review*.

Chartchai Na Chiangmai, PhD, is Professor in Political Science, National Institute of Development Administration. He received a BA in Political Science with honors from Chiangmai University in 1974, an MA in Government from Chulalongkorn University in 1976 and a PhD in Political Science from University of Wisconsin-Madison in 1983. Prof. Chartchai started his teaching career at Chiangmai University in 1976 and moved to teach at the National Institute of Development Administration (NIDA) in Bangkok in 1983. He was a research fellow at the Kenan Institute of Private Enterprise, University of North Carolina-Chapel Hill, in 1990–1991.

In administrative service to NIDA, he was a Director of the Training Center, the first Director of the Graduate Program in Human Resource Development, the first Director of the Center for Development of Graduate Studies, Acting Dean of the School of Social Development and Vice President for Planning of the National Institute of Development Administration. He was appointed to serve as the first Director of the Institute for Good Governance Promotion, Office of the Public Sector Development Commission.

Prof. Chartchai was granted a PhD scholarship from Harvard-Yenching Institute, Harvard University and was named the national distinguished researcher of the year 1989 by the National Research Council.

He was awarded the most distinguished alumnus of Montfort College in 2004; of the Faculty of Political Science, Chiangmai University in 2006 and of Chiangmai University in 2009. He received the national award for the most distinguished social sciences university professor in 2009. He was granted a decoration of Cavalier de l'Ordre National du Merite from France in 2010.

Prof. Chartchai was a consultant of the United Nations Development Program in people-centered development and poverty alleviation. He has been involved extensively in policy research on human development and rural development and was an active planning committee member of the National Economic and Social Development Plan from 1985 to 1999. At present, he is a committee member of the National Decentralization Committee, a sub-committee member of the Public Sector Development Commission.

Prof. Chartchai has published many research reports, books and articles in areas of Thai politics and governance, development management, decentralization policy and administration, rural development and human resource development.

Dr. Nicholas Clarke has developed a significant body of work researching human resource development in organizations from a relational perspective over the past ten years. This began with identifying the significance of relationships with supervisors as influencing training outcomes, which then broadened to include relational dimensions associated with organizational climate influencing training and learning in the workplace. Recently he has focused on how qualities associated with relationships in the workplace influence organization and leadership development in networks and projects. Over the past five years this has expanded to focus on how emotional intelligence might be developed and how emotional intelligence affects learning and behavior. He has published extensively in these fields in journals including *Human Resource Development International, Human Resource Development Quarterly, Human Resource Development Review, Leadership Quarterly* and *the International Journal of Human Resource Management*. He is a Visiting Professor at both Toulouse Business School and the Work Employment Research Unit at the University of Greenwich and sits on the editorial boards of the *Journal of European and Industrial Training* and *Team Performance Management*.

Larry M. Dooley is Associate Professor of Human Resource Development (HRD) in the Department of Educational Administration and Human Resource Development at Texas A&M University. He is Past-President of the Academy of Human Resource Development (AHRD). Additionally he serves as Vice President and Treasurer of the Academy of Human Resource Development Foundation. He has keynoted five major international conferences, co-authored two books and multiple book chapters as well as over 50 articles appearing in journals and other sources. He serves as Associate Editor of the *International Journal of Management Education* and is past-Chair of the Board of Directors for Human Resource Development International. Moreover, he was a visiting professor in the School of Business & Law at Napier University in Edinburg, Scotland and the Center for Human Resource Management Research at Peking University in Beijing, China.

Thomas Garavan is Professor and Associate Dean, Postgraduate Studies and Executive Education, Kemmy Business School, University of Limerick. A graduate of the University of Limerick (BBS, 1982; MBS, 1985) and the University of Bristol (DEd, 1996), he has authored or co-authored 14 books and 100 refereed journal papers and book chapters. Thomas is a Fellow of the Irish Institute of Training and Development (FIITD) and a Member of the Chartered Institute of Personnel and Development (MCIPD). He is also a member of the Society of Industrial and Organizational Psychologists (US) and a board member of both the Academy of Human Resource Development (AHRD) and the University Forum for Human Resource Development. Thomas is currently Editor in Chief of the *Journal of European and Industrial Training*. He has examined doctoral theses at a number of leading universities and business schools, including the University of Swinbourn, Australia, University of Leicester, University of Plymouth, University of Leeds and Northumbria University.

Professor Nigel Haworth trained as an economist, became a specialist in Latin American Studies and the international labor market and focuses his research in part on the Pacific Rim in the areas of national policy toward internationalization, the role of WTO and the development of the ASEAN economies. He has also written for many years on various aspects of the international labor movement. Active in APEC networks, Nigel has led the Capacity Building Network of the APEC HRD Working Group since 2001. He also works with the ILO and is currently a member of the ILO Century Project, producing the ILO's account of its role since 1919. He is currently Chair of the Partnership Research Centre, located in the Department of Labor, and was, for six years until 2009, Chair of the Centre for Housing Research, located in the Housing Corporation of New Zealand. He was National President of the Association of University Staff for three years between 2005 and 2008. He sits on a variety of committees and boards.

Paul Iles is a Professor of Leadership and HRM at Salford Business School, University of Salford UK. Formerly Running Stream Professor of Human Resource Development and course leader of the Doctorate in Business Administration at Leeds Business School, he provided academic leadership in HRD, leadership, talent and change management. He was formerly Professor of Strategic HRM and Head of the Centre for Leadership and Organizational Change and MBA program leader at Teesside University, Teesside Business School. He is a Chartered Psychologist, Associate Fellow of the British Psychological Society, and Chartered Fellow of the CIPD.

Paul is the author of many refereed publications in such journals as *Leadership,* the *Journal of World Business,* the *International Journal of Human Resource Management,* the *British Journal of Management, Human Resource Development International,* and *Human Relations.* He is Co-Editor of the *Journal of Organizational Transformation and Social Change* and on the Editorial Boards of the *Journal of Managerial Psychology* and the *Journal of European Industrial Training.*

He has a particular interest in leadership development, publishing a number of articles in recent years in such journals as *Leadership* and *Personnel Review* as well as giving seminars at international conferences and the Leadership Trust. He also has an interest in talent management, publishing several recent articles on talent management in China in the *Journal of World Business, International Journal of Human Resource Management* and *Management Research News.* He is currently working with Rotherham MBC and Morrisons plc on leadership and career development issues, and has co-edited a recent book on HRD (*HRD: Theory and Practice,* Palgrave), which includes chapters on developing leadership, teams and talent.

K. Peter Kuchinke is Professor and Director of Graduate Programs in the Department of Education Policy, Organization and Leadership at the University of Illinois at Urbana-Champaign. He holds appointments in the Division of Human Resource Development and the Division of Global Studies in Education. He is a member of the Center for East European and Russian Studies, East Asian and Pacific Studies Center, and Center for Caribbean and Latin American Studies.

He is the immediate past Editor for *Human Resource Development International* and has served on the Board of the *Academy of Human Resource Development* for two terms. A native of Germany, he earned his master's degree at the University of California in Los Angeles in Education and Work Policy and his PhD in Human Resource Development and Strategic Management from the University of Minnesota. Prior to his faculty appointment to Illinois in 1997, Dr. Kuchinke served as Director of Education for United Education and Software and as consultant for Process Management International, a Deming-based quality management consulting firm.

Professor Kuchinke's current research focuses on two areas: first, the education and training of educators working in human resource development settings in for-profit and not-for-profit organizations around the world, as these professionals lead learning interventions to foster organizational and individual growth and development. Second, he further explores the changing meaning of work, as technological, economic, political and social forces bring unprecedented rates of change to individuals, families, organizations and countries. He has published widely in national and international journals and has a long record of successful funded projects, including, most recently, a grant from the US Department of Education's FIPSE program to establish an education consortium for four US and Brazilian research universities.

Monica Lee is Visiting Professor at Northumbria University, and is a Life Member of Lancaster University, UK. She is a Chartered Psychologist, and is a Fellow of CIPD, and Associate Fellow of the British Psychological Society. She is Founding Editor in Chief of *Human Resource Development International* (1998 to 2002), and is Chair of the Board of Directors of HRDI. She is editor of the Routledge monograph series 'Studies in HRD,' and is Executive Secretary to the *University Forum for HRD*. She came to academe from the business world where she was Managing Director of a development consultancy. She has worked extensively in Central Europe, CIS and the US, coordinating and collaborating in research and teaching initiatives. She is intrigued by the dynamics around individuals and organizations, and most of her work is about trying to make sense of these. This can be seen in over 100 journal articles, and in books such as *HRD in a Complex World*.

Yvonna S. Lincoln is Ruth Harrington Chair of Educational Leadership and Distinguished Professor of Higher Education at Texas A&M University, where she also serves as program chair for the higher education program area. She is the Co-Editor, with Norman K. Denzin, of the journal *Qualitative Inquiry,* and of the 1st, 2nd, 3rd and now 4th editions of the *Sage Handbook of Qualitative Inquiry,* and the *Handbook of Critical and Indigenous Methodologies.* As well, she is the co-author, editor or co-editor of more than a half dozen other books and volumes, including *Effective Evaluation, Naturalistic Inquiry* and *Fourth Generation Evaluation,* all with Egon Guba (her late spouse), and *Organization Theory and Inquiry.* She has served as the President of the Association for the Study of Higher Education and of the American Evaluation Association, and as the Vice President for Division J (Postsecondary Education) for the American Educational Research Association. She is the author or co-author of more than 100 chapters and journal articles on aspects of higher education or qualitative research methods and methodologies. Her research interests include development of qualitative methods and methodologies, the status and future of research libraries, and other issues in higher education. She currently writes an occasional column for the higher education blog, www.21stcenturyscholar.com, where she comments on the rapidly-evolving status of research universities in the US.

Sharon Mavin is Dean of Newcastle Business School and Professor of Organization and HRM, Northumbria University, Newcastle upon Tyne, UK. Sharon was Vice Chair of the University Forum for HRD, Chair of the Practitioner and Organizational Activities Committee and Chair of the 10th International Conference UFHRD and AHRD 2009, HRD Research and Practice across Europe, Complexity and Imperfection in Practice. She has a sustained interest in people management and development, learning, studies of organization, gender in management and women leaders. Sharon has published widely in women in management and leadership and gender research. Recent research includes learning and development experiences of expatriate women in the United Arab Emirates, conceptualizing and theorizing disability, impairment and ableism, doing gender well and differently in dirty work and a critique of gendered media representations of women political leaders. Sharon's recent publications can be found in *Human Resource Development International, Gender, Work and Organization, British Journal of Management, International Small Business Journal, Gender in Management: An International Journal,* and *Management Learning.*

Gary N. McLean is Senior Professor and Executive Director of International Human Resource Development programs at Texas A&M University, and Professor Emeritus at the University of Minnesota, St. Paul. He has served as President of the Academy of Human Resource Development and the International Management Development Association. As an OD practitioner in McLean Global Consulting, Inc., he works extensively globally. He has been installed in the International Adult and Continuing Education Hall of Fame (2006) and the Academy of HRD Scholar Hall of Fame (2007). He received an honorary PhD in HRD from the National Institute of Development Administration (NIDA) in 2010.

David Megginson is Emeritus Professor of HRD in Sheffield Business School at Sheffield Hallam University. With others, he founded the European Mentoring and Coaching Council, and is an Ambassador for EMCC and an Honorary Vice-President for EMCC UK. He is a long-standing member of the Continuous Professional Development Working Party of the Chartered Institute of Personnel and Development, and author of their CPD text. He has published 17 books and numerous journal articles. David is a Quaker and is Clerk to the Nottinghamshire and Derbyshire Area Meeting in the UK.

AAhad M. Osman-Gani is Professor of HRD and International Management at the Faculty of Economics and Management Sciences of IIUM University in Kuala Lumpur, Malaysia. He has taught for more than thirty-five years in several universities including Nanyang Technological University, Singapore, Ohio State University and the University of Chittagong. He is also a Distinguished Guest Professor of East China Normal University, Shanghai, and was a Visiting Professor of Peking University, China; UTM, Malaysia; and KFUPM, Saudi Arabia.

Professor Osman-Gani is the Editor (Asia) of *IJTD* (Wiley-Blackwell), managing board member of *HRDI* (Routledge) and a member of the editorial boards of several international journals. He is the Founding Chairperson of the Asia Chapter of the Academy of HRD, and was the Conference CEO & Program Chair of all the International Conferences on HRD in Asia (held in India, Thailand, Korea, Taiwan, Malaysia, China and Bahrain). He has published more than 150 journal articles, conference papers, book chapters, case studies and research monographs. In recognition of his distinguished records of continuous publications in high-quality scholarly journals, the Academy of Human Resource Development has conferred the *"Outstanding HRD Scholar"* Award at its Annual International Research Conference in 2010.

In 2011, his alma mater, Ohio State University, recognized him with a *Distinguished Alumni Award*. Last year, he was inducted as a Director of the IBSTPI (International Board of Standards in Training Performance and Instructions). In 2008, one of his research papers was published in the prestigious *"Best Paper Proceedings"* of the Academy of Management. He has also received the *"Cutting Edge Research Awards"* presented by the Academy of HRD for authoring best research papers in 2010 and in 2005. He was presented the 2007 Leadership Award at the 14th Annual International Conference on Advances in Management (ICAM) held in Niagara, Canada. In 2006, he was honored for his contributions to the development of HRD research and practice in China. He had also received the President's Citation, Charles Mendenhall Award from Ohio State University and the Public Service Award from the Public Utilities Commission of Ohio. Professor Osman-Gani's expertise and research interests span the areas of International Human Resource Development, Cross-Cultural Management, Spirituality in Management, and Leadership and Talent Development.

Rob Poell is Professor of HRD at Tilburg University (Netherlands) and has extensive experience as editor, reviewer and author. He is Editor of *Human Resource Development International,* having been Associate Editor for more than four years, and has been Editor of the Dutch quarterly *Develop* (previously *HRD Thema*) for almost eight years. He co-edited a number of textbooks in English (*Continuing Professional Development in Europe,* with Geoff Chivers, 1998; *Facing Up to the Learning Organization Challenge,* with Barry Nyhan, Peter Cressey and Mike Kelleher, 2003) and in Dutch (*Human Resource Development,* with Joseph Kessels, 2001; *Competence Based Vocational Education,* with Martin Mulder, Harm Biemans, Loek Nieuwenhuis and Renate

Wesselink, 2003). He acts as reviewer for three international HRD journals and many other journals (including *Management Learning, Journal
of Management Studies, Personnel Review,* and *International Journal
of Management Research*). He has published more than thirty articles
in international peer-reviewed journals, more than twenty chapters in
international edited books, and more than sixty articles, book chapters
and research reports in Dutch.

Dawn Robinson is Head of Learning and Development at Sage (UK) Limited, a subsidiary of the Sage Group plc, with more than 5 million customers worldwide and the Global HQ situated in Newcastle upon Tyne,
UK. Sage is a remarkable Northeast success story, founded in 1981 on
the Quayside, through a group of local students and entering the FTSE
100 in 1999. The UK business is a leading supplier of business software
and services to more than 700,000 UK customers and employing more
than 2,000 people. Dawn's focus is to be a driving force for the business
in all learning and development solutions and to continuously improve
Sage's people's capabilities through the design and development of corporate programmes. The challenge to attract and resource the right people,
support them with their development and careers and to build a talent
pipeline for future roles in Sage are high on Dawn's agenda. Dawn's HR
and HRD career has spanned more than twenty years in the private and
public sectors, including private-public partnerships, covering generalist
HR, development and commercial roles. Her experiences have included
retail with Marks and Spencer and Boots, manufacturing with De La Rue
and the IT sector with Spring.com. Dawn is a member of the Advisory
Board for Newcastle Business School, Northumbria University, UK.

Gene L. Roth is Professor of Adult and Higher Education and a NIU Distinguished Teaching Professor at Northern Illinois University, DeKalb.
His research interests include learning to learn, international adult education, workforce preparation and development and humor and adult
learning. Dr. Roth has been the principal investigator of more than
thirty externally funded research projects that have totaled more than
$1.5 million. His articles have appeared in *International Journal of Life-
long Learning, Training and Development Journal, Human Resource
Development International, Journal of Vocational Education Research,
Journal of Industrial Teacher Education* and *Journal of Research on
Computing in Education*. He has directed study abroad programs in
Finland, Estonia, Taiwan, South Korea, Malaysia, Singapore, China,
Russia, Hungary and the Netherlands. He was awarded an Honorary
Professorship from the Shanghai Second Institute of Education, Shang-
hai, China. He received the NIU *Outstanding International Educator
Award* in 2004. Dr. Roth recently completed seven years of service on
the Board of the Academy of Human Resource Development (AHRD),

including a term as President. He also has served on the Board of the Foundation of the AHRD as well as on the Management and Editorial Boards of *Human Resource Development International*, and the Editorial Board of the *Asia Pacific Education Review*.

Darlene Russ-Eft, PhD, is Professor and Chair, Adult Education and Higher Education Leadership in the College of Education at Oregon State University. Her teaching focuses on issues related to learning and learning theory, program evaluation and research. Prior to coming to Oregon State University, she was Director of Research Services at AchieveGlobal, Inc., and previously director of research at Zenger-Miller. She received the 1996 Editor of the Year Award from Times Mirror for her research work, was named Scholar of the Year of the Academy of Human Resource Development and received the Research Article Award from the American Society for Training and Development (ASTD).

Dr. Russ-Eft is President of the Academy of Human Resource Development (www.ahrd.org) and a current Director of the International Board of Standards for Training, Performance, and Instruction® (www.ibstpi.org). She has served as Vice President for Research for AHRD, past editor of *Human Resource Development Quarterly*, past board member of the American Evaluation Association (www.eval.org) and past Chair of the Research Committee of ASTD.

She has published more than fifty research articles and co-authored several books on training, development and adult education research, most recently *Evaluator Competencies: Standards for the Practice of Evaluation in Organizations* (Jossey-Bass, 2008), *A Practical Guide to Needs Assessment* (Pfeiffer, 2007), *Building Evaluation Capacity: 72 Activities for Teaching and Training* (Sage, 2005) and *Evaluation in Organizations: A Systematic Approach to Enhancing Learning, Performance and Change* (Perseus, 2001).

Sally Sambrook is Professor of Human Resource Development and former Deputy Head of School at Bangor Business School.. She is also a Visiting Professor at Toulouse Business School in their Work, Employment and Health Group (Management Research Groupe Travail, Emploiet Santé). With a background in nursing and nurse education and training, Sally joined Bangor University in 1999. After several years as lecturer in Human Resource Management (HRM), she joined the Faculty of Health, where she developed the MSc in Health and Social Care Leadership. She was awarded an Honorary Teaching Fellowship in recognition of her excellence in teaching and enhancing the student learning experience. Sally returned to the Business School in 2006 as Director of Postgraduate Studies for Business and Management. Sally is a member of the University Forum for HRD and of the American Academy of HRD, serving as an elected member 2008–2011, and the Chartered

Institute of Personnel and Development. She has been Associate Editor of Human Resource Development International since 2005 and assumes Editorship in 2012. Sally is on the editorial boards of the *European Journal of Training and Development*, and the *International Journal of Management Education*. She reviews for several HRD journals and other nursing, healthand qualitative research journals. Sally has published widely on HRD, co-authoring three edited texts, including 'HRD in the Public Sector: The case of Health and Social Care,' in 2007, 16 book chapters and over 30 journal articles, and was awarded Outstanding Paper, for her work on critical HRD in 2005. Her research interests focus on learning and development, particularly management learning and leadership, in small and large organizations and in the health care and higher education contexts. She is currently Principal Investigator on a £1.2 million WEFO-funded project, in collaboration with Swansea University, delivering and evaluating the LEAD programme for SME managers, developed at Lancaster University. Sally is also currently developing a critical and autoethnographicapproach to management and organizational research, including doctoral supervision.

Darren Short is Director of Global Learning and Development at Avanade, a 10K-employee high-tech consulting firm based in Seattle. He has been an HRD professional since 1992, based in the United Kingdom and then the United States. His practice specializes in consulting skills training, and he has led training for more than 2,000 people in over 20 countries. Darren is currently the President-Elect of the Academy of Human Resource Development, having previously been the organization's Vice President of Membership and Marketing and also the Chair of the Scholar-Practitioner Committee. He has been published twenty times in academic journals, and presented at more than twenty conferences worldwide. His research focuses on the link between HRD research and practice and the role of the scholar-practitioner.

Jim Stewart is Running Stream Professor in Human Resource Development at Leeds Metropolitan University. Jim designed and developed the doctorate in Business Administration at Leeds Business School and is currently Director of DBA Programmes and of the HRD and Leadership Research Unit in the school. He is an internationally renowned researcher and writer who has authored and co-edited thirteen books and conducted research projects on HRD and talent management funded by the UK Government, the European Union, the Economic and Social Research Council, the Chartered Institute of Personal Development and many employers in the private and public sectors. Jim is Chair of the University Forum for HRD, an international network of universities, and holds three appointed national roles with the Chartered Institute of Personnel and Development.

Professor Sharon Turnbull is an independent academic who specializes in leadership, executive education and organizational development. She is a Visiting Professor at the University of Gloucestershire, and the University of Worcester; Senior Research Fellow at Lancaster University, and Teaching Fellow at Durham Business School. Having spent fifteen years in managerial positions with a variety of companies and consultancies, Sharon changed direction and became an academic before joining The Leadership Trust in 2003 where she could combine both worlds to connect theory to practice. As Director of the Centre for Applied Leadership Research at The Leadership Trust until January 2011, Sharon became known for her research into Worldly Leadership—uncovering ancient and indigenous leadership wisdoms for a more sustainable world, a project that created a network of scholars from around the world to co-create alternative leadership models for addressing the complex challenges of today's world.

Chanin Vongkusolkit is an economics graduate from one of the most renowned universities in Thailand—Thammasat University. Chanin Vongkusolkit obtained an MBA. (Finance) from St. Louis University, Missouri. In 2006, he was bestowed an honorary doctorate degree in Economics from Chiangmai University in recognition of his success in applying economics in his career that brings growth and prosperity to his company and the society.

Mr. Vongkusolkit started his profession as one of the founders of Banpu Public Company Limited and has been Chief Executive officer since the establishment of Banpu in 1983. With his foresight and vision, Mr. Vongkusolkit has turned Banpu into a truly international company, winning recognition as one of the 100 firms listed by *Forbes Magazine* in its global ranking of "Best under a Billion" in 2004 and 2006, and Asias Fab 50 Companies in 2010.

As a highly ethical professional, Mr. Vongkusolkit has been well recognized by both local and international investors, thanks to his strong commitment in corporate governance and corporate social responsibility, which are widely practiced at Banpu. As a result, Mr. Vongkusolkit and Banpu have been bestowed with a lot of awards, a few of which include the Best CEO in Asia's mining companies by the Institutional Investors, and the Board of Directors of the Year by the Stock Exchange of Thailand (SET). The recognition also includes the fourth rank on the Best Managed Company by Finance Asia, the third rank on the Best Corporate Governance and on the Corporate Social Responsibility (CSR) in Thailand. He was also bestowed "Thailand Top 100 HR Award 2009" in CEO category by the Human Resources Institute, Thammasat University.

Jonathan Winterton is Professor of Employment and Director of International Development at Toulouse Business School, where he was Director of Research between 2000 and 2010. He also coordinates the research group *Travail Emploi Santé* and is Visiting Professor at the Universities of Auckland, Leeds and UNIRAZAK Graduate School of Business in Malaysia. Formerly Professor of Employment and Director of the Employment Research Institute in Edinburgh, he has been researching vocational training issues for twenty years, often in association with the trade unions and the European Commission and its agencies. A product of the VET system, after an apprenticeship in engineering he gained his BSc(Hons) in Industrial Technology from Bradford, MSc(Econ) in Industrial Relations from the London School of Economics and PhD in Economics from the University of Leeds. He is currently editing a book, *Trade Union Strategies for Competence Development*, which compares union-led learning in eight European countries and will be published by Routledge.

References

Chapter

Abbott, Andrew. (1988) *The system of professions: An essay on the division of expert labor*. Chicago: University of Chicago Press.   22

Academy of Human Resource Development. (1999) *Standards on ethics and integrity*. Baton Rouge: Author.   22

Academy of Management Review. (2010) 'Special topic forum call for papers: Understanding and creating caring and compassionate organizations,' Academy of Management Review 53(1): 199–200.   22

Ackerman, P.L. (1996) 'A theory of adult intellectual development: Process, personality, interests, and knowledge,' *Intelligence* 22: 227–257.   8

Adler, Nancy. (1997) *International dimensions of organizational behavior (3rd ed.)*. Cincinnati: South-Western College Publishing.   9

Adler, Paul. (1974) 'Beyond cultural identity: Reflections on cultural and multicultural man,' *Topics in Culture Learning, Vol. 2*. Honolulu: East-West Culture Learning Institute.   1

Adnett, Nick. (1996) *European labor markets: Analysis and policy*. Longman: London.   7

African Evaluation Association. (2002) *The African Evaluation Guidelines: 2002*, Retrieved on January 11, 2005, from http://66.165.73.167/afrea/content/index.cfm?navID=5anditemID=204.   17

Aggarwal, Vinod, and Charles Morrison, eds. (1998) *Asia-Pacific crossroads : Regime creation and the future of APEC*. St. Martin's Press: New York.   7

Aguilera, Ruth V., Deborah E. Rupp, Cynthia A. Williams and Jyoti Ganapathi. (2007) 'Putting the S back in corporate social responsibility: A multilevel theory of social change in organizations,' *Academy of Management Review* 32(3): 836–863.   22

Alexander, Bryant K. (2005) 'Performance ethnography: The reenacting and inciting of -culture,' in *The Handbook of Qualitative Research, 3rd ed.*, Norman K. Denzin and Yvonna S. Lincoln (eds.), Thousand Oaks, CA: Sage, 3:411–442.   2

Alimo-Metcalfe, Beverly, and John Alban-Metcalfe. (2001) The development of a new Transformational Leadership Questionnaire, *Journal of Occupational and Organizational Psychology* 74(1): 1–28.   4

Alkire, Sabina. (2002) Dimensions of human development, *World Development* 30(2): 181–205.   22

Alkire, Sabina. (2002) *Valuing freedoms: Sen's capability approach and poverty reduction*. Oxford: Oxford University Press.   22

Alkire, Sabina, and L. Chen (2004, September 18) 'Global health and moral values,' *The Lancet* 364: 1069–1074.   22

Alvesson, Mats, and Stefan Sveningsson. (2003) 'The great disappearing act: Difficulties in doing 'leadership,' *Leadership Quarterly* 14: 22.   18

Alvesson, Mats, and Willmott Hugh. (1996) *Making sense of management: A critical introduction*. London: Sage.   5

American Evaluation Association (2004, July) *Guiding Principles for Evaluators*, retrieved January 11, 2005, from http://www.eval.org/Guiding%20 Principles.htm.   17

Ang, S., L. Van Dyne, C.K.S. Koh, K.Y. Ng, K.J. Templer, C. Tay and N,A. Chandrasekar. (2007) 'Cultural intelligence: Its measurement and effects on cultural judgment and decision making, cultural adaptation, and task performance,' *Management and Organization Review* 3: 335–371.   8

Ang, S., L. Van Dyne and S.K. Koh. (2006) Personality correlates of the four-factor model of cultural intelligence, *Group and Organization Management* 31: 100–123.   8

Ardichvili, Alexandre, D. Jondle and B. Kowske. (2010) 'Dimensions of ethical business cultures: Comparing data from 13 counties of Europe, Asia, and the Americas,' *Human Resource Development International* 13(3): 299–315.   22

Argyris, Chris. (1991) 'Teaching smart people how to learn,' *Havard Business Review* 69(3), 99–109.   14

Argyris, M., and D. Schön. (1974) *Theory in practice. Increasing professional effectiveness*. San Francisco: Jossey-Bass.   17

Attwood, Margaret, Tom Boydell, John Burgoyne, David Clutterbuck, Ian Cunningham, Bob Garratt, Peter Honey, Andrew Mayo, David Megginson, Alan Mumford, Michael Pearn, Mike Pedler and Robin Wood. (2000) *A declaration on learning: A call to action*. Maidenhead: Peter Honey.   14

Avolio, Bruce J., and Fred Luthans. (2006) *The high impact leader: Moments matter in accelerating authentic leadership development*, New York: McGraw-Hill.   12

Avolio, Bruce J., and William L. Gardner. (2005) 'Authentic leadership development: Getting to the root of positive forms of leadership,' *Leadership Quarterly* 16(3): 315–338.   12

Avolio, Bruce J., William L. Gardner, Fred O.Walumbwa, Fred Luthans and Douglas R. May. (2004) 'Unlocking the mask: A look at the process by which authentic leaders impact follower attitudes and behaviors,' *Leadership Quarterly* 15: 801–823.

Avolio, Bruce J., and Bernard M. Bass. (1999) 'Re-examining the components   12
of transformational and transactional leadership using the Multifactor Leadership Questionnaire,' *Journal of Occupational and Organizational Psychology* 72(4): 441–462.

Bailey, Ronald. (2004) *Why technology will be the defining battle of the 21st centaury*, available at http://reason.com/rb/rb081303.shtml.   21

Bandura, A. (2000) Cultivate self-efficacy for personal and organizational effectiveness,' in E. A. Locke (ed.), *Handbook of principles of organizational behavior*. Oxford: Blackwell.   8

Barley, Stephen R., and Gideon Kunda. (1992) 'Design and devotion: Surges of rational and normative ideologies of control in managerial discourses,' *Administrative Science Quarterly* 37(3): 363–399.   22

Barnard, Chester. I. (1938) *Functions of the executive*. Cambridge: Harvard University Press.   18

Barsoux, Jean-Louis. (1996) 'Why organizations need humour,' *European Management Journal* 14(5): 500–508.   16

Baskerville, Rachel F. (2003) 'Hofstede never studied culture,' *Accounting, Organizations and Society* 28(1): 1–14.   3

Bass, Bernard. (1985) *Leadership and performance beyond expectations*, Cambridge: Harvard University Press. 4, 18

Bass, Bernard, and Bruce J. Avolio. (1994) *Improving organizational effectiveness through transformational leadership*. Thousand Oaks: Sage. 18

Bass, Bernard, and Bruce J. Avolio. (1994) 'Shatter the glass ceiling: Women may make better managers,' *Human Resource Management* 33: 549–560. 18

Bates, Reid A., Timothy Hatcher, Elwood E. Holton III and Neal Chalofsky. (2001) 'Redefining human resource development: An integration of the learning, performance, and spirituality of work perspectives,' in Oscar A. Aliaga (ed.), *Academy of Human Resource Development Conference Proceedings*. Baton Rouge: AHRD. 19

Baumol, William J., and Edward N. Wolff. (1998) 'Side effects of progress: How technological change increases the duration of unemployment,' *Public Policy Brief, No. 41*, Jerome Levy Economics Institute of Bard College, 7–30. 21

Becker, Wendy S., Jerry A. Carbo II and Ian M. Langella. (2010) 'Beyond self-interest: Integrating social responsibility and supply chain management with human resource development,' *Human Resource Development Review* 9(2): 144–168. 22

Bellah, Robert N., et al. (1985, 1996) *Habits of the heart: Individualism and commitment in American life*. Berkeley: University of California Press. 2

Berger, Nancy O., Marijke T. Kehrhahn and Martha Summerville. (2004) Research to practice: Throwing a rope across the divide, *Human Resource Development International* 7(3): 403–409. 12

Bhaskar-Shrinivas, P., D.A. Harrison, M.A. Shaffer and D.M. Luk. (2005) Input-based and time-based models of international adjustment: Meta-analytic evidence and theoretical extensions, *Academy of Management Journal* 48: 257–281. 8

Bierema, Laura. (1996) 'Development of the individual leads to more productive workplaces,' in Robert Rowden (ed.), *Workplace learning: Debating Five Critical Questions of Theory and Practice,* New Directions for Adult and Continuing Education 72: 21–30, San Francisco: Jossey-Bass. 20

Bierema, Laura, and Michelle D'Abundo. (2004) HRD with a conscience: Practicing socially responsible HRD, *International Journal of Lifelong Education* 23(5): 443–458. 5

Bierema, Laura, and Maria Cseh. (2003) 'Evaluating AHRD using a feminist research framework,' *Human Resource Development Quarterly* 14: 5–26. 5

Billett, Stephen. (2001) *Learning in the workplace: Strategies for effective practice*. Crows Nest, Australia: Allen and Unwin. 20

Billig, M. (2000) 'Towards a critique of the critical,' *Discourse and Society* 11(3): 291–292. 5

Black, J. Stewart. (1988) 'Work role transitions: A study of American expatriate managers in Japan,' *Journal of International Business Studies* 30(2): 119–134. 8

Black, J. Stewart, and H.B. Gregersen. (1999) 'The right way to manage expats,' *Harvard Business Review* 77(2): 52–63. 8

Blake, Robert R., and Jane Mouton. (1964) *The managerial grid*. Houston: Gulf Publishing Company. 18

Borman, W.C., and S.J. Motowidlo. (1993) 'Expanding the criterion domain to include elements of contextual performance,' in N. Schmitt and W. C. Borman (eds.), *Personnel selection in organizations*. San Francisco: Jossey Bass, 71–98. 8

Bourg, Chris, and Mady Segal. (1999, summer) 'The impact of family supportive policies and practices on organizational commitment to the Army,' *Armed Forces and Society, New Brunswick* 25(4): 633–652. 21

Bowie, Norman E. (1998) 'A Kantian theory of capitalism,' *The Ruffin Series of the Society for Business Ethics* 1998:37–60 Briggs,Vernon N. (1987) 'Human resource development and the formulation of national economic policy,' *Journal of Economic Issues* 21: 12–36.   22

Brislin, R., R. Worthley and B. MacNab. (2006) 'Cultural intelligence: Understanding behaviors that serve people's goals,' *Group and Organization Management* 31: 40–55.   8

Brookfield, Stephen. (2001) 'Repositioning ideology critique in a critical theory of adult education,' *Adult Education Quarterly* 52: 7–22.   5

Brookfield, Stephen. (1994) 'Tales from the dark side: A phenomenography of adult critical reflection,' *International Journal of Lifelong Education* 1 (3): 203–216.   5

Brown, Duncan. (2002) *Evaluating human capital.* London: Chartered Institute of Personnel and Development.   21

Burrell, Gibson. (2001) 'Critical dialogues on organization,' *Ephemera* 1(1): 11–29.   5

Butler, Judith. (1993) *Bodies that matter: On the discursive limits of 'sex.'* New York: Routledge.   2

Calas, Marta B., and Linda Smircich. (1991) 'Voicing seduction to silence leadership,' *Organization Studies* 12: 567–602.   18

Callahan, Jamie. L., J. Kori Whitener and Jennifer A. Sandlin. (2007) 'The art of creating leaders: Popular culture artifacts as pathways for development,' *Advances in Developing Human Resources* 9: 19.   18

Cameron, Kim S., Jane E. Dutton and Robert E. Quinn, eds. (2003) *Positive organizational scholarship.* San Francisco: Barrett-Koehler.   12, 22

Carmeli, Abraham, Batia Ben-Hador, David Waldman and Deborah Rupp. (2009) 'How leaders cultivate social capital and nurture employee vigor: Implications for job performance,' *Journal of Applied Psychology* 94: 1553–1561.   13, 18

Carroll, Brigid, and Lester Levy. (2008) 'Defaulting to management: Leadership defined by what it is not,' *Organization* 15: 21.   18

CASSE: Centre for the Advancement of the Steady State Economy, available at http://steadystate.org.   21

Ceci, S.J. (1996) *On intelligence: A bioecological treatise on intellectual development.* Cambridge: Harvard University Press.   8

Chakraborty, S.K. (1986) 'The will-to-yoga: Key to better quality of work life,' *Vikalpa*: 113–124.   19

Checkland, Peter. (1994) 'Conventional wisdom and conventional ignorance,' *Organisation* 1.1: 29–34.   1

Chen, H. T. (1994) 'Current trends and future directions in program evaluation' *Evaluation Practice*, 15(3): 229–238.   17

Chen, H. T. (1990) *Theory-driven evaluation*, Newbury Park, CA: Sage.   17

Chia, Robert (1997) 'Process philosophy and management learning: Cultivating "foresight" in management,' in John Burgoyne and Michael Reynolds (eds.), *Management Learning.* London: Sage, 71–88.   1

Cho, Eunsang, and Gary N. McLean, (2004) 'What we discovered about NHRD and what it means for HRD,' *Advances in Developing Human Resources* 6: 382–393.   19

Cho, Eunsang, and Gary N. McLean. (1998) 'Gainsharing plan for the 21st century Korean economy.' *Human Resource Development International* 1: 189–206.   15

Clark, George, Suzanne Moser, Samual Ratick, Kirstin Dow, William Meyer, Srinivas Emani, Weigen Jin, Jeanne Kasperson, Roger Kasperson and Harry Schwarz. (1998) 'Assessing the vulnerability of costal communities to extreme storms: The case of Revere, MA, USA,' *Migration and Adaptation Strategies for Global Change* 3(1): 59–82.   21

Clarke, Nicholas, and Malcolm Higgs. (2010) 'Leadership training across business sectors: Report to the University Forum for Human Resource Development,' (UFHRD), Southampton, UK: University of Southampton.   13, 18

Clarkson, Max B.E. (1995) 'A stakeholder framework for analyzing and evaluating corporate social performance,' *Academy of Management Review* 20: 92–117.   19

Collins, Brandi. (2001) 'Organizational performance: The future focus of leadership development programs,' *Journal of Leadership Studies* 7: 43–54.   13

Collins, Randall. (1993) 'Emotional energy as the common denominator of rational action,' *Rationality and Society* 5: 27.   18

Commission for Education and Human Resource Policies. (2001) *National human resource development policy report to initiate 21ˢᵗ century knowledge state.* Seoul: Author. (Korean)

Conger, Jay. (1992) Learning to lead: The art of transforming managers into leaders. San Francisco: Jossey-Bass.   13, 18

Cooper, Cecily. (2008) 'Elucidating the bonds of workplace humor: A relational process model,' *Human Relations* 61(8): 1087–1115.   16

Cooper, Robert. (1976) 'The open field,' *Human Relations* 29(11): 999–1017.   1

Copa, George H. (1984) 'Organizing knowledge for use: A basis for expanding the focus of research in vocational education,' *Journal of Vocational Education Research* 9(4): 1–7.   22

Costa, P.T. Jr., and R.R. McCrae. (1992) *Revised NEO personality inventory (NEO PI-R) and new five-factor inventory (NEO FFI) professional manual.* Odessa, FL: Psychological Assessment Resources.   8

Coyne, B., Ed Coyne and Monica Lee. (2003) *Human resources, care giving, career progression and gender.* London: Routledge.   21

Crosby, Barbara, and John Bryson. (2010) Integrative leadership and the creation and maintenance of cross sector collaborations. *Leadership Quarterly* 21: 211–230.   13

Cutter, Susan, Jerry Mitchell and Michael Scott. (2000) 'Revealing the vulnerability of people and places: A case study of Georgetown County, South Carolina,' *Annals of the Association of American Geographers* 90(4): 713–737.   21

Dales, Margaret, and Paul Iles. (1992) *Assessing management skills: A guide to competences and evaluation techniques.* London: Kogan Page.   4

Day, David. (2000) 'Leadership development: A review in context,' *Leadership Quarterly* 11(4): 581–611.   4

de Vries, Kets, and R.F. Manfred. (1997) 'The leadership mystique,' *Academy of Management Executive* 8: 73–92.   18

Deci, E.L., and R.M. Ryan. (1985) *Intrinsic motivation and self-determination in human behavior.* New York: Plenum.   8

DeNisi, A.S., and R.D. Pritchard. (2006) 'Performance appraisal, performance management and improving individual performance: A motivational framework,' *Management and Organization Review* 2: 253–277.   8

Denison, Daniel R. (1990) *Corporate culture and organizational effectiveness.* New York: Wiley.   12

Denison, Daniel R. and Aneil K. Mishra. (1995) 'Toward a theory of organizational culture and effectiveness,' *Organization Science* 6(2): 204–223.   12

Dewey, John. (1938) *Experience and education*, New York: Collier Books.

DiMaggio, Paul, and Walter Powell. (1991) *New institutionalism in organizational analysis.* Chicago: University of Chicago Press.   1

DiMaggio, P., and W. Powell (1991) *New institutionalism in organizational analysis*. Chicago: University of Chicago Press.   4

Dixon, Nancy. (1998) Dialogue at work. London: Lemos and Crane.   14

Doloriert, Clair, and Sally Sambrook. (2011) 'Accommodating an autoethnographic PhD: The tale of the thesis, the viva voce, and the traditional business school,' *Journal of Contemporary Ethnography* 40 (5), 582–615   5

Doloriert, Clair, and Sally Sambrook. (2009) 'Ethical confessions of the 'I' of autoethnography: The student's dilemma,' *Journal of Qualitative Research in Organization and Management: An international journal* 4(1): 27–45.   5

Drath, Wilfred, Cynthia McCauley, Charles Palus, Ellen Van Velsor, Patricia O'Connor and John McGuire. (2008) 'Direction, alignment, commitment: Toward a more integrative ontology of leadership development,' *Leadership Quarterly* 19: 635–653.   13

Drucker, Peter. (1999) *Management challenges for the 21st century*. New York: Harper-Collins Publishers, 44.   21

Eagly, Alice H. (2005) 'Achieving relational authenticity in leadership: Does gender matter?' *Leadership Quarterly* 16(3): 459–474.   12

Earley, P.C. (1987) 'Intercultural training for managers: A comparison of documentary and interpersonal methods,' *Academy of Management Journal* 30: 685–698.   8

Earley, P.C., and R.S. Peterson. (2004) 'The elusive cultural chameleon: Cultural intelligence as a new approach to intercultural training for the global manager,' *Academy of Management Learning and Education* 3: 100–115.   8

Earley, P.C., and S. Ang. (2003) *Cultural intelligence: Individual interactions across cultures*. Palo Alto: Stanford University Press.   8

EC. (2003) *The future of the European Employment Strategy (EES):* 'A strategy for full employment and better jobs for all.' Brussels: European Commission.   7

EC. (2002) *The European social dialogue: A force for innovation and change: proposal for a Council decision establishing a tripartite social summit for growth and employment*. Luxembourg: European Commission Office of Official Publications of the European Union.   7

EC. (1997) *Towards a Europe of knowledge*. Brussels: European Commission DG XX11.   7

EC. (1996) *Teaching and learning: Towards the ;earning society*. Luxembourg: European Commission Publications Office.   7

EC. (1994) *Growth, competitiveness, employment: The challenges and ways forward into the 21st century*. Luxembourg: European Commission Publications.   7

Edwards Deming, W. (1986) *Out of the crisis*. Boston: MIT Press.   19

Elliott, Carole, and Sharon Turnbull. (2002) 'Critical thinking in HRD: A panel led discussion,' *Proceedings of the Annual AHRD Conference, Honolulu, Hawaii: Academy of Human Resource Development*: 971–973.   5

Ely, Katherine, Lisa Boyce, Jonathan Nelson, Stephen Zaccaro, Gina Hernez-Broome and Wynne Whyman. (2010) 'Evaluating leadership coaching: A review and integrated framework,' *Leadership Quarterly* 21: 585–599.   13

Eschbach, D.M., G.E. Parker and P.A. Stoeberl. (2001) American repatriated employees' retrospective assessments of the effects of cross-cultural training on their adaptation to international assignments, *International Journal of Human Resource Management* 12: 270–287.   8

ETUC, UNICE/UEAPME and CEEP. (2004) *Framework of Actions for the Lifelong Development of Competencies and Qualifications: Second follow-up report*. Brussels: ETUC, UNICE/UEAPME and CEEP.   7

ETUC, UNICE/UEAPME and CEEP. (2003, March 14) *Framework of Actions for the Lifelong Development of Competencies and Qualifications: First follow-up report*. Brussels: ETUC, UNICE/UEAPME and CEEP. 7

Evison, Rose, and Richard Horobin. (2000) The Therapeutic Uses of Laughter: Research, Theory and Applications, British Psychological Society Scottish Branch, scientific meeting, October 14. 14

Fenwick, Tara. (2005) 'Conceptions of Critical HRD: Dilemmas for theory and practice,' *Human Resource Development International* 8(3): 225–238. 5

Fenwick, Tara. (2004) 'Toward a critical HRD: In theory and practice,' *Adult Education Quarterly* 5 (3): 193–209. 5

Fenwick, Tara. (2003) *Learning through experience: Troubling assumptions and intersecting questions*. Malabar, FL: Krieger. 20

Fenwick, Tara, and Laura Bierema. (2008) 'Corporate social responsibility: Issues For human resource development professionals,' *International Journal of Training and Development* 12(1): 24–35. 22

Fetterman, David. (2001). Foundations of Empowerment Evaluation. Thousand Oaks, CA: Sage. 17

Fiedler, Fred. E. (1964) 'A contingency model of leadership effectiveness,' in L. Berkowitz (ed.), *Advances in experimental social psychology*, vol. 1. New York: Academic Press. 18

Fine, Gary, and Michaela De Soucey. (2005) 'Joking cultures: Humor themes as social regulation in group life,' *International Journal of Humor Research* 18(1): 1–22. 16

Finnis, John. (1993) *Natural law and natural rights*. Oxford: Clarendon. 22

Flavell, J.H. (1979) 'Metacognition and cognitive monitoring: A new area of cognitive inquiry,' *American Psychologist* 34: 906–911. 8

Foden, David, and Jonathan Winterton. (2001) 'The role of trade unions in the European Employment Strategy,' *Proceedings of the 6th European Industrial Relations Congress*, Oslo: 25–29. 7

Fogel, Alan. (1993) *Developing through relationships: Origins of communication, self and culture*. Hemel Hempstead: Harvester Wheatsheaf. 1

Fournier, Valerie, and Chris Grey. (2000) 'At the critical moment: Conditions and prospects for critical management studies,' *Human Relations*, 53(1): 7–32. 5

Fox, Matthew. (1994) *The reinvention of work: A new vision of livelihood in our time*. San Francisco, New York: Harper. 14

Freidson, Elliot. (1988) *Professional powers: A study of the institutionalization of formal knowledge*. Chicago: University of Chicago Press. 22

French, J.R., and B. Raven. (1959) 'The bases of social power,' in D. Cartwright (ed.), *Studies in Social Power*. Ann Arbor: University of Michigan Press. 18

Friedman, Milton. (1970, September 30) 'The social responsibility of business is to increase its profits,' *The New York Times Magazine*. 22

Friedman, Thomas. (2005) *The world is flat*. .New York: Farrar, Straus and Giroux. 10

Friedman, Thomas M. (2000) *The Lexus and the olive tree*. New York: Anchor Books. 19

Fuller, Buckminster. (1973) *Operating manual for Spaceship Earth*. New York: Penguin. 19

Fuss, Diana. (1989) *Essentially speaking: Feminism, nature and difference*. New York: Routledge. 2

Garavan, Thomas N. (1995) 'HRD stakeholders: Their philosophies, values, expectations and evaluation criteria,' *Journal of European Industrial Training* 19(10): 17–30. 12

Garavan, Thomas N., Noreen Heraty and Bridie Barnicle. (1999) 'Human resource development literature: Current issues, priorities and dilemmas,' *Journal of European Industrial Training* 23(4/5): 169–179.   12

Gardner, Howard. (1993) *Frames of mind: The theory of multiple intelligences.* New York: Basic Books.   2

Gardner, William L., Dawn Fischer and James G. (Jerry) Hunt. (2009) 'Emotional labour and leadership; A threat to authenticity,' *Leadership Quarterly* 20: 466–482.   12

Gardner, William L., Bruce J. Avolio, Fred Luthans, Douglas R. May and Fred O. Walumbwas. (2005) 'Can you see the real me? A self based model of authentic leader and follower development,' *Leadership Quarterly* 16(3): 343–372.   12

Gelfand, M.J., M.E. Erez and Z. Aycan. (2007) 'Cross-cultural organizational behavior,' *Annual Review of Psychology* 58: 479–514.   8

Gemmill, Gary, and Judith Oakley. (1992) 'Leadership: An alienating social myth,' *Human Relations* 45: 16.   18

Gergen, Kenneth J. (1991) *The saturated self: Dilemmas of identity in contemporary life.* New York: Basic Books, 68–69.   2

Gibb, Steve, and David Megginson. (2001) 'Employee development,' in Tom Redman and Adrian Wilkinson (eds.), *Contemporary Human Resource Management.* London: FT/Pearson.   14

Giddens, Anthony. (1989) *The consequences of modernity.* Cambridge: Polity.   2

Goffee, Robert, and Gareth Jones. (2006) *Why should anyone be led by you? What it takes to be an authentic leader.* Cambridge: Harvard Business School Press.   12

Gold, Jeff, Rick Holden, Paul A Iles, Jim Stewart and Joyce Beardwell, eds. (2009) *Human resource development: Theory and practice.* Basingstoke: Palgrave.   4

Goldman, Daniel. (2000) *Working with emotional intelligence.* New York: Bantam Books.   2

Goldman, Daniel. (1996) *Emotional intelligence.* London: Bloomsbury.   4

Gosling, Jonathan, and Henry Mintzberg. (2003) 'The five minds of a manager,' *Harvard Business Review* (November): 54–63.   9

Goulder, Lawrence. (2004) *Induced technological change and climate policy.* Arlington,VA: Pew Centre for Global Climate Change.   21

Graen, George B., and Mary Uhl-Bien. (1995) 'Development of leader-member exchange (LMX) theory of leadership over 25 years: Applying a multi-level-multi-domain perspective,' *Leadership Quarterly* 6: 28.   18

Grant, Barbara. (2003) 'Mapping the pleasures and risks of supervision,' *Discourse: Studies in the Cultural Politics of Education* 24(2): 175–190.   5

Gregory, James. (1989) *American exodus: The Dust Bowl migration and Okie culture in California.* New York: Oxford University Press.   21

Gronn, Peter. (2002) 'Distributed leadership as a unit of analysis,' *Leadership Quarterly* 13(4): 423–451.   4

Gudykunst, W.B., S. Ting-Toomey and E. Chua. (1988) *Culture and interpersonal communication.* Newbury Park, CA: Sage.   8

Habermas, Jurgen. (1984) *The theory of communicative action: Reason and the rationalization of society,* vol.1. Cambridge: Polity Press.   5

Hale, Ellen. (2000, December 22) 'The greying of Europe has economies in jeopardy,' *USA Today,* p. 14A.   21

Hall, E.T. (1959) *The silent language.* New York: Doubleday.   8

Hall, Edward T., and Elizabeth Hall. (1976) 'How cultures collide,' *Psychology Today* 10(2): 66–74.   3

Halvorsen, Helge. (1998) Role of Social Partners in the Development of Training, Proceedings of the ETF Seminar, Bucharest, October 2–3.   7

Hammill, Greg. (2011) 'Mixing and managing four generations of employees,' *FDUMagazine*, available at http://www.fdu.edu/newspubs/magazine/05ws/generations.htm (accessed June 17 2011).   10

Hansen, Carol D., and Ann K. Brooks. (1994) 'A review of cross cultural research on human resource development,' *Human Resource Development Quarterly* 5(1): 55–74.   3

Harbison, Frederick H. and Charles A. Meyers, (1964) *Education, manpower, and economic growth: Strategies of human resource development*. New York: McGraw-Hill.   15

Harrison, Rosemary. (1997) *Employee development*. London: Institute of Personnel and Development (IPD).   12

Hatcher Timothy. (2002) *Ethics and HRD. A new approach to leading responsible organizations*. Cambridge, MA: Basic Books.   22

Hatcher, Tim, and Monica Lee. (2005) 'HRD and the democratic ideal: The conflict of democratic values in undemocratic work systems,' in Carole Elliott and Sharon Turnbull (eds.), *Critical Thinking in Human Resource Development*. London: Routledge.   5, 21

Haworth, Nigel. (2003) 'Potential in search of achievement: APEC and human resource development,' in *APEC as an institution: Multilateral governance in the Asia Pacific*, Singapore: Institute of South East Asian Studies.   7

Hechanova, R., T.A. Beehr and N.D. Christiansen. (2003) 'Antecedents and consequences of employee's adjustment to overseas assignment: A meta-analytic review,' *Applied Psychology: An International Review* 52: 213–236.   8

Heidemann, Winfried, and Wilfried Kruse (1998) 'Validation and recognition of competences and qualifications,' *European Discussion Paper for the Social Partners*. Düsseldorf: Hans Böckler Stiftung.   7

Hepburn, Aden. (2011) 'Facebook statistics, stats and facts for 2011,' Digitalbuzz, 2011, available at http://www.digitalbuzzblog.com/facebook-statistics-stats-facts-2011/ (accessed June 17 2011).   10

Hersey, Paul, and Ken H. Blanchard. (1969) 'Life-cycle theory of leadership,' *Training and Development Journal* 23: 26–34.   18

Hofstede, Geert. (2001) Culture's consequences: Comparing values, behaviors, institutions, and organizations across nations. San Francisco: Sage.   19

Hofstede, Geert. (1984) *Culture's consequences: International differences in work-related values*, vol. 5. London: Sage.   3

Hofstede, Geert. (1980) 'Culture and organizations,' *International Studies of Management and Organization* 10(4): 15–41.   3

House, Robert J. (1971) 'A path-goal theory of leader effectiveness,' *Administrative Science Quarterly* 16: 321–328.   18

Huselid, Mark, Richard Beatty and Brian Becker. (2005) 'A players or A positions? The strategic logic of workforce management,' *Harvard Business Review*, 83(12): 110–117.   4

Iles, Paul, David Preece and Chuai X. (2010) 'Is talent management a management fashion in HRD? Towards a research agenda,' *Human Resource Development International* 13(2): 125–146.   4

Iles, Paul, Chuai X and David Preece. (2010) 'Talent management and HRM in multinational companies in Beijing: Definitions, differences and drivers,' *Journal of World Business Special Issue 'Global Talent Management'* 46(2): 179–189.   4

Iles Paul, and David Preece. (2006) 'Developing leaders or developing leadership?' *Academy of Chief Executives' Programmes in the North-East of England Leadership* 2(3): 317–340.   4

Ilies, Remus, Frederick P. Morgeson and Jennifer D. Nahrgang. (2005) 'Authentic leadership and eudemonic well-being: Understanding leader–follower outcomes,' *Leadership Quarterly* 16: 373–394.   12

Illich, Ivan. (1971) *Deschooling society.* Harmondsworth: Penguin.   14

International Labour Organization. (2010) '*Decent work for all,*' retrieved online on August 12, 2010, at http://www.ilo.org/global/About_the_ILO/Mainpillars/WhatisDecentWork/lang—en/index.htm.   22

IPCC. (2001) '*Intergovernmental panel on climate change: Summary for policy makers,*' www.ipcc.ch. Accessed 1ˢᵗ September 2004   21

Jacobs, Jane. (1961) The Death and Life of Great American Cities. *New York: Random House.*   4

Jacques, Roy. (1996) *Manufacturing the employee.* London: Sage.   14

Jamal, Karim, and Norm E. Bowie. (1995) 'Theoretical considerations for a meaningful code of professional ethics,' *Journal of Business Ethics* 14: 703–714.   22

Janssens, M., and J.M. Brett. (2006) 'Cultural intelligence in global teams: A fusion model of collaboration,' *Group and Organization Management* 31: 124–153.   8

Joint Committee on Standards for Educational Evaluation. (1994) *The Program Evaluation Standards,* 2nd ed. Thousand Oaks, CA: Sage.   17

Kafka, Franz. (1994) *The Collected Aphorisms*, trans. Malcolm Pasley. London: Syrens.   14

Kanfer, R., and E.D. Heggestad. (1997) 'Motivational traits and skills: A person-centered approach to work motivation,' *Research in Organizational Behavior* 19: 1–56.   8

Karl, Thomas, and David Easterling. (1999) 'Climate extremes: Selected review and future research directions,' *Climate Change* 42(1): 309–325.   21

Katz, Robert L. (1955) 'Skills of an effective administrator,' *Harvard Business Review* 33: 33–42.   18

Kelleher, Michael. (1996) 'New forms of work organisation and HRD,' in Jim Stewart and Jim McGoldrick (eds.), *Human Resource Development: Perspectives, Strategies and Practice,* London: Pitman.   21

Kessels, Joseph, and Rob Poell. (2004) 'Andragogy, social capital theory, and implications for human resource development,' *Advances in Developing Human Resources* 6(2): 146–157.   20

Kets de Vries, Manfred R.F. (1994) 'The leadership mystique,' Academy of Management Executive 8: 73–92, esp. 75.   18

Kiefer, Tina, (2002) 'Understanding the emotional experience of organizational change: Evidence from a merger,' *Advances in Developing Human Resources* 4: 39–61.   18

Kim, Jang-Ho (Ed) 2000) *Major policy diagnosis, analysis, and development of national human resource development*. Seoul: Korean Research Institute for Vocational Education and Training.   15

Kirkpatrick, D.L. (1994) *Evaluating training programs: The four levels.* San Francisco: BerrettKoehier.   17

Kluckhohn, C. (1967) 'Values and value-orientations in the theory of action: An exploration in definition and classification,' in T. Parsons and E. A. Shils (eds.), Toward a General Theory of Action, Cambridge: Harvard University Press, 388–433. (Original work published 1951.)   17

Korean Education Development Institute. (2000) *The direction and tasks of national human resource development*. Seoul: Korean Education Development Institute.   15

Korean Research Institute for Vocational Education and Training (2000) *Major Policy Diagnosis, Analysis, and Development of National Human Resource Development*. Seoul: Korean Research Institute for Vocational Education and Training.   15

Kotthoff, Helga. (2006) 'Gender and humor: The state of the art,' *Journal of Pragmatics* 38: 4–25. 16

Krishnamurti, Jiddu. (1999) *This light in oneself: True meditation.* Boston: Shambhala. 14

Kuchinke, K. Peter. (2010) 'Human flourishing as a central value for human resource development,' *Human Resource Development Quarterly* 13(5): 575–585. 22

Kuchinke, K. Peter. (2004) 'Contested domains: human resource development programs in colleges of education,' *Workforce Education Forum* 3(1): 43–60. 22

Kuchinke, K. Peter. (2004) 'Theorizing and practicing HRD: Extending the dialogue over the roles of scholarship and practice in the field,' *Human Resource Development International* 7(4): 535–540. 12

Ladkin, Donna, and Steven S. Taylor. (2010) 'Enacting the 'true self': Towards a theory of embodied authentic leadership,' *Leadership Quarterly* 21: 64–74. 12

Landis, D., and R. Brislin. (1983) *Handbook on intercultural training,* vol. 1. New York: Pergamon. 8

Law, K.S., C.S. Wong and W.H. Mobley. (1998) 'Toward a taxonomy of multi-dimensional constructs,' *Academy of Management Review* 23: 741–755. 8

Lawless, Aileen, and Sally Sambrook. (2008) 'Critically reflective practice and peripheral participation: A powerful or a powerless position?' *9th International Conference on HRD and Practice across Europe.,* Lille: IESEG. 5

Lee, Monica. (2010) 'Shifting boundaries: The role Of HRD in a changing world,' *Advances in Developing Human Resources,* ed. Thomas Garavan and Dave McGuire, 12(5): 524–535. 21

Lee, Monica. (2010) 'Some thoughts on the diffusion of boundaries and borders,' academic response to keynote HRD Strategies in a European Borderless Postal Market: A Hungarian Perspective, Ildikó Szűts, CEO, Magyar Posta Zrt. 11th *International Conference on HRD Research and Practice across Europe,* June 2010, University of Pécs. 21

Lee, Monica. (2009) 'On the loss of a room: An autoethnographic assay of fact,' *Human Resource Development International* 12(3): 343–349. 1

Lee, Monica. (2007) HRD from a holistic perspective,' in David McGuire, Thomas Garavan, Sandra Watson and David O'Donnell (eds.), *Perspectives On Human Resource Development; Special Issue of Advances in HRD* 9(1): 150–168. 21

Lee, Monica. (2004) 'A refusal to define HRD,' in *New Frontiers in Human Resource Development,* Jean Woodall, Jim Stewart and Monica Lee (eds.), London: Routledge, 27–40. 1

Lee, Monica. (2004) 'Complex archetypal structures that underlie the "Human Condition,"' *Organisational Transformation and Social Change* 2(2): 49–70. 1, 21

Lee, Monica. (2004) 'National human resource development in the United Kingdom,' *Advances in Developing Human Resources* 6(3): 334–345. 21

Lee, Monica. (2003) 'On codes of ethics: The individual and performance,' *Performance Improvement Quarterly,* 16(2): 72–89. 1, 21

Lee, Monica. (2003) 'The complex roots of HRD,' in *HRD in a Complex World,* M. Lee (ed.), London: Routledge, 7–24. 21

Lee, Monica. (2002) 'The complex roots of HRD,' in T. Rocco (ed.), *Defining the Cutting Edge—Top 10 Outstanding Papers of 2002,* 3–12. Bowling Green, OH: AHRD 1

Lee, Monica. (2002) 'The evolution of HRD,' in U. Pareek, A.M. Osman Gani, S. Ramnarayan and T.V. Rao (eds.), *Human Resource Development in Asia: Trends and Challenges,* New Delhi: Oxford and IBH Publishing, 695–702. 1

Lee, Monica. (2001) 'A refusal to define HRD,' in Rob Poell (ed.), *Defining the Cutting Edge—Top 10 Outstanding Papers of 2001*, pp 3–12. Bowling Green, OH: AHRD. 1

Lee, Monica. (2001) 'A refusal to define HRD,' *Human Resource Development International* 4(1): 327–341. 1, 5, 20

Lee, Monica. (2001) 'On seizing the moment as the research question emerges,' in Jim Stewart, Jim McGoldrick and Sandra Watson (eds.), *Understanding Research into HRD*, London: Routledge, 18–40. 1

Lee, Monica. (1999) 'The lie of power: empowerment as impotence,'*Human Relations* 52(2): 225–262. 1

Lee, Monica. (1999) 'Text, gender and future realities,' in Richard Goodman, (ed.), *Modern Organisations and Emerging Conundrums: Exploring the Post-Industrial Sub-culture of the Third Millennium*, Lanham, MD: Lexington Books, 109–125. 1

Lee, Monica. (1998) 'Understandings of conflict: A cross-cultural investigation,'. *Personnel Review* 27(3): 227–242. 18

Lee, Monica. (1997) 'The developmental approach: A critical reconsideration,' in John Burgoyne and Mike Reynolds (eds.), *Management Learning*, London: Sage, 199–214. 1

Lee, Monica, (1997) 'Strategic human resource development: A conceptual exploration,' *Academy of Human Resource Development Conference Proceedings,* ed. Rich Torraco, Baton Rouge, LA: Academy of HRD, 92–99. 1

Lee, Monica. (1996) 'Action learning as a cross-cultural tool,' in Jim Stewart and Jim McGoldrick (eds.), *Human Resource Development: Perspectives, Strategies and Practice,* London: Pitman, 240–260. 1

Lee, Monica. (1996) 'Competence and the new manager,' in Monica Lee, Hugo Letiche, Robert Crawshaw and Michael Thomas (eds.), *Management Education in the New Europe: Boundaries and Complexity*, London: Routledge, 101–117. 1

Lee, Monica. (1994) 'The isolated manager: Walking the boundaries of the micro-culture,' *Proceedings of the British Academy of Management Conference*, Lancaster: 111–128. 21

Lee, Monica, and Tim Hatcher. (2003) 'HRD and the Democratic ideal: The conflict of democratic values in undemocratic work systems,' in J. Winterton (ed.), *International, Comparative and Cross-Cultural Dimensions of HRD*, ESC Toulouse: Toulouse,. ISBN 1–86220–149–8 1

Lee, Monica, Hugo Letiche, Robert Crawshaw and Michael Thomas, eds. (1996) *Management Education in the New Europe*. London: Routledge. 5, 21

Lepak, David. P., and S.A. Snell. (1999) 'The human resource architecture: Toward a theory of human capital allocation and development,' *Academy of Management Review*, 24(1): 31–48. 1

Lewis, Robert, and Robert Heckman. (2006) 'Talent management: A critical review,' *Human Resource Management Review* 16(1): 139–54. 22

Littrell, L.N., and E. Salas. (2005) 'A review of cross-cultural training: Best practices, guidelines, and research needs,' *Human Resource Development Review* 4(3): 305–334. 4

Liu, X., & Shaffer, M. A. (2005). An investigation of expatriate adjustment and performance: A social capital perspective. International Journal of Cross-Cultural Management, 5, 235–254. 8

Lizotte, Ken. (2001, March) 'Are balance benefits for real?' *Journal of Business Strategy* 22(2): 32. 21

Lovelock, James. (2000 [1979]) *Gaia: A new look at life on Earth*, 3rd ed. New York: Oxford University Press. 9

Luthans, Fred, and Bruce J. Avolio. (2003) 'Authentic leadership: A positive developmental approach,' in *Positive Organizational Scholarship*, ed. Kim S. Cameron, Jane E. Dutton and Robert E. Quinn, San Francisco: Barrett-Koehler, 241–261.   12

Lynham, Susan A., Kenneth E. Paprock and Peter W. Cunningham, eds. (2006) *Advances in developing human resources 8(1): National human resource development In transitioning societies in the developing world.* Thousand Oaks, CA: Sage.   15

Lynham, Susan A., and Peter W. Cunningham. (2004) 'Human resource development as national policy and practice—The South African case,' *Advances in Developing Human Resources* 6: 319.   15, 22

Madsen, Susan. (2001) The Effects of Home-based Teleworking on Work and Family Conflict. Unpublished doctoral dissertation, University of Minnesota, St. Paul.   19

Mark, Melvin M., Gary T. Henry and George Julnes. (2000) Evaluation: An Integrated Framework for Understanding, Guiding and Improving Public and Nonprofit Policies and Programs. San Francisco, CA: Jossey-Bass.   17

Marshall, R. (1986) The Role of Apprenticeship in an Internationalized Information World,' Conference on Learning by Doing Sponsored by The International Union of Operating Engineers, the US Department of Labor, and Cornell University, Albany, NY, April 6: 1.   15

Marsick, Victoria J., and Karen E. Watkins. (1999) *Facilitating learning organizations*. Brookfield, VT: Grower.   10

Marsick, Victoria, and Karen Watkins. (1990) *Informal and incidental learning in the workplace*. London: Routledge.   20

Martin, Rod. (2007) *The psychology of humor: An integrative approach.* Burlington, MA: Elsevier.   16

Mavin, Sharon, Phil Wilding, Brenda Stalker, David Simmonds, Chris Rees and Francine Winch. (2007) 'Developing "new commons" between HRD research and practice: Case studies of UK universities,' *Journal of European Industrial Training* 31(1): 4–18.   12

Mayer, J.D., R.R. Caruso and P. Salovey. (2000) 'Emotional intelligence meets traditional standards for an intelligence,' *Intelligence* 27: 267–298.   8

McCarthy, James, Ozvaldo Canzani, Neil Leary, David Dokken and Kasey White. (2001) 'Climate change 2001: Impacts, adaptation and vulnerability,' Intergovernmental Panel on Climate Change, Geneva, Section 14.1.21.5.   21

McCracken, Martin, and Mary Wallace. (2000) 'Exploring strategic maturity in HRD—Rhetoric, aspiration or reality?' *Journal of European Industrial Training* 24(8): 424–467.   12

McFerrin, Bobby. (1988) 'Don't Worry, Be Happy,' album. New York: Simple Pleasures, EMI.   18

McLagan, Patricia A. (1989) *Models for HRD practice: The models.* Alexandria, VA: American Society for Training and Development.   19

McLaughlin, John A., and Gretchen B. Jordan. 1999. "Logic Models: A Tool for Telling Your Performance Story," Evaluation and Program Planning, Elsevier Science 22 (1): 65–72.   17

McLean, Gary N. (2010) 'The need for indigenous theory and practice in human resource development in Thailand,' *NIDA HROD Journal*: 1–19 (Thailand).   19

McLean, Gary N. (2008, April 5) 'National HRD: Challenges and implications,' Keynote presentation at the Texas A&M University Chautauqua Roundup, College Station, TX, Slide 5.   15

McLean, Gary N. (2005) 'Examining approaches to HR evaluation: The strengths and weaknesses of popular measurement methods,' *Strategic HR Review* 4(2): 24–27.   19

McLean, Gary N. (2004) 'National human resource development: What in the world is it?' in Gary N. McLean, A.M. Osman-Gani and E. Cho. (eds.), *Human resource development as national policy.* Advances in 3, 22 Developing Human Resources 6(3): 269–275.

McLean, Gary N. (2001) 'Ethical dilemmas and the many hats of HRD,' *Human Resource Development Quarterly* 12(3): 219–221.   22

McLean, Gary N., Susan A. Lynham, Ross E. Azevedo, John E. S. Lawrence and Frederick Nafukho. (2008) 'A response to Wang and Swanson's (2008) article on national HRD and theory development,' *Human Resource Development Review* 7: 241–258.   15

McLean, Gary N., Aahad M. Osman-Gani and Eunsang Cho, eds. (2004) *Advances in developing human resources 6(3): Human resource development As national policy.* Thousand Oaks, CA: Sage.   15

McLean, Gary N., and Laird D. McLean. (2001) 'If we can't define HRD in 3, 15 one country, how can we define it in an international context?' *Human*   19, *Resource Development International* 4 (3) 313–326.   20, 22

McLeman, Robert, and Barry Smit. (2004) 'Climate change, migration and security,' *Canadian Security Intelligence Publication*: Commentary no. 86.   21

Megginson, David. (1996) 'Planned and emergent learning: Consequences for development,' *Management Learning* 27(4): 411–428.   14

Mendenhall, M., Stahl, G., Ehnert, I., Oddou, G., Osland, J., & Kühlmann, T. (2004). Evaluation studies of cross-cultural training programs: A review of the literature from 1988–2000. In D Landis, & J Bennett (Eds). The Handbook of Intercultural Training. Thousand Oaks,CA: Sage   8

Mendenhall, Mark E., G.K. Stahl, I. Ehnert, G. Oddou, J.O. Osland and T.M. Kuhlmann. (2002) 'Evaluation studies of cross-cultural training programs,' in D. Landis, J.M. Bennett and M.J. Bennett (eds.), *Handbook of Intercultural Training*, Vol. 3, Thousand Oaks, CA: Sage.   8

Mendenhall, Mark, T. Kuhlmann and G.K. Stahl. (2001) *Developing global business leaders: Policies, processes, and innovations.* Westport, CT: Quorum Books.   9

Mendenhall, Mark, and Gary Oddou. (1985) 'The dimensions of expatriate acculturation: A review,' *Academy of Management Review* 10: 39–47.   8

Mestrovic, Stjepan. (1997) *Postemotional society.* Thousand Oaks, CA: Sage.   18

Metcalfe, Beverley D., and Chris. J. Rees. (2005) 'Theorizing advances in international human resource development,' *Human Resource Development International* 8(4): 449–465.   3

Michaels, Ed, Helen Handfield-Jones and Beth Axelrod. (2001) *The war for talent.* McKinsey and Company, Inc. Harvard: Harvard Business School Press   4

Mintzberg, Henry. (2004) *Managers, not MBAs: A hard look at the soft practice of managing and management development.* San Francisco: Berrett-Koehler.   9

Mitchell, Matthew. (2002, April) 'Technological change and the scale of production,' *Review of Economic Dynamics* 5(2): 477–488   21

Mokyr, Joel. (2002) *The Gifts of Athena: Historical origins of the knowledge economy.* Princeton and Oxford: Princeton University Press.   21

Morris, M.A., and C. Robie. (2001) 'A meta-analysis of the effects of cross-cultural training on expatriate performance and adjustment,' *International Journal of Training and Development* 5(2): 112–125.   8

Mumford, Michael D., Stephen J. Zaccaro, Francis D. Harding, T. Owen Jacobs and Edwin A. Fleishman. (2000) 'Leadership skills for a changing world: Solving complex social problems,' *Leadership Quarterly* 11: 11–35. 18

Ng, K.Y., and P.C. Earley. (2006) 'Culture and intelligence: Old constructs, new frontiers,' *Group and Organization Management* 31: 4–19. 8

Nonaka, Ikujiro. (2001) 'The knowledge-creating company,' *Harvard Business Review* (November–December): 96–104. 19

O'Donnell, David, David McGuire and Christine Cross. (2006) 'Critically challenging some assumptions in HRD,' *International Journal of Training and Development* 10(1): 4–16.5. 5

Ones, D. S., & Viswesvaran, C. (1999). Relative importance of personality dimensions for expatriate selection: A policy capturing study. Human Performance, 12, 275–294. 8

Oring, Elliott. (2003) *Engaging humor.* Urbana: University of Illinois Press. 16

Osman-Gani, A.M. (2000) 'Developing expatriates for the Asia Pacific region: A comparative analysis of multinational enterprise managers from three continents,' *Human Resource Development Quarterly* 11: 213–244. 8

Osman-Gani, A.M., and T. Rocksthul. (2009) 'Cross-cultural training, expatriate self-efficacy, and adjustments to overseas assignments: An empirical investigation of managers in Asia,' *International Journal of Intercultural Relations* 33: 277–290.8. 8

Osman-Gani, A.M., and T. Rocksthul. (2008) 'Antecedents and consequences of social network characteristics for expatriate adjustment and performance in overseas assignments: Implications for HRD,' *Human Resource Development Review* 7(1): 32–57. 8

Osman-Gani, A.M., and W-L. Tan. (2005) 'Expatriate development for Asia-Pacific: A study of training contents and methods,' *International Journal of Human Resources Development and Management* 5:41–56. 8

Ospina, Sonia, and Erica Foldy. (2010) 'Building bridges from the margins: The work of leadership in social change organizations,' *Leadership Quarterly* 21: 292–307. 13

Paige, R.M. (2004) 'Instrumentation in intercultural training,' in D. Landis, J.M. Bennett and M.J. Bennett (eds.), *Handbook of Intercultural Training*, 3rd ed., Thousand Oaks, CA: Sage, 85–128. 8

Patton, M.Q. (2008) *Utilization-focused evaluation*, 4th ed., Thousand Oaks, CA: Sage. 17

Patton, M.Q. (1997) *Utilization-focused evaluation: A new century text.* Thousand Oaks, CA: Sage. 17

Pearce, Fred. (2004) 'Climate change heralds thirsty times ahead for most,' *New Scientist* 2448: 16–17. 21

Pearce, Fred. (2002, July 20) 'Mamma Mia,' *New Scientist*: 38–41. 21

Perkmann, Markus, and Andre Spicer. (2008) 'How are management fashions institutionalized? The role of institutional work,' *Human Relations* 61(6): 811–844. 4

Peterson, Lori. (1997) 'International HRD: What we know and don't know,' *Human Resource Development Quarterly* 8(1): 63–79. 3

Petonsk, Annie, Daniel Dudek and Joseph Goffman. (2001) 'Market mechanisms and global climate change: An analysis of policy instruments,' in *Transatlantic Dialogues on Market Mechanisms*, Arlington,VA: Pew Centre on Global Climate Change. 21

Pfeffer, Jeffrey, and John F. Veiga. (1999) 'Putting people first for organizational success,' *Academy of Management Executive* 13(2): 37–48. 22

Pittinsky, Todd L., and Christopher J. Tyson. (2005) 'Leader authenticity markers: Findings from a study of perceptions of African American political leaders,' in *Authentic leadership theory and practice: Origins, effects, and development*, ed. William L. Gardner, Bruce J. Avolio and Fred O. Walumbwa, Oxford: Elsevier, 253–279.   12

Poe, Andrea. (2000, July) 'The baby blues,, *HR Magazine* 45(7): 78–84. Alexandria, VA: Society for Human Resource Management.   21

Poell, Rob. (2007) 'W(h)ither HRD? Towards a self-conscious, self-critical, and open-minded discipline,' *Human Resource Development International* 10(4): 361–363.   20

Poell, Rob. (2006, December 15) 'Personeelsontwikkeling in ontwikkeling: Naar een werknemersperspectief op Human Resource Development' [Developing human resource development: Towards an employee perspective on HRD], Inaugural lecture as Professor of HRD, Tilburg University, Netherlands, Rotterdam: Performa.   20

Poell, Rob. (1998) Organizing Work-related Learning Projects: A Network Approach. Doctoral thesis, University of Nijmegen, Netherlands.   20

Poell, Rob, and Ferd Van der Krogt. (2010) 'Individual learning paths of employees in the context of social networks,; in Stephen Billett (ed.), *Learning through Practice: Models, Traditions, Orientations and Approaches*, Dordrecht: Springer, 197–221.   20

Poell, Rob, and Ferd Van der Krogt. (2009, February 19–22) 'An empirical typology of hospital nurses' individual learning paths,' in Jennifer Calvin and Shani Carter (eds.), *Top Ten Best Papers from the Academy of HRD International Research Conference Held in Panama City, FL*, Bowling Green, OH: AHRD.   20

Poell, Rob, and Ferd Van der Krogt. (2007) 'Tailoring learning programmes to every-day employee learning: Customisation strategies of HRD practitioners in health care,' in Sally Sambrook and Jim Stewart (eds.), *Human Resource Development in the Public Sector: The Case of Health and Social Care*, London: Routledge, 239–252.   20

Poell, Rob, and Ferd Van der Krogt. (2006) 'Workplace learning reviewed: Confronting the rhetoric with empirical research,' in Jan Streumer (ed.), *Work-related Learning*, Dordrecht: Springer, 71–94.   20

Poell, Rob, and Ferd Van der Krogt. (2003) 'Learning-program creation in work organizations,' *Human Resource Development Review* 2(3): 252–272.   20

Poell, Rob, Geoff Chivers, Ferd Van der Krogt and Danny Wildemeersch. (2000) 'Learning-network theory: Organizing the dynamic relationships between learning and work,' *Management Learning* 31(1): 25–49.   20

Poell, Rob, Ferd Van der Krogt and Marjolein Berings. (in preparation) *Development and validation of the Workplace Learning Structures Quetionnaire (WLSQ)*.   20

Porcu, Leide. (2005) 'Fishy business: Humor in a Sardinian fish market,' *Humor: International Journal of Humor Research* 18(1): 69–102.   16

Postman, Neil. (1993) *Technopoly: The surrender of culture to technology*. New York: Vintage Books, 13.   2

Preece, David, Paul Iles and Chuai X. (2011) 'Talent management and management fashion in Chinese enterprise: Exploring case studies in Beijing,' *International Journal of Human Resource Management*. Volume 22, (16): 3413–3428.   4

Preece, David, and Paul Iles (2009) 'Leadership development: Assuaging uncertainties through joining a leadership academy,' *Personnel Review* 38(3): 286–306.   4

Preskill, H., and D. Russ-Eft. (2005) *Building evaluation capacity: 72 activities for teaching and training.* Thousand Oaks, CA: Sage.   17

Preskill, H., and D. Russ-Eft. (2003) 'A framework for reframing HRD evaluation practice and research,' in A.M. Gilley, L. Bierema and J. Callahan (eds.), *Critical Issues in HRD*, Cambridge, MA: Perseus, 199–257.   17

Preskill, H., and D. Russ-Eft. (2001) 'A systems model for evaluating learning performance,' in D.H. Redmann (ed.), *Academy of Human Resource Development: Defining the Cutting Edge,* Baton Rouge, LA: Academy of Human Resource Development, 57–63.   17

Preskill, H., and R.T. Torres. (1999) *Evaluative inquiry for learning in organizations.* Thousand Oaks, CA: Sage.   17

Ramdhony, Allan. (2011) A Conceptual Expansion of Critical HRD: Towards a Post-Reflective Understanding of HRD? 7th CMS Conference, Naples, July.   5

Ramdhony, Allan. (2010) A conceptual expansion of critical human resource development: insights into practice in a healthcare organisation. PhD thesis, Napier University, Edinburgh.   5

Renger, R., and B. Bourdeau. (2004) 'Strategies for values inquiry: An exploratory case study,' *American Journal of Evaluation* 25(1): 39–49.   17

Reynolds, Michael. (1999) 'Grasping the nettle: Possibilities and pitfalls of a critical management pedagogy,' *British Journal of Management* 9: 171–184.   5

Reynolds, Michael. (1997) 'Towards a critical pedagogy,' In John Burgoyne and Michael Reynolds (eds.), *Management Learning: Integrating Perspectives in Theory and Practice*, London: Sage, 312–328.   5

Richardson, Laurel. (2000) 'Writing: A method of inquiry,' in *The Handbook of Qualitative Research*, 2nd ed., ed. Norman K. Denzin and Yvonna S. Lincoln, Thousand Oaks, CA: Sage, 1:516–519.   2

Rigg, Clare. (2005) 'Becoming critical: Can critical management learning develop critical managers,' in Carole Elliott and Sharon Turnbull (eds.), *Critical Thinking in Human Resource Development*, London: Routledge, 37–52.   5

Rigg, Clare, Jim Stewart and Kiran Trehan, eds. (2007) *Critical human resource development: Beyond orthodoxy.* Harlow: Pearson Education FT Prentice Hall, 3–8.   5

Rippin, Ann. (2007) 'Stitching up the leader: Empirically based reflections on leadership and gender,' *Journal of Organizational Change Management* 20: 209–226.   18

Rodel, Berel. (1994) 'The environment and changing concepts of security,' *Canadian Security Intelligence Publication*: Commentary no. 47.   21

Rodgers, Jimmie. (2001) 'Human resource development: A crucial challenge for the Pacific Island,' Second Meeting of the Conference of the Pacific Community, Noumea, New Caledonia: 2.   15

Rogers, Carl. (1959) 'A theory of therapy, personality, and interpersonal relationships as developed in the client-centred framework,' in Sigmund Koch (ed.), *Psychology: A Study of a Science*, Vol. 3, New York: McGraw-Hill.   1

Rogers, Carl. (1951) *Client centred therapy.* Boston: Houghton Mifflin.   1

Romanelli, Elaine, and Michael Tushman. (1994) 'Organisational transformation as punctuated equilibrium: An empirical test,' *Academy of Management Journal* 37: 1141–1166.   1

Rossett, Allison, and Ken Sheldon. (2001) *Beyond the podium: Delivering training and performance to a digital world.* San Francisco: Jossey-Bass/Pfeiffer.   19

Rowley, Jennifer, and Frances Slack. (2009) 'Conceptions of wisdom,' *Journal of Information Science* 35(1): 110–119.   9

Rowling, Joanne K. (2003) *Harry Potter and the Order of the Phoenix*. New York: Scholastic.   15

Russ-Eft, Darlene. (2005, May) 'In search of evaluator competencies. Human resource development across Europe' [Abstract]. Abstracts of the Sixth AUHRD/AHRD Conference, 81. Leeds, England: University of Leeds.   17

Russ-Eft, Darlene. (2004) 'Customer service competencies: A global look,' *Human Resource Development International* 7: 211–231.   17

Russ-Eft, Darlene. (2004) 'Ethics in a global world: An oxymoron?' *Evaluation and Program Planning* 27: 349–356.   17

Russ-Eft, Darlene. (2003) 'Corporate ethics: A learning and performance problem for leaders?' *Human Resource Development Quarterly* 14(1): 1–3.   22

Russ-Eft, Darlene. (1997) 'Looking through a different lens: Views of human resource development,' in H. Preskill and L. Dilworth (eds.), *AHRD in Transition: Finding the Cutting Edge, International Society for Performance Improvement and the Academy of Human Resource Development*, 107–114. Bowling Green:AHRD   17

Russ-Eft, Darlene. (1986) 'Evaluability assessment of the Adult Education Program (AEP),' *Evaluation and Program Planning* 9: 39–47.   17

Russ-Eft, Darlene, and Hallie Preskill. (2005) 'In search of the holy grail: ROI in ROI evaluation in HRD,' *Advances in Developing Human Resources*: 71–85.   17

Russ-Eft, Darlene F., Bober, Marcie., de la Teja, Ileana., Foxon, Marguerite, & Koszalka, Tiffany. A. (2008). Evaluato competencies: Standards for the practice of evaluation in organizations. San Francisco: Jossey-Bass.   17

Russ-Eft, Darlene, and Timothy Hatcher. (2003) 'The issue of international values and beliefs: The debate for a global HRD code of ethics,' *Advances in Developing Human Resources* 5(3): 296–307.   22

Russ-Eft, Darlene, and Hallie Preskill. (2001) *Evaluation in organizations: A systematic approach to enhancing learning, performance, and change*. Cambridge, MA: Perseus.   17

Salas, Eduardo, Dana Sims and Shawn Burke. (2005) 'Is there a 'Big Five' in teamwork?' *Small Group Research* 36: 555–599.   13

Sambrook, Sally. (2010) 'Critical pedagogy in a health service management development programme: Can "critically thinking" managers change the NHS management culture?' *Journal of Health Organisation and Management* 23(6): 656–671.   5

Sambrook, Sally. (2004) 'A 'critical' time for HRD?' *Journal of European Industrial Training* 28(8/9): 611–624.   5

Sambrook, Sally. (2001) 'HRD as emergent and negotiated evolution,' *Human Resource Development Quarterly* 12(2): 169–193.   5

Sambrook, Sally. (2000) 'Talking of HRD,' *Human Resource Development International* 3(2): 159–178.   5

Sambrook, Sally, Jim Stewart and Clair Roberts. (2008) 'Doctoral supervision: A view from above, below and the middle,' *Journal of Further and Higher Education* 32(1): 71–84.   5

Sashkin, Marshall. (2004) 'Transformational leadership approaches: A review and synthesis,' in A.T.C.J. Antonakis and R.J. Sternberg (eds.), *The Nature of Leadership*, Thousand Oaks: Sage, 171–196.   18

Schalkoff, Robert J. (2011) 'Metaphor as used by noted HRD scholars at the Pecs 2010 conference,' *Human Resource Development International* 14(3): 347–351.   1

Schmidt, F L., and J.E. Hunter. (2000) 'Select on intelligence,' in E.A. Locke (ed.), *The Blackwell Handbook of Organizational Principles,* Oxford: Blackwell, 3–14.　　8

Schmidt, R.E., J.W. Scanlon and J.B. Bell. (1979, November) 'Evaluability assessment: Making public programs work better,' Human Services Monograph Series, no. 14.　　8

Schnurr, Stephanie. (2008) 'Surviving in a man's world with a sense of humour: An analysis of women leaders' use of humour at work,' *Leadership* 4(3): 299–319.　　17

Schön, Donald. (1983) *The reflective practitioner: How professionals think in action.* London: Temple Smith.　　16

Schwandt, David R., and Michael J. Marquardt. (1999) *Organizational learning: From world-class theories to global best practices.* Boca Raton, FL: CRC Press, LLCSchwartz, Shalom. (1994) *Beyond individualism/collectivism: New cultural dimensions of values.* Newbury Park, CA:Sage.　　19

Selmer, J. (2005) 'Is Bigger Better? Size of the Location and Expatriate Adjustment in China', International Journal of Human Resource Management, 16(7): 1228–42.　　10

Scriven, M. (1994) 'Product evaluation—The state of the art,' *Evaluation Practice* 15(1): 45–62.　　17

Scriven, M. (1991) *Evaluation thesaurus,* 4th ed. Thousand Oaks, CA: Sage.　　17

Scriven, M. (1974) Standards for the evaluation of Educational Products and programs' in G.D Borich (Ed) Evaluating educational programs and products. Englewood Cliffs, NJ: Educational Technology Publications.　　17

Scriven, M. (1973) 'Goal-free evaluation,' in E.R. House (ed.), *School Evaluation,* Berkeley: McCutchan Publishing.　　17

Scullion, Hugh, and David Collings, eds. (2011) *Global talent management.* New York: Routledge.　　4

Secretariat of the Pacific Community. (2001) *Population and development planning in the Pacific.* Noumea, New Caledonia: Author.　　15

Selmer, J. (2005) 'Is Bigger Better? Size of the Location and Expatriate Adjustment in China', International Journal of Human Resource Management, 16(7): 1228–42.　　8

Senge, Peter M. (1990) *The fifth discipline: The art and practice of the learning organization.* New York: Currency/Doubleday.　　19

Shaffer, M.A., D.A. Harrison, H. Gregersen, J.S. Black and L.A. Ferzandi. (2006) 'You can take it with you: Individual differences and expatriate effectiveness,' *Journal of Applied Psychology* 91: 109–125.　　8

Shamir, Boas, and Gad Eilam. (2005) ''What's your story' A life-stories approach to authentic leadership development,' *Leadership Quarterly* 16(3): 395–417.　　12

Shin, S.J., F.P. Morgeson and M.A. Campion. (2007) 'What you do depends on where you are: Understanding how domestic and expatriate work requirements depend upon cultural context,' *Journal of International Business Studies* 38: 64–83.　　8

Short, Darren. (2010) 'Better know an HRD scholar: A conversation with Monica Lee,' *Human Resource Development International* 13(3): 361–374.　　1

Short, Darren C. (2004) '2004: A significant year for research-practice links in HRD,' *Human Resource Development International* 7(4): 541–454.　　12

Short, Darren, and Thomas Shindell. (2009) 'Defining HRD scholar-practitioners,' *Advances in Developing Human Resources* 11(4): 472.　　16

Skinner, B.F. (1948) *Walden Two*, Indianapolis, IN: Hackett.

Smit, Barry, and Olga Pilifosova. (2001) 'Adaptation to climate change in the   19
context of sustainable development and equity,' in James J. McCarthy,
Osvaldo F. Canziani, Neil A. Leary, David J. Dokken and Kasey S. White,
eds. *Climate change 2001: Impacts, adaptation and vulnerability*. IPCC
Working Group II. Cambridge: Cambridge University Press, 877–912.   21

Smit, Barry, and Yunlong Cai. (1996) 'Climate change and agriculture in
China,' *Global Environmental Climate Change*, 6(3): 205–214.   21

Sparrowe, Raymond T. (2005) 'Authentic leadership and the narrative self,'
Leadership Quarterly 16: 419–439.   12

Spencer, L.M. Jr. (1997) 'Competency assessment methods,' in L.J. Bassi and
D. Russ-Eft (eds.), *What Works: Assessment, Development, and Measurement*, Alexandria, VA: ASTD, 1–36.   17

Spencer, L.M. Jr., and Spencer, S.M. (1993) *Competence at work: Models
for superior performance*. New York: Wiley.   17

Sternberg, R.J. (2004) 'Culture and intelligence,' *American Psychologist* 59:
325–338.   17

Sternberg, R.J. (1997) *Successful intelligence*. New York: Plume.   17

Sternberg, R.J. (1986) 'A framework for understanding conceptions of intelli-
gence,' in R.J. Sternberg and D.K. Detterman (eds.), *What Is Intelligence?
Contemporary Viewpoints on Its Nature and Definition*, Norwood, NJ:
Ablex, 3–15   8

Sternberg, R.J. (1985) 'Implicit theories of intelligence, creativity, and wisdom,' *Journal of Personality and Social Psychology* 49: 607–627.   17

Sternberg, R.J., and E.L. Grigorenko. (2006) 'Cultural intelligence and successful intelligence,' *Group and Organization Management* 31: 27–39.   8

Sternberg, R.J., R.K. Wagner, W.M. Williams and J.A. Horvath. (1995)
'Testing common sense,' *American Psychologist* 50(11): 912–927.   17

Sternberg, R.J., and D.K. Detterman. (1986) *What is intelligence? Contemporary viewpoints on its nature and definition*. Norwood, NJ: Ablex.   8

Stewart, Jim, Monica Lee and Rob Poell. (2009) 'The University Forum for
Human Resource Development: Its history, purpose, and activities,' *New
Horizons in Adult Education and Human Resource Development* 23(1):
29–33.   0

Stewart, Jim, and Jim McGoldrick, eds. (1996) *Human resource development: perspectives, strategies and practice*. London: Pitman.   12

Storberg, Julia. (2007) 'Borrowing from others: Appropriating social capital
theories for 'doing' HRD,' *Advances in Developing Human Resources* 9:
312–340.   13

Stroh, L.K., J.S. Black, M.E. Mendenhall and H.B. Gregersen. (2005) *International assignments: An integration of strategy, research, and practice*.
Mahwah, NJ: Lawrence Erlbaum Associates.   8

Summers-Effler, Erika. (2002) 'The micro potential for social change: Emotion,
consciousness, and social movement formation,' *Sociological Theory* 20: 19.   18

Sveningsson, Stefan, and M. Larsson. (2006) 'Fantasies of leadership: Identity work,' *Leadership* 2: 21.   18

Swanson, Richard A., and Edward. F. Holton. (2009) *Foundations of human
resource development*. San Francisco: Berrett-Koehler Publishers.   3

Tao, Fulu, Masayuki Yokozawa, Yousay Hayashi and Erda Lin. (2003) 'Future
climate change, the agricultural water cycle and agricultural production in
China,' *Agriculture, Ecosystems and environment* 95(1): 203–215.   21

The Commission for Education and Human Resource Policies. (2001)
*National human resource development policy report to initiate 21st cen-
tury knowledge state*. Seoul: Author.   15

Thomson, Andrew, Christopher Mabey, John Storey, Colin Gray and Paul Iles. (2001) *Changing patterns of management development in Britain.* Oxford: Blackwell. 4

Thorndike, R., and S. Stein. (1937) 'An evaluation of the attempts to measure social intelligence,' *Psychological Bulletin* 34: 275–285. 8

Tillich, Paul. (1965) *Systematic theology, Volume III: Life and the spirit, history and the kingdom of God.* Chicago: University of Chicago Press. 19

Tiryakian, Edward A. (1995) 'Collective effervescence, social change and charisma: Durkheim, Weber, and 1989,' *International Sociology* 10: 269–281. 18

Torres, R.T., H. Preskill and M. Piontek. (2005) *Evaluation strategies for communicating and reporting: Enhancing learning in organizations,* 2nd ed. Thousand Oaks, CA: Sage. 17

Travitian, Roland. (1995) *Vocational training I/1992.* Thessaloniki: CEDEFOP. 7

Trehan, Kiran. (2004) 'Who is not sleeping with whom? What's not being talked about in HRD? *Journal of European Industrial Training* 28(1): 23–38. 5

Trehan, Kiran, and Clare Rigg. (2011) 'Theorising critical HRD: A paradox of intricacy and discrepancy,' *Journal of European Industrial Training.*35(3): 276–290, esp. 276. 5

Trehan, Kiran, Clare Rigg and Jim Stewart. (2002) 'A critical turn in HRD,' *Call for papers for the Critical Management Studies 3 Conference,* available at www.cms3.org. Last accessed July 2002 5

Triandis, H.C. (2006) 'Cultural intelligence in organizations,' *Group and Organization Management* 31: 20–26. 8

Triandis, H.C. (1994) *Culture and social behavior.* New York: McGraw-Hill. 8

Trompenaars, Alfons, and Charles Hampden-Turner. (1998) *Riding the waves of culture: Understanding cultural diversity in global business:* New York: McGraw-Hill. 3

Tuhiwai Smith, Linda. (1999) *Decolonizing methodologies: Research and indigenous peoples.* London: Zed Books. 2

Tung, R.L. (1981) 'Selection and flaming of personnel for overseas assignments,' In M. Wilkinson and M.A. Devanna (eds.), *Columbia Journal of World Business* 16(1): 68–78. 8

Turnbull, Sharon. (2002) 'The planned and unintended emotions generated by a corporate change program,' *Advances in Developing Human Resources* 4: 16. 18

Turnbull, Sharon. (1999) 'Emotional labour in corporate change programmes: The effects of organizational feeling rules on middle managers,' *Human Resource Development* International 2: 21. 18

Tyler, T.R. (1994) 'Psychological models of the justice motive: Antecedents of distributive and procedural justice,' *Journal of Personality and Social Psychology* 67: 850–863. 17

Uhl-Bien, Mary. (2006) 'Relational leadership theory: Exploring the social processes of leadership and organizing,' *Leadership Quarterly* 17: 654–676. 13

Uhl-Bien, Mary, and Russ Marion. (2009) 'Complexity leadership in bureaucratic forms of organizing: A meso-model,' *Leadership Quarterly* 20: 631–650. 13

United Nations. (2010) *The universal declaration of human rights,* retrieved online on August 20, 2010, at http://www.un.org/en/documents/udhr/index.shtml. 22

Valentin, Claire. (2006) 'Researching human resource development: Emergence of a critical approach to HRD enquiry,' *International Journal of Training and Development,* 10(1): 17–29, esp. 24–25.   5

Van Maanen, John. (1985) 'Spinning on symbolism: Disquisition,' *Journal of Management* 11: 119–120.   18

Van Maanen, John, and Gideon Kunda. (1989) '"Real feelings': Emotional expression and organizational culture,' *Research in Organizational Behavior* 11: 43–103.   18

Vasilyuk, Fyodor. (1984) *The Psychology of experiencing: The resolution of life's critical situations* (English trans., 1991). Hemel Hempstead: Harvester Wheatsheaf.   1

Vince, Russ. (2005) 'Ideas for critical practitioners,' in Carole Elliott, and Sharon Turnbull (eds.), *Critical Thinking in Human Resource Development*, London: Routledge, 26–36.   5

Visser, Wayne, and Nick Tolhurst, eds. (2010) *The world guide to CSR: A country-by-country analysis of corporate sustainability and responsibility.* Ogdensburg, NY: Greenleaf.   22

Wainwright, Delia, and Sally Sambrook. (2009) 'Working at it: Autoethnographic accounts of the psychological contract between a doctoral supervisor and supervisee,' *4th Annual International Ethnography Symposium*, Liverpool University.   5

Walster, E., G.W. Walster and E. Berscheid. (1978) *Equity theory and research.* Boston: Allyn and Bacon.   17

Walton, John. (2003) 'How shall a thing be called? An argumentation on the efficacy of the term HRD,' *Human Resource Development Review* 2(3): 310–326.   5

Walumbwa, Fred O., Bruce J. Avolio, William L. Gardner, Tara S. Wernsing and Suzanne J. Peterson (2008) 'Authentic leadership: Development and validation of a theory-based measure,' *Journal of Management* 34(1): 89–126.   12

Wasti, Arzu, Rob Poell and Nigar Çakar. (2008) 'Oceans and notions apart? An analysis of the U.S. and European human resource development literature,' *International Journal of Human Resource Management* 19(12): 2155–2170.   20

Watkins, Jeff, and Lynn Drury. (1999) 'New organisational structures: skill implications for professionals,' *Human Resource Development International* 2(3): 181–204.   21

Watson, Tony. (2004) 'Human resource management and critical social science analysis,' *Journal of Management Studies* 41(3): 447–467.   5

Weinberger, Lisa. (1998) 'Commonly held theories of human resource development,' *Human Resource Development International* 1: 75–79.   19

Wenger, Etienne. (1991) *Situated learning.* Cambridge: Cambridge University Press.   4

Whitehead, Alfred North. (1933) *Adventures of ideas.* Harmondsworth: Penguin.   1

Whitehead, Alfred North. (1929) *Process and reality.* New York: Free Press, 240.   1

Wholey, J. (1979) *Evaluation: Promise and performance,* Washington, DC: Urban Institute.   17

Wholey, J.S. (1994, 1974) 'Assessing the feasibility and likely usefulness of evaluation,' in J.S. Wholey, H.P Hatry and K.E. Newcomer (eds.), *Handbook of Practical Program Evaluation*, San Francisco: Jossey-Bass, 15–39.   17

Willmore, Joe. (1999) 'Four HRD scenarios of the future,' *Training and Development* 53(12): 38–41.   19

Winterton, Jonathan. (2004) 'Improving the effectiveness of social partners' involvement in VET,' Proceedings of the CEDEFOP Agora Conference VET Research: To what end? Thessaloniki, February 16–17.

Winterton, Jonathan, and T. Strandberg. (2004) 'European social dialogue: Evaluation and critical assessment,' in *The Unification of Europe: The Role of Social Dialogue in the Enlargement Process of the European Employment Strategy*, Brussels: SALTSA/ETUI.   7, 7

Wood, Martin. (2005) 'The fallacy of misplaced leadership,' *Journal of Management Studies* 42: 1101–1121.   18

Woodall, Jean. (2005) 'Convergence and diversity in HRD,' *Human Resource Development International* 8(1): 1–4.5.   5

Woodall, Jean. (2004) 'Why HRD scholarship runs ahead of HRD practice,' *Human Resource Development International* 7(1): 3–5.   12

Worrell, Les, and Cary Cooper. (1999) *Quality of life: 1999 survey of managers' changing experience*. London: Institute of Management.   21

Yamazaki, Y., and D.C. Kayes. (2004) 'An experiential approach to cross-cultural learning: A review and integration of competencies for success expatriate adaptation,' *Academy of Management Learning and Education* 3: 362–379.   8

Yammarino, Francis J., Shelley D. Dionne., Chester A. Schriesheim and Fred Dansereau. (2008) 'Authentic leadership and positive organizational behavior: A meso, multi-level perspective,' *Leadership Quarterly* 19(6): 693–707.   12

Yamnill, Siriporn, and Gary N. McLean. (2010) 'The application of action research model in community development: The case of Lumpaya Village, Thailand,' *Human Resource Development International* 13: 541–556.   15

Yorks, Lyle. (2005) *Strategic human resource development*. Mason, OH: Thomson South-Western.   20

Young-sik Ahn, and Gary N. McLean. (2006) 'Regional human resource development: The case of Busan City, Korea,' *Human Resource Development International* 9: 261–270.   15

Zanko, Michael, and Matt Ngui. (2003) 'The implications of supra-national regionalism for human resource management in the Asia-Pacific region,' in Michael Zanko and Matt Ngui (eds.), *The Handbook of Human Resource Management Policies and Practices in Asia-Pacific Economies*, vols. I and II, Cheltenham, UK: Edward Elgar, 5–22.   7,15

Zhai, Panmao, Anjian Sun, Fumin Ren, Xiaonin Lui, Bo Gao and Qiang Zhang. (1999) 'Changes in climate extremes in China,' *Climatic Change* 42: 203–218.   21

Zhang, Mian, Wei Zheng and Jun Wei. (2009) 'Sources of social capital: Effects of altruistic citizenship behavior and job involvement on advice network centrality,' *Human Resource Development Quarterly* 20: 195–217.   13

Zohar, Danah, and Ian Marshall. (2000) *SQ—Spiritual intelligence: The ultimate intelligence*. London: Bloomsbury.   14

Abbreviations

ABAC	APEC Business Advisory Council
ADHR	Advances in Developing Human Resources
AHRD	Academy for HRD
APEC	Asian and Pacific Economy Countries
ASEAN	Association of Southeast Asian Nations
ASTD	American Society for Training and Development
BPR	Business Process Review
CCT	Cross-Cultural Training
CEDEFOP	European Centre for the Development of Vocational Training
CEEP	Centre Européen de l'Entreprise Publique (European Centre of Enterprises with Public Participation and of Enterprises of General economic Interest)
CEO	Chief Executive Officer
CES	Confédération Européenne des Syndicats (European Trade Union Confederation)
CG	Corporate Governance
CHRD	Critical HRD
CIPD	Chartered Institute for Personnel and Development
CMS	Critical Management Studies
CP	Critical Pedagogy
CQ	Cultural Quotient
CSR	Corporate Social Responsibility
CT	Critical Theory
CTI	Committee on Trade and Investment
ECOTECH	Economic and Technical Co-operation
EES	European Employment Strategy
EFL	English as a Foreign Language
ESRC	Economic and Social Research Council, UK
ETUC	European Trade Union Confederation
EU	European Union

EURESFORM	*(Forum européen d'appui a la formacion des professionals du développement des resources humaines : A European Forum for HRD)*
FDI	Foreign Direct Investment
HRDI	Human Resource Development International
HRDQ	Human Resource Development Quarterly
HRDR	Human Resource Development Review
HRM	Human Resource Management
Ibstpi	International Board of Standards for Training, Performance, and Instruction
ICFTU	International Confederation of Free Trade Unions
IHRD	International Human Resource Development
ILO	International Labor Organisation
ITD	The Institute of Training and Development
MENA	Middle East and North Africa
MNC	Multinational Company
MNE	Multinational Enterprise
NGO	Non-Governmental Organization
NHRD	National HRD
NVQ	National Vocational Qualifications
OAA	Osaka Action Agenda
OB	Organizational Behavior
OD	Organization Development
OECD	Organization for Economic Co-operation and Development
ROI	Return-on-investment
SME	Small / Medium Sized Enterprise
Studies in HRD	Monograph Book Series, Routledge
TILF	Trade and Investment Liberalization and Facilitation
TM	Talent Management
UFHRD	University Forum for HRD
UNICE/ UEAPME	Union des Industries de la Communauté Européenne/ Union Européenne des Ateliers et Petites Moyennes Entreprises (European Association of Craft, Small and Medium Enterprises/Union of confederations of Industry in the European Community)
VET	Vocational and Educational Training
WTO	World Trade Organization

Index